The Biography of "The Idea of Literature"

SUNY Series in the Margins of Literature
Mihai I. Spariosu, Editor

The Biography of "The Idea of Literature"
from Antiquity to the Baroque

Adrian Marino

Translated from Romanian by
Virgil Stanciu
and
Charles M. Carlton

STATE UNIVERSITY OF NEW YORK PRESS

Published by
State University of New York Press, Albany

For information address State University of New York Press, State University Plaza, Albany, NY 12246

Production by Laura Starrett
Marketing by Bernadette La Manna

ISBN   0-7914-2893-1 (hc.)   0-7914-2894-X (pbk.)
LC   96-068194

10   9   8   7   6   5   4   3   2   1

Contents

viii *Contents*

Organizing Letters
The Totality of Letters   159
The Book   160
The Library   162
The Bibliography   163
The Encyclopedia   164

The Classicization of Traditional Definitions
"Human Letters"   166
"Liberal Letters"   166
"Good Letters"   167

The Coordinates of Letters
Ancient Versus Modern Letters   168
National Versus World Literature   170
Popular Letters   173

Estheticizing Letters
"Beautiful Letters"   174
Beautiful Literature   176
Literature or Poetry?   177
Poetic Literature   178
Literary Art   179
Literary Versus Poetic Specificity   180
The Autonomy of Literature   182

The Heteronomy of Literature
"The Republic of Letters"   183
Society   185
Economy   187
Ideology   188

Hierarchy in Literature   189

The School of Literature
Literature with Literature   190
Literature on Literature   192
Critical Literature   193

Denying Literature   197

Conclusions   200

Notes   201

Name Index   317

Thematic Index   335

Acknowledgments

I should like to express my gratitude to my translator, Virgil Stanciu, who applied himself with great courage and dedication to a difficult text, as well as to Charles M. Carlton of the University of Rochester for a careful, step-by-step revision of the English version. I am also indebted to the latter for having checked—and, in some cases, provided—the English translations of the citations from classical authors used in chapter 1.

I am very grateful to my old Romanian friends, Matei Călinescu and Virgil Nemoianu, for their moral support, as well as for the help they offered me in some difficult moments.

I should like to assure Mihai Spariosu, who accepted with generous intellectual solidarity, the publication of this book in the series he edits for the State University of New York Press, of my most sincere feelings of gratitude.

Carola F. Sautter, my editor at the State University of New York Press, has shown much understanding and sympathy for the various obstacles and technical difficulties that an East European scholar, working in conditions that cannot be compared to those provided by American libraries, was bound to run up against. She is most deserving of my thanks for her patience and cooperation, and for her graceful acceptance of occasional deadline infringements.

Miss Elena Mosora has been extremely patient and competent in typing the successive versions of this manuscript.

A. M.
Cluj, October 1994

Preface

This book deals with the birth and formation of the "idea of literature," and with its evolution from Antiquity to the Baroque. It is the first part of a vaster project, a "history" or "biography" of the idea of literature from ancient times to the present. It covers two millenniums of the "history" of the idea of literature, the genres, development, structure and articulation of which have never been studied in sufficient detail, a situation, one might add, oftentimes deplored.[1]

The existing contributions are fragmentary. Some of them—unsatisfying, simplifying, incomplete—are predominantly or exclusively lexicographical.[2] The period extending from Antiquity to the Baroque is almost untouched, in spite of the fact that the foundations of the European idea of literature were laid then. Most studies, some of real documentary value, focus exclusively on the nineteenth and twentieth centuries.[3] There is one traditional synthesis, nonetheless, but it is limited to a single national literature, German, the evolution of which is surveyed very quickly here.[4] The notion accredited by contemporary (particularly French) criticism—that the idea of literature in its "present-day sense" (What sense may that be? Can "literature" be limited to one sense in our day and age?) only emerged in the nineteenth century—is completely mistaken.

A few brief notes on methodology may prove useful. While the traditional and, in the last resort, conventional division of material into chapters corresponding to "historical ages" is preserved, in essence, the strict chronological order is replaced by the systematic one. I found the term "biography" more appropriate to my kind of study than "history." "Biography" refers to the meaning and organic evolution of an existence (in this case, of an idea), to an inner logic, a series of symbolic gestures and privileged moments, a growth marked by decisive stages and crucial moments; it refers, above all, to an accomplished evolution. History, on the other hand, presupposes a strict chronology, a chain of causes and effects, of "*corsi e ricorsi*," progress, stagnation or decadence, maybe even certain "laws of development."

Basically, my interpretation of the idea of literature is typological, structural and, to all intents, modeling. I think I discovered, from the very outset, an immanent logic of the idea of literature, corresponding to, or identifying with, the notion of "biographical identity." One can perceive an evolution, a meaning, a progression, an intrinsic finality of the idea, a drive toward self-realization in every historical period, through a historically limited and contextualized redistribution of the basic elements. These elements are all generated by and grouped around literature's fundamental etymon, *littera*. My point of departure, then, was etymological, but combined with a sustained interest in the "ontological" aspects of the problem. The basic elements—having the values of constants, of invariants—can be defined by an older term, suggested by the American history of ideas. In A. O. Lovejoy's terminology, they are *unit-ideas*.[5]

The inevitable structural tension between the ahistorical stability of the schematic, typological view and the concrete, mobile life in history of the idea of literature can be appeased, in this instance, by a "historicized" variant of hermeneutics, to be achieved through two convergent methods. First, the "biography," the history or the "hermeneutics" of the idea of literature, can hardly be written without a *preconcept*, a preexistent idea (German, *Voraussetzung*), without a Weberian "ideal type," an operational mental pattern. In the case in question, it will be the same as the systematic and analytical definition of the idea of literature and the planned projection of the "biography" or "history" of this idea. One cannot write about the history of an idea—in our case, the idea of *literature*—without a workable definition of its status, its essence and structure. In my case, the preconcept was formulated in a previous work, the schema of which informs the present study step by step.[6] The preconcept, therefore, does away with the essential *aporia*: the history of a literary idea is necessary to understand its significance. But that such a significance should exist and be assumed is a prerequisite for perceiving and writing such a "history." So we know not only what the idea of literature *is*, but also *how* it will evolve in time.

The second method, which is difficult, in fact, to distinguish from the first, presupposes the simultaneous reading of the entire historical life of the idea of literature, seen in *contextus ordo saecularum*, to use St. Augustine's formula (*De Trinit.*, IV, 10, 21). A twofold synthesis, systematic and at the same time historiographical, thus becomes possible. The history of the idea of literature is identified with the definition of literature, which is always diversified, always in the making. All the particular acceptations of the idea of *literature* historically attested can be gathered and grouped into a systematic assembly of "parallel," but ultimately converging historical series. Each traces the history of one single acceptation of the idea of literature, part of the master idea of *literature*, seen in it semantic and historical entirety.

This device, employed since the Renaissance, is important from another point of view as well. It is the only way one can assess the actual enrichment of the idea of literature, not only through the new acquisitions of a given period in history, but within the whole history of the idea of literature, seen in its decisive moments and articulations. Thus, a synthesis can be elaborated in and through the very mechanism by which it functions and is being developed. Beginning with T. S. Eliot (for whom European literature had a "simultaneous existence and composes a simultaneous order",[7] the "method" has had its somewhat "classical" advocates, particularly in German (Ernst Robert Curtius, Hans Robert Jauss) and Anglo-American (Ezra Pound, E. M. Forster, N. Frye, etc.) criticism.[8] We must also add René Wellek. I think it has yielded good results in this case, and of the idea of literature, as well. Through it, historical changes and semantic mutations—occurring in very precise historical contexts— become coherent and can be integrated into a master matrix, permanently constituted by a hermeneutical dialectic: *whole/part, synchrony/diachrony,* I risk declaring that it is, probably, the first time that the history of the idea of literature has been subjected to such a treatment.

Thus, the basic etymological principle presiding over my philological investigations, at the level of the essential texts read in the original, finds its most thorough application. "The best concept of a thing," Herder had already said, "is provided by its origin."[9] In this sense, the basic *etymon* (Leo Spitzer also resorted to such a method) and the *unit-idea* become one: an absolute beginning, a fundamental reality–fundamental truth, of self-evident origin. To know the origin of a thing is to dominate, reproduce, recreate it. And to recreate it is to perceive it, to prescribe its meaning, finality, direction of development. Thus, *litteratura* acquires a meaning, a final global perspective.

On the same grounds, I affirm the priority of the literal sense over the spiritual one, as the former is the prerequisite and compulsory support of the latter, and not the other way around (Thomas Aquinas showed this in the Middle Ages, cf. p. 80), which points to the priority and superiority of explicit over implicit meanings, of strong over weak meanings, of stable meanings over variable ones, while neglecting none of the nuances. But everything starts from and reverts to the fundamental finding, that all the acceptations of *literature* start from and invariably return to *littera.* All the denotations and connotations of the idea of literature are naturally set forth and regulated, in one way or another, by *letters.*

In such "pioneering" investigations, with their inherent satisfactions and risks, the problem of sources is paramount. It is these sources alone that can offer, through accurate citations, all the basic meanings and significations of the idea of literature. A philological, methodical, well-oriented close reading will oblige the text to yield all its meanings. This is the reason I have used a great number of texts and numerous quotations, almost all of them taken directly from the primary sources. Ideally, this "biography" of the idea of literature could have written itself, it could have constituted and described itself as "in the making." The author's role could have been limited to directing the "montage" and supervising its rhythm and progression. I practice, in fact, a personal form of "intertextuality," within a general reference framework. Thus, I endeavor to compose, from all the "books" containing the idea of literature, a unique book: the "biography of the idea of literature," which might contain all the others and possibly "replace" them.

Antiquity

The biography of the idea of literature boasts a modest, banal and rather belated beginning: a lexical "accident," as fecund as it was unforseeable. For the time being, nothing permits us to glimpse the extraordinary destiny, abounding in unexpected turns and spectacular creative developments, of historical life of the idea of literature. All, or almost all of the basic acceptations of literature are revealed now, whether explicitly or in filigree.

FIRST DEFINITIONS

Written Literature

The starting point is to be found in the idea of *writing* and *written text* that offers, from beginning to end, the original, central and prevailing acceptation of the idea of *literature*. The relationship is defining and permanent, although constantly subjected to historical conditioning. As Hellenic was the cultural language of Antiquity, the basic etymon can only be *ta grámmata* (= letters), the first main meaning of which is the graphic sign: "the written character or form." It represents graphically, visually, the elements of language *(ta stoichea)*,[1] first of all, the sound. *Ta grámmata* = sign + sound (written + spoken).[2]

The Latin word *litterae*, used to translate this notion beginning with the second century (series opened by Cicero, *Ad. Fam.*, V, 8, 5), takes over the same meaning, while adding others to it. The restricted sense—hence St. Augustine's *litterae scripta*—remains essential: *litterae seu scribendi ars* (see the same source.)[3] It is for the time being (and will be for a long time) a neologism, as those who use it always feel the need (even after one and one-half centuries) to explain it, to expand it, to implant it explicitly in the linguistic consciousness of the age:[4] *Grámmata enim Graeci litteras vocant.*[5]

The crucial event—the actual begetting of the biography of literature—was the transition from *grámmata* and *litterae* to *litteratura*, a term that inevitably takes on the original specific meaning. The phenomenon is easily observable with Cicero, the "author," or, in any case—judging by the evidence—the popularizer of this unforeseeable and extremely fecund lexical calculus. He assimilates the memory of wax tables,[6] on which written characters are inscribed, *genuina litteratura*. Cicero, too, uses the synonym *ingenium litteraturae*.[7] It is not only once that those who copy the Ciceronian manuscripts assimilate *litterae* to *litteratura*. It is a clear indication that the newer concept has become more powerful than *litterae*, which it absorbs.[8] *Litteratura*, in the sense of the alphabet, is also found with Tacitus.[9] An accurate comment on the problem can be found in the work of the late grammarian, Audax: *litteratura vel litteralitas*.[10] The sense becomes stable: Literature = the realm of (written) letters.

The second outstanding development experienced in ancient times by our biography is the transition from the idea of writing to that of literature, in the present (even if embryonic) sense of the word or, better said, the assimilation of the former by the latter. The apology of writing is quite frequent (for example, Lucretius, V, 1444–1448), but only for practical, that is, economic, judicial reasons: recording, *aide-mémoire*, consecration, "testimony,"[11] etc. *Epistula (= litterae) non erubescit*, "a letter does not blush," says Cicero.[12] Writing is the "trustworthy guardian of the memory of past events" (Livy).[13] Because of that, for a considerable time the transition to "literary" significances was only tacit, implicit. Writing produces writings (written texts) that are "worlds" of various genres. It is these—in their totality—that literature is made up of: a body of writings, that is, of literary writings.

Greek etymology also takes us close to "literature" in its later sense: *grámmata* (and the related words, such as *sin-grámmata*) also means "short writings, written verse," *Sammelrolle*. The basic sense of *graphe* (from *graphein* = to scratch, to draw lines) is ambivalent: "Writing," but also "drawing" or "painting." Similarly, in patristic Greek, *graphe* means "writing," "individual books," in general.[14] The meaning is inevitably preserved by the Latin word *litterae*, a notion with an obvious tendency to expand its meaning: To begin with, *litteris* is used to mean "letter," "epistolary communication."[15] But *littera(ae)*, in the sense of "work," "text," "written work," "literary work," is attested at the same time.[16] This last notion will soon be separated from that of "letters" = written signs, as St. Augustine already speaks of *litteris monumentis*.[17] In Pomponius Mela (1, 12) we came across *litteras et (litterarum) operas* (but what he means is not certain). At any rate, Tertullian will later refer to *litteraturae operibus*, a term that will assert itself with all its implications and ambiguities.[18] The philology of later Antiquity also records this semantic evolution: *grámmata* = *litteratura* has three meanings: "letter," "writing,"[19] and, of course, "literary work." An ancient type of writing, something in between "record" and "short poem," will even be called *epigrámma*.[20] It is a typical illustration of the way in which a purely graphic notion acquires a poetic, literary meaning. This incipient tradition will gradually efface the mere "graphology" of the original meaning.

The idea of "literary work" is ever more firmly consolidated by the alternation and eventual substitution of the *litterae/scripturae* pair. In the beginning, "scripture" is the equivalent of the written letter, of the graphic sign, of the alphabet. Then it becomes the synonym of the "art" of writing, to become, eventually, "public or private writings," *scrittura pubblica o privata*.[21] A qualitatively superior meaning is "written monuments," *monumenta, scriptorum monumenta*,[22] as well as that of poetic products of a similar kind, also connotated by the word *scriptura*.[23] It again results that *literature* = the realm of written letters, an ancient, fundamental, hard sense, maintained uninterruptedly until today.

Finally, the first definition of a "writer," *lato sensu*, will inevitably be that of a *scriptor*, at the beginning, as *scriba*—scriveners, secretaries, accountants; then *poetae*—"writers" in a "general sense,"[24] rhetorists,[25] and even those who write on oratory, *artis scriptor*.[26] Just like "letters," "writer" has, *ab initio*, a polysemy of its own. It will accompany *literature*, in its spirit and letter, until our own times.

Oral Literature

This fairly rapid semantic and terminological evolution occurs in a context still decisively dominated by a powerful orality. Ancient culture is preeminently dependent on the live word, on *logos*. The emergence of writing brings about a great rupture, hence a series of an ever more complex relationship between writing and orality. What will be named "oral literature" appears, by implication, exactly when these relationships, rich in semantic and terminological consequences, are formulated. This acceptation, however, remains marginal, and will only become relevant when examined against the whole pattern that recuperates it and underlines its value.

In a way, the *oral* versus *written* dispute is characteristic of Antiquity's entire spiritual life. It is relevant, at any rate, for the birth and evolution of the definition of literature. For a long time, eulogizing the word, the superiority of orality and of eloquence, was part of a dogma (Quintilian: "Nothing is worth more than live uttering," II, 2, 8; Diodorus Siculus: "The power of eloquence is man's most wonderful trait," I, II, 5, etc.)[27] It is therefore natural that *scripture* should adopt the oral model, knowing that the "science of style" is so closely linked to speaking.[28] The enormous importance of oratory also constantly pushes writing aside and, to a certain extent, makes it guilt-laden.

This has direct consequences for literary notions and terms. Poetry is conceived of as a form of speech, "speech with meter."[29] There are no poets who can be only read.[30] Reciting or reading poetry out loud is essential and obligatory. "The poet is a very near kinsman of the orator."[31]

As yet, writing is not implied in fundamental poetic acts: "inspiration," "reciting," "pleasure," "agreement," "performance" ("audience," "crowd of spectators").[32]

Hence exists the rhetorical acceptation of poetry, which redoubles the idea of *litterae* through what may be called the "literaturization of rhetoric."[33] For the time being, in any event, rhetoric takes over the definitions to and functions of literature. Assimilating poetry to a form of rhetorical "diction" (*bene dicendi scientia*)[34] is a central aspect of this process. Another, of particular relevance, is that the notions *litterae* and *eloquentia* are tacitly equalized. One of Tacitus's formulas, *omne eloquentia*,[35] has precisely this meaning: "All literature, that is, all literary genres."[36] The equalization of the two types of discourse, written and oral, points to the same thing.[37] Similarly, we observe the confusion between "retor" and "poet" and the setting up of Homer as a model of eloquence among others.[38] The (no less rhetorical) question regarding whether Virgil had been an orator or a poet (Anneaeus Lucius Florus)[39] is part of the same outlook. In any case, the definition of rhetoric as the "art of speech," oral or written (found in Plato's *Phaedrus*, 260 a–b) is the first recognition of literature as language art. So, the rhetorical acceptation has marked literature from the very beginning and, under its many guises, has been a central and, for many, an essential definition of *literature*.

All these confusions and interferences, typical of the Ancient World, point to a deepening crisis of orality. This crisis has several stages. The final one is the complete dismantling of the "oral definition" of literature, the assertion, in this domain as well, of the values and definitions of *writing*. In the beginning, it is voice alone that lends superior status to a piece of writing: the table, the letter "sings" or "cries aloud."[40] Tragedy, originally oral, becomes, gradually, written. In his turn, the orator must speak as he writes; written practice benefits him entirely.[41] Later, a separation, a neat delineation is effected. By transcribing orality, the language of conversation becomes distinct from the written language.[42] The written style (*inscribendo*) becomes specialized in *poetico* and *oratorio*.[43] According to this logic, "poet," "orator," and "writer" are distinct, specialized literary professions, enumerated in this order (Hermogenes).[44]

The natural and decisive outcome of this process is that orality is replaced by the written word. From the seventh century B.C. on, poets resort to writing ever more often. They are no longer satisfied with the initial stage of improvisation and declamation. Even more spectacular for the ancient mentality is the literaturization of rhetoric, in the form of a written draft of the speeches. The new procedure is sanctioned by the moral philosophers,[45] and especially by the rhetoricians themselves.[46] The old hierarchy is turned upside down: Written discourse is deemed superior to oral.[47] Written oratory is more accurate.[48] Written discourse is the "archetype" of oral discourse[49]—a conclusion one could hardly have anticipated at the time when logos held exclusive sway. The most important and far-reaching consequence is the structural change in the nature of literary composition: the transition from orality, from "song" and "dictation,"[50] to written composition, achieved quietly, in seclusion. Literature is slowly turning into a secluded, private activity, just like writing, but increasingly so in a particular and stylistic sense, rather than merely a graphic one. This is the direction in which the most important, implicit as well as explicit, definitions of literature will further develop.

Sacred Literature

Of utmost importance in accurately understanding Antiquity's view of letters and literature is the overwhelming influence of the spiritual context, focused on sacrality, that supreme value of the primitive and ancient mentality. Part of the primeval structure of human consciousness, hugely efficient, tenacious and malleable, sacrality is also the first value to consecrate "letters" and their product. Literature's dominant and original prestige is far from having that of a cultural, let alone esthetic, nature. It has a sacred, mystical, magical nature. This phase—though obsolete in the spiritual history of Europe—cannot be profitably ignored, so numerous and decisive are the proofs of its existence.

The immense prestige of divine *logos* speaks to the importance of sacred orality, the real source from which literature sprang. Everything is created, invested, named, sanctified by the sacred word. It is the genesis of any creation, and *causa sui* as well. The Judaic,[51] Orphic and especially Christian traditions confer an outstanding efficiency, creativity and communicative power to the sacred words,[52] pouring all its demiurgic magic into words—the instruments of literature. Nothing is more natural, then, that literary endeavor, in its entirety, should acquire deeply sacralized meanings and significance.

Poetic creation is preeminently divine. Gods serve as inspiration, bestow poetic acumen, reveal, and dictate. All Hellenic Antiquity, from Homer[54] to Plato,[55] cultivates the myth of creating through the use of words of ecstatic and frenetic inspiration. Demons, divinities, and the muses of the poet's divine genius serve as agents. *Est deus in nobis* (Ovid)[56] is a professed belief and an *ars poetica* characteristic of the age.

Needless to say, the selfsame divinity creates letters, the alphabet, writing. There is a total misunderstanding or, better said, overlooking of the practical, graphic function of the *letter*. This honor is conferred upon (or claimed by) a long series of divinities: Toth, Saturn, Hermes, Orpheus, Cadmus, Wodan, Ogham, etc. Irrespective of the geographical or national position (Egypt, Crete, Phoenicia, etc.), letters are the product of divine creation and divine revelation. Sometimes, they drop straight down from the sky.[57] Divinity conceived them so it might use them to its own advantage. Divinity writes, edits, "circulates." The Bible is replete with such testimonies, the law tables are "the writing of God."[58] God often inscribes things "on hearts," upon the table of thine heart."[59] Divinity "writes" in the hearts of true believers.[60] Its written message is priceless. "The age of communications"—to indulge in a pseudo-anachronism—has, therefore, an illustrious ancient patron and predecessor.

The direct result is the sacralization of the poet, leading, for the first time in European history, to the consecration of literature. The huge collective prestige, so typical of the ancient frame of mind, that the "divine singer" and *sacrus vates*[61] enjoyed, shall never again be reached. What he writes is called *vatum carmina*.[62] Homer's origin is divine.[63] This (entirely symbolic) situation defines in its essence, from an ancient perspective, the complex issue of the origin, status, and functions of literature.

This explains the belief, unanimously held at the time, in the divine nature of poetry.[64] It is expressed by poets (Pindar, Ovid, etc.), historians (Plutarch), and philosophers who generalize the *sacrarum opera* formula (Seneca, etc.).[65] The outlook confers prestige and sets up a stable value scale. It paves the way, in modern terms, to what will later be called the "morphology," even the "phenomenology" of poetry.

In the same spirit, the letters themselves, graphic art proper, will be considered no less sacred: *hierogliphica*, *grámmata*, *ierográmmata*,[66] sacred inscriptions,[67] generally. In Latin-Christian terminology (extended to all the sacred monastic texts), they are translated by *sacris litteris*.[68] Antiquity identifies in these "sacred letters" a number of traits that already begin to take on the shape and coloring of what is later to be called "literature." Later on, they will be absorbed in definitions *expressis verbis*. "Sacred letters" are esoteric, therefore initiatory, undivulgeable. Their secret nature implies obscurity, an enigmatic style, a hermetic language. We find ourselves at the origins of incantations, of the poetic ineffable, of systematic symbologies, of a *je ne sais quoi* with a great career ahead. References are abundant.[69] Other traits also have, by undergoing complex derivations, a brilliant future: texts will acquire a fixed, typified character, leading inevitably to code and dogma. The setting up of Rome's pontifical annals *(litteris pontifex)*[70] provides the classical example. They reform Roman history, imposing a form, a content, and an inalterable, definitive chronology upon it. Sacred writings are radically, intransigently opposed to innovation. They are by nature conservative: *nomina nemo novit*.[71] What will be called "classicization" has its roots in this ancient phenomenon.

As Christian faith becomes predominant, the product of "sacred writing" will be known as *divina Scriptura*.[72] Christianity acknowledges (and incorporates, in its own spirit) *Ta grámmata*, which, in the New Testament, provides the "laws," the "Holy Scripture." With the apologists we come across the term *propheticae litterae*,[73] which designates the Old Testament. On the whole, these writings make up *Sancta Scriptura*, through canonizations, *scripturis canonicis*.[74] Christian connotations are and shall remain predominant in all of the lexical field of "scripture" (letter and content). This does not hinder the emergence of oral religious genres typical of patristic Christianity such as hymns, martyrs' lives, and homilies.[75]

In the same context, the phrase *divina litteratura* appears as a matter of course in Tertullian.[76] It is the first attestation of the idea of "sacred literature" introducing and generalizing this notion, in an exact, stable, lexical form. Such synonyms as *littera Dei*,[77] *ecclesiasticae, sacrae* or *apostolicae litterae*,[78] and *littera Christi*[79] enrich this terminology, inspired—completely—by one and the same crucial notion. It encompasses, through natural assimilation, the idea of poetry as well: *Christumque et sacro carmina*.[80] For Christianity, *vates, propheta,* and *poeta* are also synonymic notions.[81]

A number of characteristic notes of sacrality will inform, through implication or tacit adoption, the entire realm of literature. "Sacred" or "venerable"[82] literature has become, by now, a superlative. It is the supreme qualification of any literary genre. The theory of divine inspiration and of creating *ex nihilo,* which, in its essence, will continue to be met at least until the Renaissance, renders impossible, for the moment, any other psychology of creativity (rational, lucid, etc.) or the emergence of a truthful, realistic conception of art. We still linger in the realm of revelation, of sheer fantasy, of the predominantly ineffable. This is the starting point of a vigorous "irrationalist" tradition, to be found again and again, with variable intensity, throughout the course of the history of the idea of literature.

Profane Literature

Equally characteristic of Antiquity is the emergence, first of the conception, then of the concept, of *profane literature,* running parallel and often at loggerheads with *sacred literature.* This is an enormous mutation, with crucial consequences. Laicizing is the end product of an equally basic process and spiritual category. One can even speak of immanent, original laicization and of a profane character, running parallel and diametrically opposed to sacrality. "Sacred" is everything that is "consecrated," separated from the rest; "profane," all that is not "consecrated" or "hallowed," all that is not included in that sphere.[83] The sacred presupposes initiation and purification; the profane = parting with the transcendent, alienation from it, or an ignorance of it. Sacred or sacralized texts are "esoteric;" profane texts are "exoteric." Ancient terminology frequently refers to *rerum humanarum et divinarum* (Varro).

One is aware that tacit laicizing was also implemented through all the practical and private uses of writing: lists, records, bookkeeping, deeds, correspondence, etc. But it also appears in the definition and economy of literary creation, in the distinction between delirious inspiration and craftsmanship,[84] in the appearance of an awareness of inspiration and of the strictly human use of poetry *(hominem pagina nostra)*,[85] in the transformation of (sacred) myth into a (profane) script, etc. If the *Odyssey* truly contains early laicized sacred poems, it again results that the process is immemorially old and, therefore, once again, original. Euhemerism, the discovery of the sacred origin of literature, the identification of the gods and goddesses of poetry and writing, the theory that deities were figments of poets' imagination—all these are important aspects that point to the same process.

As in the case of *sacred literature*, the conception and terminology of *profane literature* are Christian contributions; more precisely, they are contributions of second- and third-century Apologetics. The aim was to defeat, at any cost, paganism, idolatry, *gloria saecularis*.[86] In the following centuries, the rift between *humanis et divinis litteraris*[87] will be even deeper. The impact on literary terms will be equally direct and important.

Perhaps the most characteristic phenomenon is the recuperation of the exclusively profane sense of *littera*. With Tertullian,[88] *de litteris* connotates "secular" or "public" writings. Similarly, in the work of the same apologist, with a keen sense of semantic precision, we come across the formula *de saecularibus . . . scripturis*.[89] This category includes Homer and Virgil. The phrasing is polemical, deprecatory. With the same Tertullian,[90] we also meet (frequently used with an identical content) the phrase *litterae saeculares*. The phrase, in current use with St. Jerome,[91] as well as Cassiodorus *(scriptures saecularum litterarum)*,[92] pairs off with *litterarum profanos*.[93] It clearly defines the bulk of non-Christian writings, that is, all ancient literature. This delineation and prohibition makes an essential contribution to the formation and clarification of a concept that will become traditional—the concept of literature.

In its present form, "secular literature" appears for the first time with the same Tertullian, a polemical vivacious spirit, endowed with a rich lexical imagination: *saecularis litteratura*.[94] A variant, *litteratura mundi*, used by St. Cassian,[95] more precisely defines both the content and its "worldly" destination. *Litteratura saecularis*, frequently used with the same meaning by St. Jerome,[96] is by now a consecrated, widespread formula. As we shall see, it tends to, more and more often, be taken to mean "literature," pure and simple, without any qualifier.[97]

The potentiality of "lay literature" is considerable. In a sense, it will even prove to be decisive for the destiny of the idea of literature. To begin with, laicization blazes a path for what will be called the estheticizing, the autonomy and heteronomy of literature. Escaping from the clutches of domineering sacrality, literature can cultivate and ponder itself and its own interests more and more freely, and can open up to as many values as possible. Both autonomy and its opposite, with all their consequences, become feasible. At the same time, laicization instills a contesting principle in literature, the idea of insubordination, of criticism, of escape from a given order. It is debunking, preeminently "modern." While the sacred hankers for worship, the profane dissociates, contradicts, judges, criticizes. Hence, a number of literary genres and devices that are totally "unholy"— polemics, satire, pamphlets—now become possible. An awareness of myths, fables and legends also appears and becomes consolidated. It is relevant that Livy (Titus Livius) distances himself, from the start, from "tales" and "legends."[98] Hence, the rationale of creation, followed by that of the ever more desacralized literary fiction, becomes a natural process. Totally absorbed by the idea of literature, laicization no longer appears evident, so original and implicit is it viewed.

LITERARY CULTURE

Grammar and Culture

However, the really decisive event, as far as the value content and the historical dynamism of the idea of literature are concerned, is a different one. It resides not only in the transliterative *grámmatiki* = *litteratura*— another borrowing and a Latin purism, "a modest name" at any rate: "Grammar translated into Latin by *litteratura*"[99]—but especially in the fact that this *litteratura (grammatica)* was seen as being an "art" or a "technique," therefore, a purely didactic subject-matter: "The art of grammar, called in our language literature."[100] *Letters, litteratura* can be studied; consequently, they become essential school subjects. This insistent, stereotyped explanation, recurrent throughout Antiquity, is a sign that the problem was seen as a neologism of a "technical" nature. As it is not in current use, it is consolidated and explained with the help of etymology, the only efficient method of the era. It can be repeatedly met with in St. Augustine[101] and Martianus Capella,[102] as well as with a number of grammarians, such as Diomedes, Servius, Priscianus, Audax, Marius Victorinus, Asper, Valerius Probus, and Donatus.[103] It is, indeed, a mere lexicographical cliché, but an essential one. It launches literature into a cultural orbit, where we can still find it today. From now on, literature can no longer be dissociated from this structure and basic meaning.

From today's perspective, this view seems minor and marginal. Not so in Antiquity, when learning to read and write was an extremely important teaching goal, of crucial importance for man's later intellectual life. At this stage, literature is called *prima litteratura*,[104] respectively *litteratio principia litterarum*.[105] The phrases refer to knowledge, to the elementary notions acquired by pupils, *primae illae litterae*,[106] or *artis litterae communes*.[107] It follows that the central, original value of literature is strictly cultural in nature, indissolubly linked to writing. In the Hellenic world as well, *téhni grámmatiki* means the "art of writing" and of "reading,"[108] that is, one elementary school skill. It is the fundamental study of Antiquity, "the speech mistress" *(magistra verborum)*, the "ornament of human genius."[109] Grammar is defined by almost every grammarian of the age as *litteralis scientia*.[110] He who teaches it is a *grámmateus* (Greek), *grammaticus*[111] (Latin), "grămătic," in the Romanian language of old, the teacher of the first notions and rules regarding speech and writing, the master of *ludus litterarius* of the "primary school," the equivalent of today's primary school teacher.

All ancient culture is ruled by a true grammatical *koiné*, not extremely prestigious, but quite fecund. Its unity is ensured by this well-organized system of teaching grammar and rhetoric in schools. It alone makes what is usually called "Romania" as a cultural territory meaningful. This is defined through a series of *equivalent* or related terms, referred to as a scale of *progressive* knowledge. *Studio* is, needless to say, reading and writing, but a little more than that: it is the first of the "literary studies," *litterarum studium*,[112] *litteraturae ingenuitatis studia*,[113] whose basic meaning is always the study of a language, the acquisition of a system of elementary, but precise, cultural, and literary knowledge. Placed on a higher level is the beginning of specialization, seen as erudition, *litteratorie eruditionis*, associated by Christian apologists with *saecularis eruditio*.[114] *Doctrine* has the same meaning as knowledge, of superior theoretical culture: *litterae et doctrina;*[115] it becomes more and more distinct from and more highly placed than the mere *litterae*. It is the incipient equivalent of "science," which includes, absorbs, and, at the same time, surpasses "reading and writing." The purely scientific connotations ("natural sciences," for example) make their first appearance: *litterata scientia*.[116] We keep treading the firm ground of accumulating and assimilating knowledge *(litteraturae fiducia)*,[117] with a perpetual tendency toward diversification and specialization.

The result is the complete identification of *literature* with the notion of culture, an obviously central definition, widespread, unanimously accepted, and preeminently classical. For many centuries, this will be the predominant and defining acceptation of literature. *Literature = written culture*. "Cultivated letters" *(litterarum cultu: non ignobilis)*[118] is, therefore, not a pleonasm, but the very synonym, the very doublet of the term "literature": an object and a method of knowing, that is, schooling, education, cultural upbringing *(Bildung)*, *plena litterarum cognitio*.[119] Grammar, in the sense defined above, is the essential instrument that institutes, transmits, and organizes culture. It is "the most beautiful foundation of letters."[120] By analogy, the cultivated, well-educated man, "well-trained in literature,"[121] is a *litteratus: vir litteratus;*[122] the one who teaches literature is called *litterator*, the equivalent of *grammaticus*, the professor of literature. Degrees of comparison are beginning to be used as a matter of course: the man with a broad knowledge is called *litteratissimus*,[123] while he who is illiterate and unread can only be dubbed *illiteratus*.

However, the orator, the rhetorician, continues to be Antiquity's loftiest ideal. "Culture is essentially literary, residing in grammar and rhetoric and tending to realize the ideal type of orator" (H. I. Marrou).[124] Letters are completely absorbed by the notions of instruction, knowledge, and culture *(cultura animi)*.[125] The literary spirit of Antiquity is original and primarily pedagogical.[126]

Vocation for Totality

This cultural spirit is at the same time engrossing, in the sense that it endeavors to express, through one work, all the writings and knowledge comprised in or derived from these writings. Before becoming diversified, specialized, classified, hierarchic, *literature* (= written culture) conceives itself metonymically, the part being conceived, defined as the total. For this reason, it "suffers" for want of a corresponding global term. This crucial moment in the biography of the idea of literature (its great ancient setback) is expressed by Aristotle in a masterly way. He deplores the fact that the art that uses simple words or words set in verses "but this has hitherto been without a name."[127] In a sense, this is the very birth certificate—negatively speaking—of the idea of literature: To lament the lack of a specific word that might refer to all literary genres. The concurrent term, *poetry*, seems to be better suited to this end. It suggests, as early as this, a substitute, a tacit, a functional synonym, acceptable for all poetic genres.[128]

The overtaking by *litterae* of the concept of totality is—from this vantage point—the decisive semantic act. It is progressively consummated within Latin culture, as the terms *litterae* and *litteratura* become ever more usual. The sum total of letters in a proper (graphic) and figurative sense, the sum total of *writings*, the sum total of *literature*, as with St. Augustine *(in omni litteratura)*[129] can, therefore, be conceived. In Cicero[130]—in every respect a true *incipit*—we already find the phrase *omni litterarum generi*.[131] Consequently, the historical memory of literature as writing becomes quite clear: It is progressively expanded to incorporate everything that can be expressed or recovered through writing, that is, the sum total of sacred and profane writings. Any literalization becomes, *ipso facto*, literature. That is to say, any discourse set on paper becomes literature.

The same cumulative mechanism is at work in the sphere of culture. It implies the transition from all writings, irrespective of genre, to all the activities and values linked to writing, as well as the connotations of any writing. According to the Greek poet, muses "know everything."[132] There are "poets knowledgeable in all the arts."[133] The Latin word, *litteratura* takes over, expresses, and determines to a better degree this integrated cultural content: *omni litteratura, omnimodae litteraturae* are usual phrases, for example with Tertullian.[134] The central cultural meaning of the word literature lends itself to an even more unmistakable identification in a formula like *totius litteraturae ac scientiae*.[135]

The Book

The basically formal content of "literature" undertakes a parallel development. First, one can notice a development, as well as an etymological updating of the terminology regarding writing material and technique. A book is "written;" it is a support, a written object by definition. This sense also is stabilized as early as Antiquity. To our day, a book has been an epiphenomenon, an avatar, a derivative product of writing. It is defined by a wide variety of technical concepts: *graphé, grámmata*, but especially *biblos* or *biblón* = document, epistle, writing; (Latin): *charta vel membrana, tabula, cortex, libellos, liber*, notions from outside the field of literature[136] (in the present, modern acceptation, then unknown, of the term). A popular etymology, seeing *liber* as derived from *liber* (= tree bark),[137] shows that we are still lingering in the same empirical, practical sphere. This is why all the material qualities of writing could be transferred to the book: pinning down the voice through "written words,"[138] memorizing *(De libris memoriam)*,[139] communication, dissemination, etc.

The great spiritual categories of the age also leave their imprint on book terminology: orphic books and others in the same class are sacred, *hieroi logoi, sepher*. Christian faith turns the Bible into the Holy Book, par excellence. Latin polytheism is also replete with *libri sacri*. Christianity is content with its *sanctus volumen*.[140] The consequence is canonization, the imperative of the *only* book, often imposing a reign of terror. Such ravages—repeated periodically in the course of history—had an effect that can still be felt today. Conversely, lay books pass for *gentillium litterarum libros, codices saeculares*,[141] or *profanus codices* (Paulin de Nola).[142] It is worth mentioning that this notion conveys disdain and intolerance.

The same spiritual horizon makes a book an essential object of "learning." Knowledge depends on orality but, after the invention and dissemination of writing, it becomes more and more dependent on the text of the written book. Inevitably, therefore, it becomes bookish and didactic. It follows that at the dawn of its cultural life, the role of the book was mainly pedagogical: a schoolbook. The book is a "mute counselor."[143] Homer (then Virgil) passes for authors of all-comprehensive books, comprising not only all literature, but all the science of the age as well. One of the inscriptions of Roman Dacia proclaims the very same principle: "Learn . . . from Homer about the events of the Trojan war."[144]

The idea of the only book is, similarly, hatched in this manner and in this period. It will embark on a long career, continuing through the modern age. For the time being, a book is conceived as a synthesis of all spiritual life, a multivalent symbol of nature, of history, of the whole world.[145] All these become, as early as this, *topoi:* "the book of nature," "the book of creatures," etc., great, widespread clichés. "The book of history" records heroic deeds, triumphs, victories, etc. This is how the concept of a total, unique, source of knowledge is born, as an archetype of books, an only text, absolute and exemplary.

At the same time, the book is increasingly identified with "literary work,"[146] that is, with "literature" proper (in the present acceptation of the term). A substitute for and general synonym of literature, the book is diversified according to genres: dramatic,[147] poetic (Homer) and many others (Honorius: *historiae, fabulae, libri oratorie et ethicae*).[148] The definition is still extensive, global, loose. But it does break new ground, paving the way for the explicit analytical formulae to be used abundantly later on.

The Library

First the material, then the intellectual organization of the book and of *literature* brings about the concept of *library*. Its meaning is equally cumulative and all-embracing; in addition, it is organizational. It sets forth the idea of collecting literature, conserving, and administering it and making it available to the public.

Derived directly from the Greek word *biblón* = book, (Greek) *bibliotheke (biblion + théke* = chest, space to deposit books) the Latin word *bibliotheca* maintains, all through Antiquity, its primary meaning of deposit, archive, thesaurus of books: "book citadel;" *bibliopolis,*[149] *librorum repositio, ibi recondetur libri.*[150] Also ancient are the words *libraria* and *librarius.*[151] To confine ourselves to the Greek and Latin world, the first libraries are the products of collecting, accumulating, even of snobbery, starting with the famous library of Alexandria.[152] Ptolemy the Philadelphian was prone to exactly the same impulse, *studio bibliothecarum;*[153] likewise, some Greek despots, among whom Pisistrates, the founder of the first public library in Athens.[154] Asinius Pollio consecrates (39 B.C.) Rome's first public library, made possible due to "war booty."[155] Varro's treatise, *De bibliothecis,* is, alas, lost.

The age's great spiritual trends provide the first qualifiers for "library." As the Bible is the prototype of all books, it will be, especially for Christian writers, the obvious synonym. *Bibliotheca divina,* or *sacra.*[156] The semantic amalgam leads to a play on words, Christian as well: *Bibliotheca mea servat meam bibliothecam.*[157] In the Imperial epoch, the idea of public editing and access, of stored and divulged writing, is also strangely asserted, *in bibliothecas referre.*[158] Similarly, a man of learning becomes, preeminently, a bookworm, *bibliothecae politus.*[159]

The ideal of reaching up to all the writings and to all culture is also inevitably included. The program of the library of Alexandria stipulates the collecting of books and histories belonging to all nations.[160] The selection criterion (Callimachus, Suidas) is not lacking either; on the contrary, it is generalized. ("I am merely selecting from the different departments of literature, not reviewing complete libraries.")[161] Hence, two long-range consequences. Selection changes into a canon, first Alexandrine and then Christian,[162] while totalization makes it necessary to use genre classification, for practical reasons mostly. We are at the still remote origins of the modern age's decimal classification.[163] Finally, the two extremes of "book" and "library"—the sum total, universal, at the one end, the unique book at the other—are also present in ancient awareness and terminology. On the one hand, the idea of a "universal library" is created and begins to take hold (Diodorus Siculus, Apollodorus); on the other hand, there is an abridgment, a summing up, a concentration in a unique digest, as in Photius's "library" ("an inventory and enumeration of the books I have read"). Cultural compilation, in just one great accumulated synthesis, becomes the supreme ideal.

The Beginning of Bibliography

In a book-revering ambience, the first techniques and reflections on bibliography were bound to appear as an activity ever more tightly bound to book production, in constant growth throughout Europe. The first catalogue of the library of Alexandria *(Pinakes)* is the world's first bibliography list. Its aim is exhaustive, "everything about everything," "the best extant writings of all men,"[164] without any selection. The organizing principle is enumeration, a book list, molded on the tables and ledgers of the same library of Alexandria.[165] The first catalogues of Christian works and writers *(De viris illustribus, de scriptoris ecclesiasticis)*[166] correspond to this cumulative-quantitative documentary record.

A banal, trivial fact, but with many consequences. The genre classification of the catalogue-bibliography of the library of Alexandria is the first typology, even "morphology," of European literature. As for the selection principle (to record what "was eminent in any kind of literature"),[167] along with classification, it can be considered one of the empirical origins of literary criticism. Similarly, the chronological order of the catalogues of Christian authors is a prefiguration of what will later be *literary history*. How poor a hold the idea of literature had at the time also results from the fact that the key notion in such a list is *auctores* alone ("nos auctores").[168] These remote, modest, purely bibliographical origins of two brilliant (and hypertrophied) future subjects are generally ignored.

The Encyclopedia

We can gain even more insight into what culture (= literature) consisted of for the ancients if we analyze its content and basic trends.

The ever-predominant didactic sense is geven more and more precise definitions. Organization of culture requires a "technical," specialized definition, which will be *encyclopedia* (Greek) *egkiklios paiadeia*, education, the sphere of knowledge. Thus, the first literary genre is the encyclopedia, the encyclopedic genre. In its original acceptation, the term only refers to the idea of ordinary schooling, primary studies, what is today understood by "general culture."[169] Latin will assimilate and at the same time incorporate the Greek term *literatura encyclique doctrinarum omnium disciplina* (= which encloses, as if in a circle, the knowledge of literature and of other sciences),[170] *orbis doctrinae* (= global science).[171] In this respect, the ancient world's first encyclopedists were, in fact, the sophists, men of a "professional" universal culture.

This is how the notion of totality, mentioned above, is given precise determination, as well as theoretical and practical legitimacy. However, ancient poetry in general is, actually, an "encyclopedia," a "tribal encyclopedia" of the community, of the *polis*.[172] The library itself is encyclopedic, by definition. So is written, cultivated, rhetoric learning. The orator's cultural and professional ideal is "to know all the questions and all the arts,"[173] a widespread desideratum in Antiquity (Macrobius, *Somnum Scipionis*, Clement of Alexandria, etc.). It sums up, in different terms, the old Hellenic ideal of universal knowledge: *polimathia*. The Hellenistic age cultivates it in the form of vast scholarly compilations. These tend to become extremely concentrated in Roman times, characterized by an eclectic syncretism.[174] Thus, compilation, universality, and synthesis become the intrinsic law of the encyclopedia. It is still instrumental today.

The cycle of knowledge consists in the study and assimilation of the seven fundamental subject matters grouped in the *trivium* (grammar, rhetoric, dialectics) and *quadrivium* (geometry, arithmetic, astronomy, music). This pattern remains intact through the course of Antiquity and is also adopted by Christian writers, including Cassiodorus, among others.[175] It is the first original systematization of European culture. The Middle Ages will take over and develop it fully.

"Liberal Art"

Culture (= literature) is not only encyclopedic, but "liberal" as well, *liberal art*. The notion appears in the encyclopedic cycle *(De septem liberalibus disciplinis)*[176] and actually enriches the idea of literature through its new, technical connotation, hence the need to gloss, to provide lexical explications: *liberali dicuntur arte*,[177] *libros artium, quas liberales vocant*.[178] The fact that a false etymology was suggested is yet another proof of incertitude: *liberales liber<libris*. This can be explained by the fact that liberal arts indeed presuppose "books," "reading," etc. The error is disseminated

through authoritative treatises as well.[179] Nor is the proposed synonym, *litterae . . . communes aut liberales*,[180] a happier choice.

Again, the basic meaning can only be the fundamental, that is, didactic, one. A series of Latin synonyms for the notion of "literary study" and "culture" express it quite clearly: *disciplinae liberales*,[181] *liberalibus artibus erudire*,[182] *liberalium scholae, liberalia < studia . . . quae Graeci eleutheria > appelant.*[183] Connected phrases are attested at the same time: *Disciplinae liberales*,[184] *liberalium litterarum scientia.*[185] The framework and cohesive factor of all these "arts" is always the supreme "art": *grammar* = source, base and integral study method: *origo et fundamentum liberalium litterarum.*[186] That it should be considered identical to the encyclopedia[187] is also quite natural. Needless to say, all these "arts" are secular, freed from the burden of consecration and initiation: *liberalibus secularis litteraturae studiis.*[188] Their recuperation *(liberales* or *seculares artes)* in a Christian sense aims at consolidating Christianity and the Church.[189] The backdrop, of course, remains the radical dissociation, perpetually invoked, already examined above.

What is really new and of great import is the social, ideological, and moral status bestowed upon literature as a liberal art. It results from discriminating between manual toil and intellectual work, that is, between mechanical and liberal arts, *illiberales, sordidae* versus *liberales, ludicra, ingenua.*[190] The former are only performed by slaves, the latter alone are "worthy of a free man": *Homine libero digna sunt*[191] and of a civilized man: it is "shameful and boorish"[192] for a civilized, cultivated man not to have known them. Literature leaves the schoolroom and permeates society and its value hierarchy ever more thoroughly.

The psychological implications and those of a spiritual hygiene are even greater. This is the direction along which, in time, all the modern notions such as autonomy, gratuitousness, disinterested or useless activity, etc., will gather momentum. The vulgar, illiberal arts, *ad usum vitae*,[193] are *sordidae*, profitable, useful, venal, mercenary.[194] They do not cultivate pleasure, contemplation, disinterested emotions; on the contrary, liberal arts provide pleasure, are not useful, and do not target personal gains.[195] Thanks to them, the spirit is freed from practical, material worries. Progress is already considerable.

"Human Letters"

Letters, literature in other words, are not only *liberal*, but *human* as well. These two notions have the same ancient origin—essentially didactic— but they acquire superior significances. Through them, the idea of literature branches out and starts to soar. Generating newer and newer meanings of the idea of literature, Classical Antiquity ever more forcibly proves its great generative and propulsive force.

This explains why, from the very beginning, "letters" and "humanities" seemed so closely intertwined (for example, the age of Cicero),[196] *de studiis humanitas ac litterarum: cum Musis, id est cum humanitate et doctrina.*[197] Literature is not only "literal," but also "humanist" and will subsequently be described as such in European cultural and educational syllabuses, *regulis artium humanorium.*[198] These "arts" are, at the same time, the expression and symbol of lay, profane culture, clearly dissociated from the sacred one, as shown by the basic structural pattern, *divinarum humanarumque rerum.*[199]

The original trait of "human letters"—another unprecedented phenomenon in the biography of the idea of literature—lies in granting culture an ethical and educational dimension. Literature is both humanized and moralized. General spiritual knowledge prepares youth for "humanity."[200] Therefore, culture, that is, literature, undertakes one essential formative role: It defines, reveals and perfects human essence. The anthropologizing and humanizing of culture overlap. *Humanitas* instructs man, morally enobles him, *politior humanitatis.*[201] It is "the Greeks' *paideia;* that is what we [Romans, our note]" call . . . education and training in the liberal arts".[202] A most fecund form of "cultivating the soul" *(cultus animi humanitatis cibo),*[203] the only one worthy of free men: *humanissimus ac liberalissimum;*[204] it is the work of the spirit most worthy of a human and most becoming a free man *(hanc animi adversionem humanissimam ac liberalissimam indicaretis).*[205]

To sum up, the essential moral effect consists of the education, shaping and, especially the acquisition of the human condition, in humanization. "May be called men, only those are perfected in the arts appropriate to humanity."[206] Only they who passionately love and cultivate arts and sciences are "the most human of humans," *humanissimi.*[207] Humaneness, kindness (philanthropy, *humanitas*) is the supreme virtue, the equivalent of civilization *(humanus cultus civilisque),* a preeminently social quality *(humanitate provinciae).*[208] In short, humanity converted, through letters, to civilization.

"Good Letters"

Antiquity experiences one other type of turning literature to good account, another definition of "letters." They are "good" not only in a cultural sense—this is self-evident as the whole theory of *grammar = culture* is based on this assumption—but also in an ethical, pedagogical sense. *Bonae sunt litterae*[209] is a profound ancient belief. Turned into a motto, it is passed on to all European culture. The synonym, *bonas artes*[210] is part of the same predominant cultural ethos. This meaning is clearly put forth, especially by Aulus Gellius as *eruditio institutioque in bonas artes.*[211] Culture can, be definition, be only "good." Never in its history—and this is not an accidental statement—will it be conferred higher honors.

It is therefore natural to invest letters with extremely exigent moral features. Literature is a "(moral) instrument of all life," *omnem vitam littera-tura.*[212] Another, later definition sees it as the supreme virtue: "A knowledge of letters is the utmost virtue": *litteratura, que omnium virtutem maxima est.*[213] The reference, of course, is to good letters, equated with sacred letters, *sacrae litterae.* Symmetrically, profane letters are by definition "bad," condemnable, *malae litterae* a typically Christian discrimination,[214] as is, for instance, the theater *(histrionis).* As can be seen, literature's guilt complex—which now gets underway—can boast of deep, prestigious roots. It will be intensified with time.

THE COORDINATES OF CULTURE

Inevitably, the first pinning down of literature in time and space also belongs to Antiquity. The spirit of history and the idea of a "national specificity" of literature begin to manifest themselves, similarly, the awareness of the universality of letters. These are new and considerably enriching dimensions of the idea of literature.

New Versus Old Letters

The conclusion that the origins of literature are quite remote in time, that poetry is by definition original, and that the inspiration for it is sacred, therefore, primordial, belongs both to Hellenic[215] and to Latin[216] spirituality. The idea of a literary tradition that can also boast of a respectable age is born in much the same manner. The current formula, *litterae antiquae*[217] defines ancient writing, in its entirety, in a double sense: graphic and cultural—literary. In time, as classical tradition is consolidated, it becomes *litterata vetustas.* The typical expression of this prestige is found in the exemplary model, the canon: Homer for the Greeks,[218] Greek literature, *exemplaria Graeca,*[219] for the Romans. The erudite, professorial, bibliographical, well-systemized origin of the ancient literary canon is quite well-known.[220] Through its very essence and mechanism, grammar invites classicism and authority. By definition, it provides and reinforces laws and rules.

Contrasting with the poet *Vetus,* we find the poet *Novus,* a well-defined category in Latin literature: *poetae novi,* or *neoterici* (first and second centuries A.D.). They oppose esthetic orthodoxy, rouse admiration, but also satirical irritation, because *omnia novat.*[221] The basic ideas are personality, freedom of inspiration, evasion from rules, originality, novelty *(carmina non prius audita),* the innovation that pleases.[222] These are essential concepts which, accompanied by ever-higher praise, will be more and more frequently associated with the idea of literature. The dialectical relationship between the two terms already raises two problems, the importance of which has been preserved, and has, indeed, been enhanced, to this day.

One is that of establishing the date, which opens the way for an argument centered upon the historical relativism of literary development and evaluation. In Antiquity, it was found that literature possessed a historical dimension, that it passed from stage to stage, in a progression. And if there is *ancient* and *new* comedy,[223] which one is better? And just how "ancient" must you be in literature to be acknowledged as such and to pass for "perfect"?[224] The confusion and perplexity of the Latins is great. The second dispute is even more fertile: in fact, it is the very source of the famous *Querelle des Anciens et des Modernes*, periodically rekindled until today. Professional, official poetry, as represented by *Collegium poetarum*, clashes with the poets *novi*, "marginal," and "non-conforming." Hence, the confrontation between two literary "ages," two value-orders[225] and, in the last analysis, between two styles: the "archaics and the innovators,"[226] followed by the polemic between "Atticism" and "Asianism."[227] The introduction into literature of a historical perspective was of prime importance: Time alone will decide whether or not satire, to take one example, is poetry.[228] History resolves everything, including the semantics of poetry, value mutation, and value reception. This incipient literary historicism will prove to be very far-reaching. Literary history becomes necessary, legitimate, possible.

National Versus Universal Letters

In Antiquity, the idea of literary totality is not limited to a cultural-encyclopedic acceptation. It also defines a consistent linguistic area, a specific historical and cultural tradition, even a spiritual "property" that can be neither alienated nor misidentified. These are the still embryonic roots of what will later be called "national literature." Prior to being written down, this literature is oral; its underlying reason is the consciousness of belonging to a spoken language. From this point of view, "national literature" appears—as an idea and term—to exist beyond and outside the sphere of literature.

The awareness of its existence is first formulated in two precise, historical-possessive syntagms: "old literature" (*litterarum veterum*)[229] and "our literature" (*nostrae . . . literae*,[230] subsequently *nostra . . . litteratura*).[231] Thus, the first step of literature's "nationalization" is its "history," assumed and assimilated collectively. The second is an open proclamation of national identity: *romanae litterae*,[232] *latine litterae*,[233] phrases that are frequently encountered, especially from the Imperial Age on. Hence, the awareness of a differentiation (Plautus: *fabula tota graeca est*), the acknowledgement of the identity of other languages, writings and literatures: *Graeca litteratura* = Greek writings and the Greek alphabet,[234] the concept of a national alphabet, *graecis litterae*.[235] Similarly, *litteratura judaeorum* = all the sacred Judaic writings.[236] However, the consciousness of a linguistic identity still prevails (Varro, *De lingua latina*).

Very closely related, and branching off from the same stem, is what is to be called "popular poetry," the vernacular language and expression, outside the sphere of cultivated expression. The concept first sprouts with the Greeks (Socrates)[237] and begins to gain ground with the Romans through phrases such as *sermus cotidianus* (distinct from the idiom *poeta doctus*) or *vernaculas litteras* = the law of the Jews, sacred literature in Hebrew.[238] A fourth-century text speaks of *scripta latina rustica*.[239] The meaning is that of "common," "current writing," below the level of *cultivated letters* or outside them. With variable intensity, this sense will be periodically rediscovered and roused, until Romanticism.

At the other end, the prefiguration of "world literature" abides by the same geographical and spiritual laws of causality: In fact, *Graecis litteris et Latinis*[240] refers to all available literature of the age, national as well as supra-national. Ideas such as a common literary culture, literary community and international civilization acquire precise contours with Cicero.[241] In the Hellenic world, a cosmopolitan current (the Stoics, the Sophists) propagates, broadly speaking, the ideal of the universal Polis[242] and of the world citizen,[243] above fatherlands or national borders.[244] The decisive factors are the dissemination of Hellenistic culture, as well as the spreading of a Roman cultural *Koiné*. Asianism, through the opening up to universality of the Greek-Roman world, as well as Christianity, which, through its apologists, extends the global categories of *Christian* and *pagan* to the writings, culture, and literature of all peoples, become decisive factors in the recognition of the universal character of culture and literature (including the present-day sense of the word). In time, the idea of a *lingua franca* more firmly consolidates this primeval universalization of letters.

The Beginning of Estheticizing

"Beautiful Letters"

Extremely fecund, in a sense even decisive for the development of this biography, are the interferences between the idea of literature and one of the central values of the Ancient world, *the beautiful*, especially when conceived as entering into a synthesis with *the good* and with *the truth*: *Kalokagathia, Kaloaletheia*. These interferences operate on several planes but, except for a few formulations that can be defined as "stylistic" or "formalist," it is hard to find, in Antiquity, definitions of literature and poetry that wholly anticipate the modern acceptations. However, there are intermittent prefigurations, some of them of outstanding interest.

All rhetoric, for example, is nothing but an intense improvement and beautifying of original orality: "For this oratory of ours must be adapted to the ears of the multitude, for charming or urging their minds. . . ."[245] Current and defining formulae for rhetoric are *ars bene dicendi*, or *peritia loquendi*. The mold is an oral one: "The true grace of Attic diction".[246] Its aim—all through Antiquity—is to instruct, but also to please, to induce emotion.[247] According to Dionysius of Halicarnassus, oratory is a genuine musical oral science.[248] In a similar manner, poetry is a "beautiful song,"[249] poets are "beautiful speakers."[250] They are praised for *suavitas vocis*,[251] for the "charm of their speech" (*verborum lenoncinio*).[252] Oral poetry is by definition beautiful.

So are writing and written poetry, though this will only be acknowledged at a later stage. Writing itself goes through two phases: That of learning the alphabet and that of acquiring calligraphy, or beautiful penmanship.[253] Though the problem has been quite thoroughly studied, it may not have been pointed out with sufficient emphasis that the famous ancient formula, *ut pictura poesis*,[254] coined by Simonides, preserves in it much of the memory[255] of pictography, or hieroglyphs, etc. One of the first *expressis verbis* definitions of poetry is, in fact, closely dependent on this seduction of the graphic image. Graduation from the strictly oral stage of rhetoric leads to the conclusion that "the value of written discourse lies not so much in the thinking behind it, as in its expression."[256] A further step toward the full literalization of expression is the observation that, "Reading verses engenders more pleasure than listening to them."[257] Thus, the letter once more imposes its own regime, its efficiency, authority, and worth. As we can see, it conquers every position, one by one.

The sacralization and desacralization of creation and of poetic beauty again confirm certain well-known fundamental directions of Antiquity: Muses are beautiful, one of them is, even, "the most beautiful."[258] Divine inspiration and celestial breath is, needless to add, "beautiful."[259] Gods can only express themselves in a beautiful manner, while some oracular verses are mediocre.[260] The beautiful is also separated from the ugly, in the field of sacred letters, in Christianity. The divine verb (John, I, 14) is eminently beautiful. Christian literature is as beautiful as the pagan, Hellenic one (Clement of Alexandria).[261] The *Septuaginta* is beautiful, while the *Vulgata* is not.[262] As the muses gradually relinquish their role as sole sources of inspiration, the beautiful becomes, to an even greater extent, the poet's own concern and interpretation. It gains priority over the expression of divine truth. The author's personality is asserted. More and more often, he speaks in the first person. Sacrality changes into the theme park of the out-of-the-ordinary miraculous.[263] The transition from an oracular verse to an accessible prose text, as in Pythia's oracles, also confirms this laicizing process. The idea that a god might express himself in any other manner but a beautiful one is rejected. Therefore, anything bland, prosaic, ugly, can only have a human origin.[264]

Letters, *letterae*, are no less "beautiful." The modern term that translates this quality is *belles lettres*. But its ancient, specific meaning is the familiar one: culture, erudition, knowledge transmitted through writing, and "literature." The present-day equivalent, used in translations, is, strictly speaking, an anachronism. The so-called ancient "beautiful letters" represent the whole cycle of knowledge (encyclopedic, liberal, human, good). Nonetheless, an equivalent for "beautiful knowledge"—the only proper phrase—is non-existent in Greek.[265] For this concept (in its present acceptation), the Romans only used formulas such as *politus litteris*,[266] *plenus litteris*, *litterarum studia*,[267] or, simply, *litteris*.[268] Relatively late, however (sixth, seventh centuries A.D.), a term is coined that comes close to the present formula: *pulcherimum litterarum*.[269] As far as the frequency of use is concerned, every one of these acceptations is quite marginal; but they are central as semantic halves, within our system of reading as well. An evolution toward qualitative values of letters and style can be noticed at the same time: from *litterarum subtilitati* ("literary knowledge"),[270] to *elegans, politus, pulcher, subtilitatis*. It is a way of saying that culture's tendency is to make expression more subtle, in modern terms, to make it more "esthetic."

Beauty (which in Antiquity is far from having the purist, formalist, esthetic-autonomous acceptations of our days)[271] has, as spheres of direct, specific applications only oratory (that is, rhetoric) and poetry (and only by implication, and through a widening of content, "literature"). There are, certainly, "beautiful speeches"[272] and poems that "say many fine things,"[273] *pulchra esse poemata*,[274] but nothing more. The idea of beauty (poetic or literary) develops quite independently from that of "beautiful culture" (the forthcoming *belles lettres*). It becomes widespread and consolidated fairly late, not before the Alexandrian and Hellenistic ages.

The way in which poetry annexes and assimilates the idea of beauty allows us to anticipate the further evolution of the notion of "literary beauty." Certain attributes (*prepon, decorum, aequivocatio*, etc.)[275] belong to composition in general. Also, the consciousness of fictionality ("many lies as if they were true"),[276] or "the embellishment of meter."[277] But the concern for metrics and euphony, as with Crates of Mallos,[278] naturally intrinsically belongs to poetic beauty in the future acceptation of the phrase, which will become current. Beautifying the writing—"the beautiful manner of writing," "beautiful words," "fine diction,"[279] are, first and foremost, attributes of the works written in metric verse. Phrases like *labor limae* (Horace), and *accurate scriptae* (Pliny the Younger) compete with rhetorical expression through the characteristic means of writing, from a perspective which is, above all, poetic.

A series of technical elements and phrases are more and more frequently associated with the idea of poetry. On the one hand, "beautiful composition" (Dionysius of Halicarnassus, *On Literary Composition*, 6–9), and "beauties of style and sublimities" (Longinus);[280] on the other, "beautiful form" (Philodemus of Gadara).[281] The latter is indistinguishable from beautiful style and the rhetorical "beautification" of discourse,[282] from *verbis pulcherimis elocutum* (Fronto) and broadly speaking, from the notion of an oral and written style:" . . . The best "literary" style is that which is pleasant to read."[283] Notions such as sonority, rhythm, variety, and harmony, become specific poetic attributes.

But all this is not yet enough to give poetry a very exact status, and especially a specific place in the order of the arts. The meaning of the word keeps oscillating between its etymon (= a creation in any literary genre, as the notion covers all the realm of literature, tragedy, history),[284] etc., and all poetic production, in which case the proper term [285] is, again, that of *literatura*.[286] The truth is, throughout Antiquity, *poetry* and *letters* remain synonymous, loosely so, but nonetheless synonymous. The link between *poeta, scriptura* and *littera* is constant and indissoluble. A remark like: Dionysius "was fond of literature and tried his hand at all kinds of poetry"[287] fully expresses the ambiguity of the situation, made worse through translation. The terms overlap—they can be used alternatively and nevertheless tend to differ and acquire specialized meanings. A real gap in the idea of *litteratura* and in its tightly closed system, however, is wrought by esthetics, by identifying a series of poetic and esthetic qualities sensibly linked to the aforementioned ones. As soon as these qualities are well-defined and associated with a given text, *poetry* tends to be directly substituted for *literature*, which finds itself outrun and outstripped. If, in Aristotle's view, philosophy is superior to *poetry*,[288] the latter takes its revenge over *literature* by pushing it—as an esthetic value—deeper and deeper into the shadows. The term *grammar* (= literature) was so specialized, so technical and minor that it could in no way have been applied to a superior poetic activity, to dithyramb, lyricism, frenetic sacred inspiration, spontaneity (*sponte sua carmen*),[289] etc.

Hence, we observe the latest tension—predicted with remarkable clarity by the distinction *esoteric* versus *exoteric* writings—between poetry and the realm of culture of *general* literature. It is the first severe crisis to occur within this concept: The separation and tearing away of poetry (a term used symbolically for everything that is "literary creation" expressed in writing, with all its characteristics) from the tradition, techniques, and exigencies of culture. Confronting the grammarian and prose writer, who is nothing more than a professional "writer," the owner of specialized knowledge, there appears a rival character, of ever-growing prestige—the composer of odes, satires, and tragedies.[290] And the poet, as Philodemus of Gadara, one of the esthetes of the Hellenistic age, accurately remarked, "need not know geometry, geography and astronomy, let alone law or navigation."[291] Creative imagination will do.

This conclusion is of capital importance for the biography of the idea of literature, as it sets forth two semantic and terminological directions quite distinct from each other and increasingly divergent: On the one hand, *literature*, which continues on its course, with all that it means for preserving, transmitting, organizing and developing culture, with all its literary implications—repetitions, stereotypy, clichés; on the other, *poetry*, which brings spontaneity, individual character, novelty, and lyricism. The two directions will permanently compete or overlap until the present day. The dispute is actually structural and eternal, therefore, inevitably undecided.

Literary Versus Poetic Specificity

Initially, the ancient acceptation of the concept of "poetic specificity" was also cultural and grammatical in nature. The conception continued to be implicit, tacit, but strong and defining, being a necessary product of all the cultural ambience of the age. The ancients' literary ideal is preeminently cultural. So, from a strictly historical perspective, the term "literary specificity" seems to be an anachronism. It is, nonetheless, justified from the perspective of the complete evolution of the idea of literature. At a given moment, we find that such a "literary specificity" really exists, and that it even has a name. It is a good instance of a latent significance that can be quite clearly foreseen.

Within this cultural-literary context, the idea of *poetry* begins to redirect literary thought. "Literary" cultural specificity is backed by a "poetic" one. It is defined by a series of new theses and propositions, beginning with Platonic logical discriminations such as: What distinguishes "the beautiful manner of writing" from what is not "beautiful"; "a poet, in verse, or in plain man's prose;"[292] What is knowledge of poetry, as distinguished from poetry itself, etc.? The *Treatise on the Sublime* is meant precisely to answer the question concerning the essence and specificity of poetry; it is, by definition, supra-, anti- and a-cultural. The idea of poetry already becomes radical. It becomes excessive and exorbitant. In parallel, letters can sometimes be thought of with the same exclusive intensity, in the superlative: *litteratissimas litteras*.[293]

The process presupposes a few typical gestures that define the poet's personality as well as his poetic creation. The personalization of inspiration (no longer attributed to a muse) is an essential condition. Archilochus depicts himself, Alcaeus makes his claims to rewards and personal glory, Alcmanus boasts of his novelty, Theognis of his originality, and Sappho is the poet of pure subjectivity, etc.[294] St. Augustine knows that some of his ideas are so personal they can hardly be put in writing.[295] With the Alexandrian poets, originality is deliberate, programmed. Poetry becomes even more specific, where certain characteristic faculties and emotions are considered peculiar to it. It has natural, unpredictable causes. It is instinctual, spontaneous, artless, improvised.[296] Poetry is the language of emotions and sentiments.[297] Its product is "creative" (= "poietic"), in the sense of creative "imitation," a pivotal concept of classical Antiquity,[298] later also defined as "fiction" (*fictis, jocari*).[299] The notion will be taken up and consolidated by grammarians and encyclopedists (Diomedes, Priscian,[300] Isidore of Seville).[301] The idea of art and poetry as "lying"[302] gains ground. Later, we will come upon it again and again, as it is made use of by almost all the anti-mimetic trends. Finally, specific poetic and literary impulses lead to specific emotions, satisfactions and responses: *otio et litteris*,[303] *dulcis otio literato*.[304] Once more, the process comprises a progressive "esthetic" drive. The idea of "play" also appears, originally connected to writing.[305] A synthesis of all these notions is found in the idea of "poetic" language" ("rhythm, lingo, and melody")[306] and poetic style ("language embellished")[307] This view is central and defining for ancient poetics. Both the future content and course of literary specificity are now traced.

Autonomy and Heteronomy

To speak about the "autonomy" of literature in Antiquity might seem yet another anachronism; still, from the perspective adopted by us, it becomes quite feasible. It cannot be a question of an optical illusion, but an incipient phenomenon, comprised by the very inner law of the idea of literature: The awareness of the existence of poetic-literary specificity forces one into ever more radical, more explicit dissociations from the dominant values. The considerations on beauty—which is in the process of being dissociated from other values—also play an important role in this respect.

The abrupt or progressive parting with sacrality kicks the process into motion, as we have seen. In a way, straightforward, mystic emotion is qualitatively the same as that provided by any formal, pure estheticism. Some interpretations of Hellenic poetry (such as Hesiod's) run along such lines.[308] Frequent reference has been made, after all, to the "esthetic" intentions of primitive people, of medicine men, Tibetan bards, and so on. The notion of "literary composition" makes its appearance as soon as visual prophesying and chaotic revelations start to become "organized." This notion implies an escape from the exclusive sway of divine inspiration. Any metamorphosis of a myth into an epic scenario, any alteration brought to an old legend, any debunking of history—attitudes that were not uncommon in ancient Greece (Hecateas of Miletus)[309]—yet another step toward laic autonomy. To admit that talent is also a "natural poetic gift" is,[310] similarly, to deny, by implication, the muse's divine inspiration. Rendering personal, subjective, erotic lyricism legitimate has exactly the same relevance.

The breakaway of poetry from literature (= culture), which we have examined, is no less a typical act of gaining autonomous status. Natural talent, nature itself, defends their rights against technique, against acquired, cultivated art. Polemics are typical of the ancient world, and their theoretical expression is really a topos (*natura* versus *art*). Dispute is, first of all, characteristic of rhetoric for which the perfect gift of speech seems to be the natural faculty itself,[311] in keeping with the idea that "the general opinion is that the untrained speaker is usually the more vigorous."[312] This extends to poetry, to which the same a-cultural "naturism" is transferred (*orator fit, poeta nascitur*).[313] Pindar makes the eulogy about the born poet,[314] and several thinkers[315] are aware of the alternative study/talent, nature/craftsmanship. The clearcut dissociation of oratory from philosophy, of wisdom from elegance of language (Socrates is the "author" to quote),[316] of philosophy from (implicit or explicit) poetry, results from the same principle of the "differences among arts."[317] The most specific dissociation between oral and written language is fully realized by the end of Classical Antiquity. A Christian poet (Sidonius Apollinaris, fifth century) affirms: "There's nothing left in me of a good orator."[318] The awareness of the autonomy of written literature is, in essence, declared.

It was too early for the terminology suitable in our day, of this autonomy to be coined, but some ancient formulas came very close to defining the concept. A proposition like: One can say "many beautiful things" but "none of the things they say"[319] is part of the very essence of value dissociation. Similarly, the remark that rhapsodists sing "to produce conviction without questioning or teaching".[320] This is the equivalent of denying the utility of art. Aristotle had admitted that philosophy also was useless.[321] Proscribing the didactic function was, in fact, quite a common attitude in Alexandrian Antiquity (Philodemus of Gadara, Eratosthenes, Dionysius of Halicarnassus, Aristarchus). Even earlier, Ovid had dissociated poetry from morals.[322] The autotelism of letters as well as the call to cultivate and honor them "for their own sake" is intuitively felt (beauty exists *per se ipsum*).[323] No less so is the existence of an absolute artistic specificity ("truly artistic").[324]

On the other hand, the tension at work between autonomy and heteronomy, fully experienced by the ancient world, continues unabated to this day. Literature is a public domain, one could already say "social." Tertullian was already aware of this great truth (*Publica jam litteratura est*).[325] Hence, the right assumed by those in power to interfere, sometimes to do good (the tyrant Pisistrates orders that Homeric rhapsodies be collected), at other times to do harm (the tyrant Critias forbids rhetoric.)[326] The authority of the written text, too, is enforced through an act of political will.[327] Censorship, propaganda, and ideological guidance were, unfortunately, quite commonly practiced during Antiquity.[328] The social function of rhetoric (the defense of the meek) is strongly emphasized, as are the texts that, through their quick, effective intervention, become quite "authoritative" in various domains, barring the literary one.[329]

A series of (quite conspicuous) intellectual facts define as early as this—even if only empirically and fragmentarily—the social dimension of culture and literature. Due credit is given to the importance of social convention,[330] in the field of language inclusively.[331] A specific institution, that of public readings, forcibly raises the question of audience and literary success.[332] It preoccupies poets (Horace, Martial) and philosophers alike.[333] The final conclusion is rather skeptical, disillusioning: *Pro captu lectoris, habent sua fata libelli* (Terentianus Maurus). Literary contests and prizes arouse great interest.[334] Some manifestations of cultural and literary snobbery (collections of unread books), the use of books as luxury *(studiosa luxuria)*, and as a sign of *social standing* are described with philosophical[335] or satirical (Lucian, *Against an Ignorant Bibliophile*) acumen. Classical Antiquity makes a clear-cut distinction between a bibliophile and a philosopher.[336]

Along with such rudiments of "literary sociology," one can also note a few budding elements of "literary ideology." Evidently, the concept of "world literature" originates (as we have seen) in the view of universal man and of a cosmopolitan, international *polis* (see, for instance, Diogenes Laertius.[337] Thus, *letters* acquire an ideological dimension and a political one by implication: *polis grámmata, civitas litterarum*. It is the "city of letters," the community of values and of literature lovers animated by mutual, universal feelings and ideas, formulated in a universal language: *sed universo loquatur hominum generi*.[338] This all-embracing, utopian order reappears periodically, in one form or another, in all the future blueprints of literary "citadels." Since Classical Antiquity, *letters* have had a strong reforming and organizing propensity, of an ideal, rational—utopic—nature. Their social relevance is already militant and rigor-seeking.

What will later be called the "economy of literature" has some starting points in the same ancient period, when *letters* became institutional and were granted social status. Their practitioners (*grammatici, servi, litterati*, etc.) belong to a lucrative profession, one defined as such. Likewise, observe the *scriba* and *poeta*, incorporated into well-defined professional guilds, especially in Rome *(Collegium scribarum et historiarum, Colegium poetarum)*. Lack of consideration on the part of *liberal arts* informs all the ancient conflict between autonomy and heteronomy in literature. Martial, a typical Latin man of letters, obsessed by publicity, literary property, plagiarism, and public success, is the best example of this antagonism. Liberal professions flatly repudiate profit and servitude, mercenary professionalism. Liberal arts define themselves as gratuitous, pure, useless (the terms are modern, but the essence is revealed early), hence the necessity of keeping one's distance. Pliny the Younger apologizes when he mixes "poetry" with "business."[339] Poetry has no utility (Philodemus of Gadara).[340] It is an Alexandrian stance, one could say an "avant-garde" one, but consistently autonomist. One can now distinctly see the power-vector of this tendency, which will be perpetuated and deepened with time.

Hierarchy in Literature

The ancient world also created the first value criteria, the first literary orientation and hierarchies. Notions such as *high* and *low, superior* and *inferior, dominant* and *dominated* make their appearance now. They go hand in hand with the great values of Antiquity, which—overtly or not, but with rigorous subordination—draw up a value-scale for all writings. Virgil is declared *princeps carminum*, "the prince of poets."[341] Sacrality is the topmost value, and this is why it is used as a literary superlative: *partes sacrae et venerabilis*.[342] Symmetrically, the profane and its epiphanies, human knowledge and science included, become inferior. Writing, too, is a crucial criterion, separating (culturally, socially, etc.) the ones who write from the ones who do not.[343] Orality, illiteracy, are made short shrift of, as signs of ignorance, uncivilized behavior, barbarism even. Latin letters—more "direct" as compared to superior Greek poetry—are plagued by a certain inferiority complex.

The history of the ancient classification of the arts has been written.[344] Broadly speaking, the existence of three levels was acknowledged: *superior* (*artes maximae*), *intermediate* (*mediocrae*) and *inferior* (*minores*) arts, as with Cicero.[345] Science, poetry, and elocution belong to the second group. But in the field of writing and literature, other criteria also apply, such as "size"[346] and "sublimity".[347] The hierarchy of styles is also established on a graded scale, according to analogous, homologated criteria: sublime (*gravem*), temperate (*mediocrem*), simple (*extenuatem*),[348] or *grandis, mediocris, humilis*,[349] respectively. This classification is taken over by Christian rhetoric,[350] which, for doctrinary and missionary reasons, makes use only of *sancta simplicitas*[351] and *sermo humilis*:[352] Even the illiterate can understand a simple style (*sermo piscatorius*). The Christian poet speaks of himself as *poeta rusticum*.[353] There is, obviously, a similar gender classification; the oratorical is at the top.[354] Poetry is more philosophical than history.[355] According to the Alexandrian poets, the cyclic, encyclopedic form is, by definition, the inferior genre.

Social hierarchy is reflected by a hierarchy of art: those cultivating *liberal* arts are shown to be above those who indulge only in servile arts. The *nobles/vulgares* classification becomes operative again. Letters are a consecrating social paradigm. Those who cultivate them secure a higher social and cultural position. Stratification, however, is not at all rigid. The great poets of the Augustan Age are not high-born, and yet their genius triumphs. Horace is a *libertus'* son. Terence is himself a *libertus*. There is a leveling out, a tendency to substitute talent for the privileges of birth. "Ranks are only bestowed by literary titles."[356] The tendency becomes more marked in late Antiquity: "The only proof of nobleness is a knowledge of letters."[357] One can already see the dawn of a democracy of letters, the only one compatible with culture's intrinsic criterion. The anonymous *Carmina popularia* are powerless to confer glory.

THE SCHOOL OF LITERATURE

Letters "Spawn" Literature

One of the direct consequences of the predominant cultural regime, of its theoretical conscience, and of the practice of letters is the natural autogenesis and self-propulsion of literature. *Letters* inevitably hatch letters. They inspire, form, develop and cultivate, in every literal way. Antiquity discovers yet another great piece of truth, a real truism, entirely—and more and more pregnantly—confirmed, until the present. There can be no literature without culture, *stricto* and *lato sensu*. Which is to say that in ancient times, literature was, pre-eminently, a product of the schools. The phenomenon is particularly obvious during the Alexandrian Age, when the role grammar played was overwhelming. It is now that the notion of "didactic"—that is, academic, dogmatic—literature is born.

We shall overlook the theories, according to which, writing and study play an essential part in the development of oratorical talent.[358] The standard grammar exercise is to copy a text, to add to it or to paraphrase it, and to compose texts based on a given model. When doctrine is systematized, grammar is invested with such a function as well.[359] Without culture, there can be no literature, no poetry. An uncultivated poet cannot possibly attain poetic expression.[360] Genius provides the basic necessities, but culture alone can consolidate them.[361] Literature is a question of *paideia*. This is the first institutional theory of literary culture. Sacred hymns can only be composed by "those who know." Literature can be acquired, the poet can be educated, and he can educate others in turn *(fabula docet)*. Studies are, concomitantly, educational and creative. This early literature is made out of literature. The architect, the artist in general, must know, so to speak, "all and sundry."[362] The *poeti docti*[363] category has taken firm hold of Roman literary awareness; so too is the device of literary contagion, of incorporating other writers' texts in one's own work.[364] Novelty and originality are a question of arrangement, of reorganization of the material.[365]

This phenomenon is of utmost importance, as it engenders a series of new literary actions and terms that actually enrich the idea of literature. Annotations, *extracts (abstracts)*, *chrestomathies (stromata, catena, litterarum penus)*, compilations are literature's very cultural birth certificate. The same impulse presides over a number of potential literary activities: *translation, text-completion, quotation, summarizing*. New species flourish, whose genesis is similarly dependent on *letter*: the *calligraph*, the *epigram*, the *palimpsest*, the *cento*-collation, the *apocrypha*, the *fake*, the *paraphrase*, the *imitation*, the *parody*, and *plagiarism*. Literary clichés (*topoi*, molds, and patterns of any kind) are similarly formed.[366] Antiquity generates all these original literary phenomena, real indexes and preludes to what the moderns will call "intertextuality," as well as most of the analogous terminology. At any rate, from the present perspective,[367] this "classroom literature" is much more than mere "decadence." The literature *on* literature, that is, the discovery that literature itself can be a literary subject,[368] appears in the same context, having similar effects, starting with a eulogy of writing in all of its guises (tables, copyists, stenographers, epigraphs, epigrams). The *book*, similarly, through the Latin poets, paves the way for one of the great European literary themes, as does the *library*, the writing primers (*ars dictaminis*), the subject matters—the "seven liberal arts." *Philology* becomes an allegorical literary character, as does *grammar*.[369] Specific genres (the legend, didactic poetry) have their starting point in this cultural act of reading and in the literary object of the latter. The product, preeminently narcissistic, of this introversion of the letter, is the *poetry of poetry*, cultivated by great poets,[370] as well as minor (Ausonius, *de suis poematis*). There is only one step from narcissism to egocentrism and megalomania, both typical literary phenomena. This direction—with ridiculous, hilarious, irritating effects—is also inaugurated in Antiquity.

Critical Literature

The basic ancient meaning of "literature" is *litteratura*, that is, the science of letters, *grammar*, which also includes the sense "criticism." Implicitly or explicity, literature is also *criticism*. It is *born*, partly, as criticism. Again, its foundations are intrinsically scholarly, cultural, closely connected to the theory and assimilation of letters. The fusion criticism-literature begins now. The "critical" acceptation of the term *literature* is both central (semantically speaking) and variable and marginal (from a contextual point of view). Its relevance will prove to be constant—in spite of some oscillations—and forever bound to literary thought and literary practice.

The following statement merits great emphasis: At its origins, criticism is a purely didactic product, an elementary, essential intellectual tool.

It is pedagogical and cultural by definition. It appears and develops in scholarly and erudite circles. This structure and this tendency, strictly speaking, are perpetuated to our days. Criticism naturally upholds, perpetuates, consolidates, and develops literature and literary culture.

The transformation of grammar—"literature"—into criticim is very rapid. Originally, it is a generic science, which becomes specialized due to a displacement of accents and a change in the priority of its activities. In the beginning, grammar is but the art of speaking and writing correctly, with a strong propensity to rhetoric: "The art of speaking well" *(recte loquendi scientia)*.[371] The definition is then completed, in keeping with the basic pattern *(reading-writing)*; the science of "correct reading and speaking."[372] We are still in the *prima litteratura* stage. The reflexive, explicative, interpretative consciousness of literature, glossing upon itself *ab origine*, has already begun to function.

The traditional forms of ancient criticism are: establishing and editing texts *(distinguere, emendare, adnotare)*,[373] the lesson, to be later called "explication de texte," and "close reading," commentary, and systematic study. Its culmination is in the Alexandrian Age. Latin terminology comprises *lectio, recitatio, enaratio* (Varro),[374] *poetarum pertractatio*,[375] and *poetarum ennarationem*.[376] Later grammarians will take over both of the terms and their glosses, extremely explicit, especially with Diomedes.[377] It is, of course, still a predominantly oral form of criticism—public professional reading on a specialized subject.

The aim is to explain texts and make them understood: *intellectu poetarum*,[378] that is, to interpret them, an operation that is brought to the fore. The definition, once again, is stereotypical: grammar is *scientia interpretandi poetas* (Palaemon, Audax, Asper, Marius Victorinus, etc.).[379]

In this manner, criticism is indistinguishable from *hermeneutics*, an operation that also evolves from the sacred to the profane. Originally, the poet is seen as a mediator and interpreter of the gods; both poets[380] and philosophers[381] are aware of this status. Thus, interpretation is handed over to grammarians, professors, "connoisseurs of literature."[382] There is a shift in perspective. Myths become the subjects of poetry (Varro). They are part "of the poet's art."[383] Aristotle failed to see the religious relevance of tragedy. His definition is, in essence, a lay one.[384] All the considerations on the genesis of myths, on the names bestowed by poets upon gods, on "theogonies,"[385] are proofs of this gradual laicization of ancient hermeneutics.

Its spirit can be seen even more clearly through the operation called *enaratio* (with Diomedes, *obscurorum sensum questionumque explanatio*):[386] the explication of obscure, enigmatic, multivalent senses. While sacrality claims spiritual, symbolic and hermetic senses, laicality prefers a literal reading, allegorical, rational-conceptual explanations. Literality *(sensus litteralis)* counterbalances and often defeats the mystical sense. Literature is, first of all, literal; literal criticism starts by being symmetrically an exegesis of the letter: a decoding of plain and figurative, literal and metaphoric-symbolical meanings. Historical evolution will only perfect this invariant situation. The question of interpretative criticism is already quite plainly raised.

After *hermeneutics*,[387] *philology* is the second classical term to define literary scholarship. The term has been preserved in the great cultures, inheritors of the Greek and Latin traditions. In a sense, philology is even more closely identified with the idea of *literature*, from which—beginning with Antiquity—it cannot even be distinguished at times: literary study, studying, and editing texts. The basic, original sense, is the cultural, scholarly one: knowledge, *polimatia*, scientific study and discussion,[388] and cultural education.[389] Little by little, it becomes more identified with the accurate, literal study of texts, taking over historical linguistic study from grammar,[390] censoring and correcting language and errors of styles with purist objectives. The typical operation is called *emendatio* (with the selfsame Diomedes: *recorrectio errorum*).[391] The first learned man of this type to be called a "philologist" is Eratosthenes, one of the "curators" of the Library of Alexandria.[392]

An even more brilliant career is that of *criticism*, a term that is, for the time being, rather marginal, but one that displays a tendency to replace the general concept of grammar and literary studies, as with Crates of Mallos.[393] Critical activity (and, implicitly, its conceptual justification) becomes fully consolidated in the Alexandrian period through glosses, reviews, commentaries, monographs (Demetrios of Phalerum: *On Homer, On the Iliad, On the Odyssey*), accurate editions, and the establishment of the classical canon.[394] The hermeneutic principle of the primacy of the text also makes its appearance now ("To explain Homer through Homer"), as well as that of authorial intention: "Each author is his own best interpreter" (Aristarchus).[395] In *ars grammatica*, the final operation is *judicium* (Diomedes: *aestimatio qua poëma ceteraque scripta perpendimus*).[396] Criticism, with its tendency of replacing, even of eliminating grammar and literature, is increasingly taken to mean a literary "appreciation," "judgment," or "verdict." However, the value/non-value dissociation is initially devoid of any narrowing esthetic implication, of the present acceptations of "taste." Criticism is first and foremost concerned with "good" texts as opposed to "bad," in the sense of textual accuracy and fidelity, and then with the dissociation between "true" (literal and allegorical) and "fake" meanings. However, these intrinsically critical operations will later be overshadowed by estheticizing. Symmetrically, the *critic* is initially considered a *grammarian*, but later, when a hierarchy of competences is established, he or she can be told apart from the latter (Crates of Mallos, Cicero).[397]

At a later date, literature lessons (introduced, in Rome, by Crates of Mallos as early as the third century B.C.) and critical activity will be confounded with what, in modern terms, will be called literary theory and doctrine. The subject-matter, by definition didactical and critical, is still designated today, in most Western languages, by the Latin term *litteratura:* "courses," "lessons," "literary theory." It is a global concept, the equivalent of the first general theoretical extension of the idea of literature, a historical product of the didactic—especially Alexandrian—milieu. This milieu—"grammatical," rather than "rhetorical"—also engenders, in an implicit and explicit manner, what will later be called a "literary specificity," or even "art for art's sake."[398] But the ancients were never interested in giving a specific, comprehensive definition to literature, which had not yet entered their "arts system." Their main concern was to define literary genres as autonomous species. As for "literary" theoretical-formalist speculations, they were encompassed by the term *poetica,* not *letteratura.* And poetics—as in the case of Aristotle—still hesitates to deal with poetry as a whole, that is, in itself, or only with poetical species.[399]

Denying Literature

Finally, what our epoch calls "antiliterature" was also anticipated by Classical Antiquity in a meaningful way, even if for reasons that are mostly extraliterary. Letters are radically repudiated, on several planes, on behalf of dominant values and concepts opposed to literature.

First, writing is rejected from the perspective of orality.[400] It is anonymous, irresponsible, uncontrollable; it weakens memory and is a real simulacrum.[401] Christianity will sharpen this critique by coining the formula: "The letter killeth, but the spirit giveth life."[402] The resistance opposed by sacrality is even greater. Religion is secret, initiatic. There are countless ancient testimonies about the prohibition of writing and of books. Even Christianity ("a bookish religion") preached the doctrine of *lex scripta in cordibus.*[403] The indictment of classical, pagan culture, gives even more depth to this radical rejection.[404] The opposition of the philosophers is older yet; in Plato, it found its most characteristic ancient formulation:[405] poetry is "imitation" (fiction, lying), it is anti-religious, immoral, it corrupts, undermines civic order, etc. A written law has no power if it has not been transformed into a virtue, if it is unassimilated by practical morality, not yet "sealed" onto people's manners.[406] Christianity abolishes rhetorical eloquence and repeals "Ciceronian" style, in favor of the *sermo rusticus humilis.* An "Attican" reaction against emphasis and artifice can be found in Rome as well.[407] Not "Athens" and "the Academy," but "Jerusalem" and "the Church" are the Christian ideals.[408] Constantine the Great bans (in 325 A.D.) Porphyrius' book against the Christians. Justinian closes the

Athens school in 529 A.D. The Christian state becomes intolerant—to use a modern word, it becomes "totalitarian."

A consistent anti-cultural reaction can also be seen throughout Antiquity. Its most characteristic form is a grim attack against erudition, pedantry, encyclopedism, and humanism. Its guises are satirical (Lucian), skeptical (Sextus Empiricus), esthetic (Callimachus: "I hate cyclical forms,"[409] "A big book is a big nuisance"),[410] philosophical (Seneca repudiates the library and bibliomania), poetic: accusations against an excess of grammar and literature,[411] against copying and compiling.[412] Nature is art's superior. Talent, genius, sublimity are above and against rules.[413] The species of myth is deeply disliked;[414] similarly, is an excess of rhetoric, "affectation" and "elegance" in style.[415] The ancient sage is, by definition, anti-literary—he condemns poetry because it is devoid of knowledge, because it does not experience and implement "goodness," it lacks "philosophy." Poetry has no place in the ideological and social outlook of Antiquity.[416] Poets are only admitted to the extent that they can be useful.[417] Political manipulation of literature is, therefore, ripe. It will score outstanding "successes." The repudiation of overinterpretation ("useless literature," "Greek disease")[418] and of an excess of loquacity, leading to the praise of silence, of the inexpressible, including its mystical forms,[419] will experience important and relevant resuscitations and will be put to significant use in modern times.[420]

CONCLUSIONS

Antiquity—a period of initiation, of tentative beginnings, and also a period when the directions of future development are set forth—already brings to the fore a goodly number of essential attributes of the idea of literature. One can notice, to begin with, a homogenous conception and definition of literature, common in spirit as well as in letter to both Greek and Latin cultures. This uniform general conception is the equivalent of an incipient universal extension of the idea of literature. Second, within ancient culture, it holds a central position. It is a key-value, a pivotal-value, symbolic of one of the fundamental yearnings of the ancient soul: cognition, culture, *paideia, humanitas*. Throughout the unfolding of its biography, *literature* will experience such a privileged position only once, maybe twice. Third, of great importance is the growth in the use and the prestige of written language, indistinguishable from now on, in all respects, from the fate of literature. The gap between literature and orality widens. The latter continues to resist, directly, indirectly or through derivation, hence a confrontation, a dialectic that will constantly manifest itself, in one form or another, throughout our biography.

The following instance is of prime importance: One can easily notice that all the questions that will prove essential for the definition of literature—including the problem of terminology—are posed, be it in embryo, from the very beginning, in Antiquity. All the basic senses and significances are given, thought out, formulated, or at least anticipated now, even if in an incipient, indistinct form, oftentimes profoundly ambiguous, even this early.

At the same time, one notices a latent indecision which, for the time being, prevents us from grasping the idea of literature other than from a "finalist" perspective. Everything is still quite indistinct, even aleatory in a sense. This indetermination that we are tempted to call "congenital," paralleled by the possibility of identifying more and more precise designs and models, is fully proven in the forthcoming phases of the biography of the idea of literature.

II

The Middle Ages

Antiquity lays the foundations of the idea of literature. The Middle Ages consolidate and unify it, give it stability and extend it to cover all Western—predominantly Latin—culture. The idea of literature is uniformly spread out over a large geographical and spiritual area. At its center one finds religion, the equivalent of a strong—one should even say "totalitarian"—conversion to Christianity. This intensive sacralization constitutes the background of literature; it permeates all its compartments and determines its essential terminology. This is the fundamental note of the medieval stage of the idea of literature, its crucial contribution to its own historical development.

SACRED LETTERS

As sacred value is the apex of medieval spiritual life, *sacred literature* becomes, quite naturally, the central "definition" of literature, the most widespread and prestigious of all definitions. It is the Middle Ages' "official" acceptation, consecrated by all official and religious written records. The result is the unanimous, solemn recognition of the primordial, substantial sacrality of literature.

The current meanings take up the terminology of Antiquity and enthrone it permanently. The Fathers and apologists of the Church take over and generalize this terminology (St. Augustine, St. Jerome, Tertullian, St. Cassian, et al.). Once again, and on a large scale, we come across *littera christi* and *mysticis litteris*[1] and, with an even greater frequency, *divinae litterae*[2] and *sacrae litterae* (. . . *tà hierà grámmata*). *Sacra scriptura* and *divina scriptura*, directly related to writing, also have a glorious career;[3] similarly, do *sacra pagina*, and, less often, *caelestis pagina*. *Divina pagina*[4] is also used occasionally. But even more infrequent is *litteratura divina*,[5] in permanent semantic and lexical competition with *littera*, which still outnumbers it authoritatively and is still, in the true acceptation of the term, the *leader*.

The enormous increase in ecclesiastical writings, backed by the scholastic, classifying spirit, has an important analytical effect upon the idea of literature. Classes, categories and species appear. It is, in fact, literature's first "genre" classification—the genres are, in principle, sacred, imposed by and projected against a theological background. One of the first criteria, to be found in St. Augustine and St. Jerome,[6] is the dissociation between *scripturas canonicae* and *apocriphas scripturas*, a question of dogma, first and foremost, but also one of authenticity and originality. On the one hand, therefore, we deal with a sacred, "officialized" literature, sanctioned by the Church, and, on the other, with a contested, repudiated literature. Using this criterion, Aimericus (*Ars lectoria*, eleventh century) distinguishes among four categories of Christian literature: *autentica, hagiographa, communia,* and *apocrifa.*[7] Two centuries later, St. Bonaventura suggests a new classification: *sacrae scripturae, originalis sanctorum, sententiae magistrorum,* and *doctrinarum mundialium sive philosophorum.*[8] Finally, an *index* consecrates the phrase *scripturae cannonicae.*[9] Biblical, patristic, and doctrinary literature belongs to the last, privileged category. It is written by *auctores nostri,*[10] by *ecclesiastici scriptoris* (Notker, *Decretum Gelasianum,* etc.).[11] The ancient *scriptor* is now invested with great dignity and authority, as an exponent of the Church. His position becomes "official." This phenomenon is entirely unprecedented in the history of the idea of literature.

PROFANE LETTERS

The rift between the *sacred* and the *profane*—specific to the ancient mentality, widened and made more systematic by Christianity—becomes even more profane and rigid in the Middle Ages. It corresponds to the dominant position of the Church and to its doctrinaire, dogmatic orientations. The basic discrimination is naturally against ancient, "pagan" culture: *Ciceronianus est non Christianus* (Gregory I, the Great).[12] God's word cannot be entrapped *in regula Donati* (Gregory I).[13] "It is one thing to speak of grammar, another to speak of God" (Smaragdus).[14]

This consistent rigor excludes, disparages, and blames profane culture as a whole, as it does not belong to the Church and is not subservient to it, hence, an extremely widespread dichotomy, typical of all medieval culture: *saecularis et divina litteratura*[15] *mundana scriptura atque divina.*[16] But even this strict dissociation admits that "profane literature" is a reality. Its existence is so obvious that it can no longer be denied.

The phrase "profane literature" oscillates between a purely "technical" (grammatical, of classroom use) meaning, and a "minimalizing," polemical, even exclusivist, one. It is widely circulated in all learned ecclesiastical circles, with its basic sense—which has become traditional—of lay culture, acquired through *litterae.* Hence, the great occurrence of the phrase *secularis litteris.*[17] Its scholastic coinage, already used by Cassiodorus and many others, becomes quite obvious in a formula like *disciplinarum saecularium studium* (sixth century).[18] The acceptance can also be found in *Vita S. Cunegundis* (chapter 7): *saecularium quoque litera-rum scientia instructerat.*[19] It is widespread through the Middle Ages.

The transition from *littera* to *litteratura* follows the already known path. The substitution of one term for another is the direct result of the intense synonymy inherent in notions such as "grammar," "letter," and "culture"—a synonymy clearly discernible as early as Tertullian and Cassian. The medieval writer Alcuin follows, quite naturally, in their footsteps: *seculari litteratura.*[20] This syntagm can be encountered in various texts, for example, in a "critical" textbook by Conrad de Hirschau, *litteratura seculari.*[21] The connotations are everywhere the same: Lay culture and literature, outside the letter and authority of the Church, through a constant separation of roles: *terrena/spiritualia.*[22] Lay literature is, by definition, "terrestrial," therefore, perpetually inferior. This explains why a double quality is often made claim to: an intellectual *(doctos, grammaticos)* and religious one *(presbiterosque pios),*[23] with a view to defense and rehabilitation. Throughout the Middle Ages, profane literature has, or is considered to have, a blatant, overwhelming *mauvaise conscience.* It is its historic handicap, difficult to overcome.

Written Literature

The Middle Ages is also the period that gives final consecration to the idea of written literature, or better said, manuscript literature, because medieval literature is really a *manuscriture,*[24] in the vernacular languages. Latin remains the language of the Church and of the chancery.[25] At the same time, the Middle Ages continue, deepen and enlarge the purely practical tradition of writing. The transition from orality to the single "manufacture" of writing, and then on to "écriture" and to writing composition[26] that is, to the culture and civilization of writing, with its increasingly complex motivation and theoretical justification, is one of the dominant notes of medieval literature. Thus, the idea of literature enters a new phrase.

One by one, all the ancient etymologies, glosses, semantic equivalents, and lexicographical explications are taken up again, beginning with *grámma = littera.*[27] Definitions that have become classical are reproduced (see Isidore of Seville; *indices rerum, signa verborum,* Alcuin: *littera est pars minima vocis articulatae.*[28] All the synonyms of "letter" are recovered: graphic sign, type, element, alphabetical sign, alphabet. We find, among others, a very precise gloss in this direction in Aimericus' *Ars lectoria* (1086).[29] *Litteratura* preserves its graphical and especially grammatical, cultural, primordial sense: *litteraturae* (that is, *grammaticae locutio* (Gregory I, the Great),[30] by extension, written Latin—the only existent language of culture that makes this homology inevitable. The awareness of literality *(litteralis)*, of writing as *exercitium litterale,*[31] becomes more and more acute. The written statement is increasingly identified with extremely convergent terms, such as *litterarius, litteralis, litteratorie*.[32] Writing *(écriture)*, respectively *scriptura*, also becomes a current word. *Ars litteraria* and *ars scribendi* are seen as synonyms, under the sign of *litteralis scientia* (Papias, *Litterae* s.v.). Its product is written discourse of any kind, *littera textualis*,[33] which is to say the text, *textus*.[34] The beginnings of the idea of text, at this elementary level of expression, are therefore modest, purely graphical.

Throughout the Middle Ages, the process of praising the qualities and values of writing, begun in Antiquity, becomes more intense. Broadly speaking, two classes of arguments are taken up again. Writing pins down, preserves, makes eternal (Alcuin: *Custos historiae*; John of Salisbury).[35] The medieval spirit is very responsive to the "mnemonic" capacity of writing. Everything that must not sink into oblivion and, for that reason, is put down in writing is called "literature." Hence, the constant emphasis given to a series of practical uses: the written letter institutes, founds, vouches for, confirms, tells the truth, invests with authority. It becomes current practice, in every domain, to refer to the written tradition. A written text is "official," *exemplary*, a matrix for future copies, a problem specific, especially, to medieval university courses.[36] As a consequence, the dichotomy *genuine* versus *fake* becomes, for the first time, a highly topical concern. The countless medieval fakes—especially forged documents—can be explained by the fact that the written text alone can aspire to win the trust of all parties.[37]

A quite widespread synonym of *sacred literature* is *sacra scriptura* or *divina scriptura* or, simply, *scriptura*.[38] In this manner, through the direct influence of the Church, the Middle Ages invest writing with the supreme value: *scriptura exhibebat in littera*.[39] The superiority of *letter* becomes incontestable through sacralization. Writing is "hallowed." *Corpus Christi* and *scriptura* are one and the same thing. Western monastic literature in its entirety—from St. Cassian,[40] the famous *Regula Sancti Benedicti* and its "supplement,"[41] to "treatises" such as *Philobiblion* by Richard de Bury (V, XVI), *De laude scriptorum*, by Jean Gerson, or *De laude scriptorum* (XIII) by Johannes Trithemius—raises writing to the rank of a true vocation and a mystical institution. Its praise is permanent, systematic, associated with the essential acts of monastic life: praying, asceticism, soul-saving, apostolic work. Spiritual hygiene and ergonomy go hand in hand. The sacralization of almost all scriptural operations[42] can be tracked down in texts, for example, with Trithemius (VI: *Quam bonum et utile sit monachis scribere*). *Textus* enjoys a similar consecration: It is a loose synonym for the Bible, Holy Writ, etc, the supreme "scriptic"-textual manifestation, in the terms of the age.

One and the same medieval mentality attributes a mystic genesis to letters and writing. The ancient explication is preserved, but in a Christian spirit. Texts are *digita dei scriptas, opus dei*. The Christian myth of writing sees God as an author and an omnipresent inspiration. His "writings" drop from the sky. Many apocryphal texts and widely circulated legends pass for works of the divinity.[43] There are numerous traditional medieval accounts of the sacred origin of writing.[44] Gothic runes and the Celtic alphabet, *ogham*, fully enjoy the prestige of being sacral and initiatory. They are "mysterious," "secret" writings, invented and watched over by deities, especially by the god of speech and eloquence (Ogmios for the ancient Celts).[45] An extremely rich folklore speaks about the magical, supernatural powers of letters. Letters know the truth, they foretell the future, deliver one from evil, conjure up spirits, and are real talismans. Celtic poets are persuaded that their art is closely connected to the sacred "letters" on which they take their oath.[46] The decoding—not yet final—of the Gothic inscription at Pietroasa points to the same conclusions.[47] By sacralization, the literary text becomes dogmatic, even ontological. For John Scotus Erigena, written law is a support of natural law.

Needless to say, "written literature" in the Middle Ages is not only sacred, but also profane. If not as active and widespread as that of sacrality, the consciousness of lay writing proves to be, by all accounts, quite well-defined. The trend to consolidate it is equally visible. In addition to its consecrated, religious meaning, *scriptura* also includes the much more modest, but no less current, sense of "letter," epistolary correspondence. This type of writing (*litterae laicorum*)[48] is given ampler circulation by the interpretation the word receives in school.

The *Christian* versus *pagan* dissociation forces all *gentilia scripta, secularium litterarum scriptis* (Abelard)[49] into this category. The most accurate terminology, however, is to be found in a phrase like *scriptura mundana*.[50] It covers a concept that is, by now, quite well-defined, and it becomes a permanent component of the idea of literature.

The transition from *littera* to *litteratura* contributed decisively to the progress of the idea through the Middle Ages. The most frequently met phenomenon is its tacit, implicit ratification, already begun in Antiquity. *Litteratura* denotes—in a broad sense—any written text, document, epistle, any *scriptura*,[51] any *litteratorum monumenta*. In Old French, *litura, letradura, lettreure, letterure*, and *lettrure* have one and the same meaning: "letter," "graphic mark" and "written text." Even more relevant is an explicit fourteenth century gloss, *ad litteram sive litteraturam*; similarly, the record of the transition from the vernacular to writing in Latin, as *vulgaria in litteraturam permutat*.[52] In Latin's shadow, the Romance languages—with French leading the way—begin, as early as the twelfth century, the transition to their written form. These semantic acceptations, indicating not so much the evolution of the spoken and written language, but rather that of the medieval view on "writing," can be followed in detail in all the specialized dictionaries.[53]

Litteratura (a term which, from now on, will increasingly mean "written literature") will define its effectively "literary" meaning within the same semantic and terminological framework. A step decisive for its future, specific evolution, is taken now. With Aimericus, *scriptura* already signifies "literary works,"[54] in the present acceptation of the word. This acceptation is confirmed and reinforced by a formula like *versificatorie atque litteratorie artis* (also from the eleventh century), all the more so as the same author also uses the phrase *litterali scientia*[55] to mean "writing." With Wace and others, *escripture* clearly means works, novel, *estorie;*[56] with Dante, *scritture* also meant that and, even more clearly, sacred and profane works.[57] His contemporaries were aware that "his noble works were produced in *scrittura*" (G. Villani).[58]

The existence of a process of progresive literaturization also results from the terminology of the writing process itself. The most current word, taken over from the patrists, is *dictare* (*dictator* = he who dictates a text, a book). The operation continues to be essentially oral, as the secretary is not involved in the effort to elaborate. When the work becomes exclusively written, the corresponding terms will be: *letter, lettrier, litterare* = to formulate, to put down in letters. *Lettré* = written, recorded in a public document. *Litteratoria, litteratorius* = put down in letters, written document.[59] Of special relevance is the fact that "composition" (in the sense of invention, creation) is closely connected to writing and letter. As early as late Antiquity, *dictare* also has this meaning: the written, re-elaborated replica of an oral sermon.[60] Phrases like *en lettre* and *la lettre* are quite frequently encountered in medieval romances, rendering the idea of "fictional composition."[61] The prologue theory in some medieval *Ars poeticae* comprises the same idea: *modi exordiendi in litteris.*[62] Dante refers to the same thing as *litterale sentenza.*[63] The various kinds of writings became, in turn, quite naturally, "literary genres." *Pagina* means writing in general, but sometimes also history, lyrical poetry, epigram, etc. *Escrit* and *romanz* are synonyms.[64]

What does such a written composition look like? It is subjected to a twofold pressure, to a contradictory inner tension. On the one hand, the Middle Ages are preoccupied, even haunted, by the idea of an accurate, pure—therefore invariable and faultless—text, an obsession inherited from late Antiquity,[65] hence, an intense obsession with reviewing, correcting, giving stability and norm to a text.[66] The installments of medieval courses, *pecia*, are *exemplaria*, that is, officially approved by the University. On the other hand, the idea of personal output, of identity and personality, begins to assert itself. An increasing number of copyists and engravers now sign their inscriptions, texts, miniatures. This can be noticed both in the case of rune engravers and medieval scribes.[67] Some *chansons de geste* even have their author named. The increasingly frequent infringement of the Christian interdiction of signature[68] has its own relevance. Copyists inevitably introduce personal variants; the intuition that there is such a thing as an individual style begins to take shape. In the Middle Ages, the literary work is "variable."[69] Thus, the ideas of "novelty" and "originality" can be vaguely perceived, even at this level of professional, mechanical, non-creative writing.

Oral Literature

Not for a moment must we lose sight of the fundamental characteristic of the Middle Ages: the notion "written literature" reappears and circulates in a period when orality is still massively and intensely predominant, as a continuation of the state of things in Antiquity. Some authors have gone so far as to doubt the very existence of "medieval literature," or, better said, to contest the propriety of the term. Such a label, they maintain, can be but abusive, erroneous,[70] given the fact this literature is, after all, not written down, does not pertain to *letter*, but is expressed, as well as received, only or mostly in an oral manner. This is a purely "letteralist" view, typical of the twentieth century.

The *oral/written* contrast is so obviously radical that it determines the first typologies of "literature." *Vox, dictio, verbum,* and *sermo* are categories opposed to *littera*. *Discere* and *scribere* are two perfectly distinct operations. The former is *per aures*, the latter, *per oculos*.[71] A concept of oral expression—if not of "oral literature" as well—therefore begins, implicitly, to take shape. On the one side, there is everyday speech, *sermonus communes;* on the other, there is writing, *litterae*.[72] The pair *sermone-scriptura* is here to stay. One is for *auditores*, the other for *lectores*.[73] In Old French, the difference is between *de bouche* and *par lettre*, between *chanter* and *rimer*.[74]

The medieval relations between the two types of expression are very complex and do not concern us now. We shall only note—wishing to call attention to them—the many interferences (already noticeable in Antiquity, especially in the transcriptions of the Homeric poems), the staunch resistence by orality, the increasingly noticeable headway made by written culture to the detriment of the oral one, and the subordination of orality to writing.[75] Some of these typical situations have a direct bearing upon literary terminology, so we shall dwell, briefly, upon them.

Composition, of any kind—sermons, theology, literature, etc.—is "oral" or "written," by which we should understand: with quill in hand. The consecrated term *(dictare, dictamen)* very accurately depicts the oral/written collaboration: *dictando et scribendo*[76] (no autograph medieval manuscripts have survived), with a strong hint of traditional orality. The author dictates orally, and the product of this operation, *dictamen*, is, from this point of view, the original type-acceptation of the idea of "oral literature" in its medieval stage. *Dictamen Omeri* is the Homeric poem in its archetypal, oral-rhapsodic form. *Dictando* = to compose poems (oral or written). Expressions such as *dictatores illustres*[77] and titles such as *Art de dictier* (E. Deschamps, toward 1400) face this ambiguity.

The definition of reading, also tightly connected to oral expression, is no less ambiguous. Are poetry and texts of any genre written to be read silently, or recited, chanted? There is an obvious transition toward reading.[78] But reading is still far from being individual, solitary and silent. The current medieval form of "reading" is still the public recitation given by professional reciters. This, however, is often based on a written text. Awareness of this fact is more than once expressed with total clarity: *escriture . . . de li reciter* (Gautier de Coinci).[79] To write for a listening audience is, actually, the medieval author's main function. As a producer of "written and oral literature," he has a specific—if embryonic or somewhat confused—view on his undertakings.

The awareness of quotation and recitation—typical of bards, minstrels, jesters, troubadours, specific to all medieval recitals, declamations and public shows in general—is in itself an implicit pre-definition of "oral literature." The corresponding phrases are of the type *gesta recitabantur*, *Las rasos de trobar* (Raimond Vidal), etc. Two typical situations are encountered. One of them—the most frequent—advocates memorization: poetry, just like discourse, must first be learned by heart, and after that declaimed (Geoffrey de Vinsauf, *Poetria Nova*, thirteenth century).[80] The other, characteristic of the *trouvères* specialized in *Chansons de geste*—though some tendencies of the kind are attested even earlier, in the ninth century—recommends a faithful reading of the written text. [81] The written support seems necessary, even indispensable. No allusions are made to improvisations and variants.

The definition's nominalism still suffers. There are other signs that "oral literature" was felt (and especially thought of) as a distinct reality. The consciousness of an oral message, of the spoken or sung discourse, of a fictitious audience (a notion that was, demonstrably, entertained until as late as the fifteenth century), of a "poetry for the ear," is quite often and clearly expressed. A medieval *ars poetica* speaks, pragmatically, of recitation, or voice modulation.[82] The very title *Cantar de mio Cid* gives away the poem's verbal, lyrical register. Also well-known (and studied) is the medieval cliché of *incipit*, of addressing a fictitious audience and capturing their attention: *oiez, seignor; écoutez, seigneurs*.[83] The pure medieval poet's oral stance is typical, with Jean de Meung, for example: *Les paroles que j'en ai dites* (*Roman de la rose*, V., 15216). Many works are entitled, in fact, *Le Dit, Dits, Detto*, etc.

In other words, an awareness of the live, phonematic word continues to challenge and overshadow the *letter*. The circumstance is plainly illustrated by a ninth century medieval formula: *Carta sine litteris* ("unwritten document, verbal order with the power of a written one").[84] Gradually, however, *litteratura* gathers (especially in glossaries) the global meaning of "written and oral word."[85] As for poets, they very clearly sense that there is an organic bond between writing and speech, letter and voice, verse and *oir*.[86] To Dante, *dire* = writing poetry. The letter is the support of oral literature: *lettres lues et entendues* (1330). The definitions for poet and poetry are similarly oriented: *dicitori in rima, quasi poeti*.[87]

Finally, the rhetoricization of the definition of oral and, by implication, written literature, is also typically medieval. It is an unavoidable phenomenon, prolonging the traditional reaction of Antiquity: rhetoric continues to be the only theoretical framework available for the delineation and study of any type of orality. *Loquendi peritia*, therefore, remains specific, in its essence, to both oratory and poetry. Marbode, a medieval poet, forsakes his youthful creation with the argument that what he had written was *nec inventu pretiosa, nec arte loquendi*.[88] It follows that the first "technical" medieval definition of poetry will be *bene dicendi scientia*, "the art of being well-spoken,"[89] and of poetic arts, *artibus rhetoricae rythmicae*. Even where poetry claims to have a sphere of its own, the traditional definition remains, for a long time, unchallenged, *seconde rhétorique*. Poets will, consequently, be *grands rhétoriqueurs*. Such concepts circulated—at least in France—until the first half of the sixteenth century.[90]

THE CULTURE OF LETTERS

Grammar and Culture

Antiquity introduces the term "culture" and defines literature in essentially cultural terms. The Middle Ages take over the definition, consolidate and institutionalize it in the same sense. Of the whole course of the biography of the idea of literature, this is the period in which grammar and the culture of letters enjoy the greatest prestige. The age is decisively dominated by cultural values, with a direct impact on the content and meanings of the idea of literature.

The main explanation is to be found in the highly sacred character of culture, a typically medieval characteristic. St. Augustine's interpretation of Psalm LXX is oftentimes quoted or paraphrased:[91] He who is not acquainted with letters *(litteratura)*[92] will not be admitted into the Kingdom of God. Another very successful medieval formula constitutes a genuine slogan: "Better be a grammarian than a heretic" (Abelard).[93] The current phrases for sacralized literary studies are: *sacrarum litterarum studium*, and *religio scientiae litterarum*. The Middle Ages could hardly have valued letters more highly. Only the "cultivated" could have sacred visions *(erudicione prediti sunt)*.[94] Christian schools, with lecturers and students, were set up as early as the sixth century, following a council (Vaison, 529).[95]

At the opposite end—but forming an indissoluble pair—again we come across *saecularium litterarum studium, saecularis disciplina*, a typology first used by Cassiodorus (sixth century). *Studium* is different in nature from *sacerdotium*. Its definition, needless to say, can only be "literal" as well: *litteraturae studia*,[96] *saecularis litteraturae scientia*.[97] This instruction is aimed at the layman, and because of that a suitable doctrine is conceived, *De institutione laicali* (Manfredo Jonas).[98]

Typically paleo-Christian and then medieval is, also, the theory of the "recuperating" of secular letters, with a view to consolidating, illustrating and propagating faith. The series is inaugurated by St. Basil, with a famous text *To the Greek Youth, on How to Take Advantage of Hellenic Letters*.[99] The phenomenon, prone to interference, often generates unprecedented, unexpected symbioses. A sort of consensus is reached, frequently reiterated in the course of time: "Even pagan letters (*gentilium litterae*) can instruct."[100] Hence, an intense "christening" of grammar and an active reassessment of profane culture: it is seen, in fact, as a "beautiful captive" which, after being purified, can even be betrothed[101]—a symbol that has its charm. It becomes obvious that the idea "literature-culture" is considerably stranger when invested with such infallible authority.[102] A synthetic formula, "Christ's *paideia*,"[103] defines, in a clear, intelligible manner for the educated clergyman, the general orientation of the Church.

Writing's essential significance is also preeminently cultural. "Writing" and "culture" could not be told apart in the Middle Ages. Knowing "letters" meant being able to read and write. *Savoir lettre = savoir lire*.[104] For Villon, *lire* means being able to read, recite, and study.[105] This somehow belated acceptation is characteristic of medieval mentality. It is a period when the culture of letters becomes the supreme intellectual ideal. *Litterae* = science, knowledge, in the fundamental ancient sense, are at the origin of the word *lateratour* (1373) in modern languages: literary culture; *letrer* = to instruct; *petite lectreure* = small amount of knowledge or instruction.[106] Literature is still an educational concept, a school product, of the *trivium* cycle and of the University. The modern term that best translates it is *literacy*. Hence, the fundamental cultural medieval typology, which continues and generalizes the ancient one: *litterata* = "those who can write;" *illitterata* = "those who cannot."[107] the *litterati* are *docti, les clercs*; the *illitterati* are *indocti, idiotas*, that is, *sine litteris*.[108] Correspondingly, *littera* and *scrittura* acquire global, cultural meanings, as well as special (doctrinal, philosophical) ones. Among the *savi de scrittura*[109] are philosophers and *altri degni scrittori*.[110]

Also typically medieval is the question (and the controversy) of the superiority of the image and of the written language. On the plane of the spirit, we witness the mightiest religious interference and redeeming of writing and of the image in all the historical existence of *letter*. In the field of culture, however, the central concern is a different one: which of the two instruments is the more advantageous, educationally the more efficient: Writing or the image?

Even within sacred culture itself, opinions are divided. The primacy and superiority of writing over pictographic image is upheld by Rabanus Maurus (ninth century).[111] Alcuin rejects "formal" satisfactions and, in his turn, proclaims the superiority of the written divine word.[112] Opposed to them is a theory that puts the two methods on equal footing: *pictura quasi scriptura* (Gregory I the Great, Isidore of Seville).[113] More than that: Painting moves the heart even more readily than scripture (Durand de Mende, thirteenth century).[114] It is a decisive argument, widely used to instruct the multitudes of illiterate faithful, mere *illiterati*, much more easily catechized with the help of icons and church frescoes (Gregory I the Great, a theoretician of the painted divine word,[115] but also Isidore of Seville, Bede and others). The doctrine is granted official status by the Council of Arras (1024).[116]

From our point of view, the dispute is important, as it effectively enriches the terminology of the idea of literature. The concept of literature as painting addressing the eye and the idea of *muta predicatio* leads to formulas such as *pictura-litteratura illiterata* (Walafrid Strabon, ninth century), *laicorum litteratura* (Honorius d'Autun, twelfth century), widely circulated in the Middle Ages.[117] Painting becomes the "literature of laymen:" it represents imagistic writing, a visual language, and a form of visual teaching. The direct literary implications of exploiting the semantics of imagery do not concern us at present. In passing, however, we shall remark upon the re-emergence of the *carmina figurata* (in a Christian sense: Rabanus Maurus: *De laudis S. Crucis*), the parallel existence and cooperation between manuscripts and miniatures, and the frequency of narrative imagery in a great number of miniature medieval texts.[118] Dante shared this view (*se non scritto, almen dipinto*).[119]

We must also note that orality gradually becomes more cultural.[120] The conflict oral versus written—even more acute in the Middle Ages than in Antiquity, which was predominently oral—is little by little resolved in favor of the latter. The two cultures exist side by side, but the absolute primacy of orality increasingly yields ground. In Old English, *heard* is already used as a technical synonym of *learned*.[121] A transition from *hören* to *lesen* and *vorlesen* can also be seen in *Mittelhochdeutsch*.[122] Improving oral expression through the teaching of grammar, dictation, *modus pronunciandi*, *legere ad pennam* is also—explicitly or not—part of medieval pedagogy. Historians agree that there was a drifting away from oral teaching, that the oral was replaced by the written, and that written sermons appeared (*manu hominibus predicare*).[123] All this leads to the redefinition, with finer shades of meaning, of the central notion of *grammar*.

First, the Middle Ages continue to use—quite naturally—the classical acceptation; *litteratura = grammatica.* The didactic, cultural meaning is not only consolidated, but also generalized and, above all, hypertrophied. It is definitively introduced into West European culture, which will be pre-eminently "grammatical" throughout the Middle Ages.

To begin with, we witness an unprecedented extension of traditional terminology, where grammar is the "art" of letters, of learning how to use them, *ars litterae communes.*[124] Other adjacent formulas include: *ars litterae, ars litteratoria,* and *litteratio.*[125] The word "letter" is obsessively reiterated in all these specific definitions of the idea of literature. Almost all grammar treatises of late Antiquity and of the Middle Ages contain an introductory chapter on *litteris.* Many glosses begin by providing an etymological explanation: *Gramatica dicitur a gramaton quod est littera.*[126] To Cassiodorus,[127] Alcuin,[128] and many others, grammar is and remains a *litteralis scientia, litterarum scientia,*[129] *scientia litterarum;*[130] formulas such as these are quite currently used. Afterward, they will change into *la science des lettres,* a term of even greater semantic heredity and wider use.

The transition to *litteratura* has one other lexical variant as well: *litteratoria scientia,*[131] *disciplina litteratoria, doctrina litteratoria, des lettres endoctrinées.*[132] The course of this evolution aims at a complete identification of *grammatica* and *litteratura.* The pair—typically medieval—possesses a twofold acceptation, summing up all the semantic evolution to date:

> 1) *Litteratura*: The knowledge, the science of written letters, that is, "ştiinţa de carte" (a knowledge of the three Rs), in the traditional sense of the Romanian phrase; it is also translated by terms such as *litteralis intelligentiae*[133] or *litteratura* (= the phonetics of letters, vowels and consonants).[134] In this respect, the Middle Ages do little more than reiterate St. Augustine's teaching: literature = a knowledge of letters, *unde etiam latine litteratura dicitur.*[135]

> 2) *Litteratura*: The "art," the "science of learning letters, that is, grammar, as a discipline and a pedagogical instrument (Oxford, 1274).[136] The object is indistinguishable from the teaching method. This is the glorious pinnacle of literature's didactic function.

This ambiguous terminology evidently predominates; it becomes saturated and redundant. Grammar, *artis infantia,*[137] is the basic school subject, the fundamental object of teaching. Its quite frequently used definition is *studium litterarum, studiis litteratorie artis;* less often, but in the spirit of the lexicographic evolution that interests us, *litteraturae studia.*[138] The study of "literature"—the study of letters. Grammar—pre-eminently a school subject-matter—is often defined as such: *litteratoria disciplina*[139] (variants: *litterarum disciplinis, disciplinis litterarum*). The encouragement shown these studies in the Carolingian Age (*De litteris colendis,* 787), gives even more weight to the "schoolroom" acceptation of the notion of literature, *littera-turae magisteris*.[140] In the eleventh century, the Benedictine friars of the du Bec abbey were described as belonging to a *litteraturae gymnasium*.[141] The notion is indissolubly bound to *disciplina scholarium, to universitas scholarium*, to *scolis*, etc. The terminology is entirely and purely didactic. To send children to school, *pono ad litteraturam* (1325).[142] It is also encountered in Old French: *clergie* = scholarly culture. School enrollment is done with a view to *apprendre lettereure*, etc.[143]

We must insist that, at this didactic, cultural stage, the acceptation of literature continues to remain minor, elementary, continuing the fundamental ancient program: *the art of reading and writing*. Hence, two other senses of the medieval definition: 1) correct "speech": *scientia loquendi sine vitio* (more concisely: *recte loqui . . . docet*,[144] Siger de Courtrai: *sermocinalis scientia*); 2) correct speech and writing *(recte loquendi et scribendi)*,[145] a definition that becomes classical and is taken over by many a medieval doctor (Hugo de St. Victor, John of Salisbury, Rabanus Maurus) and by their disciples. We are at the source of one of the most fecund ideas: *literature* = to write correctly, that is, "well." The notion will gradually open up, in every sense of the word, and will be found—in embryo—in many of the future definitions of literature. With this basic acceptation, *grammatica* is taken over by all Romance and Germanic medieval languages.

A process of semantic contraction, begun in Antiquity, is eventually achieved in the Middle Ages: literacy, grammar, and culture become one and the same notion, expressed through a single word: *litteratura*. It is the supreme criterion by which, in the Middle Ages, the cultivated man *(litteratus)* is distinguished from the uncultivated one *(illiteratus)*: to be literate = *in litteratura competens*;[146] to be illiterate = *litteratura defectu* or *illiteratura*.[147] The admissions examination for various notarial or administrative jobs (competence, titles, training) consecrates the same criterion: It is an *examen de litteratura*.[148]

The Totality of Letters

The aspiration to totality and synthesis, typical of *letters* and of *literature*, manifested since Classical Antiquity, had to reappear in force in the Middle Ages. The spirit of the age—dominated by Christian Weltanschauung—is, in fact, tempted by global significations, a tendency that has both merits and demerits. *Litteratura* tends to become a unique value and a unique formula for the "literary" and cultural phenomenon in its entirety.

In this respect, *litterae* refers, first of all, to the totality of *sacred* and *profane* letters, according to the circumstances: *litteris sacris, scripturis sacris*, as well as *litteratura mundi*. At the same time, *litterae* connotes the totality of writing and of writings, one of the fundamental acceptations of *literature* = anything written, any written text, anything ever written.

Through metonymy, letter and content become inseparable; the page and the message it conveys are one and the same thing. Particularly *litterae*,[149] but also *scriptura*, any kind of *litteralia instrumenta*, means any kind of writing, writ, letter, document, inscription.[150] The lexis used by the great doctors of divinity confirms this terminology.[151] Consequently, *litteratura* has an identical acceptation (= everything written), it defines the whole domain of writings, regardless of esthetic categories. *Opera, Scriptura* are the equivalent of *tota scriptura*.[152] On that basis, the opinion held by some historians of the idea of literature, that the notion "totality of writings" disappeared in the Middle Ages, needs to be amended.[153]

We have now seen what is the cultural—and essential—significance of letters. Encompassing all the knowledge acquired through *letters* (reading and writing) with a view to achieving as high and diversified a level of knowledge as possible can only be the natural, generalized consequence of this tendency. Therefore, the Middle Ages make a clear-cut distinction between those who "know," at a suitable level of knowledge (= *litterati*), and those "who do not know." The latter remain *illiterati* "even though they might know the letters."[154] *Letters (lettres)* therefore means, essentially, science, knowledge acquired through study, globally speaking, integral culture, the totality of intellectual acquisitions. The plural of these notions *(art, savoir, Wissenschaft)*[155] signifies this very sense and effort to acquire extensive, if possible universal, knowledge.

Litteratura follows the same extensive qualitative evolution toward totality. The basic meaning is known: Knowledge, culture: *cultura litterarum*,[156] litteratura = knowledge of the three Rs),[157] in short, *litteratura sufficientia*,[158] etc. But, as in the case of letters, knowledge again tends to become total. And then it is called *omnis litteraturae*,[159] *totius litteraturae fundamentum*.[160] The aspiration to totality is not only confirmed, but amplified. The apparition of degrees of comparison speaks in the same sense. The inferior category is that of the uncultivated, of those who do not know literature: *Je ne cunui littérature*,[161] Commynes: *aucune littérature*. The cultivated are defined by phrases such as: *litteratura insignem, conspicuus*,[162] *competentis, sapientis, eminentis, notabilis*, etc. He who is extremely cultivated is a *vir multe litterature* (twelfth century).[163]

The well-known, fundamental cultural meaning of *literature* reveals the same aspiration to totality. *Litteratura* = total culture: object and method, integral sacred and profane ideal: "We serve Christ when we know everything there is to know, *qui totum scibile scivit,*" (Gilbert de Tournai).[164] The University *(super artium et litteratura fundamentum*, the one in Paris, for instance),[165] as well as the literature of the age, its great epic poems *(Beowulf, Chanson de Roland, Niebelungenlied)* are also essential instruments for the transmission of ideas, information, and values. Medieval literary culture wants, to a higher degree than the ancient one, to become "total." It is ruled by the ideas of absolute knowledge.

This aspiration is expressed by two central symptoms. The first, evidently, is the Latin language, *latinitas*. It corresponds not only to the written tradition, but especially to *litterae*. To be "literate," cultivated = to know Latin. What is today defined as *literacy* means, first and foremost, knowing and using Latin: *litteratus* = he who knows Latin; *illiteratus* = he who does not. You may be able to read and write, but if you cannot read and write Latin you are still an *illiteratus*.[166] Latin, it follows, is the content, the emblem, and the zenith of medieval culture, hence, the essential "Latinizing" of grammar = *grammatica litterarum latinae*.[167] The study of grammar = the study of Latin. *Lettre, la lettreüre*[168] (*littérature*) will have one and the same meaning in the Romance languages (French, Italian, etc.).[169] In Middle English, *to read* = to read Latin.

The second symbol of total culture—in the medieval sense—is the eternal *grammatica*, a pilot-science of enormous intellectual and academic prestige. This view, typical of late Antiquity ("grammar as school and foundation for belles lettres")[170] is taken over, through Isidore of Seville (*origo et fundamentum litteralium artium*),[171] in almost identical terms (*origo omnium liberalium disciplinarum*)[172] by all the medieval doctrine. It presides over all the arts of speech (*artis semocinales*),[173] all the arts *literales quam mecanicas*.[174] Such an integralism of grammatical literature is hard to imagine and particularly hard to explain theoretically today. In medieval thinking, however, the *letter* stands both for a part and for the totality of its representations (Grosseteste).[175] Grammar (*fundamentum scientiae litteralis*),[176] necessarily rules over all intellectual operations (*in omni doctrina grammatica precedit*).[177] Everything is interconnected, defined, and consecrated through grammar, an integral, absolute science.

The obsession with grammatical totality may take other guises. *Artes ancillae grammaticae* is one of the most typical.[178] "Arts" are "servants" to grammar. More exactly, its equivalents—philosophy, logic, ethics, the complete cycle (*trivium* and *quadrivium*) are "grammatical" in every sense of the word. From this perspective, literature itself is seen as an indistinct whole, grouping *omnia poetarum carmina* (tragedies, comedies, satires, etc.)[179] Of course, there is an awareness of the existence of literary genres (*genera scripturarum*), each with its own name. But *litteratura* (*poesia*) includes authors of every genre, just as each genre defines all its compartments and, therefore, has all its meanings. *Sermones Bonaventurae*, for instance, contains no fewer than six different species.[180] The very act of writing, viewed as recording of data predisposes one to complete collections (miscellanies, anthologies) within a genre or, more often, of texts belonging to all genres.

Other frequently met ancient and medieval catch phrases are: *scientia, eruditio*, which express the same intellectual ideal of totality: global, exemplary knowledge. However, the medieval syntagm with the most prestigious career in this field is *res litteraria*. Ever more often attested, the equivalent of all the species of *dictamen* (Alberick von Monte Cassino: *res litteralis*),[181] *res litteraria* expresses—through its very ambiguity—the aspiration to totality of literature of every kind. We shall follow its ascending career.

The Book

A similar remark must be made about the book, which, from the Middle Ages on, is the symbol not only of literature, but of culture in general. We are now in the incipient stages of what will be known as "book civilization," a spiritual life *sub specie libri*. The book's immense cultural and historical prestige—a typical characteristic of medieval culture—originates in this medieval age of writing, manuscripts, and book reading.

The traditional magical and sacred prestige of the book, so typical of "book religions," enjoys a maximum of popularity and consecration during the Middle Ages, which, in this respect, continue and amplify the tendency visible in Christian Antiquity: The sacred book—*scriptus digito Dei*[182]—becomes a cult object and, above all, the object of a supreme intellectual, theological, and mystical experience. The book is, *par excellence, Scriptura sacra*,[183] *sacra pagina*, "God's book," "the Holy Book,"[184] "the Holy Book written by God."[185] Under this sign, the book becomes the absolute prototype of all books and, therefore, the spiritual core of mankind's whole cultural life.

At the same time, the reality of the profane book—that asserts itself in a very energetic manner—leads to a partial desacralization of the book, which is more and more evident during the Middle Ages. The sacred versus profane dissociation inevitably takes the form of the *libri catholici/libri gentiles* dichotomy.[186] The latter category is quite appropriately defined by St. Jerome as *saeculares libri*.[187] When the *letter* versus *image* controversy becomes extremely acute and topical, alongside concrete formulas for one illustrated Bible (*Biblia pauperum, libri pauperum*), we shall come across the doublet: *picturis-libri laicorum* (Albertus Magnus).[188] It is the current figurative expression for the uneducated, even illiterate, "consumption" of biblical imagery.

The handwritten, graphical, manuscript character of the medieval book is faithfully mirrored by the same bipolar terminology. On the one hand, there is *liber* (= the Bible), *Liber textus, Codex Gottes*, etc. Broadly speaking, there is an evolution from the ancient *volumen* to the medieval *codex*. Another remarkable medieval phenomenon—a direct consequence of the original orality—is the book that introduces itself, that recommends itself ("I am written"), that speaks for itself.[189]

Also very lively, acute, everywhere present, is the conception of the book as a specific cultural instrument, as a teaching method and teaching object (*scolasticalium libri*). In the *Chevalerie et Clergie* controversy (Chrétien de Troyes, *Cligès*), knights are urged to study books; such references are quite frequent. Books and literacy are the decisive criterion of the *clericus/laicus* dissociation, the specific trait of the former. Not to know how to put books to good use (*tenens librum*) is the clearest and gravest sign of ignorance.[190] The book lover (*amator librorum, amator scriptorum*) appears as a species, inspiring the great medieval book eulogies. The most famous and complete of these is the *Philobiblion. Tractatus Pulcherimus de Amore Librorum*, by Richard de Bury (completed in 1345).

The aspiration to global culture, so vivacious in this period, finds its most straightforward expression in the concept of the total book, whose model, in every circumstance, is the Bible. The age, then, will be haunted by the idea of the only book (*Opus majus, Thesaurus, Speculum majus*, etc.), by the utopia of a universal book that can include all existing knowledge in one volume. This program, expounded with great assuredness and with a lucid assessment of its intellectual and pragmatic goals, fills one with amazement today (Pierre Lombard,[191] Vincent de Beauvais.[192] Thomas de Cantimpré, B. Latini, etc.). The theme of the universal book— the alpha and omega of knowledge—makes inroads in literature as well, with Dante, for instance.[193]

Finally, such a total book has enormous symbolic possibilities. It is, for the first time, that the idea of *book* (by implication of *literature*) becomes, in a deliberate, planned way, intensely multivalent. Its mysterious meanings fascinate, scare, even terrify at times. Compared to the great abundance of senses and significances yielded by the symbolism of the predominantly sacred book[194] a textual, purely formal, profane book, when conceived, appears extremely poor.

A few species of total books can be easily identified. The first to assert itself is the image of life, the book of life. Man's life is a "book," in the words of a poet of the time (Alain de Lille: *Omnis mundi creatura/Quasi liber et pictura*). The fate of man, his predestination, the "memory" of his good deeds and trespassings are all "written" in it. At doomsday (*dies irae*), when "books are open," judgment will be passed on everyone according to the "book of his conscience" and his deeds. The divine judge will read *in libro conscientiae, in tabula cordis*.[195] *The Book of Nature*, in its turn, symbolizes the cosmos, with its many signs and tokens. *Natura* and *Scriptura* are the two great medieval emblematic books: *liber creaturae/liber scripturae*.[196] Both are laden with secrets. The difference is that *Liber creaturarum* begins to open up, not only to a symbolic interpretation, but to observation and exact experience as well.[197]

The conception of such a total, absolute book is rich in consequences for the biography of the idea of literature. On the one hand, the thesis of the unique books is put forth. Imposed as an exemplary model, it promotes orthodoxy and dogma. In the Middle Ages, we see the emergence of a type of authorized, dogmatic book, *recipiendis*, which gains "authority" and indexes—as did *Decretum Gelasianum*—each and every *non recipiendis* book. This is where the theory of the "heretical," "bad," forbidden book comes from. This is the origin of hateful censorship. On the other hand, the conservative content has a correspondence in the theory of the intangible, *ne varietur* (forever fixed) text. A faithful copy is much more important, in the Middle Ages, than a "personal"[198] composition—which is beginning to claim, though timidly at first, the status of "book." The concept evolves from a written composition to the composition of personal works, in the spirit of an author *qui faic un livre*.[199] Chaucer—and other medieval authors—introduce themselves as professional authors of "books."

The Library

The cultural cycle of writing and of the book is repeated completely in the case of *bibliotheca*. The Middle Ages also use the doublet *libraria* or *liberaria*[200] (*librairie, library*). But the classical, fundamental term, inherited from Christian tradition, remains until the fifteenth century (when the Bible becomes established for good,[201] *biblioteca Divina, coelesta bibliotheca*.[202] It expresses the prevailing idea of a sacred, absolute, exemplary book, which makes any other book appear useless or inferior. By analogy, the manuscript texts of the Bible "books" are called *codex, codices de bibliotheca*, sometimes even *l'escripture*. Terminology, then, remains traditional. In this matter, especially, the Middle Ages display a remarkable lack of imagination. The *sacred/profane* dissociation is translated in the same spirit: *tum regularium, tum saecularium librarios*.[203]

Another medieval meaning of the word (also taken from Christian Antiquity) is that of depository, a number of books gathered at the same place, *librorum reposito*.[204] With this acceptation, the term becomes general, beginning with the ninth century.[205] Its equivalent, *armarium*, is largely attested even before (sixth-seventh centuries). In the tenth, we find an explicit and complete definition: *bibliotheca, vel armarium vel archivium* (the Saxon Aelfric).[205b] *Armarium* (also *armaria*) even becomes part of a dictum *Claustrum sine armario, castrum sine armentario)*. In a broad sense, the medieval manuscript is itself a portable "library." Most often it is a *codex*, a collection, an anthology of texts. But private libraries also appear in academic circles; a medieval poet evokes with irony the way in which, in his roaming, he squandered away all his books.[206] The idea of the single, laicized book also takes the form of an "inventory of the books I have read," as in Photius' *Biblioteca* (ninth century),[207] an *aide-memoire* also mentioned by the Christian tradition (*cantos libros in memoriae meae biblio-teca considerat*).[208] The imagined plan of an ideal library (Richard de Four-nival, *Biblionomia*, thirteenth century) meets the same aspirations: to encompass, write down all knowledge, that is, all books. Hence, we find the first blueprints of general libraries, such as *Heptateuchon* or *Bibliotheca septem artium* (Thierry de Chartres (twelfth century), *Bibliotheca mundi* (*Speculum Majus*) (Vincent de Beauvais (1260), and *Bibliotheca universalis sive catalogus omnium scriptorum* (Guillaume de Pastrengo, 1350). At this stage, *library* becomes a very complex notion, fusing bibliographical, eru-dite, and (particularly) encyclopedic concerns. The consequences of this tendency, not clearly perceived for the time being, are extremely impor-tant, as we shall see.

The Bibliography

The beginnings of an "organized" European bibliography are to be sought in the Middle Ages as well. Its analytic, systematic, and classifying spirit is a very good incentive for such an initiative. It is the direct consequence of stocking and classifying books in libraries. Libraries, which were, origi-nally, strictly monastic institutions, were later taken over or reduplicated by royal courts and the aristocracy.

The first, decisive step in this direction is the drawing up of catalogues. As we know, the catalogue is an invention of the Alexandrian Age, but in the Middle Ages it becomes a universal, obligatory working tool. Its useful-ness and widespread use are proven by the multitude of terms defining it—*thesaurus, descriptio librorum, registrum librarie (librorum), inventarium librorum, nomina librorum* and even *catalogus*—are among the most com-mon. No less obvious is the obsession with totality—there is a book cata-logue entitled *Bibliotheca Magna alia Bibliotheca in ista tabula nominatur omnia scripta* (Bernhard Gui).[209]

Organizing these libraries proves to have far-reaching effects. It is based on a few empirical principles, from which the first classification of writings (that is, of literary genres, therefore of literature itself) is derived. Though modest, this event is nonetheless decisive for the evolution of literary history, even of literary theory. The first step consists of carving out a path in the unprecedented thicket of religious writings. One pioneer is St. Bonaventura,[210] another, much later, is Hugo de St. Victor.[211] This way, medieval catalogues begin to include not only the great traditional compartments (*scripturae sanctae/hereticorum libri*), but also sections de-voted to lay disciplines (for example, Konrad von Mure, *Repertorium voca-bulorum exquisitorum oratorie, poesis, historiarum*, 1272–1273; the idea of selection is also included). In some classifications, we meet philosophy, "lucrative" sciences, theology, etc.; in others, *libri poetarum, libri juri civilis, libri istoriografi, libri naturales*, etc.[212] For the first time, the idea of literature meets with an energetic organizing principle, capable of disciplining and framing it. It is not in the least important that it is, for the time being, administrative, bureaucratic, and purely pragmatic.

Even more relevant in this respect is the development of literary history, whose beginnings are inevitably bibliographical. In the initial stages, taking stock of books and of writers could only be done in a chronological manner. The lists of writings naturally change into historical repertories. The road opened by Christian Antiquity (the first inventories of ecclesiastic writers) is continued and greatly broadened in the Middle Ages (*De scripturis et scriptoribus sacris*,[213] *De scriptoribus ecclesiasticis*, *De scriptoris virorum illustrum*, etc.). One innovation is the personal catalogue, the bibliography of one's own works, for example, *Catalogus brevior librorum suorum* (Giraldus Cambrensis).[214] What emerges is a "literary history" that is cumulative, purely quantitative, documentary, without system or organizing principles, still embryonic and empirical, but destined for great, unsuspected future evolutions.

The Encyclopedia

In European culture, the Middle Ages are the climax of the encyclopedic ideal. Subsequently, this ideal will only reappear in the eighteenth century. There is a monstrous hypertrophy, and projects are entertained on a gigantic scale. The desire to encompass all knowledge is practically boundless. And then, following this moment of ardent intensity, the encyclopedic idea dies, either through fragmentation, or because of the appearance of different organizing principles. Little by little, the concept of the division of labor and the principle of cooperation begin to take hold. Also worth mentioning are the recourse to ideology and the increasing involvement in everyday reality.

In essence, this is a re-evaluation of the pattern of any medieval cultural creation. In many cases, the plan of an encyclopedia tends to reduplicate (chapter by chapter) the layout of Holy Writ. Initially, the encyclopedia is erected on a sacred foundation. The grammatical foundation is also worth noting. The classical conception of total grammar, of the encyclopedia of knowledge,[215] boils down to the formula, "Grammar is the foundation of all sciences" (Vincent de Beauvais).[216] To embrace them all, *universitas litterarum*, is the main concern. The ideal, as with Brunetto Latini's *Li livres dou tresor*, will be an encyclopedic "thesaurus" of books, a notion which is, in fact, quite explicit.[217] It is achieved by gigantic, universal Western works such as *Speculum Universalis* (Vincent de Beauvais), a programmed repertory of all the sciences of the age (*Apologia de universitate scientiarum*), *Summa Theologica* (Thomas Aquinas), a digest of all Catholic doctrine. All titles suggest gigantism, completeness, an attempt at global synthesis (John of Salisbury: *omnia legenda sunt*): *Speculum Majus*, *Speculum Mundi*, *Speculum doctrinale*, etc. A similar effort can be discerned in the Byzantine culture of the age, especially in the tenth century. The idea of a unique, total, cumulative, exhaustive book reappears in a new guise.[218] An apology of Dante's work will praise it as being *una libreria in un libro*.[219]

An inner tension, leading to the disintegration of the encyclopedic principle, can already be felt at work. On the one hand, *orbis disciplinarum* begins to branch out: *Arbor sciencia, Arbre de Ciència* (Ramon Llull). On the other, each "branch" tends to specialize in certain genres. Hence, specialized encyclopedias: of nature *(De naturis rerum)*, linguistic *(Janus linguarum)*, lexicographical (Papias, Jean Balbi, Giovanni di Genua: *Catholicon*). At the same time, one can note an indecision between "scholarly" concerns and the didactic concern for "school students and medium-cultivated readers" (Barthelemi l'Anglais, *De proprietatibus rerum*). In their turn, vocabularies (Papias, etc.) tend to become school primers. Let us remark, nevertheless, that *literature* is not mentioned in any of the great medieval encyclopedic surveys, not even in the section *grammatica*.

DIVERSIFICATION OF PROFANE LETTERS

"Liberal Letters"

The confusion *literae* = *literal*, which was introduced and used on an ever broader scale in Antiquity, is taken up again and given final consecration in the Middle Ages. Strict etymology is forsaken, in favor of tacit, general identification: *litterae* = *artes liberales; litteralibus* = *liberalibus studiis* (1168).[220] All the basic texts speak of *artibus et disciplinis liberalium artium,*[221] *artes dicantur liberales,*[222] *liberalium literarum* (Vincent de Beauvais), etc.

A perusal of the sources reveals other typically medieval aspects, first, the current fundamental opposition: *liberal / ecclesiastical* writings *(tam liberalium quam ecclesiasticarum,*[223] *libri sacri / libri de arte (liberales), sacras disciplinas / disciplinas liberales.*[224] Then, there is the tendency to redeem liberal letters, so that they can be assimilated by the Church and by Christian faith (St. Bonaventura, *Opusculum de reductione artium et theologiam)*; this is done also by "reconsidering" them, by adopting them,[225] in a selective manner, as underlings.[226]

Grammar, too, undergoes similar metamorphoses. From *litteralis* (Diomedes) and the totality of literary studies, it becomes, from Cassiodorus onward, "the origin and foundation of liberal letters,"[227] a formula that will soon become a stereotype,[228] introduced in glossaries, etc. The content, naturally, is encyclopedic, global: *omnia litteraria studia*, foundations of *totius studii.*[229] The definition, itself currently used, sometimes includes the idea of cycle (another discovery of Antiquity), of "interlocked arts" *(entrelacies).*[230]

The basic medieval meaning of "liberal letters," we must repeat, can only be cultural. *Liberal letters* = *culture (liberalium cultura litterarum),*[231] what today is called "general knowledge." This is acquired in schools *(scholae liberalium litterarum).*[232] Higher than "reading and writing" *(litterae com-*

munes/liberales)[233] it is the equivalent of literary studies *(liberalis exercitii studium)*,[234] an expression that is commonly used in this age. To acquire the liberal letters you must go through the entire cycle *(trivium* and *quadrivium)*, whose definition is also a stereotype: *septem liberalibus artibus*,[235] *litterarum septem columnis*,[236] *septem disciplinas, quas philosophi liberalis appellant*,[237] etc. A widely circulated treatise by Thierry de Chartres is entitled *Heptateuchon*, "the manual of the seven liberal arts" *(septem liberalium artium)*. Re-adapted and converted, these "seven pillars" of human wisdom support Christian faith as well.

"Human Letters"

The classical terminology of letters, inherited from Antiquity, has certain variations in the Middle Ages: *litterae humaniores, humane litterae,* and *studia humanitas.* It is a critical heritage and, at the same time, a product of the dissociative spirit typical of the Christian Middle Ages, *divinarum humanarumque rerum.*[238] Humanities are a lay, didactic discipline, corresponding to today's "humanist" and "social" sciences. Their finality goes far beyond the mere cultivation of the intellect. As we know, study— grammar, the humanities—humanize. In an ancient phrase, they are *ad usum vitae, ad omnem vitam litteratura.*[239] A *grammaticus* can no longer be a *simpliciter homo.*[240] Therefore, the seven pillars of "literal arts" have a very well-defined humanistic aim: *ad cultum humanitas conducta* (Thierry de Chartres).[241] This type of culture implies new civil and oral values: *urbanitas, curialitas,*[242] and *humane civilitatis.*[243] We are on solid, familiar ground.

"Good Letters"

The expressions *bonae litterae* and *bona studia,* also coined in Antiquity, go hand in hand with the theory and technique of medieval culture. No longer used, they are the product of medieval didactic and philosophical surveys, in which a special chapter, *ad bonarum artium studia,*[244] is included. The basic interpretation, needless to say, is Christian. But *scripta bona* begins to display particular value connotations. A *troubadour,* for instance, will distinguish himself not only by his *ben letras,* but also by his capacity of *ben cantar e ben trovar.*[245] "Good letters" can be not only "cultivated," but also esthetic (lyrical, poetical). On the horizon, then, even if still timid and inconsistent, there is a glimmer of what can already be called "literary specificity." Later, we shall become aware of other, more precise clues, pointing in the same direction. Such discriminations are plainly encouraged by the ambiguous quality of these *bonae litterae,* invested with every possible quality. They gauge, ever more accurately, the degree of complexity reached by the idea of literature in the Middle Ages.

THE COORDINATES OF LETTERS

New Versus Old Letters

In the Middle Ages, the dissociations occurring in the field of literature and of the idea of literature may acquire other dimensions as well. The characteristic tendency is that they become ever more precise and well-delineated in time. This essential criterion, referring to both chronology and value, sums up, amplifies, and reformulates all the *vetus/novus* dialectics. For the medieval Christian, whatever precedes Christianity is "old," while all the values brought about by Christian faith are "new." When a historical perspective is acquired, "pagan" Antiquity and the Church Fathers are relegated to the ancient age *(antiqua)*, while the new authors and doctors of divinity (especially) are *modern*. The process becomes more distinct between the ninth and twelfth centuries, but its connotations are far from being merely "literary." Theology, grammar, logic, and natural sciences are also involved.[246] Historical awareness itself entails terms of comparison and stages of evolution. Compared to *actas aureas* (a criterion already used by Velleius Paterculus), all that follows is decadence. Medieval thinkers reason along similar lines: They look up to the ancients and suffer from an inferiority complex, brought about by an awareness of their status as epigones.[247]

In the field of literature, categories that are by now traditional reappear: *antiquis libri, humaniora modernis, priscus poeta* and *novelli poetae, vetustiores litterae* and *modernae litterae*, which, according to tradition, include mostly literary studies, grammar studies in the first place. Innovation *(innovelatur grammatica)* in this field is frowned upon.[248] The reverse opinion is also heard: "The younger the grammarians, the more perspicacious."[249] *Recentiores non deteriores*. This antagonism has purely literary facets as well. The right to innovate and rejuvenate is openly claimed: "By writing up things, we rejuvenate old texts" (Alain de Lille). The radical rejection of old dogmas can also be seen.[250] This opposition goes even deeper with poets who use a vernacular language to write works of profane or erotic inspiration *(Vagantes, Goliardes)*, completely ignorant of and indifferent to *Ars versificatoria*.

National Versus Universal Letters

As medieval culture was uniformly Latin in expression, the concept of "national literature" could not make its appearance until national, vernacular languages, which were then undergoing a period of full development, began to produce differences and contrasts. The concept is therefore blocked by the universality and pre-eminence of Latin letters. As we know, all that falls outside the sphere of *litteratus* is considered ignorant, *illiteratus*. Those who speak no Latin are *illiterati*, that is, inferior, of no importance.

Underneath, however, the split becomes more radical: *lingua laica* becomes—through the dissemination of writing—an increasingly cultivated means of literary expression: *scripta latina rustica* or, simply, *(romane) scripta*.[251] In the service of native, vernacular languages, the alphabet inevitably produces a new, national species of literature.

For the moment, those who want to give it a name can only take their bearing from these distinctions: *libri grammatici/libri vulgari*,[252] *scriptores litterati/scriptores vulgaris*. Consequently, the theory of expressing oneself in the "vulgar," national language will be called *De vulgari eloquentia* (Dante), *Trattati delle Rime Volgare* (Antonio da Tempo). Language becomes the symbol of nationality. A different language = a different nationality, that is, a mark of national identity: *eyne dutsch Buch (Buoch)*[253] = a book in German, that is, belonging to German literature. Symptoms of a competition appear, regarding the superiority of one modern language over another. The emergence of nationality undoubtedly precedes the apparition of writing, but its existence can only be proven by writing, which is not quite sufficient for it to be recognized and established, literarily speaking. Throughout the Middle Ages, national vernacular literature is little appreciated and, therefore, little used. The enormous prestige of Latin keeps it permanently on the fringe, where it receives little attention.

On the other hand, the concept "universal letters" remains predominant. It is the expression of the global, encyclopedic culture of Antiquity and of the Middle Ages and of its traditions. It is the great age of universal languages: First Latin, then French and Italian. *Lingua franca* is the most "internationalist" cultural and linguistic concept of the age. At the same time, the prevailing cultural ideal remains the economic—cosmopolitan one in the sphere of lay culture and the economic-Christian one in the sphere of religious culture. In tenth-century Byzantium, Constantine VII Porphirogenitus proposes to "gather books of any kind from all the parts of the *oikumené*."[254] In Dante, one can clearly observe both the tension between universality and an ever more acute national *prise de conscience*, and the interference of the epoch's true spiritual structures.[255]

Popular Letters

While developing the idea of popular language—already formulated in Antiquity—the Middle Ages also amplify the concept of "popular literature." It is an important original contribution to the biography of the idea of literature. Literature begins to show signs of emancipation from under the wing of exclusively Latin letters, grammar, and culture. The undermining of these monopolies and prestige will have far-reaching consequences, especially in the concurrent, alternative zone to literature—that of poetry.

The terms by which "popular literature" begins to be defined clearly indicate the gradual dissociation from *litterae*: on the one hand, *litteratura*, on the other, *idiomate linguae terrae*, the native tongues of the planet. Within this terminology, *popular = uncultivated*. This process is fueled and amplified by culture: The written, cultivated language of the Church is opposed to the oral, laic, "vulgar," uncultivated popular idiom (*vulgaris locutionis usus*).[256] As Latin becomes increasingly difficult to understand, culture in the native tongue is felt as a necessity to which the Church begins to pay heed. Even having a vernacular version of the Bible is now possible. The genesis of such a literature is "cultivated," but there are also clerics who endeavor to cater to the taste of an uncultured class.[257]

In fact, there could hardly be a different essential criterion of identifying the new popular literature, a different certificate of (semantic) birth: writings by *illiterati*, for *illiterati*, ungrammatical, *en romans* and not *en livre*,[258] a "book" being written, invariably and, by definition, in Latin. Latin continues to be used exclusively in religious, philosophical, and didactic texts. Grammarians write in a "prosaic or metric style," while chroniclers pretend to lack proper education and write only in the *inculto effatu* style.[259] The typology will be consolidated and will already become "classical:" *litterati poete* (writing in Latin) versus *volgari* (writing in the national tongues, especially Italian).[260]

That popular literature is for a long time defined in Latin terms can be explained by the fact that it was perceived by and filtered through the predominant cultural medium, hence formulas like *barbara et antiquissima carmina*,[261] *fabulose popularium narrationis*.[262] Conversely, translation from the "vulgar" language is done into *litteratura* (that is, Latin).[263] The monopoly on terms continues to exist, but *romanz, de latin en romaunz* (Marie de France) is more and more often used to translate the new notion.[264] It's clear that "oral" is not one and the same thing as "popular." However, the traditional cultural pressure of *letterae* remains quite strong. Using the classical, Latin mode, Chaucer divides his work into "books." Popular poetry (of the troubadours) reveals a concern for correctness and code in the language that probably emulates the champions and defenders of the cultivated, Latin poetic language.[265]

ESTHETICIZING LETTERS

"Beautiful Letters"

A new lexical formula that will have a brilliant European career—in the eighteenth century, *belles lettres* will be the central definition of literature—is *pulcherrimae litterae*.[266] We are now at the medieval origins of a new acceptation of the idea of literature, which Antiquity only prefigured: *beautiful letters*. At first, the notion covers the whole of culture, science, and education: *grammatica, litteralis litterae*. It is further remarked that medieval "beauty" is very far from having the formalist-esthetic sense currently associated, from the nineteenth century on, with literature. Its career is entirely speculative, metaphysical.[267] However, by becoming sacred, the idea of beauty plays a much more important role than in Antiquity: central, exemplary, canonical. Beautiful forms are but the creation or the reflex of divine beauty (Thomas Aquinas: *Ex divina pulchritudine esse omnium derivatur*).[268] In its medieval acceptation, the intrinsic or formal beauty of letters can only be secondary, completely unessential.

This is not to say that during the Middle Ages there were no attempts at "formal estheticizing" of letters. In fact, not only was such a beautifying intensely cultivated but, through the art of calligraphy, it enjoyed its greatest period of European glory. It is the great age of calligraphy and miniature, of treatises on calligraphy and pictographical poems, of *scribere pulchre, litterae pingere, pulchritudo chartarum, versus scripti litteris aureis*, etc.[269] The illumination of medieval manuscripts rises to unprecedented levels of refinement. Medieval illumination, a synthesis of *scriptura et pictura*, is a typical demonstration of *pulchra scriptura* (Witelius).[270] The symbolism of ornate letters and of allegorical calligraphic composition is one of the delights of the hermeneutics of such manuscripts today.

Medieval grammar, an extension of the ancient tradition, is conceived of in a similar way: the sovereign art of speaking and writing "well," that is, "beautifully," in an eloquent, reductive, rhetorical manner: *peritia pulchre loguendi*, according to the formula of the late grammarians of Antiquity (Cassiodorus,[271] Diomedes, etc.). *Venustatem grammaticae*, though contested from a rigorist Christian perspective,[272] is another, no less legitimate and natural concern of the age.

The conception of verbal beauty and beautiful composition (shaped within this framework) casts a direct light on the idea of literature, on literary expression in general: *dulces litterae, elegantissima scriptura, pulchrae historiae, pulchris secundum litteram, pulchris verbis, venustas sententiae verbum bonum et suave, carminibus suavissima condimenta*,[273] *schoener Kunst* (*Tristan*, verse 7733), are some of the more frequent phrases. Notice, especially, a formula like *praetermissa litteratura* (Giraldus Cambrensis), translated by *well-written books*.[274] In Old French, its equivalent is *bele conjointure*.[275] Poetics treatises (for example, Bede, *De re metrica*) also speak of *pulcherrimo positio*, some of *venustate dictaminum*. The strong ancient rhetorical reminiscence is more than obvious: Literary beauty is viewed as *color rythmicus, colores rhetorici, flores rhetorici, rhetorica dictus*,[276] a terminology bearing upon ornamental style. *Beautiful = ornatus, forma pulchritudinis* (Mathieu de Vendôme, *Ars versificatoria*),[277] *verba splendida, oratio ornata*[278] and others of the kind. The stylistic theory is called *De ornamentis verborum, de lege dictamen ornandi, ars de difficili ornatu*. The corresponding phrases in Romance languages are *belles histoires, beaux dits* (with troubadours), *belleca de parole, belle stile, bei modi di dire, ornamento delle parole* (especially with Dante: *bello stilo*).[279] Literary beauty enjoys full recognition and, even more important from our point of view, a rich terminology.

Literature and Poetry

In equal measure, the medieval spirit is aware of the alternative *literature/poetry*, which it summarizes and resolves—predictably—in keeping with the traditional ancient pattern, but in a more organized manner, with more abundant and varied arguments. *Literature* is a discipline, a form of knowledge, a "science" and, at the same time, an art of words.[280] Dante associates poetic composition with grammar, whose cultural, erudite meanings are notorious.[281] But it is this very polarity that tends to make poetry evade the sphere of culture, of "literature," respectively. Goliards and troubadours take their distance from, or break off completely, with the Greek and Latin tradition and its didactic prescriptions. Chaucer is plainly aware of this separation (*Clerk's Tale: Franklin's Prologue*, 709–729). Poetry becomes a personal undertaking (*Troilus and Cressida*, I).

This poetry that asserts its rights continues to be, evidently, an *ars scribendi*, an *ars litteraria*, a *litteralis sermo*: a composition that is, first of all, written, done quill in hand. The oral tradition of great improvisation, of medieval poetry, introduces the first legitimate criterion for dissociation, which also establishes the specificity. There also exists an oral, vernacular poetry, "devoid of rules," distinct from grammar.[282] Even if the frequency of terms such as *poems, poesis, poetria* is not yet great in the Middle Ages, their listing in glossaries, well apart from *litteratura*, speaks volumes about their specific character being recognized: *quod poeta composuit* = a work of poetry, a work of imagination in verse etc.[283] *Scriba* and *poeta* are also well-delienated in the Middle Ages.

Poetic Literature

In any case, at this stage of historical development, "popular letters" and "beautiful letters" can only be marginal, minor, subordinated notions. Medieval literary consciousness continues to be dominated, like the ancient one, by the prestigious, authoritative *litterae*. These "letters"—being relied upon to define and give name to new, poetical forms of written expression—find a suitable equivalent in the formula *litteratura poetarum*.[284] It constitutes a new key word, which assumes ever more numerous determinations and special connotations. The essential, fundamental meaning, however, continues to be the etymological one: "The poets' written literature." One must specify that to define this notion, consecrated, traditional notions and categories must be resorted to, as before.

Dictamen is another classical term that conveys the basic condition of any kind of composition, including poetic composition. This is a typically medieval genre, derived directly from the act of writing (*dictare* = composition, editing, any kind of writing) which aims, through education and imitation, to raise any "composition" to the dignified level prescribed by "rules" (*Ars dictaminis, Summa dictaminis*).[285] Throughout the Middle Ages, it will be a characteristic form of "literary culture" and of "writing." Homer's work will be defined as *dictamen Omeri*.[286] For Dante, poetic work is also "dictated" (*dictandis verba*).[287] When scrutinized from this vantage point, the idea of "writing" continues to be stronger and more precise than any "content": a poetic text is defined, first, by its being *poetica scriptus*,[288] while the definition of poetry is different: *carmina est quando poetae conscribunt*.[289] Generally speaking, at this elementary but basic stage in the terminology, poetry, literature, are viewed as nothing more than particular ways of writing. What is, in effect, the poetic manner of writing, as viewed by the age? First and foremost, a form of "cultivated style," of *sermo scolasticus*, characterized by rhetorical estheticizing: a colored *modus dicendi*—*dicendi color*[290]—adorned with rare words and imagery, *figurae verborum*. We witness a tremendous recrudesence of rhetoric, solemnly extolled as the *soavissima di tutte le altre scienze*,[291] even personified (*Dame Rhetoryke*).[292] Therefore, the main radical discrimination (be it implicit) between poetic and everyday usage belongs to the Middle Ages, a crucial moment, the importance of which has not always been duly emphasized. This dichotomy will become stronger and more finely nuanced, theoretically, throughout the historical evolution of the idea of literature.

Thus, poetry—dubbed since Antiquity as *pulcherimum carmen*[293]—gains the full status of "beautiful letters." It follows that, from this perspective, the aim of grammar can only be *ex poeticis*,[294] and the poetic attribute *par excellence* will be *pulcherimus*[295] ("beautiful"). *Poetarum carmina, poetica carmina*, and *pulchra poemata* become synonyms. *Litteratura* continues to preserve its strong meaning: grammatical, erudite, cultural. Instead, *poesia*, a form of *sermo*, is an art, a composition that abides by the rules of "poetic art," *ex arte*,[296] a written verbal act: *poetice scribentis et dictandis*.[297] It has its source in imagination, a trait granted to any work of imagination in verse. All through the Middle Ages, the concept will be rendered through one and the same notion that will have deeper and deeper roots: *poetria, poetrye*.[298] Its star climbs higher and higher on the horizon of the idea of literature. Its products, *fabulosi litteris*, are mere fictions, *fabulationes, fabulae poetarum* (Theodulf).[299] Later, Dante will share the opinion, *fictio rhetorica*,[300] even *bella menzogna*.[301] The estheticizing of fabulation is therefore given proper consideration and it is satisfied.

An art of literary fabulation (*a poetis fictae*), poetry is a relatively new form of creation. Although nuances are not always well dissociated (they cannot be, at this stage in the semantics of the problem), it is not only a question of chronological "novelty," of the type *novus/vetus* mentioned above, but of a qualitative novelty, that is, originality: *anima facit novas compositiones* (St. Bonaventura);[302] both meanings of the notion must be taken into account. The qualitative sense, however, prevails with medieval poets: "new song" *(noel)*,[303] "renewed word" *(mutatio verbum)*.[304] The *dolce stil nuovo* poets give final consecration to both a new school and a new literary manner.

Literariness: Sacred Versus Profane

Another little-known aspect, which becomes quite obvious to the scholar who surveys the whole historical evolution of the idea of literature, is that, during the Middle Ages, the problems of the literary specific gain more clear-cut contours than in Antiquity. It is, certainly a "literary specific" defined in implicit or explicit medieval terms. However, these terms are relevant enough for marking a visible progress and a notable mutation in literary awareness.

An essential, typically medieval characteristic is that divinity is seen as an archetype of the creator, that is, of the poet. God is the supreme *dictator*, he who dictates "the book," having the tables of law as an archetypal model. He is *deus artifex*, the first artist, the exemplary creator by definition. As we know, the notion of divine inspiration has a great tradition in Antiquity. But it does not lead—as it does in the Middle Ages—to the total, personal sacralization of the poet and of his work, which is, in broad terms, identified as *verbum deus* or *deus verbis, verbum patris*.[305] The granting of such a status is, simultaneously, a humiliation and a great consecration: *Spiritus sanctus est auctor, homo vero instrumentum* (Thomas Aquinas).[306] The great career of the poet who is hallowed and also personalized through and in the name of all his attributes is only launched, strictly speaking, in the Middle Ages. His inspiration is acknowledged as being at the same time transcendental and human, real and true in both senses of the word.

The traditional discrimination between *sacred* and *profane*—the first possible medieval form of indicating literature's essentially "specific" nature—has other similar implications as well. First, a more precise definition of poetry becomes possible by marking off the "sacred" and "profane" territories *(divinis litteris/verbis poeticos)*.

This current dissociation strengthens the idea of the profane personality of the poet and of poetry, as well as that of the existence of specific themes of goliards and troubadours. At the same time, it begins to implement a reversal of the classical ratio: the Bible can now be read as a literary work, just like any pagan author,[307] a very bold and crucial initiative. To acknowledge or at least to tolerate profane inspiration, poetry seen as entertainment and play *(ludicra, jocularis)*, "jesters," *voluptas poetarum*,[308] is to further delimit and delineate the field of poetry, to a great extent assimilated by lay spiritual activity.

But the prevailing poetic style continues to be the sacred one, with its specific traits: symbolic, initiatory obscurity, secret, hermetic language—an obvious reminiscence of oracular uttering, borrowed by profane poetry, especially by the troubadours. This style can be found with "hysperics" such as Virgilius Maro Grammaticus, with troubadours (*trobar clus*[309] or Dante *sotto il velame*).[310] At the same time, as we know, *sermo humilis* has its champions in the exponents of religious catechizing. A good example of semantic displacement in the same direction is the following: the initial, sacred meaning of *ligare* is gradually identified, in the Middle Ages, with the lay idea of poetic *composition*.[311] *Poétique* signifies "inventions," "fables," "fictions," in a broad sense, constructions of the spirit.[312] Finally, a form of dissociation is to uphold and defend new poetry, in one form or another. Usually, it is a defense of novelty, of innovation, which irritates rigorist, dogmatic Christian classicism (*veterum dogmata*).[313] This is cause for controversy and argument both in the West and in the Byzantine world.[314]

The appearance—even if tacit, implicit—of an awareness of a specific nature of poetry is not without important consequences. Conversion—or, better said, the fusion with the idea of sacred poetry—is the most important of them. As seen above, this is not a medieval discovery either, but it is only now that the foundations of truly mystical poetry—destined to build up a great tradition in Western literature—are laid. The most frequent expressions start from *hymnus, ut Scriptura canit*,[315] *carmina sanctorum*,[316] and gradually progress to *carmina sacra, religiosa poetmata, cantica spiritualia*, etc. Through recuperation and mutual assimilation, theology itself becomes "God's poetry." Hence, we witness the coining of the concept *poetae theologi*[317] (another medieval combination, quite typical of the spiritual context of the age), and of its equivalent, *divine poetae*. As a final conclusion, the existence and efficiency of *Deus Poeta* are acknowledged. He alone is the Creator, therefore, the creator of poetry as well.[318]

One of the most specific aspects of medieval literary consciousness is the following: The characteristics of sacred poetry are transferred onto poetry in general, and this concept, in its turn, becomes sacred. We even witness an incipient process of "estheticizing" the Bible. To St. Bonaventura, *tota Scriptura est quasi una cithara*. St. Thomas Aquinas is moved by its poetic imagery.[319] The ancient idea of divine "madness" or "fury" is taken up by the Middle Ages; so is that of the prophetic text. The tradition of esoteric, "initiatic" poetry takes firmer hold. Its symbolism must also be seen as an important characteristic (*aenigmatibus fabularum*).[320] Dante is clearly aware of symbolic letters,[321] of Adamic language.[322] Religion and the Church may slow down personal poetic style, but the awareness of its existence and, above all, its empirical implementation, continues to be kept alive with vernacular poets, skalds, etc.[323]

The Beginning of Autonomy

It would seem an anachronism, as in the case of Antiquity, to speak of the "autonomy" of medieval literature and poetry in a period when sacrality is overwhelmingly and intolerantly dominant. But a close reading of the texts proves that this is not so. There is even more: To point out this "autonomy" is a typical example of the hermeneutics of the latent, implicit signification of the idea of literature. From the perspective of the completed biography, it becomes more and more perceivable. Questions that seem to be typically modern are raised—firmly enough—even in the often too obscure, or too eliptical, language of the Middle Ages.

The first sign of relative autonomy is provided by the permanent, inevitable, historical and ahistorical separation of the sacred from the profane. The general consensus is that poetry is not theology, that love of *superflua* is directly connected to *rerum saecularum aura*.[324] Dante himself declares his work to be that of a poet, not of a theologian.[325] The assimilation by *Poësis* of *Theologia*, which it can even replace (Alberto Mussato),[326] points in the same direction. This is, in fact, also the thesis of the apology of poetry, which begins to take shape now and which will become fully developed during the Renaissance: Poetry is justified in that to ignore it is to be unable to understand holy works (Richard de Bury).[327] On the other hand, all the medieval theory of writing implies a dissociation from oral and pictographic expression. The eulogy of writing (verse, poem) also implies separation from song *(chans, chanso)*.

Logical and methodological dissociations play an important role in medieval literary theory. It is common knowledge that grammar was included in the *trivium* cycle, and conceived of as independent of rhetoric and dialectics. The content of the *quadrivium* cycle is even further removed from the domain of letters: philosophy, arithmetic, geometry, etc. Classification in these two cycles becomes usual, beginning with the ninth century. But even in this indistinct, "grammatical" form, "literature" tends to acquire an individual being, to become an independent concept, which is still a difficult process, as the supremacy of logic and dialectics, as well as the allegorical-symbolical conception of poetry, continue to be very serious obstacles.[328]

The key to the whole process is the dissociation from grammar, that is to say, from culture. In the Middle Ages, this problem is part of the issue of defining the status of poetry. The spirit of the age does not look upon it yet as a self-contained art. It is seen as belonging to rhetoric, rather than grammar.[329] But the mere appearance of the phrase, combined with the hypothesis of a separation from adjacent disciplines, proves that the issue was, at least, raised. Other formulas are even more revealing: *pulchritudo ordinis aut litteraturae*.[330] The confrontation between *trivium* (= style, rhetoric) and *quadrivium* = doctrine) leads to identical conclusions. An old gloss (dating back to the sixth century) clearly specifies the identity of the poet. He is neither a historian, nor a prophet, but belongs to another category of writers.[331] Later, the "poet" will be scrupulously dissociated from "historiographers."[332] Other such distinctions are on record: poet versus philosopher, poet versus rhetorician—with Dante, for example.[333] The same meaning is to be found in the classification: *poeta/versiloqus, versificatores/vero electi*,[334] *versificatorie atque litteratorie artis;*[335] versification = cultural work; poetry = work of talent. The ever-wider circulation of the notion "prose"[336] *(De modo prosandi, Rationes dictandi prosaice, prosaicum dictamen)*, etc. further consolidates, by contrast, the idea of poetry.

In this sense, the often-quoted ancient dispute *utile/dulci, delectare/edificare* also has "autonomist" causes and effects. The most characteristic moment is that of the *Bataille des set ars* (Henri d'Andeli, ca. 1250), a dispute over the liberal and mechanical arts. Beyond the controversy over curricula and over the excellence of Universities (Paris/Orléans),[337] what is in fact debated is the problem of the finality and specific character of the "arts." It is obvious that "literature"—even if seen as a hypostasis of grammar—remains, by definition, a "liberal" art, defined in familiar, classical terms. This "liberality" belongs to the category of *dulci*, not of *utile*. During the Middle Ages, frequent reference (more frequent than is generally believed) is made to *dulcissima litterarum*,[338] *amor litterarum*[339] (St. Columbanus, sixth century: *delectatio litterarum)*,[340] or simply to *delectare* or *dulcitudinem litterarum.*[341] The adjective *dulciter/dulcedo* is also quite frequently used. *Otium* (a notion also inherited from Antiquity, from Seneca, among others)[342] is the specific state of mind, and the emotion defining it is pleasure *(delectare)*, seen as an *appendentia artium*,[343] as something that enchants the soul *(juvare animas)*.[344] In their turn, medieval trouvers often allude to *sequences plaisans et belles*, to that which *plaît*, to the *gracieux plaisir de la joyeuse lecture*, etc. Medieval delight, in fact, covers a fairly wide emotional spectrum, from the thrills induced by *jongleurs*, to the pleasurable, entertaining (*Fioretti: dilettar, con maraviglia l'uditore)*, even ineffable reading of "I do not know what" *(non sai cui)*,[345] to reading in a "purely literary vein" (attested in the Byzantine world as well),[346] or to the voluptuousness of book collecting (Richard de Bury, *Philobiblion*, VIII). These significances of "letters" are not, even contextually speaking, altogether marginal. They add to the major senses of the age's view on literature, by providing parallel or alternative acceptations, in keeping with the intrinsic, structural logic of the idea of literature. This logic works within the context, but it always has wider significances.

It is, therefore, possible to extract and expose an incipient medieval notion of "autonomy." Its roots are simultaneously philosophical—scholastic and moral—psychological, and well-attested in both cases. A first, radical definition, *opus naturale/opus artificiale*[347] places letters among poetic, *sive artificiales*, arts. The dichotomy will become classical: art/nature, in medieval terms *ordo naturalis/ordo artificialis*. Formal medieval preoccupations, especially those connected with *trobar clus*, identical with *ornatus difficilis* (a consciousness that troubadours have)[348] are identical in nature, similarly, the one about *la fratraisie*.[349] On this ground, poetic consciousness scorns popular poetry, considered too "natural" and "artless,"[350] too *rustica verba*. The autotelic criterion is naturally born: spiritual (including literary) values are *propter suam*,[351] literati use *la lettera per lo suo uso*, not to economic, or lucrative ends.[352] The dissociation from other values and activities even leads to the acknowledgment of the "purity" of poetic creation, which is to say that it is seen as specific, autonomous, unmistakable: Lucan (cf. Arnulf) *non est iste poeta purus sed poeta et historiographus*.[353]

Vaguely, then, one can already have a glimpse of what is called, in modern terms, "art for art's sake." At any rate, the idea of games, of gratuitous playing, inherited from Antiquity is now being consolidated, by being theoretically justified. The point of departure is to be found in the *spectacula, ludicra*, in the theater show (*De ludis*).[354] The theory of the theater (*Theatrica*) is the *scientia ludorum*.[355] It includes recreation, amusement, the joy of relaxation. *Jocum, joculum, musa jocosa, ad jocunditatem* refer to an activity and a frame of mind that are not only approved of, but also praised, especially by troubadours (in Occitan: *joy, joie*). But the concept that best renders this idea—as it also includes the inalienable cultural background of medieval letters—is that of *gay saber, gaya ciencia, gay savoir, fröhliche Wissenschaft*. It is "science" that amuses and charms, remaining within the sphere of culture, but leaving the territories of abstract intellectualism. This dissociation, which will develop steadily through the entire course of the biography of the idea of literature, collects its life-giving sap through medieval roots.

THE HETERONOMY OF LETTERS

The arborescent polysemy of *letters* is not confined to a *verbi gratia* autonomist orientation. The opposed conception of the heteronomy of letters also develops during the Middle Ages, to a much greater extent than in Antiquity. It considerably enriches the idea of literature, by defining the collective coordinates and the objective frames of "literature." They now receive a much more appropriate formulation, in increasingly specialized terms.

a) *The "Republic of letters"*. The theory of a universal, cosmopolitan motherland and, of a budding "world literature," which, as we have seen, was already sensed in Antiquity, is resumed and emphatically reformulated in the Middle Ages. The unitary character of medieval culture is a fact. The awareness of it could hardly find a more exact definition than that offered by the phrase *republica litterarum:* the community of letters and of the men of letters: *res publica clericorum.* Equally widespread is the variant *civitas litterarum*[356] = the citadel of letters, a metaphor referring to the union of thought and of the organization of world culture. European culture is conceived of as a spiritual entity, under the emblem of unifying, integrating "internationalist" letters. "Ignorance is man's exile, knowledge is his motherland" (Honorius d'Autun).[357] Dante himself has a notion of "human universalism" *(humane civilitatis).*[358]

All definitions speak of a common "citadel" as "motherland" of grammar *(civitas grammatica),*[359] humanities *(humanitas communitas),* and clerics *(universitas litterarum),* conceived of as an autonomous, fraternal, prestigious corporation. Unity is achieved through a vast epistolary network, through copies *(ad rescribendur),* and through the free circulation of ideas and men of letters. Due to these many channels, the basic operations, *translatio studii* and *studium generale,* become social and intellectual acts. A peaceful, independent, exigent, a kind of "dominant intellectual class," situated above frontiers and barriers of any kind, now becomes self-aware. In part, *letters* become potentially cosmopolitan, acknowledged and defined as such in the spirit of universalism. Thus, the notion "universal letters" acquires a truly communitarian content and acceptance.

b) *Society.* A series of fairly accurate considerations regarding the social role played by letters and, by implication, men of letters, are made in the Middle Ages. A consciousness of the institution of literature and of its specific functions begins to take shape, in a fairly direct manner, in Western Europe at the time.

The first configuration is that of the organization and stratification of society into two great categories, followed by a radical social-cultural classification: *vita regularis/vita saecularis,* or *clerics/laymen* respectively, according to the principle *duo sunt genera christianorum.*[360] There are two lifestyles, two activities, and two functions: *terrena/spiritualia,* everything being indissolubly linked to *litterae* and *litteratura.* Social promotion to public offices (notary's office) also requires *suffisance et literature d'iceux.*[361] The controversy—already classical—between *arms* and *letters, clericus et miles,* exploits this quality, very scarce at the time, to the advantage of the *clerics.* But it is extended over the entire social hierarchy, the monarchy included. Hence, the typically medieval saying: *Rex illiteratus est quasi asinus coronatus.* Uncultivated kings—or, by extension, state leaders— resemble crowned jackasses. One of the *defectu principium* is *illitteratura,* the lack of culture.[362] The social role of the poet is more precisely defined in this period. He is invested with important official attributes *(skald, filid, bard).* First and foremost, he is the court-poet, the singer of the glory of the monarch, of his heroic deeds, of the historical memory of his nation; he is the connoisseur of royal genealogy.[363] At the same time, in the best Indo-European tradition, vindicated throughout Antiquity, the poet is a counsellor and a magician, a *vates* who interprets, utters prophecies, gives penance, and pronounces anathemas ("The bard's curse"). His satire irremediably compromises, his verdicts have the value and force of a moral law.

The existence of oral, popular poetry implicitly points to the existence of a popular audience, in parallel with the one consisting of *viri litterati*. It is impossible to conceive of *courtoise* poetry, or the *chansons de geste*, without an audience, without public performances, without the idea of success. All the many dedications and invocations, some of them written, clearly point to literary patronage, to the protection of the illustrious, and of the elite literary public, above all.[364]

c) *Economy*. Another medieval contribution, exceeding the formulations and levels attained by Antiquity, is the incipient—but fairly precise—definition of literature's relations with the economic system, with economic ideas and values. The traditional point of view is quite well known: "literal arts," neatly distinguished from "mechanical" (*mechanicae id est adulterinae*), utilitarian arts, cultivated by "free" people,[365] opposed professionalism and, especially, profit-making. This exclusivism, however, is amended by social and economic necessities. The economic advantages of "letters" are promptly discovered and put to good use (trade, business), hence, the emergence of ever more advanced forms of secular, practical instruction, sometimes done in Latin, as early as the Merovingian Age.[366]

It follows that the science of letters becomes more and more profitable. Scribes, notaries, copyists, secretaries—*les clercs* in general—enjoy, if not consideration, at least economic appreciation. New concepts emerge: *litteratorie professionis, mercenari literati*, "professional writers" whose consciousness expands. Today, one may speak of them as "white-collar workers."[367]

The poetic realm, however, puts up strong resistence. The tradition of gratuitousness, so vigorous in Antiquity—and which, in one guise or another, will remain active throughout the biography of the idea of literature—tries to stave off venal profit, the author's "rights." Dante is even sarcastic to those who turn *la litteratura* into a "prostitute," a *donna meretrice*.[368] But, in his case, the target is a completely different kind of "literature." It is the one turned out by secretaries who compose love letters, and by accountant-clerks who keep the books of trade companies. Also clearly expressed is the idea of the economic value of libraries, manuscripts, and books, seen as good investments, even as treasures.[369] The most precious assets of a monastery are hidden away in *scriptoria, armarium, libraria*. This is why the ravages of wars and the destruction of books are seen as horrendous calamities (Richard de Bury, *Philobiblion*, VII).

d) *Ideology.* Ever since Antiquity, the bulk of literary ideas has included an "ideological" dimension, more specifically a relationship between the literary, on the one hand, and the political and social, on the other. In the Middle Ages—an age of great cultural, philosophical and conceptual leveling—the process becomes more meaningful and far more general. We shall refer only in passing to the purely ideological aspects of Charlemagne's cultural policy—which turned writing, school, *litterae*, into a first-rate administrative and governing instrument—to observe two general trends, both derived from a direct involvement of "letters" with the new social-political or ethical background. In the latter case, *litterae* are raised to the dignified status of a true *Weltanschauung*.

The Middle Ages is the period in which all the latent "liberal" possibilities of letters and of literature begin to develop (a development that, however, will not be brought to completion). Practiced only by free people, liberal arts are unencumbered by practical necessities, they escape economic servitude and compulsion. They are characterized by the idea of liberty—which appears for the first time, clearly formulated, in the field of literature. Glossaries put it bluntly enough: Liberales = *a libertate dictae*.[370] The idea is expressed in other texts as well: *In libertatem vocati sumus*, "In freedom we are called upon to serve [the king] through liberal studies."[371] At the same time, "letters" define an entire way of life, predominantly contemplative. For this reason, medieval scholars often quote or paraphrase Seneca's aphorism: *vita sine litteris mors est*. Letters are life, spiritual life, the substance and final goal of an existence.

Containing vital, decisive social, economic and ethical aspects, the medieval heteronomy of letters exceeds in importance and efficiency the aspects of "autonomy" pointed out previously. The latter will develop fully later in history.

HIERARCHY IN LITERATURE

Medieval literary thought consolidates and develops the basic pattern inherited from Antiquity in the field of literary hierarchy, too. The first precise literary hierarchies (implying a value-scale and classification criteria that will prove to be genuine invariants) are set up in this period. The social, ideological framework can be seen quite clearly, as can the logic of the *letter* system, with all its implications.

A first—rigid, structural, typically medieval—hierarchy has as its object sacred and profane writings and values. The classification is invariably the same: What is sacred is *top*, what is profane is *bottom*. Biblical writings are superior to any other writings. The Bible is a *culmen Scripturarum*[372] (countless references). Written, as well as oral works, are grouped according to the same criterion. Written culture, predominantly ecclesiastic, is considered superior to the oral, popular, folk one. Orality does not decay, but loses its legitimacy as a unique value. "There is nothing more becoming for a cleric than the study of letters, than to hold a book in his hand."[373] A direct consequence is that the Church's language (sacred, Latin) is deemed superior to the profane, vulgar one, the latter being declared primitive, underdeveloped, uncultivated. Dante, himself a "vulgar" poet, wavers on this point. The pro-vernacular argument is itself formulated in Latin.[374] When the Cyrillic alphabet is adopted by the Slavs, it is declared man's most valuable possession, the supreme "gift," the greatest "treasure."

A symmetrical social stratification, based on the same criteria, again brings the two great medieval categories to the fore: *litterati* and *illitterati*, cultivated and uncultivated people, the clerics and the laymen.[375] Cultural hierarchy accurately reproduces social hierarchy: on the top, the cultivated elite; at the bottom, the illiterate, uncultivated masses. It is worth noting that the medieval social system (*oratores, bellatores, laboratores*, that is, *clerics, knights, peasantry*) scrupulously observes and consecrates the hierarchy, even though knights refuse to be considered clerics. In the Middle Ages, "arms" look down on "letters."

Cultural disciplines are the object of a similar hierarchy. According to circumstances, the *trivium* and *quadrivium* prevail upon each other. The foremost science, the instrument of any kind of cognition (*literatoria disciplina*),[376] continues to be *grammar*,[377] "the first liberal art,"[378] the first of the "cleric's sciences,"[379] "the first art,"[380] etc.

The dichotomy *major/minor*—notions destined to play an important role in the philosophy of modern culture—is imposed by identical considerations. Terminologically, at least, their origin is medieval, having their roots in the classification *auctores majores et minores*, the latter being *sine litteris rhetoricis et arte grammatice*. We come across it in Conrad de Hirschau (*Dialogus super auctores*), in Aimericus (*De arte lectoria*), where the classification is extended to include profane writers. Symbolical, metaphorical equivalents, in a descending order, are found for the value-ranks of each: gold, silver, tin, lead.[381] The same degrees of comparison are applied to *litteratura: modicae litteraturae/excellentis litteraturae*.[382] We learn about the existence of a *petite letreure*. The same hierarchy is at work in Byzantine medieval culture: "elementary letters"/"superior knowledge."[383]

The medieval theory of literary styles departs from the fundamental hierarchy set up during the Christian period of Antiquity. The Church turns the traditional, rhetorical value-scale upside down, and extols, with disputative humility, *sermo humilis, rusticus sermo, sancta rusticitas*; not *sublimitas*, but *humilitas*. The reasons are well-known: The necessities of evangelizing demand simple sermons, accessible to the illiterate. "The rhetoricians' philosophy is understood by few, but the rustic style *(loquentem rusticum)* by many."[384] As a consequence, Christian ideology rejects cultivated, "arrogant" speech, as well as the "pomp of secular literature" *(in secularis litteraturae pompa gloriantium)*.[385] Christian writers even fake a careless style *(rusticitatis meae litterae)*.[386] The traditional diagram, lofty style/low style, is therefore reversed.

None of these are new ideas. However, the systematizing of styles, in keeping with the speaker's social origin, is typically medieval. An explicit text (John of Garland, *Rota Vergilii*) establishes the social categories corresponding to each style, *gravis, mediocris, humilis*. It is probably the best example of a "literary sociology" that the Middle Ages can provide.[387] The classification is quite widespread, with only minor variations in terminology, *grandiloquus* for *gravis*. The *hierarchy* is gradient: lofty medium and humble style: *semplice, temperato (medio)* and *sublime*. Social referents and esthetic connotations appear. The reversal of values is complete; *sermo humilis* (= *piscatorius*) is not only rehabilitated, but also placed at the top of the hierarchy, in the same position as "lofty style." It is only toward the conclusion of the Middle Ages that one can notice a return to lofty style, in its classical, rhetorical sense.

The "literary proper" applications introduce new hierarchies and significances. *Grosso modo, oratio plana* corresponds to prose, while *oratio pomposa fabricata* corresponds to rhetoric and poetry. In another variant, *sermo simplex/artifex*. The poets themselves begin to distance themselves (sometimes enormously) from prose (Henri d'Avranches). E. R. Curtius even speaks of a medieval *Dichterstolz*.[388] Dante exalts popular language *(nobilior est vulgaris)*,[389] probably having himself in mind. Literary genres occupy their well-defined slots in this hierarchy. Tragedy is considered *alta*, comedy "inferior and humble," because of its style. The *Grail* cycle is declared *haut livre*, etc. All the rigid classifications and hierarchies, already dogmatized, that will constantly resurface in European literary thought have their beginnings, sometimes even their sources, in these generally overlooked medieval "compartments" and "ranks."

THE SCHOOL OF LITERATURE

The Study of Literature

The Middle Ages consolidate the idea—formulated in Antiquity—that literature is, preeminently, a cultural, literal and literary product. It is a discipline of "letters," resulting from the study of letters, of all the aspects of "literary" tradition. The French *geste* continues and, to a certain degree, imitates, ancient epos. The medieval poet knows himself to be, wants to be, a *clerc*. The cultural concept is much more powerful than the poetic one. Being illiterate, uneducated, is the blight of the moral and intellectual consciousness of the age, its inferiority complex. This phenomenon is easy to observe, as early as the sixth century, with the Christian poet Fortunatus. Throughout the Middle Ages, Virgil is considered a great poet, an initiate, and a sage.

Three factors are synthesized in the medieval ideas on creation: *natura, doctrina, usu*,[390] in a different formulation: *natura, exercitium, disciplina*.[391] It is a combination of "nature" (talent) and "art," which can be acquired through "science" and "studying," in the spirit of Horace's *recte scribere procedit ex sapere*.[392] The basic principle, *ars sive scientia nihil est*,[393] is applicable to all arts. Poetry is equated with *versificandi studio*,[394] with *il lungo studio*,[395] *estude, long estude* (a conviction found in Chrétien de Troyes, Christine de Pisan and, prior to them, with Celtic bards, etc.). In eleventh-century Byzantium, Michael Psellus learned *The Iliad* by heart.[396]

The "school" is the place where one learns poetry, how to write it, and what to read in order to be able to write it. It is another typical literary site, a symbol and an institution at the same time. So, in the Middle Ages, writing had a predominantly cultural motivation: it was exercise, imitation, compilation. Literature is the consequence of *lectio auctorum*. Virgil is also, by definition, a medieval school character:[397] *Tota poetarum venit ars et norma scholarum* (Abelard).[398] Chrétien de Troyes invokes the authority of Macrobius, who "teaches" him.[399] "We only write down what we have read" (Berceo).[400] This is a problem of literary imitation and emulation, of typical bookish autogenesis.

The fundamental subject-matter, the main object of study is, naturally, grammar, an essential cultural and literary implement, a mover in every direction. It cultivates, inspires, imposes norms, points out issues. The pupil will approach poetry through grammar. (Etienne de Tournai: *Venit at Grammaticae Poesis hortatum*.)[401] "Poetry belongs to grammar, which is its begetter and source of life."[402] Medieval poets apply the strictures of grammar to vernacular poetry.

The Middle Ages is, above all, the great age of literature textbooks. Along with grammar, the school teaches a series of *artes*, ranging from the "verbal" (*de arte sermocinandi, de arte praedicandi*, preaching treatises) to the "written" (*ars dictaminis, rationes dictandi*). The latter comprise composition and versification patterns, *de modo et arte dictandi et versificandi* and, even epistolary models, *ars epistolandi, ars scribendi epistolas*. Throughout the Middle Ages, as we know, *dictare* has the meaning of literary composition (*art d'écrire, art de la dictée*). It resurfaces as such in the neo-Romance languages (Eustace Deschamps, *Art de dicter et de faire chansons, balades, virelais et rondeaux*, 1392).

Literary Composition

Conceived of as a faultless reproduction, an imitation of given models, composition becomes one of the basic components of medieval pedagogy and literary production. It appears in the early Middle Ages (*prosalem met-ricamque componere*),[403] to become (in the ninth century) the common phrase that will gain more and more ground: *litterarum compositio*,[404] *viz.* "literature with (grammatical) literature." Poetry has the same definition: *scientia componendi carmine metrica*.[405] It implies memorizing verses and prose, style and composition drills, observing rules (*causa scribendi*) of a rhetorical nature (*invocatio, propositio, narratio, amplificatio*, etc.). It becomes necessary to learn an entire catalogue of *topoi* and *tropes* (hence the medieval predilection for allegory and symbolic characters). Within this scholastic, codified context, the personal element is very difficult to distinguish from the received didactic convention (a typical example of a mixed, grammatical-poetic work, with an added autobiographical, satirical and creative ingredient is *Laborintus*). Arnold de Liège writes an *Alphabetum narrationum*, a compilation of examples, of narrative patterns (1308–1310).

The ratio between oral and written composition fully illustrates the same mechanism. Both these forms of literary endeavor take up and develop pre-existing elements of traditional literary culture. All medieval epic literature draws heavily on the oral formulaic style (a typical circumstance).[406] Public recitals are held *selon la règle*, observing the ritual. Conversely, the *chanson de geste*, written to be sung, adopts the oral style, being declaimed by professional bards. All this technique is far from being purely empirical. It is dependent on a "program" and on a culturalized literary consciousness.

Also characteristic is the manner in which literature is produced *out of* literature, through specific literary acts and literary species, starting from the literal level, from playing with letters. The existence of a specialized terminology is yet another testimony to the advancement of the idea of literature during the Middle Ages, even if many terms are, inevitably, of ancient origin. From a purely graphic point of view, we witness, first of all, the reappearance of the calligram, *carmina figurata*, a "written" poem meant to be as close as possible to its graphic representation, to make use of poetic-literary games (acrostics, lipograms, etc.). Text production relies, however, on *copying*, seen as a fundamental device and praised as such.[407] It is the first cultural act. In the Middle Ages one copies, transcribes zealously and, at the same time, annotates, "writes glosses to the letter"[408]—a marginal form of personal reflection and contribution. Typically medieval is the continuation, paraphrase, correction of the text transcribed, and the collaboration with it—an operation repeated with each new act of copying, hence, the "essential variation" of a medieval manuscript text.[409] It becomes natural to continue a preexisting text, to add to it or fill in the gaps. At times, this is done pragmatically (that is, Richard de Fournival, *Liber de . . . epistolas Ovidii, ad quas scilicet ipse non rescripserat*, 1250).

On a higher plane, we find the quotation, then the combination of quotations—implying selection, repetition, conservation, recuperation and summarizing—at the same time. It certifies authenticity, accuracy, but in the sense of equivalence through reelaboration,[410] not of reduplication. Quite widespread is the *centon*,[411] a poem consisting of lines quoted from the classics (Homer, Virgil, *Centoni virgiliane*), plucked out of context, distorted, often used with an enlightening Christian purpose.

What is called in our days "intertextuality" is, already, a medieval practice (even, partially, a notion): *versus intexti, versi intessuti, farciture*. *Carmina figurata* and *centones* are typical examples. The phenomenon is verifiable not only on a textual level, but also on a cultural (*translatio studii*) and literary one: literature and poetry made with books (Ugucione da Pisa: *poesis est opus multorum librorum*),[412] through bookish continuation and derivation (*Es livres . . .*)[413] through a fusion of mythological and Christian protagonists, etc.

There are also other methods, on a graded scale of complexity, through which books spawn books: from mechanical copying to imitation in the freest of manners. The *index* and the *summary* are two other elementary devices, tantamount to a condensed, indexed "book within a book." At the same time, *compilation (compilatio)* implies a critical selection, the restructuring and reorganizing of texts (*ordinatio*).[414] The result is an enormous number of anthologies and collections (*Florilegium, Liber Floridus, Hortus Deliciarum, Fioretti*, etc.), with a neat delineation of every category of "writers": *scriba* (= *non de suo*), *compilator, auctor, commentator*.[415] Again, we come across the idea of a "unique," "total," "encyclopedic" book—medieval compilations, extremely eclectic aim (typically) to "extract, from all branches of philosophy, a condensed summary." Hence, their title *Tresors*.[416] Other titles—*Collectanea, Excerpta*—express the same idea of totalizing knowledge through compression, summing up.

As for translation (*translatio*), in the medieval mind it is also more than a literal or cultural-literary operation. A verse translation of a prose text is already a processing of that text, an adaptation. Many medieval romances are adaptations of Greek, Latin, even Eastern works (*Varlaam and Joasaph*). This prompts a theoretical discussion about the adaptation of difficult texts, with a sense of personal contribution (*carmina fingo*), as in the case of Mathieu de Vendôme, who adapts *Pyramus and Thisbe*.[417] The process implies elimination, interpolation, completion, in other cases, *tropes* ("the introduction of a new text, void of authority, into an authenticated official text").[418] Imitation is also frequent, openly assumed through titles pointing to the source (*Pseudo-Ovidiana, Pseudo-Apuleius*, etc.). Such collaboration is tantamount to a merging of personalities (Vitalius de Blois: *Haec mea vel Plauti comedia*),[419] promoted to the status of method.

The ruling cultural spirit, as well as the fact that medieval authors work within a fixed framework, carrying on a very strict tradition, determines a more and more widespread use of paraphrase. This is seen as a continuation through imitation and pseudo-fidelity, in the sense of a Christian recuperation (*Opus paschale*) or of a laical assimilation of the great models, hence, an entire "pseudo-ancient" medieval literature, written under the influence and as an extension of Greek and Latin classics.[420] The *exemplum* is another didactic and rhetorical device that produces literature: *Liber examplarum*, illustrative stories, "creative" illustrations of a sermon, *exemplum* as *digressio*, *amplificatio*, *inventio*, in an edifying spirit, but with long-lasting literary consequences. It was one of the many sources from which the European novella sprang.[421] Parody is another bookish derivation; it has its compulsory point of departure in another text, ironically, satirically turned upside down. Sacred literature is this genre's great victim (*Evangelium secundum*, *Cena Cypriani*, *sermons joyeux*, etc.), a typical phenomenon of laicization and spiritual emancipation.[422] Plagiarism and faking—oftentimes a devout or patriotic fraud[423]—complete this medieval picture of "literature written with literature." The device is to have a great further career, as is its theoretical consciousness.

Literature on Literature

The other "bookish" side of the idea of literature is defined by an identical situation. It was inevitable that the Middle Ages—a period of intense manuscript activity, in fact the most prolific in the entire history of writing—should make of writing a literary subject, a literary theme. It is symbolic, in this respect, that the oldest record of the Roman language (800), known as the *Indovinello veronese*, should be a riddle about . . . writing.[424] Poems on writing (eulogies, instruments, texts) appear with great frequency, as widespread are the metaphors and symbols inspired by writing.[425] Emblematic in this respect are *Versus de docte scribere*, the poem of the scribe and of the inscription, a poem by Alcuin on *sic celeri currens calamo dictare libellum*,[426] and another on *Amor scriba*, etc.

The library—the preeminently bookish space—is also a source of inspiration, as with Isidore of Seville, *Versus in Bibliotheca*, or Theodulf, *Versus in Fronte bibliorum*.[427] The very medieval concept of "library" is set to verse. We have already examined the "theory" of this concept, often accompanied by poetry dedicated to books (for example, Dudon de St. Quentin, *Allocutio de Librum*. *Philobiblion* (I) by Richard de Bury, a work displaying great laic awe for books, is characterized by true bookish lyricism.

Therefore, the turning of grammar into a literary subject is not only natural, it becomes necessary. It is the typical, exemplary expression of "literature on literature," in the fundamental, etymological acceptation of the idea of literature. It assumes several forms, one of which is that of the

ABC poems (the first of which appears in the seventh century), written for predominantly mnemotechnical reasons (De Alphabeto, Incipient Versus per Alphabetum composti, etc.). Grammar—dialogated (Alcuin), versified (Alexandre de Villedieu), Doctrinale (in hexameters), eulogized (Theodulf, IV), as catechism, personified, as allegory (a tradition inaugurated by Martianus Capella)—is the classic expression of this "literature." It includes everything: the didactic intention of learning and memorizing, as well as composition starting from the text, exemplification and, at the same time, imitation and bookish invention. Similarly, rhetoric inspires eulogies (De laudae metricae artis), personifications, panegyrics, etc. Allegory engulfs all literal arts, inspiring such long poems as De Septem Liberalibus in quadam Pictura Depictis (Theodulf),[428] and Le mariage des sept arts (Jean Teinturier d'Arras), etc.

The aridity of these long versified endeavors must be examined and understood in their specific context. As we now know, in the Middle Ages, literature means, essentially, culture, and this wants to be described, praised and, above all, acquired. Poetry conveys knowledge, ideas, "philosophy," acquired in a "didactic" spirit. Didascalion de Studio Legendi by Hugo de St. Victor is a title specific to this essentially didactic, typically medieval kind of poetry.[429] "Poetry" is indistinguishable from "schoolbook" or "treatise," Litera docet remains the basic principle of the age.

This didactic-literary osmosis is best illustrated by a purely medieval genre, the legend. It contributes a new significance to the medieval idea of literature. Originally, the term indicates that which must be read and learned (De usu legendi et prelegendi,[430] lecturus, legendus). But it also points, simply, to everything that is being read, in a general or restricted sense (the inscription on a medal, the captions on a drawing, map, plan, etc.). That acceptation has been preserved to our day. As for the content of compulsory "reading," in the context of sacred literature it can only be religious—the lives of saints, to be read in cloisters and churches according to an annual calendar. Jacobus de Voragine's Legenda aurea is the most famous of these texts. By extension, "legend" gradually comes to mean an imaginary, popular tale.[431] There are proofs that the term was becoming markedly laicized as early as Antiquity. It enters such combinations as "legendary tales," "legends regarding Dyonisios," etc.[432]

A panegyric to creative writing, conceived of as a literary and poetic theme, could already be detected in the texts dedicated to writing, such as Laus literarum (Ennodius),[433] Ad Bonnossum (Rabanus Maurus),[434] etc. The Middle Ages also boast of other, more evolved, forms: creation diaries, poetic introspections, even specimens of "poetry on poetry," such as Cum modo carmina non scribat (Theodulf),[435] Alcuinus Abbas compossuit hos versus qui in hac pagina continentur.[436] An entire implied poetics can be deciphered in these lines. The gesture is repeated by some of the vernacular poets, by trouvers, by Guillaume de Machaut, by the "new-style" poets, such as Guido Cavalcanti, who wrote a famous sonnet (XVIII) on the writer's "tools" (quill, scissors, sharpening knife), which all tell about what the poet is writing, as all suffer on his behalf. In all these instances, the consciousness of "literature as literature" appears with maximum clarity.

Critical Literature

The structures of sacred literature—predominant in the Middle Ages—raise more acutely (compared to Antiquity) the question of literary criticism. Naturally, in terms of the period, *literature* continues to contain *criticism*, but there is a different distribution of emphasis. Not philology—the establishing of texts and the "explanation" of poets—but the interpretation of sacred writings now comes to the fore. Therefore, the central concern is of an exegetic, hermeneutical nature. In the Middle Ages, *criticism* (= *literature)* is, first and foremost, a question of hermeneutics.

Naturally, stereotype definitions—already classicized—sum up the ancient formula or grammar, which includes the *scientia interpretandi poetas atque historicos*.[437] The systematizing and development of literary interpretation brings about a flowing of the typically medieval genre *Accesus ad poetas, Accesus ad auctores,* and *Dialogus super auctores* (Conrad de Hirschau). There are compulsory, normative and restrictive lists of *auctores consultos,* a real university canon.[438] They constitute, at the same time, the first systematic, theoretical or applied "keys," "introductions," critical "methods" to be used in Europe. As is known, the starting point is to be found in the lesson, *lectio* (= what is being read), which develops into the "art of reading" (Aimericus, *Arte lectoria*), with the amendment that *Lectio divina* is more important and more frequent than the scholastic one and that the *Ars Lectoria Ecclesie* (John of Garland) has first priority. In its turn, classical rhetoric is replaced by Christian rhetoric.

The other fundamental literary notions are also circulated in the didactic-profane zone of culture: *poetics*—partly a prolongation of grammar,[439] the theory of written or spoken, correct or figurative discourse, in fact, *rhetorica*—and the lecture, *lectio,* that offers, simultaneously, models of literary composition *(imitatio poetarum)*. The tendency toward schematism, norming, dogma, becomes stronger and stronger. It is the heyday of *Ars dictandi* and *Ars predicandi,* considered to be normative treatises. In the Middle Ages, *grammatica* and *litteratura* have a prototypal value, in the sense of both an exemplary *latinitas* and a theory of a pure, unique, undifferentiated, universal, "inalterable" language.[440] On this ground, preoccupations of speculative grammar burgeon: systems of logical rules, valid for all languages, but of no consequence in the field of literary theory. Grammar extends its range to the maximum: from the science of reading and writing, of figures of speech, to the explication of nature and of the laws of language.

Although greatly overshadowed in size and importance by sacred hermeneutics, in the Middle Ages, secular hermeneutics enjoys its first European flowering. It is a point of fact in this period that the real basis of hermeneutics, of the technique of explaining senses and significances, therefore of interpretative criticism, is laid. Some methods already prove to be very efficient and become classical. The first of these is of an etymological nature, and Martianus Capella, who provides a systematic explication of the etymology of *Litteratura* (220) establishes, in fact, the model for the entire Middle Ages. John of Garland also speaks of *litteratorie vel ethiomologice exponendo*.[441] Of the key literary notions, *the book* will be explained, in this fashion, through *liber-liberare-liberando-liberalis*, as a "free" document, a document of "liberty."[442] In this manner, a book of criticism becomes a *liber explanationes*. Prototypal schemes of editing—and of interpretation—also appear, to be rediscovered and reinstated by modern journalism (especially American), forced to answer the following questions: *qui, quid, cui, cur, quomodo, quando, ubi.* Albertano da Brescia), that is, *who, what, to whom, why, how, when, where?*

Of capital importance is the theory of the senses of *letters* (*intentio litterae*): literal, allegorical, tropological (moral), anagogical (mystical)— the central summit of medieval critical literature (*ad litteram, ad sensum, ad allegoriam, ad moralitatem*).[443] In fact, the basic meanings can be reduced to two: the literal and the spiritual (Thomas Aquinas: "The spiritual meaning is always based on the literal and derived from it"),[444] which lends the literal text great dignity and relevance. The discrimination between literal (*ad litteram*) interpretation, applicable only to profane text, and the spiritual one, typical of the text of the scriptures, for which literality would be "fatal" (Hugo de St. Victor), becomes, thus, natural. It is fundamental and defining for the entire condition of literary criticism, authorized to discover allegories in profane poetic myths as well.[445] Any text can have a parallel language and therefore a parallel relevance, clear or obscure, on one plane or another. Thus, the Middle Ages consolidate and systematize the plurality-of-meaning theory that lies at the basis of European literary criticism. Even impressionistic "poetic" criticism can identify its source in such a method of turning the interpretation of language and of etymology to poetic account.

There is, however, another "discovery" of medieval criticism, destined to play a spectacular role much later, in the modern literary criticism of the second half of the twentieth century: plurality of meaning presupposes ambiguity, multivalence, a phenomenon both necessary and inevitable. If any *littera* has four basic senses, identifiable in all the written texts, it follows not only that any "pagan" poet can be simultaneously Christian (to operate with the terms of the age), but also that any laic *or* religious text can have multiple meanings when read from various angles. Thus, the relative character of interpretation is given a first justification. Also justified is the original polysemy of the text, claimed by obscure, symbolist, mystical poets, who write in "secret languages" (troubadours, Dante, stilnuovoists).[446] In essence, all these constitute what much later, in this century, has been called an *"opera aperta."*

DENYING LITERATURE

One of the most violent denials of literature, in the entire biography of the idea, occurs in the Middle Ages. It is by far more radical than Antiquity's antiliterary reaction. The explanation is quite simple: this is the period when Christianity's intolerance of profane, "pagan," "literary" culture reaches its climax. All the fundamental arguments are extraliterary, pushed to the brink of rigid, totalitarian fanaticism.[447]

To begin with, the theory according to which *gratia vivificat, litera mortificat, littera . . . occidit, spiritus vivificat,*[448] a true dogma, is revived, all lay (that is, "heathen," "heretic") culture will be repudiated, essentially on these grounds. It will be repressed in every possible way: council, canonic, monastic bans,[449] excommunications, book burning, etc. One of the darkest chapters of medieval culture unfolds underneath the motto on the crest of St. Bernard: "Beware of books:" *prohibere studia litterarum,*[450] *non magis luxuria quam litteratura.*[451] Prohibition applies to all *saecularis litteris,* all *gentilium litterae,* all *artes liberales.*[452] Literature—in the classical, traditional acceptation of profane culture—is banned as a whole. This refusal is associated with the laical outlook and way of life, defined, with a no less typical formula, as *contemptus mundi* or *contemptus saeculi.*[453]

Within such a restrictive, intolerant frame, profane literature proper (prose, poetry, etc.) is no more than a fragment of the global object of spiritual censorship . . . but it is a well-defined, clearly delineated target. Thus, medieval literary denial is directed at precise targets: *laicorum cautus obscenus, carmina diabolica, poeta vanos, Virgilii et poetarum, ineptis nugatorum,*[454] in general. Even in the frequent instances when it is recuperated, adjusted, and reinterpreted in the Christian spirit, classical poetry continues to be mistrusted. For a long series of reasons (dogmatic, heretical, disciplinary, and so on) *litteraturae studia* became totally incompatible with medieval Western Christian mentality.[455] A Franciscan friar is denounced as a *saecularium cantionum curiosus inventor.*[456] The Eastern church seems to be somewhat more lenient toward "letters;" to a certain extent, they are even praised.[457]

Therefore, the refusal of *grammar* has, first of all, a symbolic value. Its repudiation provides us with the best possible vantage point from which to examine the antiliterature of the age. It falls prey to the new scale of intransigent values: *mea igitur grammatica, Christus est* (Gregory I, the Great).[458] To the same author, it is blasphemy to subject divine words to grammar rules, *sub regulis Donati*.[459] Such formulas, true medieval clichés,[460] start from the principle *non est Deus grammaticae curiosus*.[461] They consecrate the absolute supremacy of theology.[462] There are other arguments against grammar—the fact that it can change into speculative logic, or objections derived from the general criticism of "liberal arts" and "humanities" (see the consequences of "The Battle of the Seven Arts") of the *clerics/laymen, clergie/cavalerie* controversy.

Antiliterary theory becomes more complex and profound than in Antiquity, owing to the fact that the very essence of poetry comes to be contested. The first specific antiliterary arguments appear now. The fictitious, playful, purely evasive nature of poetry is repudiated, while its quality of an *infima doctrina* and *defectus veritas* (Thomas Aquinas)[463] is sanctioned. In fact, the entire theory of the rustic, uncultivated style, the eulogy of *sancto simplicitas* and *sancta rusticitas*, is antipoetic, antiliterary, in a broader sense. The rhetorical style is fought off by all the Church Fathers. The spiritual message by far outweighs the love of words, in *verbis verum amore non verba* (Rabanus Maurus).[464]

Some antiliterary arguments from the sphere of lay culture are also incipient, intermittent, but with far-reaching effects—anticipating the modern age. A whole category of medieval intellectuals place themselves quite overtly outside official culture, outside disciplined schooling. They are the so-called *vagantes, ordo*, or *secta vagorum, fugiti clerici*, cultural outcasts who produce nonconforming, "contesting," "antischolastic" verse.[465] Medieval parody, including the antigrammatical type, belongs to this group, which will also produce the celebrated *carmina burana*, replete with antiliterary accents.[466] The irregular genres (*fatrasie, flamenco*) are the products of the same nondogmatic, or openly antidogmatic, mentality.

Of special interest are the claims to uncultivated spontaneity, to writing devoid of a cultural memory (Aimericus: *Ego sine libro patrono . . . scribendo dictando et dictando scribendo*),[467] the refutation of imitation and the praise of originality (the troubadour Pierre d'Auvergne: "A song is never good if it resembles another").[468] In Chaucer's work,[469] we come across a violent, categorical rebuttal of "learning" and "rhetoric."

The antirhetorical praise of "silence" is also worth noting; it had already been anticipated by Christian Antiquity (*tacitae orationis*),[470] and was to foster well-known texts, such as *Tractatus de arte loquendi et tacendi* Albertano da Brescia (1245). For the time being, it is a question of Christian meditation, and also of the "literature of silence," of written literature,[471] to a certain extent. The modern implications of "silence" will undergo interesting avant-garde developments, in an absolutely negative sense. The limits of uttering are sensed as early as this: the best lines, compared to those one has dreamt, can only be the "mute" ones.[472] This is Keats, antedated by several centuries. Greatly anticipatory is also the inkling concerning the poetry of "nothingness," the tendency to suspend meaning and to cultivate empty form (the troubadour Guillem IX, *Farai un vers de dreyt rien*).[473] The paradox of this experience is expressed with great intuitive clarity.

CONCLUSIONS

A final conclusion asserts itself: The Middle Ages is not only the period when the idea of literature—focusing on sacrality and culture—becomes stable and homogenous, settling definitely into its structure as *letters*, but also the period when it becomes analytically diversified and produces all its basic terminology. Almost all the fundamental meanings and significances of *literature* have appeared by now, even if some acceptations continue to be rare and are seldom used.

At any rate, the consolidation of the first acceptations—all of them fundamental—is definitive. There will be little further essential progress, limited mostly to nuances. One could say that almost all the creative capacity of the idea of literature has been exhausted. If we add to all these the fact that the idea of literature, thus defined—even if cloistered in monasteries and universities—develops into a crucial European notion, especially in the West, into a genuine master idea, one can say that the Middle Ages is a period of remarkable importance in our biography. It is an epoch of great semantic and terminological genesis.

III

The Renaissance and Humanism

The idea of literature is discovered, consolidated and diversified in Antiquity and during the Middle Ages. During this stretch of time, the idea, organized around sacred cultural values, gains stability. The situation will change from the Renaissance on. The essential cultural background remains inevitably the same; nevertheless, it undergoes a significant change: the definition of "literature" becomes more technical, more learned. The matter enters into the hands of men with access to libraries: scholars, philologists, lexicographers, renowned humanists. This is the essential characteristic of the idea of literature during the Renaissance and Humanism.

Letters Are Humanized and Spiritualized

"Human Letters"

Of all the acceptations of the idea of literature, the one that best conveys the bookish, learned spirit of the Renaissance and of Humanism is that of *litterae humanae*. This notion—forcibly brought forth by the enthusiasm fostered by the rediscovery of the old values and ideals of Antiquity—promptly becomes a genuine catchphrase of the age. From a mere technical phrase, it becomes invested with the value of a full program for leading an intellectual and moral life, symbolic of man's dedication to culture and letters.

Reintroduced at first by Italian humanists and afterwards by the French (L. Bruni Aretino, L. Valla, B. Guarini, M.-A. Muret, etc.), inclusively in the form of *litteris humanitatis*,[1] *litteris et humanitatis artibus*,[2] *litteris humaniores*[3] (sometimes with a hint of incertitude, leading to a desire for lexicographical accuracy: *litterae, illa quae . . . humanae vocantur*),[4] these *litterae humanae* appear often, especially from Erasmus' nib, for whom they seem to have the value of a slogan.[5] In the same humanists' work, one can plainly notice a transition from *litterae* to *humaniores litteraturae*,[6] a phrase that becomes quite current itself. Its philological, didactic meaning is precise: all the letters (texts, knowledge) that preserve, hand down, and teach cultural data and values: *Humanitas = eruditio in literatura*.[7] Modern languages take over both the formula and its significance: *lettres de humanité*

(Rabelais), *lettres humaines* (J. Amyot), *lettras humanas* (Pedro Juan Núñez), etc. Its frequent use is attested in France in the sixteenth century.[8]

How "cultural" this basic acceptation remains also results from the alternative synonymous phrase *studia humanitatis*. It forcefully reaffirms the original meaning of the idea of literature: *letters* are *learned* (didactic subject-matter), but also "studied" (as a field of research and intellectual passion). The term is ever more insistently used, in both senses, from the fourteenth century on, by Petrarch (*Fam.*, I, 9), among the first to be then made popular by all the humanists: L. Bruni Aretino, C. Salutati, Erasmus. In the next century, it will also be used to define an object of academic study, whose newly bestowed name, *humaniora*, will be inherited by the centuries to follow. Both phrases will enter Western school tradition, to be academically perpetuated to our day. For the time being, however, they are just marks of superior education, intellectual distinction and the humanistic fraternity. *Studere in humanitate:*[9] a new branch of knowledge, a modern profession, and, at the same time, a modern passion, forever part of the consciousness of the age and of human history.[10] To a certain extent, these ideas become known in Southeast Europe as well.[11]

The purely didactic relevance is backed by the ideal of systematic knowledge in the sphere of culture. The notion incorporates all the basic "disciplines;" *studia humanitatis id est poetarum, oratorum e historiographorum* (Peter Luder, 1456), according to the principle *connexa sunt humanitatis studia* (Coluccio Salutati).[12] The programs of the age are comprehensive (frequently referred to are those of Pope Niccolo V and of Gargantua, in his famous letter to Pantagruel, Rabelais, II, 8). They coincide with the two cycles which, in the meantime, have become traditional, the *trivium* and the *quadrivium*,[13] followed by the domains inspired by the *humaniores Musa*.[14] Modern languages have tended, rather, to favor the synthetic formula: the ideas of classical literature, of the *trivium* and the *quadrivium*, inclusively, will be globally called *humanité* (Jean Boucher, 1527),[15] *lectré en art d'humanité,*[16] *studi che chiamano d'umanità*[12] (the first reference, in Italian, dates from the third decade of the sixteenth century).[18] For Montaigne, to write *humainement* is to write in a "cultivated style," *Essais*, (I, 56).

An original lexical coinage of the time is *humanist, humanista* (Ulrich von Hutten: *isti humanistae:*[19] the professor of literary studies, of humanities, (classical languages and literatures, grammar, rhetoric), sometimes the student of such disciplines or the man of science who has made the *studia humanitatis* his specialty. The term is in circulation beginning in the fifteenth century.[20] In modern languages, the first attestation (Italian) dates back to 1522 (Ariosto, *Sat.*, Vi, 22–27). Speroni Sperone speaks of *la nostra umana professione,*[21] of an *Accademie alli Humanisti* (1542). *Humaniste* in French, and *humanist* (professor of *humanitie*) in English (1598) are other usual words circulating in Europe. One notch higher one finds the highly qualified *humanista*: a man of erudition, an interpreter of classical texts, as he is defined in the general repertory of the professions of the age.[22]

For the first time in the history of the idea of literature, the *studia humanitatis* are invested with a real pedagogical finality. The moral effects of literature had been stressed before, as we have seen. But this conception only becomes generalized during the Renaissance. It is now organized, systematized, turned into an ideal, a way of life. "My home is my paper, my quill and my ink" (Petrarch, *Fam.*, XII, 7). In this acceptation, *litterae humanae* are seen as an act of vital, intellectual, and ethical living. Their transference to the world of values is completed: "Letters are the documents of virtues, manners lie hidden in them, everything lies hidden— *latent mores, latent omnia*" (C. Salutati, *Ep.*, VIII, 12). This conception, typical of the Renaissance and of Humanism,[23] has been theoretically discussed by L. B. Alberti, L. Bruni Aretino (*De studiis et litteris*),[24] and others. Superlative intellectual life is the equivalent of supreme moral virtue, hence, the formula, frequent with Erasmus and others, *honestis litterarum studiis*,[25] *honestissima litterarum studia.*[26]

Consequently, the identification of literature (= *studia humanitatis*) with the fundamental virtue of *humanitas* becomes inevitable. This old notion, abundantly glossed over and explained away since Antiquity,[27] is rediscovered in the second half of the fifteenth century[28] and changed into an absolute conception of life, no less modern and fecund. Its eulogy becomes a ritual (as in Gregorius Chrispus' *De cultu humanitatis et honestatis*). Its aim is erudition and education through arts and letters—an education principle based on utmost moral rigor (C. Salutati, *Ep.*, XII, 18; X, 25). One of the epoch's definitions sums up the whole doctrine: "Literature . . . is the instrument necessary to our lives."[29] In modern languages, this idea becomes known and is circulated as *umanità, Humanitet.*[30]

Man alone is endowed with the capacity for perfecting himself through knowledge, culture, and education. This capacity alone confers on people the quality of *vir humanissime*. This old idea is also taken over and circulated.[31] *Letters* humanize; they restore man to his true nature, pluck him out of "barbarism." Such ideas were widely circulated in the period (L. Bruni Aretino, C. Salutati,[32] Erasmus,[33] etc.). In a parallel Slavonic-Romanian acceptation, those "who are not familiar with the Scriptures are like cattle."[34] "Literature must improve (*migliorare*) any man."[35] It makes him "subtle" and gives him plenitude. "Sciences, letters, make real people (out of people)" (Erasmus, *Querela pacis*, XI), "studies without which we are not humans."[36] A good, complete and explicit definition is provided by G. Budé: "These letters of which the ancients speak were called human or humanist (*humaniste*) letters because, without erudition, without these disciplines, people would live like brutes (*brutalement*), not like humans (*humainement*).[37]

The entire conception is governed by the ideal of a man with a thorough education, therefore, perfect. This paragon of humanistic thought is inextricably linked to *litterae*, the means by which man comes to know himself, to develop all his faculties and to acquire all the virtues. Culture "makes people perfect, almost divine" (Guicciardini, *Ricordi*, 47, 128). A complete catalogue of virtues accompanies this achievement and adds to it: *benignitas, facilitas, suavitas, justitia, pietas, constantia, magnanimitas, prudentia, moderatio*, etc.[38] To live in their spirit is to achieve harmony, equilibrium, happiness: *vita contemplativa* dominates *vita activa*. An *ottimo umanista* cultivates an individual, spiritualized, esthetic, exquisite brand of Epicurism. Such an ethical-intellectual integralism confers on *humanitas* all possible meanings: *vocabulum enim polysemum est litterae, scientia, virtua*.[39]

Now it is even easier to understand why the polysemy of the age makes of *litterae humanae* the basic meaning of the idea of literature in the period of the Renaissance and of Humanism. Letters define a complete man: *humanitatis autem litteras*.[40] Never before has literature been granted such a dignified status, nor will it ever achieve it again. Never since has the idea of literature contained the integrated definition of man, never again will it be the total expression of his aspirations, the symbol of spiritualization, of thorough humanizing. And, to the extent that *human letters* mold man and restore him to his true essence—which is not merely fulfillment, but also regeneration—we find the source of yet another fertile European idea: that of the "new man," so celebrated in our own day, but who seems to have forgotten (or not yet discovered) his true origins, which are, in fact— who would have expected it—Renascentist and humanistic.

"Liberal Letters"

The epoch digs up another ancient definition of literature, closely connected to *litterae humanae* (of which it is an empirical synonym): the letters *liberales et ingenuae*.[41] This phrase enjoys wide circulation, with minor terminological variations, all from the sphere of liberal-literary studies, disciplines, arts or sciences: *Litteris et liberalibus studiis* (B. Guarini),[42] *disciplinis liberalibus* (Erasmus),[43] *De artibus liberalibus* (Melanchthon), *scientiarum liberaliumque artius*.[44] The syllabus is the one we already know, with a strong emphasis on the *trivium*, from grammar and poetry to oratory, painting, sculpture, and architecture (M. Ficino, *Ep.*, XI). As for semantic identification, it is vividly felt and clearly defined in the same period: *Disciplinae autem liberales, humanae quoque ideo appelantur*.[45] Another synonym, *eruditio-eruditionis*,[46] which will provide another of the definitions of the humanist—*liberalibus artibus eruditus*—once more confirms the strong cultural sense of the idea of literature in this period. Also well attested is the traditional didactic sense (Ramus, *Scholae in artes liberales*, 1553).

The Western language equivalents are even more important, as they set up the critical-literary terminology of modern European culture. Consecrated by famous texts, the French phrases become classical: *savoir libéral et honneste, arts libéraux* (Rabelais, *Pant.*, II, 8), *arts libéraux et sciences humaines*[47] (first attested in 1542).[48] The corresponding Italian formula is quite similar: *liberali studii* (Boccaccio, *Vita di Dante*, 4). Even more important for the biography of our idea is the fact that, in translating Plutarch, Amyot renders *encyclos paideia* (that is, "encyclopedia") by *science et littérature libérale*.[49] The renowned translator also uses the phrase *honeste littérature*.[50] This is not only a newly coined syntagm (which it quite obviously is), but one of the first attestations and definitions of the idea of literature in a modern language of widespread circulation, supporting a great culture, which definitively stabilizes its *etymon* and its lexical physiognomy. As we shall see, in the age of the Renaissance and of Humanism, this phenomenon will be repeated at the level of other significations of the idea of literature.

The pedagogical and ethical implications of *liberal letters* are extremely important. This is the phase when literature starts appropriating, more and more systematically, moral and educational functions, and the idea of literature becomes "moralized." Its didactic background makes such an evolution unavoidable. Renaissance pedagogy establishes a direct link between "manners" and "liberal studies" (P. Paolo Vergerio, *De ingenuis moribus et liberalibus studiis adulescentiae*), identifies the notion of "education" with that of "liberal education" (Maffeo Vegio, *De educatione liberorum*). The old etymology of *liberal letters* (*Artes Eleutherias i. liberales, liberalitas litteraria*), as well as the idea of *liberty* are rediscovered and adopted enthusiastically: "Liberal arts make people free" (P. Paolo Vergerio),[51] *"homines libri i philosophye"* (Thomas Lodge);[52] *Litterae* are the "genuine food for a free soul" (L. Bruni Aretino).[53] They alone are "worthy of a free man" (L. Bruni Aretino).[54] Finally, of the same ancient inspiration is the praise—no less frequent—of the "liberal" way of life, viewed as free of worries, of material obsessions, as having secured inner freedom, as being far removed from such ambitions as fame, money, career, etc. For Erasmus, living liberally (*liberaliter*) means living a life devoid of privations and needs, in a carefree, Epicurean style, indifferent to political turmoil, to justice, trade, and so on. It is the old *otium* of peace of heart, made topical and integrated in European liberal thought, first as a spiritual, then as a political dimension.

"Good Letters"

During the Renaissance and Humanism, the basic definition of literature has a third formula, semantically very similar to and contextually not very far removed from *human* and *liberal* letters, that of *good letters*, *bonae litterae*. A very accurate translation is difficult, because of the great ambiguity of the phrase. It has, at the same time, a global, cultural meaning, as well as an ethical, esthetic and even a literary-poetic one. At any rate, all these senses overlap in the work of the notion's most celebrated apologist, Erasmus.[55] He frequently speaks of *bonae litterae*[56] in every possible acceptation: didactic, intellectual, linguistic, moral, Epicurean.

The phrase can be found, without fail, in all the humanists, from Petrarch to Poliziano, from G. Budé to J. Reuchlin, and constitutes a genuine program of the age. Its profoundly cultural sense results from the fact that the *bonae litterae* are constantly associated with the effort of acquiring knowledge, with the idea of study (*bonarum litterarum studio*),[57] of doctrine, discipline;[58] erudition, education, and learning. It works its way into titles, such as *De honesta disciplina* (Piero Crinito, 1504). L. B. Alberti sets himself the task of writing *de literis, de doctrine, de ingenio, de bonis artibus*.[59] The complexity and tightly knit connections of the notion become evidence once again. Accordingly, it will be very frequently equated with *human letters*.[60] So will the typically Erasmian thesis of humanizing: *bonae litterae redunt homines*.[61] Finally, these *good letters* (just like the *human* and *liberal* ones) had to find their equivalent, too, in a corresponding formation of the kind of *litteratura*. In this particular case, the equivalent could be *litteratura melioris*, attested especially in Erasmus.[62] This transition from *littera* to *litteratura* is an important lexical mutation in the biography of the idea of literature. It contributes to the stabilization and consolidation of its classical terminology.

The *bonae litterae*—a real semantic nexus—comprise, apart from many possible ambiguities, a true dialectic of the sacred and the profane, about which more will be said hereafter. Sacred value, which is so indissolubly linked to *litterae*, will make its first appearance in the Renaissance and Humanism in this indirect way. Erasmus' position is once more exemplary. On the one hand, his main aim is to bring about a cooperation and eventual synthesis of religion and culture, of the church and *litterae: magnam concordiam inter theologiam et bonas litteras*.[63] A similar attitude can be found with Ulrich von Hutten, Melanchthon and other champions of the Reformation. On the other hand, though, as the *bonae litterae*, increasingly associated with "heresy," begin to be persecuted, and theologians become more and more dogmatic, intolerant, and obtuse (there are numerous negative reactions to this in the correspondence of Ulrich von Hutten and, especially, of Erasmus),[64] such a position is bluntly denounced as "barbarian," as a proof of *odio bonarum litterarum*.[65] As a consequence, from this perspective the *good letters* are attributed a strongly laicized connotation, sometimes a dissenting, polemical one, at any rate neatly dissociated from theology. On the other hand, it is quite obvious that the notion of *bonae litterae* could only be conceived, from the very beginning (by semantic self-determination, that is, by acknowledging its own qualitative potential) as being completely separated from the sphere of sacred letters. The first known English secular poet, Adhelm, the first to write in Latin, passes for a *bonus auctor*.[66]

As in the case of *human* and *liberal letters*, the polysemy of *good letters* has a rich ethical and educational content, often expressed in radical forms. The humanist's vision on literary studies is almost ascetic: they are to be cultivated in seclusion, in complete indifference to material well-being. The *litteris ac moribus* theory is the axis of the entire conception; the *good letters* will improve manners, they have a urifying effect on those who cultivate them, "whose nature (*leur nature*)"[67] they tame and soften. "Good" spirits become "perfect" (Guicciardini, *Ricordi*, 313). *Bonae litterae* and *ingenuitate morum* become, in fact, synonyms.[68] By definition, humanism is wise, it is a paragon of virtue. It is characterized by *bona sapientia*.

All these significations find their equivalents in modern Western languages in phrases that are equally general and weighty. The French formula, *bonnes lettres* (attested in Rabelais, Montaigne, Malherbe;[69] but also in many other authors: J. du Bellay, J. Amyot, Commynes, etc.), becomes current. It conforms entirely to the spirit of the Renaissance and of Humanism, which sanctions it. Many equivalent and solitary formulas (*bones disciplines, bonnes lettres et érudition, bonnes lettres et disciplines libérales*)[70] testify to the vitality of the idea and determine a considerable expansion of its lexical sphere. The situation is the same for the Italian *le buone lettere* (Bandello, *Nov.*, I, 8) and *le buone scritture* (P. Bembo),[71] for the Spanish *las buenas letras*, etc.

The transition to *bonne littérature* contributes to an even greater extent to literature's becoming firmly establushed in European consciousness and lexicography. Even though the term is not yet frequently attested in its primary form (*Bonne licterature*),[72] its appearance at the end of the fifteenth century (1490–1495) shows that the scales oscillating between *lettres* and *litterature* are increasingly tipped in favor of the latter. Eventually, the notion will be stabilized as *bonne littérature* (1549),[73] or, more rarely, as *pure et sincère littérature* (J. Amyot);[74] in English, *good literature*, this time with a manifest didactic connotation.[75]

The age of the Renaissance and Humanism is a period of great glory and vitality in the lifespan of the idea of "good letters." Then the idea becomes classical and academic and, little by little, it withers away. Eventually, it will end up as a venerable, more and more fiercely contested, academic relic.

PROFANE LETTERS

As a result of the desacralization of these values, profane letters come to the foreground of literary consciousness. Consequently, the alternative to *sacred literature*—that is, its opposite, *profane literature*—reasserts itself in force, in keeping with the inner logic of the idea of literature and of its polarities. We will note that, in this period, the lay spirit is remarkably more lively and more active than in the Middle Ages. The very existence of *human letters* and the consciousness of their existence—so typical of the Renaissance and of Humanism—reveals the sense of this spiritual revolution.

The signs are clear: the old dissociation, already systematized by Cassiodorus, becomes, once again, inevitable. We come across it again in titles of treatises (Pico della Mirandola, *De studio Divinae et humanae philosophiae*)[76] in the current definition of a humanist: *homo literis tam humanis quam divinis eruditus*.[77] There is progress in the terminology, as the distinction clearly refers to *religio sancta* and *vera litteratura*,[78] to *litteratura divina et umana*.[79] This is an obvious acknowledgment of the existence of two spiritual structures: *moi/dieu* (Montaigne, I, 56), of two types of culture, two forms of letters and of literature. Of necessity, modern letters will use the same bipartite formula: *lettres saintes et humaynes*,[80] *literature and erudition, divine and human*,[81] *divinas letras / humanas letras*, etc.

The generalization of the term *profane* (or *secular*) *letters* can be explained in the same way. It is the product of the lexical tradition, but also of the in-depth dissociation specific to the age. With Erasmus, the idea appears as *profanae litterae*,[82] with G. Budé as *secularia studia*.[83] Italian humanists use very similar phrases, which we shall nevertheless list, in order to recompose the entire field of literary ideas: *doctrina litterarum secularium* (L. Valla),[84] *seculis et ultra litterarum studia* (C. Salutati, *Ep.*, III, 20–23), *saecularibus* (L. Bruni Aretino, *De studiis et litteris*), *poetria saecularis*. Even more relevant is the appearance and consolidation of *seculari litteratura* (with Erasmus),[85] and especially of *litteratura profana* (1548),[86] a term that will assert itself. The English term, *profane literature*, has a slight precedence over it (1545).[87] It becomes natural to think of "secular" letters as "liberal."[88] A current phrase to be met in the same period (with J. Amyot and others) is *Auteurs profanes*.

The process of spiritual and cultural laicizing, which makes considerable headway (with which we are not concerned here) is mirrored directly by literary terminology. For instance, through an obvious laicizing of the term *mystères*, the existence of "honest, licit profane mysteries" (1548)[89] becomes possible. Above all, it is possible that "sacred letters" should exist, "whose style observes the laws of grammar" (Erasmus, *Laus stultitiae*, LIII). It is clear that the hierarchy has been reversed. The way in which this hierarchy is formulated is exemplary.

Written Literature

The literal tradition of *literature*, which the Middle Ages had taken over from Antiquity, is not only kept up, but intensified in the philological, lexicographic age of the Renaissance and Humanism. The fundamental meaning, that of *written literature*, is now consolidated and gains circulation throughout European culture. "Literature" (the acceptation is repeatedly verified), can only be primarily and essentially "written." Whatever is "literary" refers to "letter," to *literalis*.[90] All the well-known elements are summed up, confirmed, and made systematic by the dictionaries and linguists of the age: the etymological tradition (*grámma*),[91] the transition from the Greek to the Latin alphabet, and the definition of "letter" (as a graphic sign and as a phoneme).[92] One does not come across new ideas, but rather generally acknowledged, clearly formulated data.

The same situation holds good for the identification *litterae = scripta*;[93] which causes an even more forceful comeback of the well-known *scriptura*, again identified as *ars litteraria*. The theory is called *De ratione scribendi* (for example, A. Brandolino Agostiano, 1546), and its equivalents in the great modern languages: *écriture* (1432),[94] *scrittura*, *Schrift*, and *Schriftkunst* (1571) will find their way into all the other languages. The great *topos* of "writing" will be resurrected with this occasion and will hold an important place in the consciousness of the age: memory (Montaigne, III, 13), testimony, truth, conservation (Castiglione, I, 29), eternizing, cognition, and culture. This, for the time being, is the decisive argument—on this plane of signification—in favor of the supremacy of literature and of its legitimate character. However, there are others, derived from the same literal origin, that remain pre-eminent.

We are still moving within the sphere of great traditional ideas and of fundamental cultural clichés. We have been acquainted, since Antiquity, with the great importance bestowed upon the sacred function of writing, rendered by another celebrated *topos*: the divine origin and significance of writing, of secret, initiatory writing. We find that it is quite widespread in this age, too, under such names as *litterae arcanae ac celestes*,[95] *De verbo mirifico* (J. Reuchlin, 1494), "God's original language" (Montaigne, III, 9). The inferences are, once more, of considerable import: secret, sacerdotal writing preserves the purity of the mystery (Montaigne, I, 56). It is symbolic, a "cipher," it justifies the obscurity of communication, it makes—as we shall see—multiple, multivalent interpretation inevitable (IX, 4). The semantic density of literature is once more acknowledged, through its very quality of written language, of an increasingly complex writing process. This phenomenon, however, is not confined to this age.

The manuscript tradition—that of imagistic writing, of the miniature—still very powerful and linked to the prevailing religious spirit, complicates the idea of *letter* even more. The tradition of the "sacred letter," of the *hieroglyph* (Horapollo, *Hierogliphica*, 1419, Latin translation 1505; C. P. Valeriano, *Hieroglyphica*, 1556)[96] is resurrected with enormous success, and occasions countless speculations on the subjects of "esoterism," the symbolism of writing, the image-sign, and particular graphisms (calli-grams, pictograms, etc.). These seeds fall on the well-furrowed field of the richly ornamented manuscript, of illumination and "book" illustration and, thus, a long series of text-image syntheses is produced. Some, like the *carmina figurata*, discovered in late Antiquity and inherited by the Middle Ages, are traditional. Nevertheless, the esoteric relation brings along a new quality: "The illustrated image . . . can be called a hieroglyphic let-ter."[97] Others are of a didactic, mnemotechnical nature: *Artes memoriae*, M. Ringmann, *De Grammatica figurata* (1509), visual alphabets, letters figured through body images. The purely cultural concern remains predom-inant.

The appearance of a genre that mixes text and images, combining them for declared symbolical or poetical ends, lends to figurative writing yet another dimension. Now, it acquires such names as *emblem* (A. Alciati, *Emblemata*, 1531), *impresa, devisa, enigma*, all varieties of illustrated epi-grams, under the sign of the "hieroglyph." The pattern is as follows: 1. a short fable or allegory in Latin verses; 2. an allegorical illustration; 3. a short *motto* that draws the conclusion. An emblem is figurative thought: message-rough idea, metaphor, comparison, concept (for example, the but-terfly that makes a line straight for the flame), image and sentence brought together for reciprocal clarification.[98] The genre enters the poetry of the age, with M. Scève, for instance (*Délie*).[99] The graphic sign tends to point to a decoded mystery, but the general meaning remains intensely signifi-cant, symbolic.[100]

However, in this period as well, the essential vocation of *letter* is a different one, the old, familiar one of statement or text written in any form, regardless of length or content. A proof that the traditional meaning of *littera* is the one used with utmost frequency: writing, letter, epistle,[101] copy (*copia*),[102] written notice (*cancionem litteratoricum*),[103] a "book" of any kind; document, written text, and letter as typographical sign. This, after all, is the implicit—at times explicit—sense in which it is used in the first texts—secular letters that have survived in Romania,[104] beginning with the letter from Neacşu of Cîmpulung (20–30 June, 1521).[105]

At the same time, written literary-literal activities of any kind can only find a modality of expression in the same, eternal *writing*. Conse-quently, through constant semantic enrichment, the latter becomes form and content, instrument and result. This phenomenon—of great ambigu-ity—can be clearly discerned, especially in the philological vocabulary of the humanists. For these learned men, the traditional meaning remains the basic one: *litteratum sive scripturae*. But the act of "writing," of *scriptura*, covers not only all the transcribing, copying, and editing operations, but also the very idea of "composition," even that of a written "work," in the sense of a personal creation.[106] They all become *writings*. To Montaigne, *se mesler d'escrire* (II, 9), already has a complex sense: gloss, confession, personal meditation, publication, etc. To B. Castiglione, *le scritture* of the ancients (II, 1) are even more clearly "works," "written compositions of various kinds." The idea of translation is included (*tradurre* is not neatly separated from *comporre*). In German, *Geschrift* acquires the same meaning (1571).[107] Lexicographically speaking, it is still difficult to mark off the purely literary work, as one and the same word may refer to both the written text (*litterarum monumentis*)[108] and to "poetical works," that is, original creation (J. du Bellay, *L'Olive*). The same indeterminacy exists in the case of *text*—a notion that is intensely circulated during the Renaissance—taken to mean, depending on the circumstances, either enunciation, written text, or literary composition, in verse or otherwise.[109] The idea of classifying writings into special literary genres also appears now, in the same terminological context (Jacques Peletier du Mans: *des g'anres d'écrire*).[110]

Predictably, the transition from *litera* to *literatura* proves to be equally hesitant and ambiguous. This cannot take us by surprise, as long as the idea of *writing* predominates, and *letter* simply connotates all the actions that will become "literary" at some other time and in some other manner, when they acquire modified, differentiated, specialized significations. At any rate, this phenomenon remains characteristic of the Renaissance and Humanism.

From the point of view of typology, there are three generic situations. They all converge toward the final, complete installation of the term *literature*, which tends to divest *letter* of most of its prerogatives: 1. the phase of assimilation and tacit glossing: *letter = literature* first of all with regard to the alphabet (*litteratura graeca*) and orthography[111] or calligraphy (*fractura = literatura*),[112] but also in problems of text editing and of the semantics of the letter (*rationes literaturae*);[113] 2. the phase of explicit assimilation, of precise glossing in lexicons (*Literatura . . . quae de literaris tractat*)[114] and in poetic treatises (*litera sive literatura*),[115] indicating a prolonged oscillation, due to the fact that the new term has not yet become quite stable; 3. the phase of complete assimilation, of the current use of the basic sense that *literatura* acquires in this age; the sum of literary writings,[116] literary culture in its entirety.[117] In all these circumstances, *literatura* seems to ignore completely its etymological, original meaning, by which it is instituted. In other words, it gives evident signs of emancipation, proving to be decisively weaned from its purely "literal" origin. We shall see later (VI, 6) how the incipient process of becoming autonomous can only benefit from this situation. Finally, let us add that all of these phases occur simultaneously, with frequent interferences and repetitions throughout the epoch.

Oral Literature

The parallel phenomenon—that of orality and its implication—cannot be conveniently ignored. The dissemination of writing and especially (as will be shown hereafter, of printing, does not yet expunge the tradition and prestige of oral expression. It continues to have considerable vitality.

In Tudor England, the "literary" style is still oral.[118] In Spain, the technique and style of recitation continue to be practiced in an age of printed chivalric romances.[119] In Italy, also, orality continues to be part of the most highly evolved literary technique: Boccaccio feigns the oral style, which is also frequently used by novella writers like Bandello, by the authors of dialogues, encouraged by the link with ancient tradition.[120] The humanists, wanting to resurrect rhetorical tradition, cultivate its devices, *verborum dulcedo* (Petrarch, *De remediis* . . . III, 97). Make-believe orality is itself a widespread literary device. Petrarch adopts the stance of the oral poet (*Rime*, I), Rabelais either mimics, or gives free rein to his instinct as an oral storyteller (*Pant.*, III, *Prologue*, 30). The story of the frozen words that start talking after the thaw (*Pant.*, IV, 55–56) is symbolic of the same predominant orality. Boiardo also pretends to be the reciting poet (*Orlando innamorato*, I, IX, 1). All these facts have an obvious explanation: While writing and printing are innovating practices, recent inventions at any rate, orality continues to be the natural, traditional, fundamental, permanent way of expression. The concept *oral literature* has not appeared yet. But the factors that make its appearance possible already enjoy explicit or implicit recognition.

No wonder, then, that the linguistic and literary consciousness of the age continues to see in writing, in editing, in composition, a form of *speech*: "To write down on paper," to "write the live word" (Montaigne, III, 1, 8); "Writing is but a form of speech" (B. Castiglione, I, 29), a "speech through letters."[121] The old definition reappears: writing is "an image of the act of speech.[122] "The quill is the tongue of the soul" (Cervantes), etc. Even more relevant is the idea of orality as the perfect form of expression: "On paper, as in the mouth," "I speak on paper just as I speak to the first person I meet" (Montaigne, I, 25; III, 1). "To write as you speak"[123] is a widespread commandment, backed by the great prestige of the rhetorical ideal.

Oscillation, indetermination, the interference of the two traditions remain, at any rate, characteristics of the age. Elocution continues to enjoy a tremendous prestige; the well-codified esthetic ideal is the rhetorical one[124] (more about this subsequently). The current expression is "in letters and in words" (Castiglione, III, 47). The poets address "the noble readers and listeners of this book" in equal measure;[125] romances should be "well sung and well read;"[126] with many authors there is still a visible hesitation between *vive voix* and *papier écrit* (1565).[127]

The ever neater dissociation, however, points not only to a separation of the two courses but also to a disjunction of the concepts, implicitly of the two types of literature. Writing and written literature will eventually emerge as victors from this controversy. Most significant is the shift of interest from the oral to the written word in religious sermons. The Benedictines, naturally, preach the superiority of the written sermon over the oral.[128] *Devotio moderna* likewise adopts the catchphrase *fratres non verbo, sed scripto predicante.*[129] The crucial fact, however, is not only that during the Renaissance and Humanism the separation of the written language from the oral is final, but also that this is discussed theoretically, with a tendency to diminish the importance of oral expression. The dissociation is very neatly operated by Sperone,[130] while in Bembo one even meets the interdiction that oral language should be continued or imitated in writing.[131] Castilian is *por uso*, Latin, *por arte y libros.*[132] Spanish linguists list the differences between *hablar* and *escrivir* in two columns.[133] Evidently, under such circumstances, the idea of "oral literature" can only be conceived through linguistic implication.

This is not to say that orality has no direct influence on written literature, sometimes translated conceptually. *Gesprächbüchlein* by Ulrich von Hutten (1521), for instance, is something new: a "conversation book." Printing codifies orality, subjects it to discipline, while at the same time acquiescing in its existence. The dissociations made by the "poeticians" of the age between *il bel parlare* and *novellare*, that is, *elocution* and *letters* also map out—if one looks from above—two distinct literatures.[134] Even Renaissance dialogues, a widely practiced written species of Platonic inspiration, suggest oral communication. An oral pseudo-literature is thus mimicked, even anticipated from the perspective of our biography.

SACRED LETTERS

We are still very close to the Middle Ages and sacrality continues to be the dominant and central value in culture. But, under the pressure of the new, increasingly powerful, cultural reality, its basic sense becomes more complicated and progressively laicized. Alongside sacred ecclesiastical culture—official, canonized—there appears a new form of highly cultured sacrality: humanistic culture. This is the outcome of a historical situation that has changed. Sacrality's sway over the entire empire of letters is never questioned. Dogma stays incontestable, but "letters" start assessing their peculiar character and intrinsic value more and more energetically. Hence, a new, ambitious, synthetic formula, in Erasmus (making its appearance in his first work, *De contemptu mundi: pietas literata*, with the variants: *docta pietas, humanitas christiana*). The new syntagm expresses a great part of the age's complex idea of *culture = literature*.

First of all, inevitably, the traditional terminology of religious *letters*—the Bible, patristic writings, Council edicts, etc.—continues to be used; *divinae litterae*[135] or *sacris litteris*,[136] *evangelicis litteris*, and *litterae arcanae* are phrases used frequently, and not only in ecclesiastical circles. These letters are the work of "ecclesiastic writers" (J. Trithemius, *Liber de scriptoribus ecclesiasticis*, 1494). In modern languages, phrases like *les saintes lettres*, *les lettres sacrées de la religion*, and *sacre lettre*, of even more intense circulation, have the same meaning. It is worth noting that in Romanian culture such formulas appear for the first time in Coresi (1569–1567): *cărți creştineşti*, *scriptură sfîntă*. The traditional belief in the divine origin of old writings, "the letter fallen from the sky," as in the old apocrypha (*The Manuscript of Ieud*),[137] seems to have been propagated even before that. In every geographical area, there exists an obvious unity of the religious mentality, of a pan-European character.

Even more important, however, is the outcome of this sacred valuation of *letters*—as a continuation of the medieval principle *reductio artium ad Sacram Scripturam*: the global sanctification of literary studies. *Sanctissima studia humanitatis*,[138] *bonnae litterae* (as seen earlier), *sanctissimae . . . omnes disciplinae*[139] and other very similar formulae become the expression of this program. (A typical title is Paulus Cortesius, *Sacrarum literarum omniumque disciplinarum scientia summi viri*, 1540). All humanists,[140] led by Erasmus, adhere to it. *La science des lettres . . . don divin*,[141] *sacri monumenti delle lettere* (Castiglione, I, 46) will define, in modern languages, the same intensive sacralization of letters.

It will assume other forms as well, all of them recuperative, against the background of the old doctrine of reconciliation and fruitful cooperation with secular letters. Selective assimilation, preparation for a superior understanding of the texts, the acknowledgment of central values (*virtus*, *charitas*) make it possible to accept, even to theorize upon "Christian humanism."[142] The transition from lay classicism to Christianity (*inter alia*: G. Budé, *De transitu Hellenismi ad Christianismus*, 1555) is a phenomenon typical of the age. The discovery—one might even say "reconsideration"—of the forerunners also becomes a perfectly feasible undertaking. Virgil and Seneca in the Middle Ages, and Socrates during Humanism (*Sancte Socrates, ora pro nobis*)[143] are salvaged and integrated, without any inhibition, into the new spiritual structure. This absorbs and reformulates practically all ancient culture.

Such a cultural and religious fervor naturally leads to what has been called a "religion of letters." The idea of literature will never experience higher forms of veneration, nor will letters ever again become the supreme spiritual value. The priests of the new "religion" are humanists. They are declared *Sacerdotes Musarum*[144] and *literature* itself becomes the object of the new cult, with the essential amendment that the religious sense, which interferes permanently, is of equal, if not superior, importance to the specific cultural sense, already touched upon.

So the Renaissance and Humanism produce another prestigious cliché: *sacred literature*, literature as a form of piety, as with Erasmus (*literaturae quam pietas*),[145] or mystical doctrine, as with G. Budé, *litteratura . . . quam mysticam doctrina*. In the latter we also meet a compromise formula: "History is the sheath, and the spirit of literature (*litteraturae spiritus*) the sword,"[146] *quasi divino-haec litteraturae*.[147] Alongside divinization, but on a lower plane, we find literature assimilated by theological theses (*ista literatura*)[148] and theology lessons,[149] which leads to the same conclusion. In the epoch, the intensely used meaning of the idea of literature has a purely mystical and religious content. It is also true that *literature* can only keep up such a degree of intensity in rare, privileged moments of its existence.

THE CULTURE OF LETTERS

Grammar and Culture

The background of these *letters*, inevitably, is the idea of *culture*. It dominates and shapes all the definitions of literature in this period, as it did during Antiquity and the Middle Ages, but with great *élan*, with a more enthusiastic educational and intellectual assiduity. To speak of a "rediscovery" of letters is therefore not enough. Letters are seen, defined, and praised as the central concept of man, of the epoch's global effort for knowledge and creativity. Literature sees itself, first and foremost, as an essential cultural act. So once again we come across the homologous pair *literature = culture*, the central axis of the biography of the idea of literature. The primacy of culture constitutes, in fact, the most specific form of the laicizing of literature in this period.

Very authoritative, in particular, is its elementary, traditional, fundamental definition, based on the ancient Greek and Latin etymology: *culture = grammar*. The prestige of classical forms is great, explaining their frequent use. The first of these forms is a "knowledge of reading and writing." We come across it everywhere, from grammarians and philologists to humanists and poets (Petrarch, *Fam.*, I, 7), or in translations (J. Amyot). A new phenomenon, it enters the epoch's dictionaries and encyclopedias (Balbus, *s.v.*, R. Estienne, *Thesaurus linguae latinae*, *s.v.*), which shows its stability and normative character. We are in a period when almost all the meanings of the idea of *literature*, consecrated by reference works, tend to become *ne varietur*. One of these significations, *recte loquendi scribendique scientia*,[150] is a real invariant, constituted as early as Classical Antiquity.

The same remark can be made about *studia* or *studium literarum*, the current equivalent of grammar,[151] of cultural activity generally. This acceptation, found in all the humanists (L. Bruni Aretino, *De studiis et litteris*

(1477); G. Budé, *De studio litterarum recte instituendo* (1557), etc., also works its way into the philological concerns and dictionaries of the age.[152] The modern equivalent, Italian, for example, is no less frequent: *studi delle lettere*. Not for a moment must we lose sight of the strictly didactic context and finality of these *litterae* and *studia*, which are, in fact, copiously discussed theoretically (B. Guarini, *De ordine docendi ac studendi*, Erasmus, *De ratione studii*, etc.) Thus, *letters* again appear—especially at such a moment in history—to be what they were originally: a typical school product, a specific subject-matter to be taught (Castiglione, I, 25; Rabelais, *Garg.*, I, 23; *Pant.*, II, 8. etc.) Such references should not be overlooked, but should be recorded with the attention due them.

These *studia* transmit "knowledge," *litteris cognosces*.[153] The Renaissance and Humanism legitimately speak of a knowledge of "letters," of "literary arts," of "good letters" and so forth, in the sense of acquiring first-rate knowledge. But the cultural and didactic content prescribed by the *trivium* is predominant in every instance, including Romania's Slavonic scholarly circles.[154] Grammar is seen as the basic condition, the "foundation of all literal arts and of all disciplines.[155] So, once more, we meet the classical, ancient definition, taken over with great faithfulness.[156] This way, the idea of literature is structured and stratified vertically, on a foundation of grammatical knowledge, made up of a knowledge of letters. Later on, grammar will detach itself from the culture of letters, to remain the normative discipline of reading and writing. The tradition of finding etymological explanations for words is also forsaken.[157]

The term *culture* itself, *litterarum cultura*,[158] is but rarely used. Much more common are its equivalents, all well attested: *doctrina literis* (E. Dolet), *de tradiendis disciplinis* (R. Agricola, J. L. Vives), *literarum peritia* (L. Bruni Aretino), *eruditione* (E. Dolet), and *prudentia literata*. The most current formula that best expresses the spirit of the times and most accurately fits the terminology, the eternal *litterae*, will be increasingly glossed and rendered as studies, sciences expressed through letters and contained in books,[159] as humanistic knowledge (1527, 1538),[160] broadly speaking, in an extended sense as culture. The entire modern exegesis of Renaissance and Humanistic lexicography is the same in this respect.

The translations of *litterae-culture* into modern languages play a decisive role in the introduction and acclimatization of the notion in Europe. It is necessary to take stock of them. *Lettres* (Montaigne, II; Rabelais, *Pant.*, II, 8), *science des lettres*,[161] *science littérale* (1531), and *science et érudition* (J. Amyot)[162] become the current expressions for the idea of literature used in this essential acceptation of "the science of letters,"[163] in a specific, narrow sense; general science, knowledge (1495), science, knowledge, in a broad sense. This is the very kernel of the idea of literature, in this period as well. In the same sense, *littéraire* = pertaining to letters and the knowledge thereof (1527).[164] An identical situation occurs in Italian, where we find *coltura, coltura d'anima* (after *cultura animi*)[165] (B. Castiglione, IV, 45), and *coltura degli ingegni* (A. Possevino, 1598). More frequently, *lettere* and *notizie di lettere*, also in *Il Cortegiano* (I, 42; III, 9), as well as *studi delle lettere* (L. B. Alberti), *scienza delle lettere* (L. Bruni Aretino), *eruditione e principi delle lettere* (G. Vasari), *dottrina delle lettere* (M. Palmieri), etc. Note that the idea of *mathesis* appears again as *mathematiche*, respectively *scienze dottrinali*,[166] *Letras, ciencias* are the corresponding Spanish terms. In English, *culture* initially had both a technical (land tillage) and a spiritual sense: *culture of the mind, taste, manners*.[167] The doublet *learning* renders even better the idea of knowledge acquired in school, of the "ability to read and write."[168] As synchronization is a current, inevitable phenomenon, the *gelehrte Kentnisse*,[169] the German equivalent to *litterae humanae*, renders the same notion. With it, we have covered the whole basic lexicography of European culture, although it is impossible to make an exhaustive survey in so few words.

An identical evolution and semantic clarification occur in the case of terms defining the man of culture as a *man of letters*. *Litteratus*[170] has the meaning—already historical, traditional—of connoisseur (in every sense of the word) of "letters." The notion, quite current during the Renaissance, tends to become redundant; *doctus et literatus*,[171] or to be narrowly specialized: *literator* = he who owns, or has a knowledge of, *multi libri*.[172] In the Byzantine world, the old term *grammaticos* is preserved: a *grammatico*.[173] In the Romanian culture of old (the fifteenth century), "ritor" and "scholastic," as in Lucaci, the author of a Slavonic-Romanian sermon book (1581),[174] are synonyms of schoolmaster, learned man, educated man; broadly speaking, he who "writes and talks with great skill."[175] Such qualities already enjoy wide appreciation.[175]

Modern Western languages make full use of this term, which covers the entire range of cultural versatility: from those who are familiar with letters and can write them, to those who "know," are educated, cultivated: *lettre, homme de lettres, homme de grandes lettres*.[176] Other variants can be found: *bien lettré, savant en lettres, gens lettrez et doctes, doctes en lettres*, etc. Some Italian humanists (A. Poliziano) claim for themselves—in the old, familiar tradition—the rank of *grammatici*;[177] others style themselves as *letterati, molte lettere . . . prudentissimo*, (L. B. Alberti), *eruditi et studiosi di buone lettere* (S. Sperone), *scientiati di poesia*, or, simply, *uomo di lettere* (M. Bartoli). In Spanish, *hombre de letras* and *letrados*—with a clear definition by Juan de Lucerna (those who know what is written in letters)[178]—have the same meaning; similarly, the English *instructed in letters* (1531),[179] or the Romanian *cărtularu*, attested as early as the sixteenth century.[180] Conversely, *illiteratus*[184] means—just as in the Middle Ages—*sine litteris, cum litera ignorant id est non latine* (L. Valla).[182] *Laicus, analphabetus* (G. Budé), respectively, *uomini volgari ed emprici, illiterati* define ignorant, uneducated people. It is more than mere disqualification: a great rip in human existence, failure to be a real human being, decay.

But the real importance of the Renaissance and of Humanism to the biography of the idea of literature is the following: It is only during this period that the notion *literature* becomes absolutely clear, that its basic meanings and significations are specified, that it is made systematic with the help of a general definition that enters every European language of widespread circulation. This is the inevitable result of the intense philological and lexicographical thought and activity that are so characteristic of the age. It is necessary to ponder at some length an analytical description of the process:

a) First, the "grammatical" definition of literature is consolidated and asserts itself. An entire classical tradition is recovered through the formula *grammatica = litteratura*.[183] The definitions are inevitably *ne varietur*; they begin by referring to the acquisition of the rudiments, with a purely didactic purpose: *litteratura seu litteratione designatur: abecedarii, syllabarii et nominarii*.[184] The object of education is *litteraturae professoribus*;[185] there is nothing new under the sun yet, but the basic meaning is settled and consecrated for good.

b) The situation of the old, traditional cultural sense is identical: *litteratura = culture*, or, as with Erasmus, *melioris litteraturae* (= *bonae litterae*), but also *litteraturae peritia, litteraturae cognitio*,[186] *litteratura et disciplina* (T. Gaza).[187] Exerting a powerful pressure, the humanist conscience makes *literature* become, at the same time, a form of *bonus animus*,[188] a pedagogy of virtues and a moral quality: *prudentia*,[189] *urbanitas*, etc. In keeping with this, the educated, cultivated man, the man of culture, will be referred to as *in litteratura instructus perfectus*,[190] *in litteratura virus* (L. Bruni Aretino),[191] *aptis litteratura personis*,[192] which is to say *vir magnae litteraturae*[193] = an extraordinarily cultivated man. This formula—turned into an ideal, a supreme term of comparison—will have a long career.

c) The "ethnic" dimension of literature is established within the same framework. As we shall see further on, it underlies the concept of "national literature." So far, this concept is only implied, in a formula like *De litteratura non vulgari* (Curio Lancilotto Pasio, Lelio Gregorio Giraldi). In the cultural *lingua franca* of the day, this means grammar and literature written in Latin. There are other attestations pointing to the same idea.[194]

d) Literature finally reaches its first lexicographic status due to the fact that it enters the great humanistic dictionaries of the day, which explain and define its sense as accurately as possible. This is an even more important event in the biography of the idea of literature, as it enters definitively the semantic and lexical stock of Renaissance literature and through it, as we shall presently see, all modern European languages. Only now does *literature* receive an "official" current definition, which may have become rather trite, but which is nevertheless "authoritative." Thus, Western acceptations become usual, referential. The series seems to be inaugurated by the *Dictionarium* of Ambrosius Calepinus (Paris, 1514), later known under the title *undecim linguarum*. In it, *Literatura* (II, p. 829) is defined by its familiar, classical meaning: the science of letters (*grammatica*) and *connaissance des lettres*, that is, *scrittura, scienza, die Kunst der Buchstaben und Geschrift*, etc. The coupling of grammar and culture and the oscillation between the two are maintained with G. Budé,[195] Etienne Dolet, and Robert Estienne, first in his small, school dictionary,[196] then in the great *Thesaurus Linguae Latinae* (1572): *de litteris tractat, literarum cognitio et scientia.*[197] These provide lapidary, exhaustive definitions for this level of signification. The semantic glosses of the age retain the same aspects for *litteratura*; elementary training (*pueris elementa*),[198] and in a negative sense, little culture (*mediocris literatura*).[199] It is therefore impossible to say that literature in this form and with this acceptation disappeared during the Renaissance.[200]

A further, even more decisive argument is that the term appears and circulates, with the same meaning, in the modern languages. The French attestations in the second half of the fifteenth century (1468–1495) connote general scientific and literary knowledge,[201] that is, "culture." The notion really takes root in the next century;[202] sciences, literary knowledge (*lettrerie, licteratiur*),[203] the object of teaching (*enseigner la littérature*),[204] intellectual and cultural background (*mon peu de sens et de littérature*);[205] the meaning "general knowledge" (*toute sorte de littérature*) appears in Montaigne as well (II, 19). So the age assimilates and sanctions in a final manner *la littérature et autre science.*[206] The quantitative side of this intellectual and cultural accumulation is quickly turned into a stereotype: *excellens, experts* and, especially, *homme de grande littérature.*[207] Conversely, the uneducated individual, regardless of nationality, is *sans littérature.*[208] The English equivalent is *illiterature* (1592).[209] The formula is a true head of a series.

Such terminology, specific to European culture, is encountered everywhere. The situation is identical in Italian; *vera litteratura* (L. Valla), appears in the same context as *studia humanitatis* and *buona litteratura.*[210] In Portuguese, *leteratura* (1507) and *sciencia e literatura* have the same general cultural meaning.[211] *Literatur*, in German (Simon Roths, *Ein Teutscher Dictionarius*, 1571), contains all the basic meanings: craft of writing, knowledge, science, intellectual pursuits.[212] Finally, an identical situation is found in English (wherein a 1425 attestation can be said to inaugurate the series):[213] *Knowledge(d) and literatured in the wars* (Shakespeare, *Henry V*, IV, 7, V. 145), with an even stronger didactic sense: *Lyterature* (John

Colet).[214] It has been said, in fact, that almost all Renaissance literature should be examined against this cultural *background*.[215]

The Totality of Literature

As we now know, as early as Antiquity and the Middle Ages *litterae* become the symbol of both total culture and the sum-total of writings. Renaissance *letters*—human and others—partake of the same meaning: a totality of cultural knowledge, expressed by a plurality of genres and works. The terminology of the age faithfully renders these global meanings of literature: a) the sum-total of knowledge; b) the sum-total of cultural and literary activities and genres not yet integrated within a general concept of "culture" or "literature" (in the general, modern sense); c) the sum-total of writings of any kind. We are still under the regimen of cumulative *letters*, reduced to the lowest possible common denominator: culture and writings of any category.

Lexicography—the only reliable source for this kind of research—again mirrors all these nuances: a) *omni literarum genere;*[216] *omnes ingenuas disciplinas et arts,*[217] etc., correspond to the ideal of total knowledge, *de omni re scribili,* of global culture and of the universal, Renaissance man; b) the long catalogues of literary and scientific disciplines,[218] quite common with humanists (L. Bruni Aretino: poets, philosophers, orators; A. Polliziano: poets, historians, orators, philosophers, etc.) are proof that, for the time being, literature fails to be a conceptual totality, and continues to be a "sum" of enumerated, countable stock disciplines; c) the purely constitutive, cumulative sense results even more clearly from such complete accounts of writers and writings as: *omnis scribentium turba* (Petrarch, *Fam.,* I, 8), *omnium scriptoribus* (L. Bruni Aretino),[219] etc.

The notion of totality finds its way, quite naturally, into modern languages; *toute bonne littérature* (Rabelais, *Pant.,* II, 8), *toutes sciences libérales* (G. Budé), *en doctrine et en tout genre de lettres,*[220] *cognoissance de toute sorte de lettres,*[221] *all literature and erudition,*[222] *all kinds of profane literature,*[223] etc. An identical situation to be kept in mind and one which, in this respect, is decisive for our biography is that of "total literature": *omni litteratura.*[224] Derived from it is *toute sorte de littérature* (Montaigne, II, 8; II, 19), *ogni genere di litteratura,*[225] etc. Then the adjective disappears, and *literature,* used alone, will henceforth carry the meanings of all its cultural attributes. Its multivalence becomes, one more time, inevitable.

Another formula expressing the same idea that is in general use—an expeditious synthesis that may be too elliptical—is *res literaria,* a phrase of medieval coinage. It will have a remarkable career. It is currently encountered in the work of humanists (Erasmus, G. Budé, Le Fèvre d'Etaple, etc.), in lexicons,[226] in the letter-writing of the age. Its meaning covers the widest possible cultural area: the activities it refers to are cultural, universal

(Erasmus: *universa res literaria*),[227] scholarly (*omnia literarum studia et universam res literarium*),[228] grammatical (*re grammatica*),[229] educational (*rei literarie gymnasium*),[230] etc. All "literary" output is obviously subsumed by this notion as well, that is to say, literary works, writings with a "creative" and imaginative character, but also all the editing and marketing operations, with their economic, material aspects. Modern translators can find no more suitable word for *re literaria* than the eternal, all-encompassing word "literature" (*la littérature*). This is one more example, not of an anachronism, but of a simultaneous reading of the idea of literature.[231]

Encyclopedic Knowledge

Another technical term for the idea of global literature (in the sense of culture) is brought to the surface by the classical cultural and lexical background of the age (predominantly Hellenic): *encyclopedic* knowledge. It is a learned, traditional formula of the *letterae humanae* family, which faithfully conveys the size and significance of Renaissance literary culture. Attested in 1529 in Germany,[232] in 1531 in England,[233] and in 1532 in France (Rabelais, *Pant.*, II, 20), the word *encyclopedia* reveals from the start its Greek etymology (Joachim Sterck van Ringelbergh, *Lucrubrationes vel potius absolutissima* κυκλοπαιδεια, 1519), and especially its intrinsic didactic-pedagogical sense. A direct, immediate relationship is found between *encyclopedia* and the notion *paideia*[234] and study (*studio encyclopaediae cult.*).[235] It expresses both the idea of global knowledge, and the way of achieving such a cultural performance. Romania's old codexes and *sbornics* had, in fact, the same function; their spirit lives on in the following centuries. The thirst for knowledge in this era was unquenchable, and drinking the fountain of knowledge dry was not yet regarded as "utopian." We are not yet in the 20th century.

It is therefore natural that the program of global knowledge—typical of pedagogues (Vittorino da Feltre, P. P. Vergerio), humanists (A. Poliziano),[236] Renaissance writers (Rabelais, *Pant.*, II, 8)—should be linked to the idea of the encyclopedia. Quantitatively speaking, an encyclopedia is the "sum of all sciences" (Domenico Delfico, 1556),[237] all the knowledge provided by "sciences" (Pierre l'Anglais).[238] To the mentality of the age, such an operation was entirely feasible. As is well known, the *trivium* and the *quadrivium* made up the complete, traditional, and necessary syllabus for acquiring exhaustive, perfect knowledge. This, after all, is the key argument of the "cyclic knowledge" method, invoked by Erasmus: "Hence the name encyclopedia, which closes the circle of disciplines" (*Adagia*). The method will therefore be defined as: *circularis disciplina*,[239] *circularis doctrina, circularem eruditionem et disciplinam*,[240] *orbis disciplinarum*, in Paul Scaliger, *Encyclopaediae seu orbis disciplinarum tam sacrarum quam profanarum Epitome* (1559). The idea enters European culture,[241] wherein it has undergone continuous developments and interpretations to this day.

The modern language transpositions will again take up, of course, the basic idea ("a circle of liberal arts"),[242] as well as the consecrated formula of spherical knowledge ("the spheric encyclopedia").[243] The effort at assimilating this neologism will have beneficial consequences, as all the suggested variants and nuances emphasize the concept of a "linked," "circular" type of knowledge. This will be integrated to the latter-day "hermeneutical circle." Knowledge is acknowledged to have a systematic, organic, circular structure. It is one of the fundamental phases and acceptations of this idea. It is also worth noting that, by substituting *literature* for *letters,* the former notion is also given a cyclical nature too: "Literature, this circle (*rond*) of sciences named by the Greeks encyclopedia."[244] The new signification in effect confirms and enriches the profoundly cultural semantics of the word *literature.* But now crisis looms: "total" encyclopedias reach their maximum capacity of absorption and organization, following which they begin to specialize. A discovery of tremendous import is made: Universal knowledge is no longer possible, except within one single field. The concept of poetry as philosophy is afforded (B. Daniello, *La Poetica,* 1536) and the eulogy of philosophical poetry gives,[245] in traditional classical terms, the same perspective. Thus, the extreme expansion of literature leads to limitation and the beginnings of specialism. The *whole/part* relation is modified in favor of a more and more accented and particular character of culture (= literature). The process will gain momentum in time.

Letters and Print

There is one other reason why the Renaissance and Humanism play an important part in the biography of the idea of literature; in the evolution of writing, therefore of *written literature*, a crucial event occurs, the invention of printing. The appearance of printing is a mere technical accident in the history of writing, but it has tremendous cultural and literary consequence. At first, the new invention is sensational because of its novelty, but it quickly becomes "commonplace" and taken for granted, so much so that printing—entirely identified with the ideas of writing—ceases to impress. It becomes definitively, indissolubly associated with the idea of *literature* in all its material aspects.

The traditional idea of *writing* is so powerful that it immediately appropriates the new invention. From manuscript, *writing* becomes typographical, even if printing is but a mere method, a new device, an uncommon way of writing and nothing more. Proof is found in the fact that frequent references continue to be made to "the manner of writing through impression,"[246] "a new art of writing with metal type," "a new sort of writing," a kind of writing "with typographic letters" as distinct from "handwriting."[247] The corresponding learned formula, in Latin, *ars artificialiter scribendi*,[248] renders the same idea clearly. The Romanian Deacon Coresi declares, in keeping with this tradition: "I have written," "I have written with printing" (1561, 1567).[249]

In the beginning, a printed book aimed at little more than the copying of a manuscript as closely as possible, or reproducing its graphic aspect, its visual image. All it wanted was a faithful image. The lure of the facsimile now appears. An incunable was meant to be a printed "manuscript," with the same initials, columns, ornaments, illuminations. Metal letters copy handwritten, calligraphic letters; the change is just lexical: *letter* was replaced by *type*: *imprimere arte characteriali*.[250] Many decorative elements are still handmade. Copyists and typesetters worked very closely together until about 1475. The circumstance is illustrated by the mixed products, *libri impressi cum notes manuscriptis*.[251] Many scholars continue to be scribes and copyists, even after the invention of printing; there are quite a number of manuscripts copied off printed texts; manuscripts continue to circulate after the invention of printing.

There are plenty of signs that the contention is—for some time at least—far from being resolved. To be more precise, for a long period the opposition of the manuscript tradition proves to be still strong and active, as it inevitably had to be. Benedictines, such as J. Trithemius in *De laude scripturorum* (c. VIII), continue to uphold the thesis of the superiority of handwriting over printing. Their arguments? A handwritten text secures the author's posthumous fame, it lasts longer than a printed one, no one can afford to buy all the books printed, etc.[252] Some Italian humanists also proclaim the superiority of the manuscript until as late as 1490.[253] It is a foregone conclusion, however. The eulogy of printing becomes current and turns into a real Renaissance and humanist *topos*. Printing equals all the arts put together.[254] It is an "admirable invention,"[255] "the Muses' sister," "the tenth Muse" (J. du Bellay), etc. It is characterized by quantity in diversity: there are many books in many languages (Erasmus).[256] Its usefulness is matchless: "This art, if not the noblest of all, is at least the most useful, as it serves, brings to perfection, and propagates all sciences and arts" (H. Estienne).[257] The supreme consecration, however, comes from religion, through sacralization. Printing is a "divine invention" (Rabelais, *Pant.*, II, 8), *haec sancta ars* (N. Cusanus),[258] a valuable ally of the Church. It is known that it played a decisive role in the dissemination of Reformation ideas. But the most important, the most direct result of its invention was the widespread circulation of the Bible. Before 1500, 45 percent of all the printed books were religious texts.[259] The typography theory is fully systematized in the second half of the sixteenth century: A. F. Doni Domenechi, *Della Stampa* (1562),[260] H. Estienne, *De sue typographiae statu*

(1569), *Artis typographicae querimonia* (1569), etc., are complex humanist essay-books, whose fundamental idea is the totality of *letters*, the totality of culture, which has finally produced its ideal instrument for recording and multiplication.

Despite all these poets, the influence of *printing* on the definition of *literature* is not—nor can it be—too great for the time being. It continues to be classified either under the heading *in Re Literaria* (Francis Bacon, *N.O.*, CXXIX), or as a form of *Schreiberei*,[261] and nothing more. A typeset-ter-editor-philologist, like Aldus Manutius, is similarly deemed, like any other humanist, *bonarum litterarum vindicator*.[262] *Scriptor* and *impresor* are used as synonyms in many an incunabula.[263] The direct effects on writing, editing, and publishing are enormous, but they will only influence the acceptations of *literature* much later. As yet, all the qualities of writing are taken up and intensified by printing. This does nothing but enrich and confer new prestige upon the known, already classical, significations of *literature*.

It is easy to observe that cultural praise continues to be most frequent and enthusiastic. Printing is among the inventions that changed the face of the earth (Bacon, *N.O.*, aphorism 129). Printed literature has a decisive role in accumulating, conserving, memorizing, and disseminating knowl-edge. Image-culture—let us remember the theory of "painting-literature" for the use of the illiterate—is definitively replaced by the culture of the written word. The printed letter confers more authority (Montaigne, III, 13). It can be repeated with accuracy (a quality that oral literature lacks), it makes the text stable and standardized, it makes it homogeneous, leveled out, "democratized." Anyone can gain access to the text of the letters (Rabelais, *Pant.*, III, 8), hence its implicit desacralization.

The first semantic manifestations of "popular" or "mass" literature, even of "subliterature," can be discerned at the same time. A manuscript is a "personal" work and form of achievement. Printing, on the contrary, depersonalizes. It is a collective, abstract, almost anonymous product. Evi-dently, neither the originality, nor the novelty of literature is annulled. These ideas reappear in force, but on different planes. For the time being, the idea of novelty and priority will only be used to refer to the technical ("miraculously discovered") invention itself and to its alleged inventor, Gutenberg, "the first man who . . . without a pen. . . ," etc.[264] We shall soon see that in the same period such praise of the purely technical or craft aspects will no longer do.

The Book of Literature

The most momentous result of the invention of printing is the final com-ing together of *literature* and *book*. Now begins the great age of the book—of the multiplied, printed literary book. *Writing, book,* and *printing* become synonymous. This is clearly visible, especially in the humanists'

vocabulary, where *liber, volumen, codex, libellus*, etc., at the same time connote manuscript and printed texts.[265] *Bücher oder Schriften*[266] are one and
the same thing. *Escriture = livre.* All the functions of writing and of the
letter are transferred to books and acknowledged as their attributes: recording, conserving, memorizing. The equation *book = literary work* ("*Finito il
libro chiamato Teseid*")[267] appears within this frame of reference.

A book is, first and foremost, the essential implement and symbol of
culture: *librorum lectio*, of the "thirst" for knowledge: *libris rationi nequeo*
(Petrarch, *Fam.*, III, 6; III, 18). Love of books *amor librorum*, and *amator
librorum*,[268] book lover, *bibliographus* in its extreme forms will define from
this moment on the man of letters and culture, the specialist in *literature*
(= culture). *Human letters*, or *libros de humanidad*[269] will be the passion of
his heart. However, the idea of book is indistinguishable from that of *studies*,[270] education, culture, discipline, intellectual upbringing in general.
Hence the German term *Zuchtbuch*, used inclusively for translations from
the ancient sages (for example, from Seneca). The idea of book, taken
over by pedagogues, becomes identical to that of wisdom (J. L. Vives).[270]
This theme is abundantly illustrated by the countless emblems of *book*
circulating during this period.[272]

The definitions of literature—which, as we can see, are becoming
more stable and more generalized—are associated with or derived from the
same idea of *book.* Literature is currently associated, first of all, with the
entire field of letters, to *re litteraria* (= *rem libros appello*),[273] books of culture, of literature in the sense of *belles lettres*, of every kind, epistles, etc.
In England, toward the end of the sixteenth century, a book, *blotting-book*,
is any kind of "book," including a personal diary.[274] The idea of encyclopedic culture gathered in one single book (*Fiore di virtù, Adagio*, Montaigne
himself, in his essays, is very close to this conception) remains dominant.
Hence: *book =* the symbol of integral, absolute culture (*arca de deposito*),[275]
that is, of "total" literature. Countless false attributions, the fluid paternity
of the circulated texts, fuel the consciousness of anonymous culture, a
global culture, with a tendency to become universal.

In its turn, the great prestige of the *holy book* helps to assert and consolidate the idea of "sacred literature." Creation is *il libro di Dio* (Tommaso
Campanella, St. Bernardino da Siena),[276] (a conception that is quite current: *libro divino*, with an archetypal value, (*libro primero, libro original*).[277]
God made the world in three books: *written, spoken, ciphered* (*simplis, pro-
nunciatis, numeralis.*)[278] Paracelsus takes a similar view (*Cyclopaedia Paracel-
sica christiana*, 1585).

The concurrent definition of "profane literature," in full expansion—
and which will assert itself to such a degree that, eventually, it will be
taken to mean "literature" proper—already has several typical and memorable expressions. They all include, inevitably, the concept of *book*, visibly

and gradually laicized: *libros ad seculum*,[279] *livres au monde* (Rabelais, *Pant.*, IV, 53). The text of the period that is most characteristic for the problem concerning us now, *Philobiblion sive de amore librorum* by Richard de Bury (1473) constantly wavers between the sacred and the profane, with a tendency to maintain a balance between the two and reconcile them. Of special relevance is the way in which the concept of *book of nature*, highly sacred at the outset, becomes laic and is frequently evoked (M. Ficino, T. Campanella, G. Bruno).[280] Through its identification with the idea of "letter," "writing," "alphabet," "language," "signature," the whole universe is turned into a profane system of graphic signs. Only a profound lay spirit can imagine a divinity so professionally dedicated to the writing of a true "book," defined in such specific terms. This is also true of such synonymous concepts as *the book of the world, the book of life, theatrum mundi*, etc., all of them metaphors with a considerable cultural meaning and motivation: a "book" that teaches, educates people. The universe has become entirely literal and literary. During the Renaissance and Humanism, *literature* becomes the central value of existence, it becomes the essence of the world. An ontology of the book, of literature, becomes possible.

A highly personal coloring, conferring new dimensions on the *book*, that is, upon *literature*, can also be noticed. In *Des livres* (Montaigne, II, 10), its functions continue to be the traditional ones: instruction, viz. culture, and entertainment. However, the concept of unique book is given a new motivation: the need of the irreducible self to confess, as the self can only speak about itself, "as long as there is paper in the world" (II, 9). Such an undertaking is seen as quite singular: "The only book of its kind in the world" (II, 8). Thus, a whole view of literature as a personal, unique, authentic, subjective experience is prefigured. The author pours himself into the book and the book "makes" its author: therefore, literature is seen as a way of life and of self-realization. In fact, one could argue that it is also this period that sees the first differentiation of *writing*—mere expression, spontaneous, unorganized testimony (Eduard Dekker: "What I am writing is not a book, but a mere rhapsody of my unquiet reflexions"—from the book as a whole (Montaigne, II, 12).[281] The notion becomes stable and increasingly professional. In the German culture of the mid-sixteenth century (though the situation is general), the writer, the author (*Schreiber, Verfasser*) is a "book-writer" (*Buchschreiber*, 1541). This is an even more interesting phenomenon, one that will have notable further developments. The personal diary and the memoirs soon seem out of place within the disciplined confines of the book, whose structure remains rigid. For this reason, these genres tend to become emancipated and eventually "deliteraturized."

The Literature Library

The concept of library, also frequent in the humanist's vocabulary, acquires new meanings too: a collection and depository of books in manuscript and printed form. However, the terminology is not noticeably enriched. *Librarium pro bybliotheca*[282] is the source of the doublet *librairie/bibliothèque*,[283] known since the Middle Ages. As for *bibliothèque* (1493), *bibliothécaire* (1518) in French, and *Bibliothek* (1532) in German, they are mere loan-words originally derived from the Latin *bibliotheca*. In any event, all these terms are definitively consecrated by modern Western languages.

The highly personal character of the "library"—a characteristic of the age—must be attributed not only to the personality of Petrarch, then to that of Montaigne, but also to the individualistic spirit of the time. The Italian poet and humanist gained fame as a passionate collector of manuscripts and copies of manuscripts; he also wrote about books and libraries (*De librorum copia, Dial.* XLIII). The tendency is even more pronounced with Montaigne, who frequently uses the term *librairie*: a secluded, private, personal, and free cultural space that can be paced in every direction. The library, installed in his famous "tower," is "the most useless place in my house." Read: disinterested, gratuitous, purely intellectual. We feel the first timid breeze of cultural independence, indeed of cultural autonomy.

In this respect, the process of making culture perfect and global gains momentum. Since the Middle Ages, the library has been an instrument and symbol of collected and stored, stratified culture. The tradition is now resumed and considerably augmented, hence, the superlative concept of *bibliotheca polienda, politia*,[284] the exemplary instrument of culture, in a laic sense, reaching the limits of the cognitive possibilities of the age. *Library*, generically used, is the term applied, beginning with the sixteenth century, not only to reading notebooks consisting of notes and extracts, such as those of Photius, but also to the notion of the unique book. The idea is anticipated and reaffirmed in connection with the *library* of Diodorus Siculus, who is reputed (1559) to have "collected," "abridged" and "summarized" other books.[285] The idea of totality, the "universal library,[286] the encyclopedia, *tanta studiorum varietate*,[287] *tutti gli autori*[288] confers on the *library* this dimension as well. The conception inspires works like *Bibliotheca Universalis* (1545) or *Pandectae Universalis* by Conrad Gessner. The first projects of "ideal libraries" are also devised now: François de la Croix du Maine submits one to Henri III in 1584.[289] Also ideal is A. Possevinus' *Bibliotheca Selecta* (1593). No matter how much parody and sarcasm Rabelais' imaginary library contains, its prestige remains (*Pant.*, II, 7). That it inspires "literature on literature" is yet another sign of a complete literary assimilation.

The Beginning of Bibliography

Compared to the Middle Ages, the basic significations do not evolve, do not acquire new, important shades of meaning, but their context is gradually changed, which makes Renaissance and Humanist "bibliography" more erudite, more philological and, in general, more laic than that of the previous age.

A typical example of a double implicit meaning is *bibliotheca universalis*, which includes the idea of *bibliographia universalis*, that is, a universal repertory of writings, without any cultural, let alone literary, character. The term defines the sum-total of references to "printed or reprinted, of all genres and from all countries," as with Conrad Gessner (1545).[290] The term used at the time, *De omni literatura*, appears in the third edition of I. I. Fries' *Epitomes* (1583) in the "Universal Library" of the same Gessner. The idea of totality, of encylopedia, is therefore understood. It is the explicit beginning of the definition that will become an uninterrupted series: *literature* = *bibliography*. Other terminological variants circulating at the time include *notitia rei litterarie, bibliopolarum omniumque rei literarie*, the erudite and exhaustive inventory as an integral part of *ratione studiorum*.[291] The religious character, however, is far from being omnipresent. "Libraries—encyclopedias" of a laic or scientific character (*Bibliotheca naturae*), as well as the first medical and juridical bibliographies,[292] were also published during the Renaissance. The tendency will be generalized, with a view to recording and systematizing all the writings of any genre. In this context, the idea of value and hierarchy has not yet appeared. This preparatory stage is a necessary prerequisite, however.

Other terms that express the notion of "bibliography," containing the first signs that it is beginning to be specialized, constitute new and important contributions to the age. A first, sizable compartment belongs to religious writers such as Johann Tritheim (Trithemius): *Liber de scriptoribus ecclesiastici* (1494), the "father of bibliography" (T. Besterman). It is the first printed ecclesiastical bibliography. In subsequent editions, the title will be changed to *Catalogus scriptorum Ecclesiasticorum*. The index-catalogue formula becomes popular. The term *Nomenclator scriptorum philosophicorum atque philologicorum* (Israel Spach, 1598), as well as the more specific one, "catalog," is also encountered now. The latter is closely linked to the beginnings of a national bibliography: John Bale, *Illustrium maioris Britanniae scriptorum summarium* (1548), Cornelis Loos, *Illustrium Germaniae scriptorum catalogus* (1581), etc. In modern languages, the corresponding titles are in Italian, *Libreria* (Antonio Francesco Doni, 1550); in English, *Catalogue of English Printed Books* (Andrew Maunsel, 1595); in French, *Bibliothèque française* (*Catalogue général . . . de tous contenant des hommes que des femmes qui ont escrit ou composé, en notre langue française maternelle*, François de la Croix du Maine, 1584). Such enumerations are inevitable. An author's bibliography is an innovation and an index of radical specialization: *Catalogus omnius Erasmi Roterdami lucrubrationum* (1523). Finally, the publisher's catalogue-bibliography also makes its appearance: H. Estienne, *De sue typographiae statu*, 1569), having an advertising function as well. Thus, in broad lines, the field of modern bibliography is already drawn.

On this foundation, the first rudiments of "literary history" are formed in the Middle Ages. It evolves in the same way during the Renaissance, even though it may bear the labels of *Libreria, Bibliotheca, Registrum* (cf. *Registrum librorum Angliae*, a sixteenth century Ms.).[293] The equality *literary history = bibliographic repertory* is thus formed: first inventory, data gathering, then "value judgments." In this context, with the same characteristic traits, the first truly national literary histories begin to be published in France: Claude Fauchet, *Recueil de l'origine de la langue et poésie françoise*, 1581).[294]

THE COORDINATES OF LETTERS

New Versus Old Letters

Neither historical perspective, nor historical dimension can be said to be, in their essence, discoveries of the Renaissance. As we know, they date back to Antiquity and the Middle Ages, and have been closely associated with the continued confrontation between old and new. The new phase is nevertheless important, as differences become radical and the historical ages are systematized. "Literary" history, that is, cultural history, works out its first operational pattern, and literature begins to be conceived of in evolutional terms as part of a unitary historical process.

What appears first is the awareness of a new moment and a new historical context for *letters: O seculum. O litterae. Juvat vivere* (Ulrich von Hutten, 1518).[295] *Seculum* is the traditional ancient phrase (Tacitus) for the "spirit of the age," of the "century." Synchronizing brings about the appearance of "new books,"[296] "new authors" (*temporis authorum nova*),[297] while trite, obsolescent letters define *leitura (literatura) antigua*.[298] Other ways of expressing obsolescence, *remotae litterae, litteris antiquis*, are also part of the same, classical, *antiqui/moderni* scenario, with its corresponding doublet, *tradition* versus *innovation*.[299]

A comparison of the historical ages of literature thus becomes possible. For the Renaissance, the critical term of comparison is the Middle Ages, a barbarous age by definition, when the "Goths" destroyed *toute bonne littérature*.[300] It is the first serious crisis in literary history: massive book destruction, ignorance, "darkness" everywhere; the formula *tenebris litteraturam*[301] defines it accurately. By contrast, the reverse formula, that of the "rebirth" of literature, *priscae litteraturae renascentis*,[302] constitutes a true emblem of the reconsideration and rejuvenation of letters, of restoring literature to its essential function and vocation. All the defining qualities of "letters" are rediscovered: *Renascuntur bonae litterae, resipiscit mundus, reflorescit politior literatura*.[303] This update is the equivalent of rescuing the very existence of literature (of letters, of culture). The crucial argument is purely cultural: "Now all the disciplines are resurrected," "light and dignity . . . are restored to letters,"[304] the "study of the disciplines" is "rediscovered,"[305] "human letters/are/restored."[306] In this way, all the related expressions, *restitutae litterae, renatae litterae Latinae, renascentium amore litterarum, litteras instauranda*, etc., will acquire the same double, even treble, significance: cultural (the cult of letters), critical (repudiation of medieval barbarity), and cyclical (recovery of Greek and Latin letters, return to literature's archetypal sources).

The first elements of a history of letters appear within the same framework and follow the same scenario. Writing and graphic arts are of two kinds: *litteris vetustis, littera antiqua*, respectively *scriptura nova*.[307] Also, the discovery is made that writing already has a history, a tradition, hence, the first considerations as to the conventional origin of "letters," the skepticism surrounding the real paternity of the invention of writing,[308] and the generalities regarding its evolution.[309] Parallel to them are the eulogies to the historical benefits to be had from writing, such as a cultural memory and a knowledge of the past centuries. When printing is invented, it is immediately acknowledged by the age. "The age of imprinting is ours." A new historical age has dawned. It greatly enhances the dimensions of the literary world. Until then, only "old books" were in circulation (*Aesop, Le roman de la rose*, etc.). Now, "new books" appear (translations of the Bible, calendars, almanacs, etc.).[310]

The confrontation between the literary ages themselves—hinted at when we discussed the parallels between Antiquity and the Middle Ages—had far-ranging consequences. This is the immediate origin of the famous *Querelle des Anciens et des Modernes*. The controversy is based on two sets of observations: 1. the "history" and "progress" of poetry,[311] indicative not only of chronology, but also of the succession of ages of poetry that are structurally differentiated, beginning with the first phase: the transition from sacred to profane poetry; 2. a "comparison of modern literature with the ancient one,"[312] regarding quality, hierarchy, typology, and emulation. As will be seen, the controversy engineers the first declared—and even theoretically discussed—breach in the idea of literature: elements of a profound differentiation (within periods, countries, styles, literary theories, etc.) are exposed with greater and greater clarity.[313] Consequently, the notion of cultural unity is more and more bitterly contested. *Literature* is no longer looked at as a *continuum*, as an organic whole or a structural or morphological entity.

National Versus Universal Letters

The acknowledgment of the existence of national "vernaculars," already manifest in the Middle ages, continues with increased intensity during the

Renaissance. It has countless "literary" consequences, even though the first concept of "national literature" is linguistic rather than literary. Before forming a cultural (let alone esthetic) whole, literature is a special form of linguistic aggregation, the sum-total of writings in a national language. This linguistic conglomerate opens the way to new concepts and significations in the idea of literature: tradition, specific traits, and national literary history. These new acceptations will make it increasingly difficult to reduce the idea of literature to a single unit. A crisis of definition—which is to play havoc later—can already be anticipated.

Literature's basic national identity—we are tempted to call it original—continues to be the classical one, more specifically the Greek and Latin traditions. It is strongly reaffirmed when the two prestigious ancient *letters*, of archetypal value, are rediscovered and recuperated, hence formulas such as *latina litteratura*,[314] *litteratura romana*,[315] *literae vere latinae*,[316] etc., respectively *Hebraica Graecaque literatura*,[317] *Graecas litterae*, etc. It is the domain of *De litteratura non vulgari* (Curio Lancillotto Pasio, 1518): the study of classical Latin grammar, distinctly delimited from the study of "Vulgar," vernacular languages.

Acknowledging the existence of popular national languages took a rather long time and was accompanied by uncertainty and controversy. The prestige of Latin culture and of the Latin language—declared "eternal"[318]—is still towering. Dante's poetic instinct urges him to compose verse in Italian, but his intellectual upbringing makes him write *De Vulgari Eloquentia* and other works in Latin. For the time being, language theory can be done in no other language. Many humanists and Renaissance men are persuaded that the language of the vulgar will never have its "Ciceroes" or "Virgils."[319] The language of "the vulgar" is also repudiated by other "writers" (Castelvetro), by the adepts of neo-Latin poetry, etc.[320] A first Italian grammar remains in manuscript.[321]

Under such circumstances, the idea of "national literature" takes shape very slowly and with difficulty, through sporadic, discontinued initiatives. *Literature* continues to be made up of *lettres tant en Latin que Francayses* (1544).[322] *Prose della volgar lingua*—a program title—by P. Bembo comes before that (1525). But it seems that the initiative of explicit nationalization again belongs to a Frenchman, Claude de Seyssel, in the manuscript preface to his translation from Justin (1509). This is described as part of a plan of setting up a *literature en françoys* through "translations into French of books written in Greek and Latin."[323] The cultural sense is still dominant, if not the only one: *national literature = national culture*, viz. in the national language. The edict issues by François I at Villers-Cotterêts, that French be used in all official documents, is dated 1539. The idea of literary compositions of French nationality appears in this context: *les bonnes escriptures françoises*.[324] But the classical, exemplary text remains

La Défense et Illustration de la Langue Françoise by J. du Bellay (1549), which
leaves behind the translation phase and enters that of imitations based on
the classics, emulations, and original compositions in the native tongue.
The ideas are older (Italian),[325] but they become more and more current
and are completely assimilated in the second half of the sixteenth century
(Montaigne, I, 31; I, 54). *The Scripture in Englyshe* is written and claimed
in England in the same period (Thomas More, 1553).[326] In this respect, at
least two other important texts appear toward the end of the century:
Richard Puttenham, *The Arte of English Poesie* (1589) and Sir Philip Sidney, *Apologie for Poetrie* (1598). In Italy, the notion is translated by the
phrase "poetica volgare."[327] Thus consolidated, the idea begins to circulate.

The notion has several other notable facets. One of them is linked to
the celebrated historiography pattern sketched for the Middle Ages, *Translatio studii*. Letters migrated from Athens to Rome and thence—during the
modern age—to several European centers. One of these is Florence, *princi-
patus . . . litterae studiaque* (L. Bruni Aretino, *Laudatio Florentiae Urbi*).[328]
Florentinorum litteratura principes[329] blooms in this city. Another is Paris.
So there appears a local patriotism, a local, even national, literary pride,
visible especially in J. du Bellay. Even more significant is the discovery of
a so-called "indigenous" literary tradition. Due to the fervor created by the
"rebirth" of national literature, the existence of Celtic or Gaelic literature
is discovered, first in France (Jean Picard, *De prisce celtopaedia*, 1556). The
conclusion? *Humanae litterae* were cultivated in Gaul as well, not just in
Greece.[330] The rise, especially in the West, of vernacular languages—
mostly in the Church (translating the Bible is justified via patriotic arguments)[331]—has this claim-making sense, doubled by a subversive,
heterodox, often political one. In conclusion, "national literature" appears
in a polemical climate and has, from the outset, a patriotic, even "revolutionary" nature, but remains insubordinate to the dominant cultural tradition. It is the case especially of the German humanist supporters of *amor
litterarum et patriae* (*Gott und Vaterland*).[331b]

However, by force of circumstance, the idea of "national letters" is
little circulated and remains rather marginal. *Litterae* are, by tradition and
vocation, universal and universalist. The cultural space they configure—
against the backdrop of Latin as a world language and of universal Latin
culture—is homogenous, unitary, undifferentiated, almost limitless. The
formula *res litteraria* expresses it best: *Latinae rei litterariae universae*.[332] This,
in fact, is the first definition of *world literature*. *Rei litterariae* are universal
by definition. Their characteristic feature is an aspiration to totality and
encyclopedism.

The "Universal man" of the Renaissance is the symbol of this aspiration. Among his "creations" are "works" of every "genre," in "various languages and of various letters" (Giannozzo Maneti).[333] It is a view that is

not so "cosmopolitan" as it may seem, but, rather, cumulative, quantitative and, especially, egocentric and narcissistic, as it expresses the individual's pride at having achieved self-fulfillment, of being the free master of all his creations and goods, in as many fields of activity as possible. *Letters* are only one—one could say a minor one—of these accomplishments. The well-known *litterae humanae* are much more universal, in the substantial, ontological sense of the word. They are the true emblem of literary universalism of the Renaissance, based on the principle *humana species est in omnibus*.[334] All humans—and, therefore, all the literature they produce—belong to one and the same species. *Literature's* substantial universalism, in all the acceptations of the age, is, in fact, made possible and guaranteed by the universality of mankind.

The idea of a concrete universalism of literature, in time and space, begins to take shape in this spiritual climate. One form is the *consensus saeculorum universitas litteram*. Another, even more precise, sees all letters, especially the Latin ones, as a real form of universalism and, therefore, an objective, referential term of literary history. At least we believe this is the way in which the remark made by a French translator of Ovid (1556) can be interpreted, which refers to a literature *tant universelle que la Métamorphose d'Ovide*.[335] Finally, the invention of printing gives an enormous boost to the consciousness of literature's universal character, by making its unlimited spatial dissemination possible. H. Estienne praises the new "art" for having spread "to the great advantage of mankind, all over the world."[336] The same memorable idea is engraved on Gutenberg's headstone: "Serving all nations and languages." The printed *letter* can only be universal. Any opposite view, any obstacle of any kind, will deny its very essence, being, by definition, anti-literary.

Popular Letters

The question of popular letters continues to have, during the Renaissance and in humanist circles, the same predominantly linguistic cultural character it had in the Middle Ages. However, some accents and shades of meaning are new. The differences between popular spoken language and written language, particularly between national languages and Latin, will be brought out in bold relief. Thus, we find the first controversies and the first apologies for literary works, written in one of the national languages. The equation *national* = *popular*—well-entrenched and of universal circulation—also dates from this period.

Due to the fact that the dissociation "vulgar, native"[337] versus "cultured" language (the only one that confers authority and prestige) becomes more radical, the traditional opposition between *persone idiote e semplici* and *grandi scrittori* appears. The first category—also of medieval origin—makes it necessary that writing also be done—for the sake of spreading the gospel—"for the stupid people," as Deacon Coresi puts it in the Romanian culture, hence, the necessity of printing in his native tongue.[338] The tension remains high nevertheless. Still very tenacious, "grammatical" prestige is hostile to the ascent of national languages. English is still devoid of any written rules. "For Grammer it might have, but it needs it not; beeing so easie of it selfe."[339] Even if the popular oral language and the written one are acknowledged to be one and the same,[340] the cultured language continues to be seen as ideal. It is the only one that can be considered "artistic." Vulgar language is allowed into literature, but only a "vulgar language that is different from colloquial (*vulgar uso*)." It is therefore possible to write "lofty" poetry in such a "vulgar" language.[341] Previously, the same point had been made by Dante: Arnaldo Danielo *fu miglior fabbro del parlar materno* (*Purg.*, XXVI, 117). The difference between the everyday, practical use of the language and the literary usage is already clearly perceived and roundly expressed: sometimes "vulgar" expressions are not rendered in an artistic form (*art certain*).[342] They are to be polished some more.

The frequent but well-attested reversal of this traditional relation will contribute to the most significant mutation of all: the "living," "vulgar," "young and new" language is eventually declared superior to "dead" Latin.[343] This leads to the conclusion that *vulgare rimare* requires greater literary mastery than *versificare litterale* (Francesco Rinunccini).[344] Here we have a true birth certificate of the idea of popular literature. At any rate, the *cultivated/popular* typology, in both language (*vulgarem linguam o literata*) and literature is already set up. For the traditional classicizing mentality, the use of the popular language in literature is a real innovation. The content of culture begins to change. The discovery of "popular culture" is made, in fact, in the same period.[345]

It is not our present concern to study the appearance and development of literary themes and literary genres that are noncanonical, marginal, minor, of "popular" inspiration, contaminated by the "popular" spirit; nor is it to trace the resurgence, in one form or another, of "folk" heroes in the literature of the Renaissance and of Humanism. Nor are we preoccupied with the problem of mutual influences: from cultured to popular literature and the other way around. But it is important to note that under pressure from "popular letters" the concept of literature is enlarged, becoming less "cultured," therefore less rigid and canonical. The sum-total of letters is proportionally increased. The oral and the written—literature's two structural axes—once again reach a coexistential equilibrium. During the Reformation and the counter-Reformation, the "civilization" of the written word makes considerable inroads in the rural areas.[346] But the vitality of orality—and especially of its self-awareness—is again demonstrated, in the midst of the glorification of learned, written letters.

An important contribution in this sense is made by printing. It has been seen that written and printed culture both kills off yet saves oral culture. At any rate, it does not finish off oral culture, though it may push it into the shadows. The best proof is provided by the printing of popular books, by the emergence of gossip literature (with no mention of author, publisher, date or place of publication). Actually, printing encourages the apparition and development of this new species of "paraliterature." The species will gradually work out its own definition and theoretical reason for being.

ESTHETICIZING LETTERS

"Beautiful Letters"

The acceptations reviewed so far do not fully exhaust the idea of literature during the Renaissance and Humanism. New significations are added to its fundamental cultural meaning, leading to a richer terminology. *Letters* are not only "human," "liberal," "good," but also "beautiful." The formula appears, first of all, as a prolongation of the traditional identity of good-beautiful, in the ancient spirit (*kalokaghaton*), which makes its vigorous comeback in the spiritual life of the Renaissance. Another cause is that the sensitivity and esthetic conscience of the cultured man of the age are considerably enhanced. Due to their harmony, perfection, and emotional power, the *letters* are also *pulchrae*. As it provides a new definition of letters and literature, this lexical initiative is quite important. The acceptation, quickly established, becomes a fundamental, "classical" one, which will undergo considerable development to the present day. In a sense, *beautiful letters* are already a constant of the idea of literature.

The link between education, study, and the beautiful—only sporadically, fugitively anticipated in the Middle Ages—is now generalized in every domain of cultural activity. Erasmus is one of the most active champions of the new terminology. He often refers to *pulcherrimae disciplinae;*[347] alternative formulae: *pulchrarum litterarum studii;*[348] *politioris littera,*[349] *blanda humanitatis studia.*[350] The doctrine—fixed under the emblem *De politia literaria libri septem* by Angelo Decembrio (1462, 1540)—is of great semantic clarity: *literariam politiam appellati . . . humanitatis studii* (1562 ed., p. 99). The superlative for a learned humanist is *perpulchre instructus.*[351] He is a cognoscente of all the kinds of "letters" reviewed by us so far.

A decisive contribution to the history of this meaning of literature is, however, the one made by the lexis of modern languages. In French, the notion is definitively assimilated as *belles lettres humaines* (Brantôme),[352] *belles sciences, bonnes lettres et la politesse de ces sciences;*[353] in Italian: *lo studio delle belle lettere.*[354] The idea will be so closely associated with the study and culture of "letters," that in the nineteenth and twentieth centuries the equivalent of *literarum studii* will be *les belles lettres*, listed as such even by modern dictionaries (Robert, s.v.). This is the best possible proof of its transformation into a true semantic invariant of the idea of literature.

The transition from *politioris litterae* to *politioris literatura*, occurring in the same period, brings *les belles lettres* even closer to *literatura*. A first (?) attestation in Pico della Mirandola, in a much quoted letter to Ermolao Barbaro ("He who is not conversant with literature is not human," *politioris literatura*)[355] is followed by the frequent use of the term by Erasmus,[356] *Politioris literatura, perpolita literatura,*[357] *tenuioris literatura.*[358] In its so-called "original" form—included in a long title as well—*politioris literatura* also has a militant, polemical meaning: a "broom" to sweep away the champions of barbarism and the enemies of humanism.[359] But the intense cultural meaning remains predominant.

Beautiful Literature

The implicit or explicit evolution of "beautiful letters" from the "cultural" to the "esthetic" is one of the important moments in the biography of the idea of literature. As we know, this was anticipated, more or less sporadically, during Antiquity and the Middle Ages. But it is only now that "letters" frequently and explicitly claim to have an esthetic dimension. Beauty becomes an important element of the definition of letters and of literature. This is the real origin of the idea of "beautiful literature," in its modern, belletristic sense, thought out and defined as such. The process of consolidating the idea is irreversible. The direction of its development tends, increasingly, to esthetic radicalism, to purism and autonomy.

This progression (in point of fact, a genuine mutation) is strongly felt even at the level of written and oral expression. Oral beauty is—by definition—rhetorical, a notion that is applied to both oratory proper and poetry (*art de rhétorique*) or the poet (*rhétoriqueur, grand rhétoriqueur*).[360] At this level, tradition is not disrupted and theoretical innovation is insignificant. Not so with *letter*. Its beautifying begins in the Middle Ages, for the time being in the domain of calligraphy. The idea of *scrittura bella, belissimo scritto, belle et sa lettre et ses traits* is continued in the Renaissance, when the theoretical treatment it enjoys is more committed and more profound. Actually, this is the age of the great calligraphy treatises, of "guides," "arts," and "sciences" of beautiful penmanship. To exemplify, here are a few titles: Geoffroy Tory, *L'Art et la Science de la due et vraie proportion des lettres* (1529), Giambattista Palatino, *Libro nuovo d'imparare a scrivere* (1540), Giovan Francesco Cresci, *Il perfetto Scrittore* (1570), Pedro de Madariaga, *Honra de escribanos* (1565), Francisco Lucas, *Arte de escriver* (1577), etc.[361] The artistic character of printing is not nullified by typography, which, on the contrary, becomes preoccupied with it (a sample quotation from Trissino: *bellissimo modo di fare con la stampa*).[362]

The synonyms of *belles lettres* are a first sign of the ever more wide-spread estheticizing of letters. The formula is increasingly felt to be predominantly or exclusively scholarly, high-brow. In fact, the process works at a deeper level: due to its ambiguous meaning ("beautiful"/"good"), *bellus* no longer renders the idea of esthetic achievement and satisfaction accurately. Thus, a series of equivalents, felt to be more specific, become used more and more often: *ad literarum elegantium,*[363] *elegantioribus disciplinis*[364] (let us also remember *Elegantiarum linguae latinae* by L. Valla), *literarum amoenitati,*[365] *amoeniores literae,* etc. Also, by natural contamination, *elegantionis literaturae*[366] = *beautiful literature,* a term that will make good. It remains to this day one of the essential definitions of literature. The tendency is also at work in modern languages, wherein terms such as *poli(s),* *politure, concinnità,* and *soavità e belezza* increasingly take over the emphatic meaning "beautiful" of *belle-bellissime lettere.*

The dissociation—ever more currently made—between *litterae . . . bonae et elegantes dictae*[367] is another indicator of a conscious estheticizing of letters reflected in a terminology that aims at being as proper and accurate as possible. "Good" and "elegant" are no longer seen as synonyms. The latter term seems much more appropriate for the idea of "beautifully written letters." The process can be seen in "modern" letters as well: *bonnes lettres et élégantes, belles et bonnes lettres, doctes et élégans écrits en belles manières,*[368] *bene e leggiadramente scrivere.*[369] It has other important consequences as well.

The most weighty one, undoubtedly, is that *belles (élégantes) lettres* are taken to mean beautiful writing, a beautiful composition or work, in the "belletristic" sense of today. Such associations have existed, sporadically, ever since Antiquity. But it is only now that the idea gets to be full-blown and stabilized and that it is used frequently and efficiently by publicists: *la beauté des lettres,*[370] *scritti belli* (B. Castiglione, I, 29), *bella scrittura.*[371] "Beautiful book," which appears at the same time, has an identical meaning: *beauls livres* (Rabelais, *Garg., Prol.*), *les beaux livres nouveaux.*[372] The distinguishing sign is the beautiful form, *pulchris velaminis* (Petrarch, Boccaccio),[373] respectively, style: *literarum ornamenta.*[374] The praise of "adorned" style, which is to reach its climax in the next baroque period, also becomes quite common. The rich terminology is already significant. Other equivalent formulae, *belle contexture* (Montaigne, II, 10) and *belles allegations* (J. Amyot)[375] give an even wider circulation to the definition of beautiful composition and beautiful expression. The definition tends to become more specialized, more nuanced. The process can be observed in the differentiation of genre as well: *belles histoires, dialogue très élégant, belle la comedie, bellezze della poesia,* etc. In the course of our biography, we shall often come across these phrases of an *incipit* value.

Literature or Poetry?

The advancements of esthetic consciousness, more and more clearly formulated, have one other important consequence. It is one of the most
significant occurrences in the evolution of the idea of literature. Latently
anticipated from the very outset, the separation and then open opposition
between *poetry* and *literature* is a "turntable" in this biography. The process
is of capital importance: *poetry* tends to express, ever more exactly and
completely, the sum-total of the "artistic" values of the *letter*, from writing
pure and simple to the most sophisticated forms of literary composition,
while *literature* is increasingly directed toward its original, essential, and
peculiar domain, culture, to which the syntagm *beautiful letters* refers with
predilection. Poetry takes over, ever more insistently, the totality of the
esthetic functions of the letter, while *literature* continues to claim as its
own a propensity for culture, intellectual and scholarly work, heredity.
Thus, *poetry* will be able to devise a history of its own, ever more detached
from and opposed to the idea of *literature*. This concerns us only to the
extent that poetry tends to break away from literature and to recuperate
it, to dislodge it from its dominant position and, eventually, as *anti-litera-
ture*, to contest it.

From the Renaissance on, therefore, the essential esthetic and literary
problems will be, more and more frequently, taken over by *poetry*. The
discovery (in every sense of the word) of Aristotle's *Poetics* was the immediate impulse. Lacking an equally prestigious term of reference, "beautiful
literature" misses a historical opportunity to undergo theoretical treatment. From this point of view, *literature* will only have a partial history,
almost marginal, tangental to the new esthetic and literary conceptions.
This does not mean that it totally abandons the historical scene. Literature
continues to defend and affirm emphatically the incontestable cultural
value and functions of *letters*. Its literal condition remains the essential
prerequisite of any "poetic" or "literary" work or theory. For this reason,
the "cultural" definition of *literature* will dominate and interfere for centuries with the still hesitant, ambiguous, and unsettled idea of *poetry*. This
phenomenon can be clearly observed now, in the Renaissance period, but
will be even more visible in the forthcoming stages.

The dominant outlook, then, continues to be the traditional, cultural,
"humanist" one: *poetry* is assimilated by literature, by encyclopedic knowledge. It constitutes a "written doctrine" (*doctrine escripte*),[376] a "science"
(*science*).[377] The formula is currently used in this period in England (*learning, good learning, humane learning*),[378] Italy (*flos scientiarum*, identical ideas
in Petrarch, Boccaccio, etc.),[379] and Germany (*seminaria omnium doctrinarum*), etc.[380] "Poetry is a part of letters;"[381] *poetica virtute et studio humanitatis* (A. Manicelli, 1518) are closely knit together.[382] The definitions of

the poet as a "cultured" and "literate" man are equally frequent: *litterati poete*,[383] that is, "learned," a "scholar," *escolier* like F. Villon. The poet is *learned*,[384] a "grammarian" (*grammatici poetales*),[385] a source of knowledge, like Virgil, from whom "any science" (*ogni dottrina*)[386] can be learned. Without any doubt, *poetry* = *literature*. The notions are still rigorously synonymous.

It follows that the first cracks in this all-too-solid façade are all the more significant. As seen before, the vein of popular, vernacular poetry has proved its vitality since medieval times. So "poetry" can also be written outside the exclusive, restrictive world of letters. The folk spirit, always effervescent, even if crushed by the marble slab of Latin culture, is the best of proofs. Thus, "the grace of vulgar poetry"[387] is being acknowledged— even if not very frequently—beginning with this period. When *tractatum poetarum* (*Fam.*, IV, 15) is translated by "poetic literature,"[388] the modern versions of Petrarch attribute to the author exactly such a thought. Even if it is still in a state of conceptual confusion, the idea is now actually given thought and expression. In its turn, the status of the poet goes through important, albeit incipient, mutations. For the time being, a poet continues to be, essentially, a "writer"[389] of an indistinct kind, even a transcriber, an editor of texts. The alternation *litterator/scrittore*[390] is also frequent. In the Renaissance, there is still no accurate delimitation of an *escrivain* from a man of science, of an astrologer from an astronomer, hence, the great importance of the first delineations of this kind, though they be quite incidental and sporadic. It is nevertheless a sign that the dissociation of ideas is at work; *poeta et humanista*,[391] "humanist and poet,"[392] "grammarian and poet" (1559),[393] "writer and poet"[394] are well-delimited categories. The last distinction is especially sharp and decisive. The essential quality of the poet who writes poems (*poeta poetando*)[395] is that of being at the same time a "man of culture" (*buon letterato*) and a "poet of value" (*di valore poeta*),[396] a "good writer" (like Virgil and Homer),[397] a "noble writer" (in the same sense).[398] The coefficient of personal, original creation is also considered: "perfect humanist" and "unique poet" (*singolare poeta*).[399] It becomes increasingly evident that poetry is looked upon as a separate activity, progressively detached from the original cultural trunk, that is, from *literature*.

Literary Art

The Renaissance is the age when the following fundamental acceptation of *literature* begins to be formulated: *the art of writing* = *literary art*. This is not devoid of ambiguities and obscurities. "Writing" necessarily oscillates—the situation will prove to be typical and recurrent—between "literature" and "poetry." "Literary art," in its turn, means to write or, respectively, to compose "beautiful" poetry and prose. Thus, the consciousness of the estheticizing of letters takes one step forward. The meaning of "literary art" is that of a more or less technical concern, one that might be called a "workshop preoccupation" today. It is, at any rate, a meaning pointing to literary "craftsmanship," "mastery," ability, talent or "industry." Thus, the nominal expression appears in this very period, long before Paul Valéry: *an industry of writers* (B. Castiglione, I, 44: *"industrie de' scrittori"*).

A strong accent is put on the idea of productive activity; "composition," the "modality of writing books,"[400] the "composition of works."[401] A writer is by definition a "book composer" (Boccaccio, *La Teseide*) and literary works ("writings," *scrittura*)[402] are well-written, that is, artistic, compositions. The idea is rendered by the recurrent phrase "beautiful writing" (*beau escrire*),[403] indiscriminately applied to any sort of literary writings. It is closely associated with those of "form" (*la forma dello scrivere*)[404] and "artifice" and the conception is preeminently rhetorical. Oratory resorts to "artificial," rather than "natural" words. To write *artificiosamente* means to use artistic devices characteristic of "literary art" (that is, "artificial").

Poetry tends to define this "literary art" and to become identified with it. In the Middle Ages, the problem is still abstract, of a taxonomic and gnoseological character. In the Renaissance, however, *poetry* is increasingly referred to as the idea and technique of "literary art." This soaring prestige can be explained, to a great extent, by the great impact of rediscovered ancient poetry. In a current acceptation, poetry continues to be a form of "writing" (*scribere unum carmen*),[405] of *dictaminis*,[406] hence the German *Dichtung*, the equivalent of *Skriptura*.[407] But Petrarch has already noted (*Fam.*, I, 1) that there are various ways of writing, that writing—meaning literature—is not, in reality, a monolith, how poetry is exactly one of the strongly differentiated, peculiar ways of writing. Essentially, poetry is an "art" ("art itself").[408] It consists, on the one hand, of "writing lyrically,"[409] on the other, of adopting specific forms of expression: verse and rime. Hence, the ever more frequent definition "writings in verse" and "riming writings" (*scriptures en ryme*)[410] but not just any verse and rime, only "elegant and beautiful verses."[411] In this way, the ideas of art and esthetic emotion are recovered and integrated with *poetry. Literary art par excellence = poetry*. An equality that has a crucial importance for the destiny of the idea of literature, which, esthetically speaking, is relegated to a secondary, subordinated plane and subjected to constant devaluation.

Literary Versus Poetic Specificity

In this context—an enhanced self-consciousness and the estheticizing of letters—one can speak of the existence, even if in incipient form, of a literary "specificity." In the terms of the age, it is identified with "true," "genuine" (*vera*) literature. According to Erasmus, this can only be ancient literature.[412] This is another important contribution of the Renaissance to the biography of the idea of literature. The road is open due to the detachment of literature from the sacred. This trend, though decisive, is not sufficient. Nor is the separation from the domain of *culture*, specifically defined by the word *literature*, sufficient any more. *Literature* and *poetry* waver and the two ideas are often considered synonyms. The decisive step will only be taken when poetry tends to absorb and, especially, to define all the esthetic values of *literature*, hence, the appearance of a new, greatly enriched, and nuanced terminology.

The first observation is that the prestige of traditional definitions is as strong and tenacious as ever. Recurrent, for instance, in this period is the conception of poetry as "painting that speaks,"[413] in the spirit of the tradition instituted by *ut pictura poesis*. The formula is inoperative, as it looks for poetic specificity in another art. Nor does bowing to the "beautiful things of poetry"[414] add anything to the concept "beautiful letters," which has in the meantime become essential. If one looks at it from the general perspective of this biography, it will be seen that the idea of "poetic specificity" can only be glimpsed, for the time being, as a formula typical of the French Pleiade: "good and true poetry" (*la bonne et vraye Poësie*.)[415] "True" is now taken to mean real, essential, specific, *per se*, in itself, "good work in itself" (*buena en sí*).[415] Dante had also spoken of a letter *per lo suo uso*.[417] The idea of "poetic essence" is not alien to Renaissance Platonicism either. Maurice Scève even invokes this *essence* in a poem. The only problem is specifying just what this essence is. The most common answer refers us to the natural character of poetry: "a purely natural trend of imagination," a "whim of nature" (according to P. Aretino's celebrated formula),[418] a "naive writing" (Ronsard: *nayve scripture*).[419] The natural thing is the most beautiful (Montaigne, III, 3). The consideration given to popular poetry is justified in a similar way.

Praising "poetic" quality and referring ever more often to the "poetic" attribute are clear signs that the idea of poetic specificity has ripened. In humanistic Latin, it is dissociatively defined *scribere rhetoricaliter et non poeticaliter*.[420] In their turn, modern languages contain phrases such as: *poeticamente*,[421] *il modo dello scrivere poeticamente*,[422] *poétique* (Amyot; *livres poétiques*),[423] *poetical* (*meere Poeticall*).[424] But what is it exactly? What does "to write poetically" mean? Why can poetry be "culture" and "literature" no more? For the simple reason that it is primarily a form of *poiein*, of "genesis," of *fattura*, a *faciatura*,[425] in short, a "creation." One of the great esthetic discoveries of the Renaissance is that poetry is the fruit of creative fantasy, of the imagination. It follows that to justify imaginative literature becomes, so to speak, one of the imperatives of the day. This type of literature only provides fiction (Petrarch: *fingere id est componere, Senilia*, XII, 2), "ingenuous fictions," "imitations," in the ancient, productive sense of the word "by its nature, poetry is nothing but imitation."[426] Which is to say, inventions, creations in the spirit and sense of "nature," molded on it. Many other phrases anticipating this incipient awareness of a "specific" character are now in use such as *carminum structura*[427] and *ingeniorum historia*.[428] Poetry has a makeup of its own. Fabulation, imaginative poetic works can have a history of their own, therefore, they can have a literary history. This enriched terminology mirrors the obvious progress made by the literary spirit toward acknowledging the existence of a zone of its own within the sphere of letters.

The most important specific feature is still a matter of language. The first precise considerations of the poetic function of language—a most fecund and generous topic, the importance of which becomes ever greater as we advance towards the modern era—are also made during the Renaissance. First, the tradition of oral poetry and language is continued, the tradition of "vulgar" language and of *sermo cotidianus*. At the same time, there is a development of the conception of a cultivated language, opposed to the plebeian one, of the esthetic superiority of the written, cultivated style over the oral one.[429] "Writers are those people who . . . ennoble languages" (B. Varchi).[430] An even more important step: language is the organ of literature, poetry—the idea already sounds "modern"—is "made of words:"[431] *la poesia di parole*.[432] It "imitates with the tongue or with language.[433] All the considerations about poetic style (elegant, imagistic, ornamental, personal, "new," etc.), more and more frequent in this period, open the way for the Baroque. The parallel, autonomous symbolic language will be excluded by Classicism as being tautological. Once again, it proves very difficult to mark off the typological and the chronological aspects of the idea of literature. We are in a historical period in which this phenomenon becomes increasingly apparent.

The Autonomy of Literature: Progress

In the same period, almost all the modern terms relating to the idea of literature can be identified and followed closely (that is, in a documentary, philological manner) in texts. Still traditional, the terminology is often approximated, imprecise. But, even if their verbal label is, for the time being, imperfect, new meanings of the idea of literature have emerged. Their dissociative senses establish limits, mark off an autonomous area, which makes it possible for the idea of literature to be thought of in "autonomous" terms, to be considered "in itself." At any rate, in the last decades of the sixteenth century, the conception of poetry comes very close to the "artistic" or "esthetic" outlook.[434] Some of the methodological recommendations of the epoch, in fact, open up the same perspective: "Let him who wants to assess a thing weigh its peculiar features, and not alien elements."[435] In this respect, an important role is played in the Renaissance by Aristotle's distinction between fable and fiction, on the one hand, and oratory, history or science, on the other.[436] Thus, latently or explicitly, the principle of the dissociation of values and autonomization of literature made its appearance. From now on, literature will tend to assert, ever more forcefully, its independence from anything that does not belong to it organically.

The first—fundamental—dissociations are again those of the polar constituents of the idea of literature. Secular literature detaches itself from sacred literature, which it comes to contest as an expression of divine inspiration, of Platonic "poetic fury" (*Ion*), a thesis of great prestige during the Renaissance, sarcastically repudiated ("folly").[437] Consequently, the human nature of poetic inspiration will be constantly and insistently proclaimed (G. Fracastoro, L. Castelvetro, T. Tasso, etc.). If the first poets were theologians, now they are mere "lay sacerdots" (A. Mussato). Their poetry is of "profane use."[438] Orality, with its rhetoric and many *arts de bien dire*, is challenged by the *arts de bien écrire* and especially by the unprecedented success of printing, which vindicates written expression for good. The same tendency is also consolidated by a prolongation of the tradition of figurative expression.[439]

Against the backdrop of the well-known, open conflict between *literature* and *poetry*, what will be termed "autonomy of values" in the future, can be seen with increasing clarity. It is, in fact, an expression of the efforts of poetry to break away from its opposite, irreducible, value: culture. Study or natural instinct? Letters or personal "genius"? The dissociation already leads to a typology of poetry, classifiable into two "species:" one originating in an inner impulse (*interna agitazione*), another in "study and artistic discipline" (L. Bruni Aretino).[440] The former belongs to creative literature, the latter to literary studies. Such doublets as *litteratura* versus *studi liberali* (L. Bruni Aretino), *littérature . . . et savoir* (E. Dolet)[441] are most relevant to the separation of the two domains.

It therefore becomes possible to acknowledge two types of poetry, one "literary," the other "natural." The former abides by rules and norms; the latter—spontaneous, natural—provides art with rules, as with Homer. In *Degl' heroici furori* (1585), G. Bruno formulates this thesis with exemplary clarity, against those called *regolisti di poesia*, "real beasts."[442] Poetry goes beyond rules (Montaigne, II, 17). Thus, the opposition "precepts, rules, doctrines" versus "natural poet" is increasingly encountered in France,[443] Italy (A. F. Doni, Fr. Bocchi),[444] etc. The praise of popular poetry, seen as "perfectly natural," should be examined in the same context. It is not "artistically perfect" (Montaigne I, 54), but merely "instinct of nature,"[445] a "naive" creation. Romanticism will rediscover and reuse this very old and basic duality: natural poetry/artistic poetry. Other concepts are linked to the natural inspiration theory, more and more frequent in the period:

invention, fiction (Boccaccio; *fictiones poeticae*, *De Genealogia Deorum*, XV, 8); even the notion of the ("artistic") "lie" enjoys widespread circulation.

In its turn, the theory of literary languages is host to other important dissociations. The object is the same, the method differs. The autonomization of poetry becomes possible when traditional classification and categories—*poetry/prose* and *poetry/verse* are left behind. Breaking away from *letters*, poetry embarks on a course of its own: It can be equally well expressed in prose.[446] The opposite idea is born the same way: When there is no poetry, all that is left is prose: "One may be a poet without versing and a versifier without poetry."[447] This discovery, insistently underlined, heralds another new concept: "prose poetry," "poetic prose." It will develop in a subsequent, modern phase of the idea of literature.

The process also has psychological effects, instrumental in defining poetic emotion. This is distinct from the satisfactions provided by study (Petrarch's "pleasure given by books" remains ambiguous, *Fam.*, III, 18) and boils down to one single idea: pleasure (*litteraturae delicies*).[448] Pleasure, frequently invoked by the translators and commentators of Aristotle's *Poetics* (A. Riccoboni, F. Robortello, L. Castelvetro, etc.: *delectation, delectare, dilletare*) becomes a key concept.[449] "Pleasure is the purpose of poetry."[450] But even as it becomes radical, tending toward hedonism and "voluptuousness," new shades of meaning appear: gratuitousness, contemplation, *De l'oysifveté* (Montaigne, I, 8), play, and *le passetemps* (III, 3), and especially unaccountable, ineffable emotion: *grâce, douceur, je ne sais quoi* (*non se qué, non so che*).[451] This last aspect especially will undertake very significant developments.

The dissociation of arts and values is also clearly formulated. Poetry occupies a fluctuating but distinct place in the classification and enumeration of the liberal arts. The *letter* is the only accurate criterion: *non in litteris modo, sed in musica, pictura* . . . (1515),[452] that is, one that is still purely empirical. Instead, there are a series of dissociations, which will become classical, that abound in justifications, implications and consequences. Despite our general lack of knowledge, it is a fact that they are all introduced as early as the Renaissance: poetry/reason (Montaigne, I, 36), truth/beauty (A. Poliziano to M. Ficino: "You are looking for truth in the classics, I for beauty"),[453] liberal arts/utility (*liberali litterarum altera est, altera rei utilitari*),[454] poetry/life (G. Veronese: "Life has one purpose, poetry another"),[455] wisdom/literature (*sapientis non litteratura seu scriptura*).[456] Other distinctions that will become increasingly commonplace appear in the same way; poetry/rhetoric, poetry/philosophy, poetry/morals, poetry/history, etc. The references are more numerous than one might suspect. In fact, all of the "apologies of poetry," frequent at the time, written by Sir Philip Sidney, Sir John Harrington, Samuel Daniel, Sir Thomas Elyot, and also by Boccaccio, L. B. Alberti, Enea Silvio Piccolomini, etc., are set up on the same basis. It is a generous theme that becomes the object of specialized research.[457] Poetry is no longer saved only as an effective form of theology, of great persuasive power, but is also acknowledged as a specific, autonomous constituent of culture.

THE HETERONOMY OF LITERATURE

The terms that define the opposite condition of literature are equally "modern" and—within a biography like this one, conceived of as a unit, with a unique line of development—relevant in retrospect. Seen from this angle, the biography is subject to extraliterary contexts and determinations, having heterogenous contents, frameworks or conditions of development. Today, this situation is rendered by the term "heteronomy." Since Antiquity and the appearance of the idea of literature, this invasion and domination of extraliterary values has been a marked phenomenon. Now it becomes crystal clear, as all its main trends of development are perfectly delineated.

"The Republic of Letters"

This term, coined in the Middle Ages, is widely circulated during the Renaissance. It defines another essential dimension of literature: its communitary character, *letters* as a well-defined cultural and social collective institution. The corresponding formula, *litteraria Republica*, seems to have been used, for the first time during the age, by the humanist Francesco Barbaro (6 July 1417).[458] It is then widely circulated, due to the patronage of Erasmus, under many terminological variants such as *litteraria civitas*, *politia litteraria, orbis litteratus, sodalitas litteraria*, and *republica scholastica*. Modern languages take over the idea under the forms *république des lettres*, *republic of letters, commonwealth of learning, repubblica letteraria* or *litterale*, and *académica república*. Its meaning develops in four converging directions.

A first acceptation—the one most closely linked to the content and essential vocation of *letters*—voices the aspiration to encyclopedism and universal knowledge, to all the data of written culture. The "city of letters" is the space wherein all the letters of the world are or can be accumulated, cultivated, systematized.[459] Their universal character is rendered by a precise figurative phrase. Once again, we come across the idea of "world" literature and culture, ideologically consolidated: *literaturam universam Poeseos*.[460]

The second acceptation is that of a moral and intellectual commonwealth, of group or caste solidarity—in friendship and spirit—of humanists (Pico della Mirandola: "Between us there is a bond stronger than blood.")[461] The "city" or "republic" of letters is an *eruditorum societas*,[462] a *literarium concilium*, a "community of liberal disciplines," a "society of good letters," animated by the thought of a noble common mission. The fervor of this ideal changes humanism into a kind of lay religion. It is a collective consciousness, setting up an ideal republic, capable of giving birth, through general consensus, to a prestigious current of opinion, an international spiritual force, that of the humanists of great learning, exerted through the medium of Latin.[463]

The institutional, "corporate" dimension must also be taken into account. The "city of letters" involves an elaborate network of "societies" and "academies," of communications venues and channels, beginning with the humanist printing press—a real technical and intellectual club. Dimensions such as "organizing" and "constitution" are inherent in its definition.[464] Group consciousness is the same thing as "literary life," *litteratorum cohors*,[465] the community of men of letters, held together by common ideals and close epistolary ties. Printing gives an even greater boost to dialogue and intellectual exchange across national boundaries.

For all these reasons, the "city of letters" is universal (*universae Reipublicae literariae*), a universal, cosmopolitan "realm of the spirit." This idea, with ancient and medieval roots, is backed by several firmly defined conceptions: the universal nature of the human spirit (M. Palmieri); the unique reality of human genius (Vittorino da Feltre);[466] and the communion of great minds across boundaries of time and space, hence the solidarity among "men of letters from any country, any century, of any profession."[467] A *concordia mundi*, embracing all nations, is thus achieved. Finally, the humanist's consciousness of himself as a "citizen of the world" is energetically affirmed, in the spirit of a resurrected ancient cosmopolitanism: (Erasmus: *Ego mundi civis esse cupio*; G. Bruno; speaking of Sir Philip Sidney: "A citizen and scholar of the world)."[468] Letters, wherever cultivated or whose praise is sung, are the humanist's only fatherland. The very term *cosmopolitan* ("citizen of the world") was coined in this period (G. Postel, 1560,[469] H. Estienne, 1578.)[470]

Society

On the social plane, *letters* also acquire new meanings, due to the influence (to a certain extent decisive) of the new developments in courtly life, leading to demands and expectations that are far more complex than the medieval ones. Stress is increasingly laid on sociability, on *letters* as a civic instrument, regulating social intercourse and granting social status. The social dimension of culture and literature is granted careful and nuanced recognition.

The age naturally inherits from Antiquity and the Middle Ages the classical social etymology of *liberal* letters, characteristic of *free* people,[471] worthy of such a condition,[472] at times seen to be as important as "high birth." The educational moral and social function of *human letters* is also traditionally viewed. *Studia humanitas* means *urbanitas* and *civilitas*.[473] They fight off "barbarism" (*vitrix barbaries*),[474] prepare man for a "civil," civilized, even fashionable life, after the *Il Cortegiano* (B. Castiglione) formula. *Politia literaria* (Angelo Decembrio) is the expression of just such a program.

Civilis cultura, civil learning[475] is the supreme ideal of the pedagogue of the age. It aims at molding man for family life and for the life of the city, as citizen (P. Paolo Vergerio, Vittorino da Feltre, L. B. Alberti, etc.).[476] The confrontation between the contemplative and the active life is heightened in the Renaissance, with the clash between *literarum otium* and *publica obligatio* at the core (L. Bruni Aretino).[477] "Letters" are increasingly preferred to "arms,"[478] *cedunt arma literis*. The social, moral and cultural stratification implied in such a division is, in its turn, rendered through two symbols: the "Quill" and the "Sword."[479]

Mention should also be made of some principles of social organization, favorable to such activities—viewed, of course, from the perspective of *letters*. The preeminently humanistic milieu is the ideal society of books, the "family of books" (Petrarch, *Fam.*, III, 18). Its universal dimension—the "City of/good/letters"—encompasses the entire planet.[480] The ancient myth of the poet-shepherd reappears in J. Sannazzaro's *L. Arcadia* (1504), a pastoral, utopian romance with a Renaissance view of the "golden age." More practical, more realistic now, however, are the new "book" institutions: public libraries (C. Salutati asks for them as early as 1339)[481] and poetic-literary Academies.[482] The ancient tradition of granting the status of official court poet is also continued. One form of social promotion is the title of *poeta laureatus*. Its erosion by satire (J. du Bellay, *Le poète courtisan*) also becomes inevitable.

Ample development can be seen in the field of the dissemination, reception and success of *letters*. The notion "literary public" (1538–1539)[483] dates back to this period: "The public, by which I mean the community of book lovers."[484] Mottoes are a *chose noblement populaire*, as everybody can understand them.[485] The size of this public is enormously enlarged by the use of printing, by the publications of the Reformation, by the ever greater popularity of *colportage*, hence, the new slogan, "No cottage without a book" (S. Brandt, 1498).[486] The "ordinary folk"[487] and the "not very literate citizens"[488] are taken into account, too. Humanists almost form a *Tiers Etat* (1598).[489] Needless to say, literary success and glory are not novel discoveries, or new aspirations, but such a phrase as "typographic glory," openly opposed to "military glory," (H. Estienne)[490] is entirely typical of the age. Poetic fame is commented on impassionedly and with considerable persuasion (Petrarch, *Fam.*, I, 2; *De remediis utriusque fortunae*). Those who denigrate it are fought off.[491]

We are in a period when the profession of letters and "literary life"—

with its "satisfactions" and "nuisances" (in L. B. Alberti's words, *commodis/incommodis*)[492]—become the objects of lively controversy. The poet's suffering and calamitous life are increasingly brought into the limelight (Petrarch, *Fam.*, I, 1). The motif can be met in E. Dolet, M.-A. Muret, L. G. Giraldi, etc. Elements of social criticism also make their appearance: any milieu becomes "hateful" to an author if it is not favorable to letters (H. Buschig).[493] It is now that the dark image of the poet as a social victim—a beggar living from hand to mouth, besieged by every possible ailment—begins to take shape.[494]

Economy

During the Renaissance and Humanism, *letters* have not only social, but also economic connotations. *Res litteraria* are part of the "business world." Historically speaking this is a crucial watershed: the awareness of literature's economic value and its relevance, merely budding in the Middle Ages, clarifies its aims and the methods for achieving them.

The theory and practice of the "professional writer," of the "master writers" (*maîtres-écrivains*) continue; artisans typical of the pre-printing era, they are grouped into corporations. Writing is still a profitable trade, one that can be learned. This accounts for the countless handbooks, previously alluded to, such as Lodovico Vincentino, *La Operina di . . . da imparare a scrivere lettere cancellaresca* (1523), Pedro de Madariaga, *Libro Subtilíssimo intitulado Honra de Escrivanos* (1565), etc. This category comprises not only paid secretaries and copiers, but also calligraphers who deal in illuminated manuscripts for private, aristocratic, or royal collections (Federico da Urbino, Matei Corvin [Mathias I Corvinus], etc.).

The economic event of crucial importance, however, is the invention of printing. The invention spreads very quickly, particularly for commercial reasons. Printing brings two essential changes to the economics of letters: cheaper, more numerous writings, and increased productivity, leading to higher profits. Its cultural and ideological import is to be felt later, produced only by the general semantic context of *letteres*. In fact, the great profits to be derived from the industrialization of printing are received with reserve, at least with mixed feelings. The main objection is that of the *liberal arts*, which continue to hold trade, however useful and lucrative, in great disdain (Montaigne, I, 24). Humanist typesetters, interested especially in philology, in the purity of texts, also put up resistance. "Illiterate," mistake-prone typesetters are severely rebuked.[495]

However, the profit-making principle gets the upper hand. Printing is able to produce a much sought-after piece of "merchandise," considerably cheaper than a manuscript copy, hence, the desire to increase productivity (still only a run of 200–300 copies can be achieved).[496] Speed is increased, proofreading and the number of proofreaders are reduced, leading to a conflict that is to become fundamental between quality and quantity; hence, the "not undeserved reputation [of the printing press] of corrupting books. . . ." (J. Lipsius).[497] This is the origin of a literary hierarchy: the commercial, industrial, for profit (cf. P. Aretino, *l'industria della pena*, "Muses need money")[498] and the cultural elitist. Commercial, utilitarian arguments become more and more persuasive, and account books and calculation handbooks are far more necessary to merchants, who are not at all interested in "philosophy."[499] The unknown factor of the ordinary reader also interferes. Printing "gives even the poorest of people a possibility of acquiring a personal library, at little cost."[500] The professional division of literary work is also accelerated, as categories are further defined ("chronicler," "poet," "storyteller," "writer," "copier," "translator").[501]

Two other "economic" elements also gain entrance for the first time into the sphere of letters and literature. One is publicity, advertising, stimulating sales through the use of catalogues and notices.[502] It is now, we daresay, that the concept *bestseller* is formed, at the Frankfurt am Main book fair, which will later become an even more important European cultural institution. The other is the concept of literary property, underwritten by the printer, a right sanctioned through a "privilege" that has become in modern times "copyright." The first such privilege is granted in Venice in 1492, the first typographic signature dates from 1457.[503] It is only now that the notion "plagiarism" acquires a specific meaning, similarly that of "author's rights"—payment and a specific number of copies.[504]

All these are especially characteristic of Western Europe. In the Romanian principalities—in the East, generally—books are still extremely scarce, not to say expensive. In the fifteenth century, a book cost one thousand *aspers*, one-third the cost of a mountain. In the sixteenth century, one paid "eight hundred and fifty aspers, one horse and twelve sheep for two books."[505] In this domain, *letters* have mostly a barter value.

Ideology

In its turn, the system of ideas, political, social and so on, of which *literature* is a part, is referred to in memorable phrases, some of which rise well above medieval formulae. The most important contribution, ideologically speaking, is the concept of *literature* as a "state," as a specific "regnum" of the spirit, separated from and even superior to other activities. This is the sense in which we think that we can interpret the modern translation *il regno delle lettere* of literature situated *supra humanas vires anteacta*.[506]

With this conviction, and most aware of the role they play in the "city of letters," Renaissance humanists claim for themselves not only a central position, but also the prerogative of direct intervention, in the spirit of *letters*, in organizing and governing the city. They ask that the state be ruled by an enlightened prince, a protector of *good letters*, acting as royal or imperial counselor. This way, the ideology of enlightened despotism and of cultural patronage is born. As we shall see, it will become extremely topical again in the eighteenth century. The idea is expressed with some insistence, especially by Erasmus.[507] In their moment of religious fervor, Renaissance men of letters believe themselves to be the peers of . . . the secretaries of the Apostles.[508] The edict issued by Louis XII in France (1513) that makes the printing trade legitimate and at the same time orders it to print only "good, salutary doctrines,"[509] is typical in this sense. Kings are inculcated with pacifist ideas. Erasmus, a real *columnist* of the age, is hyperactive. *Letters* condemn *arms* openly.[510] Two conceptions of utmost importance tower over the intellectual life of the period.

At the very core of humanist-renascentist "ideology" is the consciousness of universal progress, through and for the sake of *letters*. All the references speak of the "flowering" or "revival" of letters, or progress *de mieux en mieux*,[511] of the advantage to be gained from printing "to the benefit of mankind everywhere."[512] The idea of an ascendant, infinite literary development is now given one of the most original formulations. The sense is overtly or covertly polemical: anticulture, antibarbarism, as in Joannes Murmelius, whom we have quoted before: *Scoparius . . . in barbarei propugnatores . . .* (1518). Despite current prejudice, St. Teresa of Avila asks for *letras* for *las mujeres* as well.[513] This is feminism budding in an unlikely context.

The idea of freedom—already vaguely present in the Middle Ages, but gaining, due to the Reformation, in clarity and power of impact—is more and more closely associated with literature and has ever greater impact in this field. This is one of the seminal ideas of the age, which all reformers invoke: "freedom of speech," "freedom of expression,"[514] etc. By contrast, repression, in the form of *Indices librorum prohibitorum*, accompanies, like a dark and seemingly eternal shadow, the idea of the freedom of letters. Looked at from this somber perspective, they become "suspect," "prohibited," "damned."[515] The vocabulary of repression, which will rise to considerable heights, made its ominous appearance with the counter-Reformation. The first humanist casualties (Etienne Dolet, burned at the stake) are the victims of this grim, totalitarian mentality.

HIERARCHY IN LITERATURE

The Renaissance and Humanism continue to set up literary hierarchies according to the principles devised in the Middle Ages. The main trends will be inevitably the same, with some particularities characteristic of the age. The essential value-criterion—the sacred on top, the profane at the bottom—is not changed. Once more, sacrality is the uppermost, supreme, superlative quality: *sanctissima litterarum religio*.[516] The *Iliad* is the sacred poem by definition. Printing, in its turn, moves even farther away, as far as value is concerned, from orality. Praise of writing is continued and amplified by the eulogizing of the printing process.[517] The printed book is declared greatly superior to oral recitation. The balance is definitively tipped in favor of the printed letter.

Enhanced literary consciousness and the diversification of literary life give a fresh boost to the establishment of the modern scale of values. Literature and the world of letters become accustomed to affirming and acknowledging some values more frequently and openly, while ignoring or contesting others. Such hierarchies are tantamount to clearly formulated value-judgements. Empirical literary criticism begins with such utterances as *primum rei literarie deus*, "the greatest man of letters."[518] Villon is "the best Parisian poet," etc.[519] The concept of literary totality is rent asunder: *optimas literas* on top, *mediocris litteratura* at the bottom.[520] There are "good" and "bad" *letters*, texts, writings.[521] The *nobilitas literata*[522] principle no longer has unanimous application. The mere quality of *letter* stops being sufficient. Value ratings are introduced, resulting in a number of consequences. The "best" writers become "models," through an inevitable cultural and pedagogical reconsideration. The canonizing process continues, but with a different set of heroes. The "major"/"minor" doublet, clearly defined in the Middle Ages, is thus recovered. The first attestation in a French text dates from 1493.[523] The latter category also comprises writers who are marginal, social outcasts, loners, nonconformists, even *avant la lettre* "dissenters" ("tenebrosi, solitari, selvaggi").[524] The Bohemian literary life, with roots in the Middle Ages, begins to acquire its classical physiognomy. It will become an essential element of European literary life.

The traditional pattern remains the fundamental one. Culture exceeds by far, in importance and prestige, literature proper (in vernacular languages). L. B. Alberti "offended literary majesty"[525] by writing in Italian instead of Latin. An outright confession in this sense is made by Montaigne (I, 39). *Higher books* = Latin books.[526] Grammar continues to pass for "the first among sciences,"[527] which, in fact, Dante agreed with as well.[528] It is the symbol of elitist culture, the culture of the cultivated classes, opposed to popular culture, subjected to repression and relegated to the wings. This social-cultural cleavage becomes quite obvious in the epoch.[529] The result is that popular literature is pushed out to the margins, *colportage* literature is totally disavowed, "entertaining" genres (comedy and the novel)[530] are seen as valueless, anecdotes, like those of Poggio Bracciolini (*Liber facetiarum*) and pornography even more so. The pressure exercised by cultivated literature is primarily responsible for the emergence of "mass literature" and "subliterature." The phenomenon gains momentum in this period and in the future, it will enjoy considerable development and acknowledgment.

Finally, another hierarchical criterion is provided by the dissociation *literature* versus *poetry*. Poetry proclaims itself superior to literature, that is, prose, for extra- or anticultural reasons. Latin, the "holy language," may be a *Hauptsprache* (1531) but, "for poetry, the native tongue is better than all the others."[531] The gap is widened when versification is seen as no better than prose. A professional writer is but a *rimatore di rima*.[532] The tripartite style-pattern inherited from the Middle Ages (*sublime, average, inferior*), frequent at the time,[533] vindicates poetry even more: "The sublime height of poetry" (T. Tasso).[534] Hence, we find the hierarchy of literary genres: the lyrical on top, farce and comedy at the bottom. Such patterns, increasingly elaborated, are still vital today.

THE SCHOOL OF LITERATURE

The Study of Literature

Compared to the Middle Ages, when literature's cultural vocation is definitively consolidated, the Renaissance and Humanism raise this principle to an even higher level: Literature is a cultural product *par excellence*. It departs from an act of literary knowledge. Any literature necessarily presupposes a prior literature. Such a view on literature is unavoidable in a period of great, enthusiastic cultural discoveries, when there was a revival of neoclassical poetry. Poetry is a *poetica humanista*,[535] those who write it are *poeta doctus, poeta eruditus*,[536] *grammatici poetales*.[537] Literature is "learned." This concept is fundamental. The epoch's poets and theoreticians are persuaded that what literature and poetry essentially need are culture, study, "good letters." "Good writing begins in science" (*le savoir*).[538] The necessity of studying is underlined by Petrarch (*Fam.*, I, 8) and numerous others. Their doctrine amounts to two principles: talent plus culture, *ingenio* and *lettere* (*litteris et stilo*, *doctrine* and *parfait artifice*). Literary creation is the "effect" and "fruit of letters."[539] The theory and technique of committing culture to memory, of *ars memorativa*, is a typical of the entire period.[540]

Literary terminology mirrors this situation with startling clarity. Poetry is "studied" (*studere in poetria*.)[541] Poets indulge in "poetic studies." Boccaccio's self-composed epitaph is quite telling: *Studium fuit alma poesis*. Everything written with a *docte plume*—to revive the syntagms of the French Pleiaide—can only be *doctement écrit*. Originality is not one of the exigencies of the erudite poet. It feeds itself from a traditional common fund that belongs to everybody. Homer and Virgil are the "source of all disciplines." We are, again, in the impersonal, objective domain of literary culture.[542] In Petrarch, one comes across the same humanist, erudite conviction: "We reformulate, in our own words, other people's ideas," books "are united with us" (*Fam.* III, 8; I, 8). Of course, the idea can be found, more than once, in Montaigne as well. The French moralist openly admits to "borrowing," "transposing," taking over "other people's opinions and science, which only need to be made our own" (I, 24; I, 25; II, 101; III, 12). The result is the "consubstantial book" (II, 18). Creative continuity and assimilation, the fruitful *translatio studii*, are the kernel of this doctrine.

Transformed into an imperative cultural ideal, it finds expression in a typical Renaissance literary genre: the encyclopedic poem (theological, cosmogonic, anthropologic), like *Microcosme* (1562) by M. Scève, based on poetic and scientific synthesis[543] and on knowledge in its entirety: "A good poem partakes, generally, of all the sciences,"[544] of all the arts, as well. The erudite poet is, by vocation and definition, an encyclopedic spirit, interested in universal science. For him, science is both a program and an essential prerequisite of creation. Looked at from such an angle, literature becomes an aggregate of knowledge. "He who wants to become familiar with all the genres of arts and sciences" should necessarily read *Le Roman de la Rose*. In the sixteenth century, they call an epic poem an "encyclopedia,"[545] and so on.

Literature with Literature

Continuity, processing, and emulation are also characteristic of all the preeminently cultural acts that necessarily produce literature. Their meanings are glimpsed as early as the Middle Ages, so all this age can do is adopt them again and consolidate them. In this respect, the idea of literature makes no further progress, it merely becomes more stable.

The starting point is, once more, the primordial operation of writing. It begins with the *copy*, the transcription (Erasmus, *De copia verborum et rerum libri duo*, *De ratione studii*), the sequel, the annotations, the glosses, the written exercise, generally speaking, that accompanies reading. Manuscripts are "written on," commented on, often rewritten.[546] Imaginary inscriptions, imitating the ancients, also appear (*Hypnorotomachia Poliphili*). Another series of "literary" arts deal with writing methods, with the "learning" process itself, beginning with the writing and calligraphy books, quite common at the time, such as G. A. Tagliente's *Lo presente libro insegna la vera arte dello excellente scrivere* (1524).

Medieval-type manuals of the *ars dictaminis* kind are closely related to these: letter models (for example, J. L. Vives, *De Conscribendi Epistolis*)— such epistolary patterns were also in circulation in Romania[547]— versification textbooks (John Stockwood, *Progymnasma Scholasticum*, 1597), etc. The tendency to reuse, recover, especially typecasting, is quite obvious. Compilations[548] also aim to instruct, by selected quotations and useful texts, grouped in anthologies.[549] This kind of book, the main purpose of which is to instruct and teach, proliferates: *Adagia*, *Florilegia*, *Spicilegia*, especially in aphorisms, sentences, maxims: *Polyantheia*, *Vividiarium*,

Flores. This was widespread in Romania, too: *Floarea darurilor* (1592), selections from ancient thought.[550]

The intention of achieving superior elaboration—not in a typical literary fashion—in the logical and rhetorical tradition of old also informs another type of commonly found collections: *topoi, loci comunes, exempla,* lists of virtues and vices, as well as of villages, towns, hill and river names, etc.[551] They are all gathered with a didactic purpose, and are further amplified through glosses and personal comment. All this pre-existent, grouped, systematized material fosters "literature." The matter of quotations is raised, during the Renaissance, in the same context. The quotation is an essential factor for the continuity of literary culture, both for taking over old texts and producing new ones. The practice and theory of quotation can be easily traced from Petrarch to Montaigne,[552] with all the humanists in between. Simultaneous reading is the method of recovering texts; ancient excerpts are reconverted and read in the same topical register as modern ones (Montaigne, III, 13). The device of simultaneous reading, once discovered, is applied fully. Reassembling quotes in a new technical order—a device already known to the ancients and widely practiced during the Middle Ages—produces a well-known genre, the *centon.* This conception can be found in Petrarch (*Fam.,* III, 4), Henri Estienne,[553] E. Taburot, Montaigne (I, 26), etc. Homer and Virgil are intensely exploited for poetic purposes (by Henri Estienne, 1578, among others), but the Renaissance *centon* also has an ideological function (see Justus Lipsius, *Politica sive civilis Doctrinae,* 1589). It is generally accepted that any text, regardless of its final aim, can be founded on another text. Literature already knows that it is—or can be—self-productive. In the last decades of the twentieth century, modern poetics will gloss and speculate intensely on this state of things, which is already quite clearly felt to have existed earlier.

From transcription and collage to the wish to continue and create there is but one step to be taken. The old Romanian chronicles followed suit. For instance: "This is where Father Macarie's rhetorical endeavors stop. Therefore let me, his former, undeserving apprentice, Azarie, take it up from here. . . ."[554] All these activities, in fact, are concomitant and concordant. Similarly, the Latin poetry of the age is written as a prolongation of classical Latin poetry. Bilingual poetry is composed, too, in the same vein of cultural interference. What we call "intertextuality"[555] today is already conceived and defined. During this period, there is much talk about "correcting old books" as a method of writing;[556] quotations are abundant and other text borrowings massive (Montaigne: "My book is made up from the remains of theirs," II, 32, and cfr. I, 25; II, 18; III, 12, 13), the epigram is again defined as "inscription,"[557] and "poetry,"[558] as an exercise on a given subject.

Rediscovered with Aristotle's *Poetics,* the mimetic theory is reinterpreted in the same cultural, bookish spirit. The main object is no longer to "copy nature," but to learn the "lesson of the good, ancient authors."[559] To use Horace's words, (A. P., 1, 318), the poet is but a *doctus imitator*, who acquiesces in the necessity, satisfaction, and usefulness of imitation. Montaigne openly admits that his "condition [is] aping and imitative" (III, 5). But his literary purpose far exceeds simple copying. Selection, creative emulation, personal exploitation of a commonly held cultural fund are some of the new ideas. The metaphor of the bee that gathers honey from countless flowers is held in high esteem (Petrarch, *Fam.*, XXIII, 19; Montaigne, I, 26). After all, the classical writers did the same. The belief is given due emphasis (B. Parthenio, *Della imitatione poetica*, 1565).[560]

Other forms of quotation and imitation belong to the same sphere of literature born of literature. Moral quotations, thoroughly explained, produce *parabolae* and *exemplae*, respectively *paraphrase* (Fr. 1525, Le Fèvre d'Etaple),[561] a familiar medieval device. With Erasmus, it is the result of annotating *The New Testament*. When the idea of writing *à la manière de* (as in a comedy by T. Nashe), of "counterfeiting the author of *The Iliad*" (Ronsard),[562] makes its appearance, *pastiche* also becomes an established fact. There is every reason to believe that it is the conceptual and literary contribution of this age. The procedure is expanded, with ironical intent, to include language: "macaronic Latin" is invented (Teofilo Folengo = Merlin Coccai, *Macaronices libri XVIII*, 1517).[563] Another form of imitation is the *parody*. On its reappearance,[564] the term is closely associated with *centon* (Fr. 1583), that is, with the idea of a preexistent text. This one is merely "moved" in the opposite direction (*inversa mutatis vocibus*),[565] disparagingly and satirically, as in Rabelais.[566]

Nothing, however, can vouch for the progress of literary consciousness in this domain better than the Renaissance's violent reaction against *plagiarism*. Condemned during Classical Antiquity as well, it is now denounced for ethical reasons (false literary glory by appropriating the intellectual property of others, stealing property that belongs to others, Petrarch, *Fam.*, IV, 15, Erasmus) and is, "juridically" speaking, looked upon as theft.[567] The cultural criterion, then, loses its footing as originality is increasingly appreciated. "Creative robbery" from other languages and literatures is recommended, but it becomes odious when practiced within one's native tongue.[568] Vouchsafing the rights over literary property,[569] through editorial privilege and monopoly, also plays an important part in this change of atitude.

This whole procedure is granted official sanction. The edict of François I, by which censorship is instituted in France (1537), explicitly mentions books "that have been or will be made, compiled, amplified, corrected and improved,"[570] that is, all the operations of "literature born of literature." One can hardly say that the judiciary of the time lacked a sense of precision or of lexical accuracy.

Literature on Literature

The Middle Ages had discovered that literature could be written *on* literature, thus enriching the idea of literature itself. The trend continues during the Renaissance and Humanism, even though this period is less "creative" in this respect.

The first thing to mention is the well-known treatises—eulogies, composed in a semimedieval spirit, of the type *De Laude scripturae*, by Jean Gerson, or *De laude scripturorum*, by Johannes Trithemius. The writing process and the writer again become theoretical and literary themes. Actually, specific, original themes, belonging to the literature of all times, are summed up, beginning with the description of the beautifully written *letter*, raising it to metaphoric status;[571] letters are then systematically dealt with in treatises on verse: Jacques de La Rue, *Alphabet, de dissemblables sortes de lettres. En vers alexandrin* (1565), John of Beauchesne, *A book containing divers sortes of hands* (1570). The frequent praise of writing and of its metamorphoses (Brébeuf, etc.) is continued by paying homage to printing and to the printed book (Rabelais, *Pant.*, II, 5), to the library (*Pant.*, II, 7), and Théodore de Bèze, *Ad Bibliothecam*, etc.

Particularly characteristic is the praise of "letters," erudition, study, in such texts as *Le Blason de l'estude*[572] by Samuel Daniel, and others.[573] A lost comedy by Petrarch was entitled *Philologia*. Once again, culture occupies the foreground of literature and the two notions become indistinguishable. As a result, the didactic genre, the genre that is literary—*par excellence*—reappears and sinks deep roots. It conveys knowledge (a great quantity of "scientific poetry" is produced during the Renaissance), moral teachings (*Disticha Catonis*), textbooks of good manners, of courtly and good deportment (*Il Cortegiano*, by B. Castiglione, and remains the classical text, but it is far from being the only one, for example, in France, *Doctrinal des filles à marier, Doctrinal des bons serviteurs*, etc.).

The final literary purpose of the didactic impulse is to instruct on composition and metrics, as does John of Beauchesne.[574] Literature and poetry again have a predominantly cultural justification, facilitated only by "letters." What is to be called the "poetry of poetry" is revived in this context (Pierre de Ronsard, *Elégie à son livre*). All the iconography of poetry, its allegorical figures, accompanied by *imprese*, by emblems and verse mottoes on poetry, cultivates the same genre, much appreciated during the Renaissance.[575] That the act of creation, with all the ensuing difficulties, is evoked, is the result of the same process of fecund cultural germination.

The *legend* that is still associated with the idea of the written text (explanatory caption, 1594) on saints' lives is gradually divested of its sacred meaning, becoming a folktale, chockfull of incredible miracles.[576] The ever-increasing detachment of the *legend* from its original sources ("free narrative" and "unbelievable narrative")[577] mirrors the tension between the written and oral traditions of creative imagination. Literature on literature, however, energetically leaves behind the intrinsic obstacle, the preceding "letter," which determines its condition and applies pressure.

Critical Literature

The constant concern for *letters*, more typical of the Renaissance and Humanism than of the Middle Ages, also reappears forcefully in the sphere of *philology*. The definition of *literature*, in its classical sense—didactical and critical, then scholarly and hermeneutical—is taken up again. Philology is the discipline specific to the age and is, to a certain extent, its "philosophy." The Renaissance is the period that displays the greatest interest in discovering texts and reading them in their spirit and, above all, letter. The equation *literature = philology* exhaustively denotes and connotes this decisive cognitive process. *Littera* is always the starting point.

The original, didactical-educational nature of philology is shown by its first technical definitions: an object of study that educates the soul (*anima instituitur*)[578] through "letters" and "true, pure, fraternal languages" (*germanas*).[579] The promulgation of the beautiful is also essential: *Philologia eandunque Calligogia.* The idea is already contained in the first philological "treatise" (G. Budé, *De Philologia*, 1532),[580] whose title is also the first attestation of the term. From France, it crosses into Germany, or is reinvented there (1536).[581] At any rate, in mid-century, its frequency is well accounted for.[582] Philology comprises all the *literal, good, human, encyclopedic* letters and these formulae are commonly used during this period, by G. Budé, among others. To L. Valla, *studia humanitatis* and *litteratura = philology*) are consubstantial notions, almost synonyms.[583]

The first evolved premodern theory on reading appears within this framework. It continues and develops the older cultural-pedagogical meaning, redoubled by the recreative, entertaining one. The notion of "implied reader" is added, followed by an ever clearer evolution from *lectio,* to the explanatory comment and then on to criticism. The foremost, cultural meaning of reading ("man of vast reading", 1581)[584] remains the traditional one: educational method, pedagogical, study instrument (P. P. Vergerio, Battista da Guarini, Guarino da Verona, etc.). Plutarch, in Amyot's translation, provides a fundamental text: *Comment il faut lire les Poètes.* In the same sense, Melanchthon composes *Epistule de Legendis Tragoediis et Commediis* (1545). Even a "reading machine" gets invented, a "rotating" bookcase, the engraving of which is often reproduced.

We shall skip the dissociation—very precise in Montaigne (III, 8)—between "books to be studied and learned" and "books to be read" (in a relaxed, entertaining, gratuitous manner), to retain the ever more widespread idea of a virtual, implied reader, with whom the author enters into a dialogue. The head of the series is probably Petrarch (*Fam.*, I, 1), followed by Erasmus and by other humanists, but especially by Rabelais and Montaigne, with his famous *L'Aucteur au lecteur* and *suffisant lecteur* (I, 24, also cf. III, 9). Finally, there is the reading as *lectio*, the instructive and exegetical explanatory lesson, made up of a *lectura humana*[585] (a briefing in the humanities) and comments. Reading is the basis of understanding texts (Trissino).[586] A *lectio* therefore becomes the prerequisite of establishing the text, that is, of textual criticism, and then of hermeneutical interpretation and literary criticism proper. Once again, the origins of European criticism show themselves to be modest, scholarly, dominated by the problems of the *letter*. Criticism will never break free from this exigent, restrictive heredity.

Thus, philology becomes the critical literature of the age. It deals with the selection and establishment of texts in their original, authentic purity. A *lectio* proposes a very faithful reading of the text, through confrontation, collation, correction, *emendatio*.[587] This is the characteristic critical approach of the age. The term *liber criticus* itself appears, for the first time, in this period (1561).[588] The principles of textual criticism are also laid down now in Francesco Robortello's *Disputatio de arte critica corrigendi antiquorum libros* [1557]). The main object is the correction of corrupted, altered[589] ancient texts, to straighten out errors.[590] The conception becomes definitively settled along these principles (Scioppius, *De arte critica*, 1597).[591]

The traditional term for describing such operations, *grammar*, makes a strong comeback. More than ever, it is taken to mean *emendatio*[592] and "explication de textes" in the form of lectures (A. Poliziano, *Praelectiones in expositione Homeri*).[593] Its object consists of the criticism and interpretation of texts. There is no difference between a grammarian, a philologist, and a critic.[594] The "literator" and the "language teacher" belong to the same category.[595] The study of "letters" and of the "poets" is one and the same thing.[596] Note that in definitions of this type, the term *literature* is used spontaneously,[597] due to the natural influence of the ancient and medieval lexicographic tradition.

At this stage, textual criticism remains indistinct from explicative and interpretative criticism. Together they form a monolith. However, the diversification in terminology, increasingly consolidated, does offer some hints as to the future trends of development. The *gloss*, the *annotation*, and the *footnote* continue to be part of the classical humanistic vocabulary.[598] The *commentary* (*commentarium*)[599] enjoys great success in a period of philological effervescence. The term is widespread and covers a wide range of critical subjects. It is, actually, the "global criticism" of the era which includes commentaries on classical and modern works (Malherbe, *Comment-*

aire sur Desportes), lessons in applied literature through *examples*, moral, social, theological meditations (initially undertaken with the same didactic purpose)[600] and what are already called *essays*.[601] Autocommentary is illustrated by Rabelais and Montaigne. All of these are still contained in the basic, original category: *ista literatura*.[602]

Due to the many ambiguities and alternatives of explication and interpretation, the question of understanding *letters* becomes topical once again. In Romania, *Tîlcul Evangheliilor*, printed by Coresi (1567), purports to meet exactly such a need. The scenario is recomposed: *sacred* or *profane* literature? Erasmus (he is not an exception), like Cassiodorus, instates *philologia sacra*. All the interpretations of sacred texts, under the aegis of the Reformation or of the Catholic Church, are erected on these foundations. Interpretation is riddled with old and inevitable dilemmas: The *sacred* or *profane* sense? The *literal* or *mystic* sense? The "causes of the difficulties of sacred letters" (*vel inscita, vel malitia*) are examined. There are no fewer than . . . fifty-one of these, for which *remedia*[603] are promptly found. From the hands of theologians, the controversy is passed on to humanists, then to writers, who are aware of the existence of "symbols," a "hard core" of expression (Rabelais, *Garg., Prologue*). The Renaissance inherits medieval allegory and symbolism entirely; there are countless texts originating from this type of poetry and interpretation (Petrarch, *Ep.*, CXVIII; Boccaccio, *Vita di Dante*, III, etc.). The theory of multiple meaning (literal, allegorical, moral) is also current.[604] It is worth noting that the literal sense is considered the most suitable for the "ordinary people."[605] This again leads to an acknowledgment of the inevitable obscurity of hidden (Boccaccio, *De general. deorum*, X, XII, XIV), ambiguous, multivalent meaning. Montaigne, an unsystematic but very lucid hermeneutic spirit, is a great champion of the variable interpretation of texts (I, 24, 26; II, 12, etc.).

This is how the conception of the multiple significations of literature, predestined to having a spectacular career, enters European criticism. It was born in this philological, symbolist milieu, in conditions that, for the time being, remain obscure. It all starts from a series of practical, immediate necessities: breaking the ciphers and symbols existing in allegorical, mystical poems, in the secret, initiatory language of the poets (for example, Pierre de Ronsard, *Discours à Monsieur Cheverny*), "Attribution of Senses,"[606] explanations of *imprese*, and *mottoes*, all similar concerns, thus can be considered the dawn of literary semiology.[607] The imagination/inscription ratio is purely semiological in nature and we are indeed surprised that modern semioticians do not refer to such first-class precursors. One should not lose sight of the fact that all this effort at exegesis is constantly placed under the aegis of *grammar*,[608] of *literature*,[609] respectively, conceived of in their fundamental, didactic-philological sense: We "learn" and interpret only texts that are well pruned and explained, so that we may decipher and understand them correctly.

This is the very project that *studia humanitatis* embarks on in the beginning. Studying the "books of the poets, orators, and historiographers" (Peter Luder, 1456) is the first, traditional form of interpretation and hermeneutics. Didactically speaking, the two notions are synonyms. It is only when the idea of *interpretation* appears and gains individuality that a certain progress, especially terminological, is made: "Grammar is not the interpretation of authors."[610] *Ratio studii* is twofold: "Reading and interpreting authors" (Erasmus).[611] In the fifteenth century, *interpreter* means "translator" as well.[612] Another step—this time considerable—is taken when philological effort (*interpretationem, explanationem*) is achieved in the critical sense, that is, of a value judgment (*ac judicium*). The grammarian becomes (or better, again becomes) a critic.[613] An accurate text only can be judged correctly and appreciated with due acumen.[614]

Rhetoric—the central literary theory of the age—continues to be equally didactic and "grammatical." Grammar is still taken to be the same thing as the "art of speaking," as discourse theory, a traditional subject of study,[615] boosted by the prestige of the old *elocutio*, of elegant oral expression (*ornata verborum*).[616] The dissociation is gradually effected: grammar reigns in the field of *recte loquendi*, while rhetoric aims at embellishing discourse: *copiose splendique discendi duc*.[617] The application of this principle to both oral and written expression is a new step. Rhetoric, the "noble art," is closely associated with writing (*coucher par escrit*)[618] and, therefore, subject to the rules of composition.[619] Let us also mention that the first notions of rhetorical art, by implication of literary theory, enter Romanian culture in this period as well.[620]

Initially, poetry and poetics are subjected to the same rhetorical and didactic regimen. The former is the *Art de seconde rhétorique* (E. Deschamps) the latter the *Traité de la seconde Rhétorique*. Both are didactic genres, *grammatica*[621] and *gaya scienza*,[622] simultaneously. Considered at the beginning an auxiliary of grammar and rhetoric, poetics gains individuality after the publication, in Latin translation, of Aristotle's *Poetics*, securing for itself a distinct slot in the Renaissance classification of sciences.[623] The normative, canonical dogmatic sense is predominant. Now, at the dawn of European prescriptive criticism, poetics paraphrases and generalizes Aristotle (*dictator perpetus*)[624] and Horace,[625] who are pre-eminently concerned with setting up models. After all, the cultural theory of literature had to lead to an esthetics of imitation, to precepts of a classical nature.

This also explains the great number of treatises on rhetoric and poetics, and textbooks produced in this period, ranging from the "mirror" (*Schriftsspiegel*, 1527) and theory of writing (C. Mylaeus, *De Scribendo*, 1551), to the art of versification (J. Wimpheling, *Ars metrificandi*, 1505) and poetry (Thomas Sibilet, *Art poétique*, 1555). Such books, in Greek or Slavonic variants, circulated in the Romanian countries as well, being "learned" there, too.[626] The notions of "rule," "instruction," and "science" are present in almost all the titles of works of this kind. But all the great "poetics" of the age (Scaliger, Puttenham, Minturno, Castelvetro, etc.) have the same blatant didactic and educational character. The only thing that goes beyond this—rather latently, for the time being—is the accent laid on the "beauty" and "artifice" of poetic discourse, of *dire*,[627] on the elegance of language, on the subjectivity and individuality of the self (Montaigne: *mon estre universel*, III, 2). This will be more and more energetically and massively affirmed, beyond grammatical and poetic categories, beyond all the rules of literary genres. It is the great theme of European literature, discovered and launched by the Renaissance.

DENYING LITERATURE

The most virulent germs of antiliterature continue to proliferate, as a prolongation of the radical, dogmatic-religious, medieval stance. The resistance opposed by sacred values takes up—in its most determined and organized form—all the traditional arguments: vain, dangerous art; literature corrupts; it circulates "heathen" ideas. *Theologia minime adversa poetica* (Petrarch, *Fam.*, X, 4). Many humanists continue to see their reading of the classics as "the antics of youth" (*taedium scriptorum gentilium*).[628] Those who continue to ask themselves whether profane authors are worth reading are still numerous.[629] The controversy is fueled by the first waves of the Reformation, then by the radicalism it brings. Intransigent Catholic orthodoxy (anticipated by Savonarola) takes on Luther and "good letters" at the same time, denouncing them with the same arguments: heresy, paganism, the laicizing of the spirit. From the opposite direction, the attack is led by reformers (Calvin, Wycliffe). Caught in the middle, Humanism is not comfortable at all. Erasmus rises against both exaggerations, though to little avail.[630] The Counter Reformation brings the Inquisition in its wake, the *Index librorum prohibitorum*, censorship, the persecution of *letters*. Literature goes through a period of great restrictions and its sense of guilt is exacerbated.

One could not possibly argue that hostile religious arguments have no direct bearing on literature and culture, on the very essence of literature. The old controversy *letter/spirit* (the latter being considered the only one that is "alive") is resumed. One of Alciati's *Emblemata* is *Littera occidit, Spiritus viuvicat*.[631] A knowledge of God is not compatible with the "alphabet and its letters" (Marsilio Ficino).[632] The thesis *De docta ignorantia* (Nicolaus Cusanus, 1440), according to which "ignoring" actually means "knowing," is also intensely debated. In other words, to ignore is to know the size and limits of one's own knowledge. Consequently, being *"doctus"* in one's own ignorance becomes the summit of wisdom.[633] Lay, human culture is also questioned directly in another treatise, which apparently deals with this thesis polemically, *De ignota letteratura*, by Jean Wenck de Harenberg: "I start from literature (= culture), from science in particular, to achieve an ignorance of it." In summation, "literature" and "human doctrines" are "the work of darkness."[634] Erasmus uses an identical formula, *inerudita eruditio*,[635] the science which, in essence, does not know anything. In the same sense, see Henri Cornelius Agrippa, *De incertitudine et vanitate scientiarum et artium atque excellentis verbi Dei declamatio* (1530). In fact, culture is now most radically contested by the lay, desacralized spirit, as a prolongation of the still powerful medieval tradition, in the form of parody or violent blasphemy even. It is interesting to note that one of the age's German characters in the parodic mode is even named *Freihart* ("freedom").[636]

Another series of antiliterary arguments is founded on the constant heteronomy of literature and of its idea. Moralizing criticism, by now well-entrenched, becomes very active during the Renaissance and Humanism. It inspires pamphlets (for example, Stephen Gosson, *The Schoole of Abuse*, 1579) and a series of other severe diatribes.[637] Poetry is hostile to the "supreme good." So powerful is the cliché of virtuous life and "literature" that it is used, for promotional reasons, even by a man of dubious literary morals, the pamphleteer, and sometime blackmailer, Pietro Aretino.[638]

On the other hand, the poet, the cleric, the grammarian, broadly speaking, the man of culture, stand out as socially and morally detestable human types, because of their many blemishes, vigorously denounced. The deference that the "poet" and "letters" enjoy at the court[639] or in the high social circles, on the part of the aristocracy and of the military, is nil. Conversation is declared superior to writing (Montaigne, III, 8). Ridiculed for his poverty—corrupt, vainglorious, flattering, and unreliable—the "poet" is a compromised character, the target of sarcasm and satire. Petrarch remains aloof from the "itching" of writing. Erasmus's *Laus stultitiae* is replete with epigrams. Other humanists also respond negatively (Ermolao Barbaro, *Contra Poetas*, 1455; Battista Mantovano, *Contra poetas impudice scribentes*, 1499). The great specialists in antipoetic diatribes are the satirical poets, who know perfectly well what they are writing about. A representative text is *Dialogo contro i poeti*, by Francesco Berni (1526).[640]

The cultural aspect of "letters" is also held in low esteem. Pedantry is deplored (Montaigne, I, 25). Grammar and grammarians are intensely disliked ("this plague called grammar").[641] The century is awash in *l'escrivaillerie* (Montaigne, III, 9). The moralist yearns to be wise, not learned (II, 10), nor a "maker of books" (II, 37). Even for Rabelais (affectation or not), *le travail d'éscrire* is "vain and totally useless."[642] Toward the end of the

Elizabethan Age, literature had become a fashion, a mania, an inflation in England, hence, a reaction to excess and a parodic repudiation.[643] The mercenary, economic, professional aspect of the trade is also detested.[644] Some poets of the period place greater value on their "scientific," "encyclopedical" work than on the literary. At any rate, the status of poetry and "letters" must be quite low if the apologists of the age (Sir Philip Sidney, M.-A. Muret, etc.) try to counter social criticism of this type as well.

Antiliterary arguments are by far more important, especially when considered in historical perspective, when they originate in the literary field itself. During the Renaissance and Humanism—a period when notions are clarified, but also dissociated—the discovery is made that "literature" can and must be effectively questioned, even denied from the inside. This process again begins with a contestation of writing, but this time the reasons for the indictment are no longer sacred; they belong to literary creation itself. The approach has become laic. Writing—due to its abstract symbology—immobilizes, "freezes" (the celebrated myth of the "frozen words," Rabelais, *Pant.*, IV, 50–51), while the spoken word is constantly updated, permanently efficient and available for creation. The conventional nature of writing, connected to the cult of the image as a simulacrum, is sometimes felt as a true "apostasy" (G. Bruno, *De magia*).[645]

The attacks against pedantry and erudition (of which but a small part has been mentioned so far)[646] imply the questioning and radical upsetting of the cultural hierarchy. For the first time, memory and book culture are the object of radical doubt. Montaigne is the symbol of this crossroads. He rejects the excessive praise of letters (I, 31), "purely bookish" knowledge (*suffisance*) (I, 26), the state of being "overburdened with books" (I, 25). There are great implications in his program of writing without the "memory of books" (II, 10; III, 5), without making use of "things ever studied" (III, 2). So culture, that is, literature, stops being a condition of creativity, even of spiritual activity. This moment in the biography of the idea of literature is downright "revolutionary." All European antiliterature is now prefigured, *in nuce*.

Denunciation of the abuse of books—in a period of great interest in philology and the printing press—is another aspect of the problem. Book inflation, or over-production, is already repudiated at the conclusion of the Middle Ages (J. Gerson, *Contra curiositatem facendi plures libros*, 1400). Such attacks become ever more frequent, from S. Brandt to Petrarch,[647] from Peletier du Mans to Montaigne. "Any book is an epitaph" (Henry Vaughan.)[648] The "folly" of the book will be one of Erasmus' subjects. The well-known myth of the "book of nature"—living, antidogmatic, the instrument of direct, intuitive knowledge, which is like paradisiac knowledge—is opposed to the "dead" printed book. Books were not known in the Golden Age or in Paradise,[649] nor obviously were libraries, now denounced and ridiculed (Rabelais, *Pant.*, II, 7). Bibliomania is already considered a vice.[650]

The antiliterature of the age is also inspired by the abuse of overinterpretation, which makes the text obscure.[651] Excessive comments, criticism, and glosses are felt to be a hypertrophy of the spirit. Montaigne laments: "We interpret interpretation more than we interpret things" (III, 13). Abusive, caricatured hermeneutics is present in Erasmus's *Praise of Folly* (LIV) as well. The proliferation of quotations, compilation, writing books with other people's books opened up in front, the text that "smells of other people's ink," are all brought into question. The "literature out of literature" has already gained, in circles that are ever more representative, a very bad reputation. The controversies between "ancients" and "moderns" also play a great part in this, as they voice strong objections to ancient literature and its imitators. The simple "writer" remains a mere *escrivailleur* (Montaigne, III, 9). Literary hierarchy is again subjected to a structural modification.

The climax of this antiliterary polemics is the direct refusal of grammar and culture, the praise of the creator "devoid of letters" (*sanza lettere*), as Leonardo da Vinci proclaims himself,[652] not without ostentation. You can be gifted and become a great artist without attending school. Dante and Petrarch can be successful substitutes for grammar (Cino Rinnuncini).[653] There are quite a few authors who admit to not having learned "school doctrines," to not having "studied grammar,"[654] in all-out defiance of the accepted literary form. B. Tasso declares his letters to be "extremely uncultured" (*si incolte*).[655] This is affectation, but also defiance. A cliché of creative counterculture begins to take shape.

The opposition, *poetry* versus *literature*, consubstantial with the idea of literature, is clearly delineated against this background. The separation we have already noted now turns into open enmity and hostility. It is therefore perfectly legitimate to speak at such an early time of *antiliterature*, the sense of a declared opposition of poetry to literature. In the first stage, poetry is, obscurely, "learning"; in the second stage, it is its opposite. Poetry openly detests erudition (Ronsard strips his works of learned allusions from one edition to the next). Some poets announce: "We have grown tired of books that teach us, give us books to stir our feelings."[656] A point that is made with great insistence in this period is that the aim of poetry is "only to please and entertain."[657] In Romanian culture, in the same period, the pleasure of reading is also discussed, even if in a rather empirical, accidental manner.[658] "Vain subtleties" are also rejected, from the perspective of popular poetry (Montaigne, I, 55). The regeneration of poetic language through the vernacular tongue becomes a fact. It is visible especially in du Bellay.

The art/nature opposition underlies this controversy. It is a central theme of the moral and esthetic thinking of the age. The "struggle of art against nature" is discussed by Montaigne (III, 5), who points out the value of "naiveté," the "natural sap" of poetry,[659] that is, spontaneous inspiration, genuine lyricism. This thesis is extended over all literary genres (written with "my heart," in conformity with the "inclinations of my own nature," by a "son of nature").[660] To Leonardo da Vinci, a "good natural talent without letters" is much more deserving than a "good man of letters with no natural talent."[661] Hence, we are confronted with two other important consequences: 1. the praise of "simple, naive language" (Montaigne, I, 26), of the "natural, ordinary" style (*mon pas*) (II, 10); 2. the rejection of artifice, that is, of "literature," viz. of erudite, "grammatical" subjects, and language. "Art," "affectation," "sought-after effects" (II, 10, 17) are openly fought off. When art vanquishes nature (I, 30), man's and poetry's natural state becomes corrupted and begins to suffer. This is a subject used by Bacon (*N. O.*, II, 39–40, Charron and Marie de Gournay, an adept of the theory that genius is invented. It does not "transverse" either rime or grammar.[662]

Denying culture, erudition, "literature"—in the classical, unanimously accepted sense—has other important consequences as well. Literary consciousness, literary attitudes, and literary technique all undergo change. The traditional idea, *letters = literature*, is at a loss. Many a Renaissance poetician (T. Campanella, F. Patrizio, P. Verri, etc.) rejects poetic rule and norm, that is, literary education. The problem is summarized by G. Bruno in this masterly manner: "Poetry is not born from rules . . . the rules derive from poetry."[663] This position is the equivalent of anticlassicism, opposing the dogmatic, Aristotelian spirit that is usually associated with "literature." Seen from this angle, *literature* is classical, potentially classical, while *poetry* is modern, potentially modern. We shall repeatedly run across this dialectical relationship. Mannerism and the Baroque profess to have a "freer," therefore "anticlassical" conception of literature. For the same reason, *poetry* is antirhetorical, while literature is dominated by rhetoric.[664] The word *rhétoriqueur* (= poet) is used in a rather negative sense. The reaction against artificial, "sophisticated,"[665] elaborated style has the same cause. Spontaneousness tends to authenticity and prosaic expression, to a type of writing devoid of artistic intentions.[666] There is theoretical comment on prose, on "affectation and abundance of useless words" (Larivey, 1579.)[667] The dissociation between literary and poetic specificity turns into manifest, clearly motivated hostility. The first signs of "classicizing" appear: rarity and excessive novelty are condemned (Montaigne, I, 54).

The amplitude assumed by the controversy *new* versus *old letters* will also have great consequences, especially from the eighteenth century on, but some of them neatly expressed even now. By their nature, the new letters are pitted against the old. The ideas of novelty and originality receive a new boost and become downright polemical. Once more, Petrarch is the illustrious forerunner (*Fam.*, XXXIII, 19). The basic modern thesis of the *Querelle* is "not to borrow anything from the ancients,"[668] not to "overuse study and letters," "to produce new inventions."[669] Imitation, borrowing (*gran pestilenza*), transmutation, *le pillage*, are all condemned.[670] In Aretino's crude language, these operations amount to *il cacar sangue dei pedanti*. He seeks originality, rather than anything else: "He is a fool who believes he can make a name for himself through other people's toil,"[671] neither God, nor a master in esthetics. One could say that the anarchist slogan of the nineteenth century is already heralded: "Modern," *avant la lettre*, means to value silence. This, an extension of ancient and medieval ideals,[672] has a predominantly ethical motivation in the period (Petrarch, Rabelais). In the last two centuries, it will become the rhetoric of the ineffable, of the inexpressible, even of "silence."

CONCLUSIONS

The period we have just covered is not, strictly speaking, a "creative" one in the biography of the idea of literature. Nonetheless, it is important, first of all because the major meanings of *literature* now become definitively settled, stable, and consecrated. The Renaissance and Humanism circulate the idea of literature all over Europe. The pattern of the development of literature becomes clear, unitary, final, and accepted by all the cultural and literary circles of the age. One may say that it is only now that the basic cultural acceptance of *literature* enters European consciousness. The learned-cultural sense is intensified to an unparalleled degree. Another characteristic phenomenon is the rediscovery of the old, didactic-pedagogical vein. The educational involvement of literature becomes even greater. As to its moral function, it is more inherent, more "humane" and, concurrently, more social than in Antiquity and the Middle Ages.

At the same time, some really new aspects stand out clearly. The first explicit etymological and lexicographical definitions of literature appear in the Renaissance and in Humanism. They are not yet to be found in special treatises, but rather in a few great lexicons and dictionaries. Also new is the ever more decided laicization of literature. The strong sacred dimension of the literature inherited from the Middle Ages begins to fade, in some cases to the point of extinction. The humanization of literature and of the idea of literature becomes, increasingly, a reality. Social involvement and the rise of the "Republic of letters" are other important contributions.

However, the most "original" aspect of our idea—which is now beginning to mature—is the separation of *poetry* from *literature*, from its essential background, which it then radically contests. We even witness the birth of *antiliterature*, through the rending asunder of the original union *culture = literature*. Poetry, a notion on the rise, increasingly takes over the "esthetic" functions of the erstwhile union. As for *literature*, its role becomes more and more marginal.

The first signs of the weariness of literature, of the "classicizing" of it, also appear. The idea already displays a tendency to become ossified, to lose its vital drive, to become academic. Culture, that is, *literature*, is institutionalized. The force of its *élan*, which has driven it forward since Antiquity, is now taxed by dogmatism and by incorporation into the official culture. The fate of *liberal letters*, potentially nonconformist, even insurgent, but eventually turned into a mere scholastic school subject, is symbolic of this situation.

IV

Classicism and the Baroque

As it is governed by a twofold sensitivity and a redoubled literary con-sciousness—Classical or, rather, Neoclassical and Baroque—the seven-teenth century can only conceive of the idea of literature in these two terms. On the one hand, therefore, we witness a moment of stasis, solidly consolidating a tradition that is taken in its entirety and turned into a dogma. The formulae become *ne varietur*, they are great platitudes which become quite commonly referred to. The terminology becomes general and "official." On the other hand, the rise, since the previous century, of the idea of *poetry* causes ever more severe perturbations in the system of the idea of literature. The esthetic meanings of the idea of literature are taken over by poetry with a renewed determination and sense of commit-ment. Literature is definitely relegated—rather, sent back—to the territory where it originated: the cultural one. Consequently, the strong, cultural sense of the idea of literature is subjected, in the hands of poetry, to a process of devaluation and marginalization, a process that has continued to this day, in what we may describe as in free fall.

TRADITIONAL DEFINITIONS

Grammar and Culture

On the surface, the first thing worth noticing is that the well-entrenched definitions of grammar continue to circulate uninterruptedly. The preemi-nently didactic meaning, in the tradition of the classical, erudite formulae (Cicero, Quintillian etc.[1]) has been known long since *bene loquendi ars, ars . . . pure loquendi,*[2] etc. Grammar continues to be seen as the "art of reading and writing" and the "art of reading and writing well."[3] In philo-logical circles, the old equation *litteratura = grammatica* is also preserved (*grammatica quam litteraturam dicimus.*)[4] This is the "popular" meaning of grammar (*grammatica litteraria*), as distinct from the philosophical (*gram-matica philosophica*), dealing with the nature and power of words).[5] It enters the great dictionaries of the time (Du Cange, Furetière,)[6] thus becoming "official."

The increasingly manifest tendency is to push the purely *grammatical* sense of literature toward the periphery and to make better and better use, with as many shades of meaning as accurately as possible, of the *cultural* sense. In this respect, Classicism and the Baroque bring about the final eclipse of the traditional, grammatical definition of literature, which is felt to be too vague, too non-specific. For A. Tassoni, "a literate person . . . is no longer [merely] he who can read and write."[7] He is, first and foremost, a "man of letters" (*personne de lettres*),[8] that is, a man of superior knowledge acquired through letters, a well-read, educated, cultivated individual.[9] The cultural publications of the age, some of them quite scholarly and erudite, address this very publicly. Consequently, they bear such names as *Il Giornale de' Litterati* (1688) and *Journal des Savants* (1665). At the time, concepts such as knowledge studies, education, and instruction were closely connected to *letters*. Though hardly new, it was only then that the idea became an axiom, a dogma even. *Avoir des lettres, nourri aux lettres* (like Descartes, *Disc. de la Méth.*, I), *connaissance dans les lettres*[10] (to confine ourselves to some current French phrases) thus better define the ideal image of the cultivated man. Synonyms from the same semantic sphere, in various languages (*doctrine et scavoir, learning and knowledge, discipline, saber, science*, etc.), taken from seventeenth-century authors, point to the perfect osmosis of the ideas of *letters* and *knowledge*. Hence, the fundamental classical meaning of the term *literary*: of or referring to *letters, cultural knowledge, science*. Classicism is fundamentally cultural.

The same notion is expressed by another widely circulated word in the seventeenth century: *eruditio, erudition, erudición*, etc. Dictionaries define it as superlative knowledge and culture and, at the same time, as a synonym of *literature* ("extensive knowledge in any kind of literature," "deep knowledge").[11] Classical philology adopts it, too: *litteratura sive vario eruditio*.[12] Its meaning tends to define the so-called technical substratum, the ensemble of specialized cultural knowledge, situated at a higher level: "Have you ever seen a doctrine without literature"?[13] Erudition is always "doctoral," "scholarly," highly competent in a delimited field of knowledge.

The persistent, generalized, direct fusion of the two notions, *culture = literature*, definitively consecrates the primordial, preeminently cultural meaning of the idea of literature. One could say that *literature* cannot even be conceived of outside the sphere of the culture within which it appeared and with which it is entirely and permanently identified. Some Latin formulae (*cultioris literature*,[14] *cultura literarum, excultae litterae, literarum cultores*, etc.)[15] preserve the mark of this semantic overlap. Most of the time, though, *litterae* and *litteratura* express, in a synthetic manner, the entire cultural content of fundamental studies. In general, they denote great intellectual distinction (*vir et litteratura . . . insignis*).[16]

The same process can be seen at work in the modern European languages. The figurative sense of the idea of culture is, first, that of a *culture of letters* (*culture des lettres, culture des bonnes lettres*,[17] which subsequently becomes *littérature, literature, letteratura, literatura* (countless references).[18] To have no literature = to be uneducated, uncultured. The notion is indissolubly linked to organized, book-based culture. The first etymological and semantic analyses of the idea of *culture*, emphasizing the same meaning, date from that period, too.[19]

It is also now that a generalization of the spiritual, metaphorical sense takes place: *cultiver l'esprit, coltura degli ingegni*, in the good Ciceronian tradition of *cultura animi* (*Tusc. disc.*, II, 5). The formula reappears in Leibniz, Pufendorf, etc.[20] The subjective, intimate, spiritual content of *culture* ensures the peculiar, subjective and, eventually, esthetic character of literature. A new and significant breach again opens up in the idea of culture-erudition by the irruption of the sensitive, qualitative criterion. The phenomenon is especially noticeable with Baltasar Gracián. He often speaks of *gustosa erudición, sabia y selecta erudición*.[21] For him and for others, culture is increasingly defined through personalized qualifications of a special nature: "An erudite is more than a grammarian," erudition is "more worthy of respect than the great science of the grammarians," etc.[22]

Nevertheless, the most current evaluation of *culture = literature* remains quantitative, and the relative and absolute superlatives of the idea are conceived of as the supreme ideal of an intellectual upbringing. It follows that the most frequent praise is bestowed on him who distinguishes himself through "great literature" (*grande littérature*, F. La Mothe Le Vayer, 1668; Charles Sorel, 1671, etc.). There are numerous variants: "vast and profound literature" (Pierre Bayle),[23] "vast and prodigious literature" (Jean Chapelain),[24] "immense literature," (Saint-Évremond), etc.[25] In other languages: *singolare letteratura, eminente letteratura, solide littérature, infinite literature, spacious literature*, etc.[26] Almost the entire series of possible cultural superlatives is attested. One should not ignore the great prestige of *reading*, seen as the process by which knowledge is acquired intensively, hence, another current phrase: *grande lecture, great reading*. In that respect, *literature* and *reading* become, in the seventeenth century, synonyms.

The consecration of this definition (*culture = literature*) in the great dictionaries of the age can be considered the culmination of this rapid process of classicization. Lexicography gives the most typical expression to the stability of a concept that has become canonical. The set of traditional, definitive, *ne varietur* formulae is now launched, to be repeatedly made use of to this day. The definition of *literature* becomes official and even acquires a certain rigidity. In the final analysis, the same acceptations and meanings of the idea of literature will be found circulating throughout cultural Europe: "science," "eruditio" (Du Cange),[27] "doctrine," "deep knowledge of letters" (Furetière),[28] *honnêtes connaissances* (Richelet). The Dictionary of the French Academy is but the last stage in this officialization. The plurilingual dictionaries of the epoch (P.Ph. Monet, A. Littleton)[29] give further extension and stability to the intensive, cultural acceptation of *literature*.

School is the medium that consecrates, employs, and generalizes this acceptation. To a greater extent than in other periods, the didactic context of *literature* plays a decisive role. It is the period when Jesuit academies (a product of the counter-Reformation) are in full bloom,[30] the period of *Ratio studiorum* (1591), of prestigious standardized textbooks (the ones from Port-Royal have acquired celebrity), of the literature of the type: John Brinsley, *Ludus Literaribus, or the Grammar Schole* (1627). This European phenomenon was, inevitably, manifest in Romanian culture too. Certain essential didactic and literary concepts now enter Romanian culture and become widespread: ştiinţa (M. Costin), *cetitul* (Dosoftei), *dăscălie* (= teaching), *cărturar, grămătic, grammatichia, filosofia, învăţătură academicească, a pedepsi* (= to teach), etc.[31] We even find a eulogy to culture (*Indreptarea legii*, 1652).[32] These are the first, discontinuous and occasional, explicit or implicit, acceptations of *literature = culture* in Romanian culture, the beginning of a long series.

Written Literature

There is yet another consequence of this process by which the idea of literature becomes stable, homogeneous and classical in the seventeenth century: the association of *letters* and *writing* becomes so close, so current and natural, that it becomes yet another commonplace, tacitly and unanimously accepted. Literature can be but written. At the same time, the cultural meaning of literature completely absorbs the idea of writing, from which it is indistinguishable. This latter notion continues to have a lexicographical and philological existence of its own, but one that is subordinated and which contains no peculiar semantic nuances.

The *letter/literature* doublet is especially characteristic of studies in philology and in the history of writing. Studies on Runic and Gothic writing (*litteratura runica, literatura Danica*),[33] or on the beginnings of writing with the Germans (*litteraturae primordiis*),[34] are published. In all of these instances, *litteratura* refers exclusively to graphic signs, which is also true of the etymological dictionaries of the age.[35] The same identity can be found in some histories of writing composed in French: *lettre* (graphic sign) = *littérature*.[36] One might say that the idea of *literature*, thus conceived and expressed, has been greatly impoverished, bereft of all the complexity acquired so far.

It is equally true that the *letter* or the graphic *type* (this notion also comes into use) preserves its great capacity for syncretism and semantic agglutination. The species of *letters* points to "literary" species. The classification of the former presupposes an attempt at literary classification, by genre: *varia scripturarum nomina*.[37] Many terms used in epigraphy (anagrams, epigrams, inscriptions, etc.) refer, in actual fact, to an equal number of literary species (that is, *De arte epigrammatica*).[38] *Literatura solidi* = the lettering on coins,[39] respectively *lettrier* = *inscription*.[40] The rendering of the idea of "written work" by *monumentis litterarum* seems to have a great future before it. The phrase—to be used with increasing frequency—already occurs in the first bibliographies.[41] *Literarum opera*, also widely attested, will be definitively consecrated. In French, it becomes *ouvrage des lettres*[42] and then, more and more often, *lettres*, in the most general possible sense, that of *literary work*. The notion *epistle*, letter, belongs to the same category (*epistola* = *littera*).[43] The dictionaries of the age—especially those of the French Academy, which enjoy great authority[44]—ensure that these meanings, converging on the *written text* of any kind, are stabilized. *Scriptor, écrivain* preserves its original meaning: copyist, scribe, secretary, public writer.[45] But a qualitative change asserts itself rapidly in the semantic evolution.

The imagistic, pictural conception of writing, rediscovered and turned to literary account throughout the period, is also traditional. As is known, the writing-image synthesis dates back to Antiquity and the Middle Ages. The Baroque, in particular, cultivates and exploits *à fond* all the confusions and multivalence of iconographic writing. Egyptian hieroglyphs, rediscovered during the Renaissance (Horapollo, *Hieroglyphica*, 1419, of which the Romanian scholar N. Milescu had some knowledge, *Cartea despre hieroglife*), provide a true archetype for the overlapping of planes.[46] This is enhanced by the systematic use of the device in the form of emblems (reminding us of another famous text, A. Alciati's *Emblemata*, 1531), a species that brings the tension and confusion between image and inscription to culmination. As a result, another mixed and utterly ambiguous form of "written literature" appears and is cultivated as such.[47] The superiority of the written text over the image is even more evident in the closely related genre of *mottoes*. An idea becomes much clearer in a scheme comprising a motto, an image, and explicative verse.[48] The basic text is *Iconologia* by Cesare Ripa (1593).[49] The subject has its devout adepts and specialists, from H. Estienne[50] to Bouhours.[51]

Capitalizing on writing—and, by extension, on "written literature"—has many other aspects. One group of meanings takes up, perpetuates and even amplifies the old medieval thesis of *pictura laicorum Scriptura*. Writing is *pictura loquens* (Du Fresnoy)[52] *graphic art* = *the art of painting* (*De graphicae, sive arte pingendi.*)[53] The relationship between *inscription, pictura, subscriptio* is simultaneously denotative and connotative.[54] In its turn, printing becomes "commonplace" and so identified with the idea of literature that its definition cannot be told apart from that of the latter. A *literary work* = a *printed work*, or *book*. What is an author? "In literature, that can be said of any person who has brought a book to light, who has had a considerable work printed."[55] The publication and existence of literature is, therefore, preeminently a question of typography. Manuscripts leave the stage of history.

The first references to *writing/writings, scripture,* and *printing* are used in Romanian culture with a certain frequency in the same period. The basic synonym remains the same: *carte* = *scrisoare* (letter and written text), symmetrical to *cărturar* = *învăţat, cultivat.* "Writing—adroit mirror of the human mind" (M. Costin). The writing/image ratio also appears in the form "written on the icon."[56] Dosoftei writes *mottoes. Izvod* = version, written text; *script* = anything written down;[57] *scrisoare,* above all, = work in prose (a chronicle, etc.) or verse (*stihuri*)[58] are terms that usher into this country the idea of literary composition, that is, of literature, in perpetuity. The author of "letters" is a writer,"[59] notwithstanding the genre.[60] For the *Psaltirea slavonă* ("Slavonic Psalter," 1637), a printing press is "more valuable than all earthly treasures."[61] This is how Romanian culture has assimilated the basic notions of written culture and literature.

Oral Literature

Compared to the rising prestige of letters and written literature, oral literature appears to be completely overpowered, marginalized, deconsidered, often made to feel culpable. At any rate, during this period, the oral is in eclipse. However, the fact that it is recycled by the letter, as well as a series of dissociations and other esthetic considerations prepares the way for the recognition of what will be called "oral literature." Some preliminary signs are relevant.

Although the rhetorical tradition does not make a clear-cut distinction between writing and oratory as yet,[62] the tendency is to see the two as different entities, to define *l'art oratoire* and to set up two distinct rhetorics (*de la parole/de l'écriture*),[63] followed by the dissociation and classification of two categories of literary genres, written and oral. This is the very embryo of the idea of "oral literature." It defines itself by a more and more precise dissociation from the written literary expression. The emergence of the notion "oral tale" (*conte oral*), which takes shape in this period and even enters dictionaries (Richelet), is quite relevant in this respect.[64] It is also during this period that the oral tale is seen as identical to the *novella.* This does not mean that the *letter* no longer reigns supreme. There is even a tendency that oral expression is absorbed, assimilated, and eventually eliminated in its entirety, on the grounds that "writing does the work of speech."[65] Hence, a more and more frequent reversal of definitions, to the benefit of writing. The idea is that "a letter is written conversation,"[66] orators are writers of prose,[67] a *performance* is a composition (*work*.)[68] The situation is typical (even archetypal) of the whole destiny of the concept "oral literature." It can only acquire sense and signification when contrasted with the notion of writing, acknowledged as a standard, a term of comparison and differentiation.

Needless to say, oral expression does take its revenge, but again it does so through writing. Revamped in written form, completely absorbed by writing, orality openly proclaims its excellence and superiority. Another reversal is thus produced: oral style becomes esthetic norm. "This precept, of writing as you speek, is not new."[69] Indeed, it is quite widespread and has been often recommended not only in France, but in Spain,[70] Germany,[71] England,[72] etc.[73] Nor is the tradition of medieval improvised, spontaneous, oral poetry lost.[74] This superiority[75] often turns—especially with nonclassical, *irréguliers*, Baroque writers like Charles Sorel[76]—into a true model, as live language, better than dead Latin, had its champions even during the Renaissance.[77] The classical historical tradition continues to provide the basic stylistic molds.[78] Some of these even enter the Romanian culture of the age.[79]

Sacred Literature

A certain "impoverishment" in the significations of the concept *religious literature* could already be felt in the later periods, the Renaissance, and the Middle Ages. The phrase becomes a mere convention, an administrative, official designation. The process starts during the Counter-Reformation, when the content of the definition becomes official, dogmatic, to a considerable extent, ossified. The Church is interested in preserving its institutional unity, rather than the religious inner life, the intimate, personal experience of the authors of such "literature." This remains outside the concerns of a political, bureaucratic, official Church, reorganized along strict lines by the Council of Trento (1545–1563).

The consecrated phrases, *sacrae litterae*,[80] *scriptores ecclesiastices*[81] continue to circulate. The equivalent in Romanian is *meşteşugul scripturilor*,[82] and especially, *cărţi*, including prophecies like *Cartea Sibilelor* (written by N. Milescu), *sfinte cărţi* (Dosoftei, etc.).[83] The European equivalent, *saintes lettres*, *lettere sante*, sanctified by tradition, is quite widespread. In parallel, the "Jesuit" notions *pietas litterata* and *religione litterata*[84]—meaning poetry on religious themes, used to instruct, catechize and covert—become increasingly well-known. This is the specific signification of the age. It incorporates and subordinates all traditional religious stereotypes related to writing and literature: the myth of the sacred, hieroglyphic letters of divine inspiration, of the bible as poetry, of nature, read with theological eyes (*liber arcana*), of the sky and the world as poem," as "divine art,"[85] of the world as an epic poem "written" by God (Calderón, *El divino Orfeo*), of the writer as "the Lord's instrument and plume."[86] Even a theory of "Christian poetry"[87] is announced: eclogues, psalms, "spiritual sonnets," "Christian muses," sacred epics, visions, prophecies, etc., all and sundry, bound to fail esthetically, but having a precise educational and propagandistic function.[88] In this respect, some particular significations of *religious literature* also appear.

The Baroque favors a less exalted piety, consisting of gravity, moralism, and controlled rigor. Prophecy and *sauvage* mysticism become suspicious, viewed as being outside the discipline of the Church. The "virtues" turn into "divinities," while the sublime constitutes a substitute for contemplation and divinity. Read from this angle, Boileau has Baroque characteristics, too.[89] The tendency is to discipline inspiration, to set it right and "calm it down" (*désordre régulier, folie raisonnable*).[90] Traditional concepts ("divine fury," *est deus in nobis*, etc.) become either trite or mere clichés. "We must soar high on wings of thought" (J. Vauquelin de la Fresnaye, 1605).[91] Baroque man keeps at an esthetic distance from divinity. Literarily speaking, it only interests him under its thematic, formal and—last but by no means least—suggestive aspects. The sense of mystical experience is lost; instead, the psychological, emotional, cathartic effect appears (*je ne sais quoi, grâce*). The Baroque, then, engenders a sort of civilian, formal, esthetic mysticism. It is spectacular, grand, ceremonial, awe-inspiring. The Mass becomes a ceremony, a performance, a "show." Such a conception has an impact upon the definition of *sacred literature*. It appropriates *ornamenta poetarum*.[92] *De stylo seu literatura scripturae sacrosanctae*[93] becomes a concern from the esthetic point of view as well. The idea of *venustà delle parole*[94] makes its way into sacred oratory. The esthetic, sensitive formalization of sacred literature is evident, characteristic and, from our point of view, well conceptualized.

Profane Literature

A similar process determines and pins down the meaning of *profane literature*. The term, it bears repeating, has a mystical, theological origin and is used, as before, in typical doctrinary dissociations, constantly reiterated, like *sacram profanamque*,[95] *lettres saintes et profanes*,[96] and others of the kind. Individualized phrases: *lettres profanes, lettere e dottrine profane*, conceived and written down by *auteurs profanes, cervelli mondani*, etc., have a restricted, usually critical, meaning, which can often be derisive (*heidnischen Scribenten*).[97] A tendency to assimilate free ("libertine") thought, *Des esprits forts* (La Bruyère) is also apparent. The suspicion of error, heterodoxy, or even heresy proves to be permanent and great.

The penetration and entrenchment of the lay mentality substantially modifies literary consciousness and the concepts with which it operates. These concepts claim to have a specific condition of their own, and this anticipates claims to the autonomy of literature. The phenomenon, as we have seen, is far from novel, and continues throughout the period in a dynamic manner. An important effect of laicization is the conviction that genuine mystic poetry is the expression of a state of grace, so rare that one cannot find more than "two or three excellent instances "of the kind, even in the most prolific centuries.[98] In other words, statistics categorically favor lay literature. From now on, it will be the natural, current, traditional form of literary expression, hence, its definitive identification as literature pure and simple. This tendency is amplified by a set of psychosocial and cultural factors (the context and the *bienséance* system of the courtier). The mixture of Christian heroes, themes and psychology[99] becomes risky.[100] Classical mythology is also banished as false, unbelievable, as an obsolescent form of irrational superstition.[101] The loss of the mystical, initiating, revealing sense (even if deplored) is a fact and becomes one of the reasons for the inferiority of the moderns.[102]

This has a specific outcome in the metamorphosis of mythological-mystical scenarios into fictional scenarios. Profane literature changes into epic fable, into a *romanzerie*.[103] The degraded myth turns into *contes de fées*.[104] Another remarkable phenomenon is that divine fury and inspiration become art, imagination is no longer seen as a miracle. Apollo is but a subject of *badinage*, etc. The controversial issues of the day—the *Querelle des Anciens et des Modernes* is raging—are taken over by lay, esthetic "sects" and "religions." Poetic language, completely desacralized, also becomes radically fashionable. Symbols and allegories (*emblèmes, blasons,* mottoes) now become mere poetic clichés, emptied of any esoteric meaning.[105] More than in the preceding periods, lay literature is equated with the estheticizing and formalization of literature.

The concepts *sacred* and *profane*, applied to writing and literature, are also attested in seventeenth-century Romanian culture. Dosoftei declares of his *Psaltire în versuri* (1673): "*Amu tălmăcitu şi am scris precum au vrutu Dumnezeu*" (I translated and wrote the way my Lord wanted me to). In its turn, Matei Basarab's *Pravila* (Code of Law, 1640) recommends that the printed text "*să nu ajungă în mînă de mirean*" (be not read by laymen).[106] The two domains are kept well apart in Romania, too. The first index of proscribed books in Romanian culture also dates from the seventeenth century.[107]

The Totality of Letters

It is the phase when the definition of literature as the *totality of letters*, in both senses, the *totality of knowledge* and the *totality of writings*, is fully accepted and consolidated throughout Western culture. These basic meanings are acknowledged as essential, obvious, unquestionable. The *totality of letters* is a solidly organized entity, of great terminological stability. All the "literary" lexicography of the age is imbued with a comprehensive, all-embracing cultural spirit.

The traditional phrase *re litteraria* continues in use in the didactic, academic sphere of classical Latin culture. We come across it in essential dissociations, such as *re et litteraria*,[108] defining at the same time scholarly studies and subject-matters and various literary information (*in re litteraria*).[109] The notion is currently employed and its global content is obvious. It appears even more forcibly in the no less widespread formula *omni litteratura*[110]—maximum, total culture, a synonym of the absolute superlative *grande littérature*. It is the definition of the ideal man of culture.

In modern languages, the phrase oscillates between *littérature* (= writings, works of any kind, as with Furetière, *Auteur*, s.v.) and *all literature and erudition* (= all-comprising culture and erudition, as with Bacon).[111] The formula *toute sorte de littérature*[112], *toute la littérature*[113] is even more explicit in that respect, and consecrated by dictionaries: "Any science and doctrine" (Furetière, *Lettres*, *Dict. de l'Acad. fr.*, *Lettres*, s.v.). *Letters* and *literature*, respectively, are a global reality, initially indistinct and include all the literal or mechanical sciences and arts. In modern terms, they involve the entire content of humanistic or scientific culture, forged by "all the illustrious men of letters."[114]

We find the same totalizing logic at work in the case of various "literary" domains: *divers genres de littérature et de science, ogni sorte di lettere, tutte le scienze, any other literature, all sorts of poetry*, etc., cited from various authors of the time. Their frequent use saves our having to seek precise reference. *Any* content can be attributed to literature. The formula becomes ever more commodious and expedient. The weakening is yet another potential cause of a terminological crisis.

The Book

The idea of *book* is also completely stable, current, continuing—with certain new developments—all the significations with which it has been invested. Its content is still of secondary importance. The hard, basic sense is that of written text (with only an implicit idea of "work"), of printed text, publication. An author—of any kind—is "he who has brought a book to light," who "has put together any printed book."[115] The writer is a *Buchdichter*, a *Buchschreiber*.[116] Some technical descriptions of the book as a typographic and ornamental object are also remarkable.[117] In a first plane of signification, the *book* is the definition and symbol of writings of any sort. The idea of the totality of written literature points in the same direction.

Sacred and profane metaphors for *book*, continuing in the Renaissance vein, are also quite frequent. They carry on older ideas, of great theological and philosophical prestige. One chapter of D. G. Morhof's *Polyhistor* is entitled *De libris mysticis et secretis* (I, c. X). The creative divinity, author of the "book of the world," is another cliché. Its symbology, transferred to mathematics, is of interest to Galileo and others. The world is a divine book, the work "written" by the Lord (Bacon).[118]

The lay interpretation of the "book of nature" is even more widespread. The cosmos is a "public manuscript."[119] It is the utmost source of knowledge and wisdom. The practical philosophy of the age (Gracián, Descartes, Galileo) admits of no other object or surer method of observation. Purely bookish culture is undermined. It is only the great book of the world that teaches us *le bon usage* of written books.[120]

This does not mean, however, that, from a didactic point of view, the idea of *book* loses ground, or that it forsakes its original, essential, cultural, and pedagogical functions. The book remains "the first instrument of education" (Comenius).[121] The tendency to cram all knowledge into a "unique" book proves to be equally strong. It is active both in the sphere of popular culture, where almanacs are widely circulated[122] and, especially, in that of refined, exalted culture. Anthologies, collections, compilations of texts, are frequently used. Of great interest is the conception of comprising and synthesizing all the science of the time "in nine or ten in-folios" (Huet),[123] of a "general index" that compresses 112 in-folio volumes into only one volume.[124] These are the beginnings of the "literary digest." The paternity of this "modern" idea is older than one might have thought.

Maybe the most important aspect of the idea of *book* in the seventeenth century—in a way, the decisive aspect—is that it is more and more emphatically differentiated from the notion of graphic record and typographical object. Now, a book is defined as "a work or composition made by a man of the spirit in order to convey to his readers or to posterity what he himself has learned, gathered, invented or experimented," (Furetière).[125] Thus, creative writing and personal invention, "composition" and "invention", appear alongside the idea of cultural accumulation and dissemination. As we shall see, these concepts will greatly contribute to the ongoing "estheticizing" process in literature. This first attempt at lexicographical precision definitively introduces the idea of book as literature into the sphere of literary creation.

The new conception takes even firmer root due to emotional and literary satisfactions—already grasped in the previous century—which are no less specific about the idea of the literary book. Books are not "dead things," but "living objects" (Milton, *a partencie of life*).[126] According to an even more widespread formula of the time, they are *animae medicorum*. Translated into social language, this means happiness, consolation, evasion from "boredom and idleness." The spiritual phrase, "paper lovers" (Pierre Bayle), was coined in the same period.[127]

An echo of all these basic significations (albeit, in elementary, embryonic form) can be spotted in the Romanian ideas of the time. Evidently, the key word continues to be "sfînta carte" (the holy Book); *Evanghelia cu învăţătură* ("Learning from the Gospel," 1624), *Carte românească de învăţătură* ("Romanian Catechism," Varlaam, 1643). From a religious viewpoint, books are "true or false." The notion of a book of lay culture is also present, as in N. Milescu: *Carte pe scurt despre cele două muze şi despre cele şapte arte liberale* ("A Brief Book on the Two Muses and on the Seven Liberal Arts"). The so-called "books of wisdom" that begin to be published in this country in the seventeenth century originate in the same educational and religious tradition.[128] To print books (*a bate din tipar cărţi*), to praise, even, the printing activity in the city of Amsterdam (*"prin chărti este. n omenie tipar"*, as Mihai Halici wrote in 1674)[129] are pioneering intellectual attitudes and concepts. They begin to exert a powerful attraction over Romanian minds.

The Library

The relationship *literature* = *culture* = *book* is organically prolonged into the seventeenth century through the already classical idea of *library*. All previous senses are maintained and amplified, but there are new acceptations as well. The *library* enters a new phrase, wherein it is intensely organized, systematized, given a theoretical basis. It becomes a true cultural institution, which stocks and disseminates culture. *De re bibliothecaria*[130] refers to the theory and practice of erudition, to the methodical, documented initiation to refined scholarship. Material management, as well as the embellishment of reading rooms, is an equally important preoccupation.[131] The library becomes the temple of the muses.[132]

The spirit of the age is administrative, bureaucratic, oriented toward disciplined, officialized cultural actions. The establishment of the French Academy (1635) has a symbolic value as well. The conservation and stocktaking of books is followed by detailed, systematic instructions on how to use them. A title like *Musei, sive bibliotheca tam privatae quam publicae extructio, instructio una, usus . . .* , by Claude Clément (1635), establishes a comprehensive programme. Similarly P. J. Granger's *Syntagma bibliothecae Parisiensis Societas Jesu* (1678). Libraries are not put together, managed or used randomly. The specialist, the book technician, must intervene, as he alone is qualified to give competent instruction. The classical text in this respect is, undoubtedly, *Advis pour dresser une bibliothèque* by G. Naudé (1627). This purely cultural conception enlarges and enriches traditional attitudes.

The pedagogical purpose—in the sense of giving a global, universal orientation to reading, through the most efficient method available—

remains a priority. Leibniz' *Bibliotheca universalis* again expresses an aspiration to global cultural knowledge,[133] indistinguishable from the idea of culture and literature. A library "must be universal" and assist the reader "to know everything."[134] The concept "general catalogue," associated with that of "library," is convergent, some think synonymous, with the latter.[135] The famous baroque portrait of G. Archimboldo, Rudolph II's librarian, consisting of books, is symbolic.

A value judgment, leading to critical selection or screening, also intervenes. One title, among many, is edifying: Charles Sorel, *La Bibliothèque française, ou le choix et l'examen des livres français* (1664), a sort of pioneering literature textbook. As will be seen, the concept "literary criticism" is closely associated with these intertwining senses. To build a library, one needs to "select the most important books."[136] It is here that the idea of preferential lists appears to be considerably developed later on: La Mothe Le Vayer, *Du moyen de dresser une bibliothèque d'une centaine de livres seulement* (1648).[137] On the same occasion, the concept of a unique book reappears, this time pushed to the "limits of utopia:" "All the Greek authors in one volume, all the Roman in another,"[138] etc. This compression is the equivalent of a *Bibliothèque des pauvres*. The problem of available living space is already raised. More serious reasons are also taken into consideration: the recurrence of ideas, thought up by only five or six geniuses and then repeated in unchanged form (Bacon, *De Studiis et lectione librorum, Sermo*, 48). There is, then, no need to collect platitudes in several copies and to cram the libraries.

The Bibliography

The beginning of the tradition of bibliography could already be noticed in the period of the Renaissance and of Humanism. A further step is taken now by the coinage of the term itself, G. Naudé, *Bibliographia politica* (Venice, 1633). It results from the semantic synonymy and alternation *bibliotheca/bibliographia* and actually enriches the idea of literature with a new term (and a new definition), a term destined for a grand career, particularly in the Germanic area, in the nineteenth and twentieth centuries.

For the time being, the notion that becomes consolidated and gains ground is that of index, inventory (Philippe Labbé, *Bibliotheca bibliothecarum*, 1664), and catalogue (Antoine Teissier, *Catalogus auctorum* . . . 1686). New terms, new techniques, and new practices define an activity in full swing, triggered, and made indispensable by the epoch's progress in erudition. The basic requirements can be seen clearly: a complete, exhaustive inventory, in both senses: universality (everything about everything, for example, Broer Iausz, *Catalogus universalis*, 1639) philosophers, historians, litterati[139] and specialization (everything on one field of knowledge), hence the publication of specific bibliographies: *Bibliotheca exotica, classica, media et phisica, juridica et politica,* etc. Once more the mechanism of total accumulation, of totalizing cultural data is set in motion, even if in only one single area of activity. On this plane too, *literature,* in its general sense and as the totality of its parts, strives to comprise all knowledge.

The historical dimension—which is now beginning to take shape and gain momentum—of *bibliography* has an even more promising future. The chronological principle opens the way not only for the history of libraries (Louis Jacob, Jean de la Caille) and the history of bibliography (a collection of catalogues and "libraries"),[140] but also for literary history proper. It is at first a mere repertory, inventory, catalogue of authors and works, listed in chronological order. This extremely interesting moment of genesis dissociates, empirically at first, two sets of data: the chronology of cultural data, in the context of a series of historical events (wherein—through complex enumeration—such information inevitably appears),[141] and a chronology of specialized biographical data, gathered from the cultural-literary sphere exclusively. Within this framework, one finds references to *historia literaria* and even to special works, such as Guillielmo Cave, *Scriptorum ecclesiasticorum Historia Literaria* (Londini, 1688). The errors of erudites are already denounced: *Ex historia literaria, de extractionibus eruditorum* by Petrus Hogier (1685). The distinction between *dictionarium* (= bibliography) and *historia litteraria* was to be made in such books, too.[142] The basic pattern continues to be the traditional one: the sacred (literary) area versus profane (literary) area. The latter is looked upon as a mere appendix of sacred history.[143]

The "critical" signification of bibliography, which appears through the inevitable introduction of selection and value-assessment, is not devoid of importance either. Not all books, but only the "good" ones, are catalogued. Thus, critical bibliography appears: V. H. Vogler, *Introductio universalis in notitiam cuiuscumque generis bonorum librorum* (1670). The new term is used quite explicitly in some titles: *Bibliographiae eruditorum critico-curiosae sive Apparatus ad historiam literariam novissimam conspectus secundus* (1681–1710). Such titles prefigure a genuine program: value judgments, cooperation with literary history, the screening of "novelties," of the latest publications. The notion of "literary criticism" appears, vaguely, in embryo, even in such dry terminology. The idea of "bibliography" appears in Romanian culture as well, in the same fleeting, casual manner, in the epilogue of *Chiriacodromion* (1699), for example. The necessity of mentioning the sources and the edition used is pointed out.[144]

The Encyclopedia

Being "total" and "bibliographical," *literature,* that is, *culture,* cannot help being encyclopedic as well. The humanistic, Renaissance foundation of this concept is of great importance, and its prestige has a direct bearing on the definition of literary culture in the seventeenth century.

Once more, the central element is the circularity and totality of knowledge. We find it reiterated in phrases like *in toto rei literariae circulus*,[145] *omnium litterarum cognitionem*.[146] Leibniz' formula, *Mathesis universalis portabilis*, is quite famous. The ideal continues to consist in "a perfect encyclopedia, or a circle in which all sciences and arts are linked" (Charles Sorel).[147] Such an encyclopedia evidently becomes a "unique book," a *liber librorum*, therefore, a *bibliotheca portabilis*,[148] a *libro de libros*.[149] In a literary-historical sense, the same task is fulfilled by a book like *Della Enciclopedia Poetica*, by Giuseppe Artale (1679), a gathering of notes on authors.[150] Concern with "universal erudition" is often praised. Literary culture "moves in a circle" to embrace every field of knowledge.

This universal "literary" spirit appears in many tactical titles, such as *Encyclopaedia, Polymathia, Pansophia, Polyhistor*, etc.[151] The modern spirit—esthetic, poetic, seeing in literature but a highly specific art—can hardly understand this universal cultural fervor. It is encountered in other specific titles, too: *Plaza universal de todas scientias y artes* (C. Suárez de Figueroa, 1629), *Dictionnaire universel* (A. Furetière, 1688), whose contents are a truly encyclopedic catalogue and, above all, the *Grand Dictionnaire Historique* (Moréri, 1674) and the *Dictionnaire historique et critique* (P. Bayle, 1690). These are gigantic cultural totals of an almost utopian character, at any rate situated at the outer limits of the possibilities of the human mind. It is the maximum experience, personally assumed, of European literary culture. After such an exacerbation, *culture = literature* can only become cooperative, and specialized work. The concept of total culture is "shattered," *éclaté*. It will never be put together again.

The inner tension of such an idea pushed to a paroxysm also results from a series of dilemmas, alternatives and divergent functionalities. The ideal, needless to say, is "universal man" (B. Gracián, *Oráculo manual*, 93), a "compendium" of all the aspects of life. *El hombre de todas horas* (*El Discreto*, VII). In the classical French variant,[152] the intellectual type, doubled by the socially and morally perfect, is *l'honnête homme*. But shaping him is difficult because of the very precise limits. Hence Pascal's compromise: *Peu de tout*: "As you cannot be universal and know everything there is to know about everything, you must know a little of everything."[153] This principle is embraced by the epoch's guides of fashionable conduct.[154] Finally, the alternative appears: private or public encyclopedism, a "public thesaurus of erudition,"[155] is this a solution to be wished for? We shall see that the future, very ages sociable, tip the balance in favor of the collective character of culture.

THE CLASSICIZATION OF TRADITIONAL DEFINITIONS

"Human Letters"

Another definition of *culture = literature* reappears naturally, stripped only of the previous Messianic passion of Humanism. The traditional concept of "literature" becomes "classical" in all its aspects. It becomes disciplined, stable, taught in schools. It is the integral expression of an official and, implicitly, laicized institution.

A first proof[156] is what has been called *l'humanisme dévot*, the glorification of human nature under the spiritual, but also social, supervision of the Church. Another is the classification, rather bibliographical in nature (in any case, administrative and widespread, especially in the Catholic area) of books like *Libri Theologici* and *Humanistae*. Hence, once again, in modern languages: *Lettres divines et humaines*,[157] *lettre humane e divine, divinas letras, humanas letras*, etc. Such nomenclature, ruled by the dichotomy sacred/profane influences literary terminology proper (for example, Lope de Vega, *Rimas humanas y divinas*, or *Poesis sacra/Poesis prophana*, as in some bibliographies of the time).[158]

The well-known and quite current formula, *litteras humanitatis, litterae humaniores, studia humanitates* do not say anything new. Nor do their equivalents have any special significations. The doublet *lettres humaines* (1635), *sciences humaines* (1661)[159] appears frequently with a stable meaning: knowledge, education, "letters" in general. The situation is the same for *lettere humane, studies of humanity, letras de humanidad*, etc. The word *humanités* is common to them all. It occurs in critical texts,[160] as well as in dictionaries, a proof of the stabilization and definitive consecration of the basic sense. The syntagm once again connotes all the activities and creations of the spirit (*les Lettres humaines, la Grammaire, la Rhétorique, la Poésie*).[161]

The notion *humanist*, also reactivated, has the same meaning. It continues to refer, on the one hand, to the popular professor of *letters* (*humaniorum litterarum professor*), the specialist in humanities (*humanitate litterator*); on the other, it is the true symbol of encyclopedic knowledge. The humanist must cover this in its entirety, according to a typified schema.[162] Certain ethical and psychological implications are also obvious; the civilizing character (*amollitur animas*), happiness (an emblem: "The study of letters and man's happiness),[163] and especially humanizing the human being (*plus humain = plus savant*).[164] Glorifying literary culture now reaches its apex. The century's anthropology is essentially "bookish," in the noblest sense of the word. But this prestige, which had been occasionally questioned before, is already beginning to fade.

"Liberal Letters"

The phrase *liberal letters* is equally frequent and equally devoid of significance. It comes into use again, closely associated (almost synonymous) with *studium humanitatis*[165] and *encyclopedia* (*ekkiklias Graeci, nosi Liberales vocant*).[166] These are the current formulas of humanist culture (literature), entirely and finally classicized. And what is their content? The two traditional cycles, the *trivium* and *quadrivium* (J. Thomasius, *De septem artem liberalibus*; N. Milescu also referred to the "nine muses"), grammar being the most important element. The idea of culture remains predominant. The acceptation we give the term "literature" today begins to surface now—but at different levels of signification—and is still hidden under a thick layer of traditional terminology.

Considerations on the status of liberal "arts" and professions, well differentiated from mere crafts, are also quite common. Similarly are considerations regarding the "culture of civilian life" (G. Naudé, *Syntagma de studio liberali*, 1632). "Liberal" study, just like the "humanist" one, teaches, civilizes, prepares the mind to accept virtue. The moral universe of *letters* has not changed since Antiquity.

"Good Letters"

Good letters are part of the same traditional lexical set (another legacy of the glorious age of the Renaissance and Humanism). They comprise all accepted and eulogized categories of *letters*, of both Latin (*bonae litterae, boni scriptori*)[167] and French (*bonnes lettres*) expression, respectively *buone lettere, good letters, buonas letras*, all frequently attested. The cultural content continues to be the decisive factor. A proof of this is the frequent use of the syntagm "a knowledge of good letters,"[168] often in a predominantly pedagogical sense.[169] This becomes a common denominator—a commonplace, even—for all literary genres and species, from epithets and fables to dramatic poetry.[170] Obviously, with this acceptation, *good letters* cannot be told apart from the *totality of letters*, which absorb them under a generic name.

The rise of the key term of *literature* proper is a real step forward. We can also record, in the Classical and Baroque Ages, the characteristic doublet, *la bonne littérature*,[171] *letteratura di buoni autori*.[172] The tendency of singling out and revaluating a certain category of literature (writings, works, authors) is evident. It will branch out, in a remarkable manner, in other levels of knowledge as well.

The same *good letters* are directly attributed a series of ethical and psychological values, which, if not new, are clearly revamped. Counter-Reformation pedagogy sees a direct relationship between cultivating spirits (*cultura ingegnorum*) and *buoni libri*. *De bonarum mentium* and *artium* is a subject of study for erudition as well. *Humanitas* is defined as love of *bonae litterae*. Hence, the complex definition—true to the socializing, fashionable, stylized spirit of the age—of the exemplary literary type: "A man of spirit and good letters," a "zealot of good letters."[173] His moral trait is

Epicurism: *gli esercizi deliciosi delle buone lettere*.[174] Precise confessions were recorded at the time to the delight (even *la débauche*) of reading and study (Gui Patin).[175]

One can notice, at the same time, a steady decline in the traditional humanist acceptations, totally classicized in their Latin expression. The phenomenon can be observed in Du Cange's *Glossarium* (1678), in which, under the entry *Litterae, bonae litterae* and *humanas letras* are no longer mentioned among the acceptations.[176] If we confined ourselves to this authoritative source, we could say that the phrases were no longer in use.

THE COORDINATES OF LETTERS

Ancient Versus Modern Letters

Although the historical perspective on letters is the original one (having been shaped in Antiquity, when the contrast between new and old in literature was grasped, to be ever more decisively underlined by subsequent ages), it is only now that the gap widens. Historical perspective becomes broader and more accurate. In the long run, the idea of a totality of letters, as well as the other global definitions (*book, library, bibliography,* etc.) seems too general, too undifferentiated. The need is now felt of a more precise determination of *letters* as a function of a certain time and place, of the actual historical conditions in which they appeared and manifested themselves. Consequently, the sense of history grows and becomes better organized. The historical content of literature is changed, and literature is "aware" of it. With an important amendment, determined by the specificity of the age, *letters* are, increasingly, the object of systematic historical research, of methodical erudition and, simultaneously, of morpho-typological parallels covering large periods of history. A new character enters the stage: the "specialist," that is, the literary historian, the erudite, the bibliographer, and—*verbi gratia*—the "phenomenologist" and "morphologist" of Greek, Latin, and modern literatures. These researchers will leave their print on the entire subsequent development of European literary studies.

Information on the origin of writing and of alphabets is abundant enough to make the first syntheses not only possible, but also necessary. Hermannus Hugo, for instance, in *De prima scribendi origine et universo rei literarie antiquitate* (1617) starts from handwriting and ends with printing and book illustration. Others deal with runes (Ole Worm, *Danica literatura antiquissima,* 1636), hieroglyphs, etc.[177] Such studies (if examined carefully)[178] speak volumes about the essential origins of literary history. The very term gains authority, both in its modern (for example, *histoire des lettres et des auteurs*)[179] and its classical (for example, *De historia literaria*)[180] variants. The following pattern is used: the history of alphabets, with illustrations in the texts, the diachronic enumeration of the first written records (the history of written texts = literary history), and the development of the concept of the totality of written texts as the final object of historical investigation. This methodological archetype will also have a long life.

For the time being, however, such a concept can only lead to two types of historiographical research. In both cases, it is simply a question of taking an inventory of writings of every sort, of making a chronological, quantitative record of *literature*, taken in its basic, totalizing sense. In its incipient, so-called "prehistoric" phase, literary history can only be a history of written culture, drawn up in two ways: 1. a chapter of cultural history, as part of a general or national history, as in E. Pasquier, *Recherches sur la France* (VII, VIII, IX) (1621), an author who is intent on demonstrating that "Gaul, later called France, cultivated the *good letters* since immemorial times;"[181] 2. bibliographies and literary encyclopedias ("theaters," "libraries," "art collections,"[182] etc.), repertoires and specialized inventories of "illustrious people," of "literate people," such as Lorenzo Crasso's *Elogii d'huomini letterati* (1666), in the general sense of men of culture but with an incipient genre specialization: *Istoria de poeti greci e di que che'n Greca lingua han poetato* (Napoli, 1678). The most specialized institution in this field is now set up in France as *Académie des Inscriptions et Belles-Lettres*, (1663), consisting of the "most versatile scholars in the knowledge of history and of Antiquity."[183]

The essential ideas of historiography are not new, but applying them to literature makes it possible for literature to become part of a clear-cut, objective, generally applicable scenario. The most fertile is the idea of the historical cycle, that is, of progress and decadence. There is an *incrementa literatura*,[184] a "blossoming and a death," a "decadence" of letters.[185] The "revival of letters"—already talked about in the previous period—discovers its intrinsic causality, its own laws, as happens with all historical phenomena.

La Querelle des Anciens et des Modernes, not so rich in new ideas as is usually believed, is part of this general process. The existence of a "modern literature" had been acknowledged for a long time.[186] Now, however, the prerequisites of any "modern literature" are formulated in a clearer manner: a) the historical criterion, that is, the existence of a new, incomparable, unique historical moment: b) the qualitative criterion, that is, the linguistic, spiritual, thematic, morphological specificity typical of every historical moment. "Each century has its own style."[187] Reference is frequently made, therefore, to *littérature moderne*,[188] in both senses of the term: the conviction of the "moderns," that they have "changed the face of literature"[189] is general and fully justified. But the strongest argument—the apparition of a new "spirit of the age" is older and has been used "in other spheres as well" (Bacon).[190] It is used again, very forcefully, to justify an acute awareness of the present historical moment (new, irreplaceable), followed by a whole set of mutations in the literary sensitivity: a new "taste," a new "fashion," new conditions of literary "success," etc.

The effects of the new perspective are also quite considerable. The ever more numerous parallels and typologies between ancient and modern literatures act directly upon the idea of literature. On the one hand, there appear the first typological, morphological and—in a wider sense— structural investigations, not only of national literatures, but, by implication, of literature in general. On the other hand, symptoms of a crisis of the idea of literature are manifested at the same time. Is a general (common, single) definition possible for literary phenomena and literary works situated so far apart in time and space? Later, in the nineteenth and twentieth centuries especially, it will be revealed that the idea of literature is divided on both of these questions.

National Versus World Literature

The problem of "national" and "world" literature in this period does not go beyond the stage of a latent definition. Though conditions are ripe, an *expressis verbis* formula cannot be found. We are offered yet another opportunity to observe the fundamental predicament of our biography: the idea of literature asserts itself and grows through significations that are first and foremost implicit and only afterwards explicit.

If the first national literary identity was Greek and Latin, during the Renaissance the process of discovering multinational literary identities was set in motion, through the promotion and cultivation of national languages. The national language is, indeed, an invariant of the idea of literature. It confers on it a precise, stable identity. The term *literature* is used to refer to national writings: *literatura Runica, Hebrea ac Graeca literatura* (Ole Worm), *litteraturae apud Germanos* (D. Ge. Schubart), and also to the whole corpus of writings in a national language: *graeca literatura, judaica literatura*, etc. (numerous attestations). Everything that falls into this sphere is the domain of *vulgaris libris*, hence, the equation: "national language" = "vulgar language" (*Poetes des Isles Britanniques en langue vulgaire*, 1686).[191] In the same period, there is a growth in the number of titles of literary works that include the idea of national identity (*Buch von der Deutschen Poeterey, Teutsche Prosodia, Teutsche Dicht- und Reimkunst*, etc.). The necessity of writing in the national languages is generally acknowledged (an Italian imperative: "You must write in your own tongue.")[192] Here, chronicler Mihail Moxa reiterates Coresi's principle: "*Mai toate limbile au carte pe limba lor*" (Almost every language has books written in it).[193] This phenomenon is also a symptom of laicizing. National languages are neither biblical, nor Adamic.

More than during the previous stage, national literature can be defined through extra-literary connotations. It is chockfull of complexes and resentments that have nothing to do with literariness. This is one of the least "literary" acceptations of the idea of literature. The first to intervene is the complex of national superiority or inferiority. The French believe that Spanish writers are uneducated, the latter (Calderón), humiliated, admit that they are inferior.[194] "The cause of modern writers is tied to the grandeur of the French nation."[195] The moderns play from the very beginning the nationalist, patriotic card, and they win.

Therefore, they will often consider themselves the equals even of Homer.[196] French comedy is ideally suited for a comparison with Greek and Latin ones.[197] The argument of equal value appears with all the moderns (Italian, English, German). Other consequences are active emulation and the competitive spirit. The moderns are on an equal footing with the ancients. The praise of national talent often takes on exaggerated proportions: "Our France has an infinity of Homers, Virgils, Euripides, etc."[198] It is the beginning of a national complex of superiority, predisposed to hypertrophy and megalomania. It will play havoc, both in literature and in the sphere of the idea of literature. A certain degree of lucidity can nevertheless be noticed in this respect ("The preconceptions of nations or of the authors' countries)."[199] Yet, as of now, literary nationalism is a reality,[200] a calamity even. It is a direct outcome of the awareness of the superiority of the moderns over the ancients, of the superiority of some moderns over others.

It is not only a question of literary egocentrism and state policy (Colbert), but also of theoretical justifications: the permanent, universal principle of emulation is extended to nations[201] and then to national literatures. *La Querelle* has such reasons as well; they can be found in France, England, Germany, and Spain.[202] On the other hand, the idea of progress beings yet another argument in favor of national literature: if the Greeks were outdistanced by the Latins, the French can naturally outdistance the Greeks and Latins. Those who are writing today are by definition superior to those who wrote yesterday. The mere flow of time perfects poetic invention. In the course of time, such arguments will often be invoked by every movement of literary regeneration, down to the twentieth century avant-garde movements. But it is this early that they appear (Johan Rist, *Musa Teutonica*, 1634).[203]

A twofold feeling of superiority eventually dominates the consciousness of a national literature. This is first toward precursors of any ilk (vernacular languages compared to the ancient ones, the new, modern, language toward the old one,[204] modern writers to classical, a very current occurrence); and second, toward other modern languages: "The beauty of the French language is greater than that of all the others."[205] There is only one step to chauvinism, autarchy, intolerance. Nationalist egocentrism and conceit made their appearance in the idea of literature: "You can be well-educated (*habile*) without speaking any language but French."²⁰⁶ A brutally put piece of truth . . . even the syntagm "literary nationalism" has been used in connection with Etienne Pasquier.²⁰⁷

Much more positive and fertile are a few other significations that will enter the essential definition of "national literature." First, the idea of a "national specificity" takes shape, and its components begin to be analyzed. Everybody is fully aware that modern, Baroque writers do not write *à la grecque*, but *à la française*,²⁰⁸ that "each nation has its own manners, laws, and psychology." In the same line of thought, they maintain that "each nation has its special character."²⁰⁹ Hence, there is a marked predilection for national themes and subjects. These cater to a differentiated national taste: "Each nation has a taste of its own."²¹⁰

That the idea of literature becomes national can be seen even more clearly if we examine the nomenclature of the instruments of study and research. These are the first national "literary histories," such as *Bibliographia Parisina* (1643–1650), *Bibliographia gallica universalis* (1644–1647, 1651–1653) by Louis Jacob de Saint Charles. National, even local bibliographies appear (Donato Calvi, *Scena letteraria de gli scrittori Bergamaschi*, 1664), as well as national syntheses (Giovan Maria Crescimbeni, *L'Istoria della volgar poesia*, 1698). Cultural-literary information becomes fragmented and specialized in ever more precisely delineated national domains.

The meaning of the opposite term, "universal letters," is first and foremost inherited from the Renaissance and Humanism: the universal character of cultural knowledge, cultural and literary universality extended in time and space. The first meaning can be easily identified in phrases like *universis litteraria, universa rei litterariae*. In modern languages, we come across "universal books that tell of many things"²¹¹ and even "world literature" (= world culture).²¹² Universalist consciousness also appears, in forms that are highly superior to the historical positivism of later ages. It is the expression of "a vast spirit/ [which is] of all time and all centuries. It sees everything at once, if I may say so, with one glance."²¹³ Happily, specialized, compartmentalized fragmentation, devoid of a vision of totality, has not yet asserted itself in literary studies. A simultaneous reading of universality is still possible.

The perpetual extension of vision, the increase in the knowledge of Oriental nations, so typical of the seventeenth century—in the case of China, the situation is paradigmatic²¹⁴—result in European concepts being applied, in a general manner, to the processing of the new, exotic data. Chinese writing becomes "Chinese literature,"²¹⁵ and liberal letters find an equivalent in the "liberal arts and sciences of the Chinese."²¹⁶ Chinese literature and culture are translated in terms that are equally classical (T. Spizelius, *De re literaria Sinensium commentarius* . . . , 1660). The idea of a universal language and a universal writing, common to all people—a central preoccupation with Leibniz—is successful for the same reason (for example, Samuel Hartid, *On Common Writing*, 1647; John J. Becher, *Character pro notitia linguarum universalis*, 1661). Along similar lines, medieval preoccupations with "philosophical" language and grammar are shown to have an equally universal character (John Wilkins, *An Essay Towards a Real Character and a Philosophical Language*, 1667). The Port-Royal Grammar has a similar orientation. It will be resumed and brought up to date only in the twentieth century (N. Chomsky).

The terminology of the age also appears in the names given the instruments of universal literary knowledge. "Library" becomes *Bibliotheca mundi* (1626), *Bibliothèque universelle*, as in Leibniz' plan: a summarizing synthesis of world culture."[217] A functional, editorial formula is *Bibliothèque universelle et historique* (1686–1683), in twenty-six volumes, by J. Le Clerc and Lacroze. *Teatro d'huomini letterati* (1647) by Girolamo Ghilini purports to be a "Teatro Universale." The textbook for initiation to Oriental studies has an identical title and structure: Barthélemy d'Herbelot, *Bibliothèque orientale, ou Dictionnaire universel . . .* (1697). Was it read by Dimitrie Cantemir? At any rate, in the *Predoslovie către cititor* (Foreword) of his poem *Viaţa lumii* (Life of the World), M. Costin invokes the principle of the universal existence of poetry: *"În toate ţările, iubite cititorule, se află acest fel de scrisoare"* (This kind of writing, dear reader, can be found in all countries).[218]

Popular Letters

The fragmentation of the idea of literature in the seventeenth century has other aspects as well, which, in time, will become traditional. The schema belongs to the prior period, the Renaissance, but is made more systematic, clearer from a conceptual point of view. As the value and importance of national—popular—languages are no longer questionable, their dissociation from and opposition to the standard cultivated language, Latin, becomes more and more evident. Hence the "difference in language between scholars and ordinary people."[219] Written literature is, by definition, cultivated; the oral one is uncultivated, vulgar. The typology *vulgar/erudite* is, in fact, characteristic not only of Classicism, but also of the Baroque.[220] It is reflected in this country, too, in the sphere of ecclesiastical culture, in the concern *"să izvodim aşea cum să înţeleagă toţi"* (let us speak in such a way that everybody will understand) (*Noul Testament*, 1648).[221]

This dichotomy has a direct bearing on literary typology and terminology. Consequently, there are *populares et illeteratas artes*,[222] even treatises *De quator artibus popularibus*,[223] by opposition, first and foremost, to *liberal arts*. Grammar, gymnastics, music, graphic arts would be of "popular usage." "Art" continues to have the ancient and medieval meaning, that of technique, craft, versatility.

At the same time, an awareness of folklore and poetry is beginning to manifest itself. It appears in England, where folk ballads are being collected.[224] On an emotional level, they appeal even to Sir Philip Sidney, Italy (G. B. Basile),[225] France—here in a pejorative sense: "Pont-Neuf verses" (Mme de Sévigné) that are "shouted in the streets" (Pierre de l'Estoile), etc. This shows disdain, the source of which is not social, but rather a great cultural superiority—an important distinction.

Finally, there is the "literary" use of popular inspiration: the *contes de fées*, the "naïve simplicity" of which is praised through the rehabilitation of the "nurses' tales."[226] Stylized and ennobled, this literature is put forth as a modern genre (Ch. Perrault). The *tale of the miraculous* is another component of this marginal, barely accepted category. Here, Miron Costin prefers Plutarch to the "Basne" of the *Alexandria* (The Exploits of Alexander the Great).[227]

The cultural connotations of the concept remain all-important. They are a direct outcome of the importance given the popularization of science by the ideology and the press of the time. P. Bayle has a very clear idea of "medium-range information," something between newspaper items and the "purely scientific news."[228] The emergence of a new reading public—fashionable and feminine, "learned" because snobbish—helps the process gather momentum. Aristotle's (then Newton's) philosophy is "divulged" to ladies,[229] astronomy to marchionesses, and so on. The concept "vulgarization" becomes even more widespread.

ESTHETICIZING LETTERS

"Beautiful Letters"

In the seventeenth century, the most characteristic definition of literature—the specific product of well-entrenched classical mentality—is "beautiful letters." The corresponding formula is still famous today: *belles lettres*. Its translation into other languages is a mere linguistic calculus: *anmuthigen Wissenschaften* (1665), *schöne Wissenschaften*, *belle lettere*, *belas letras*, etc. The term becomes official when Colbert sets up (in 1663) the *Académie des Inscriptions et Belles-Lettres*, which we have already mentioned. The name of the new institution, which parallels the already famous *Académie Française* (1635), consecrates the superior, cultural, erudite, learned acceptation of the term. After 1671,[230] it is attested with increasing frequency. At the same time, the ambiguity of the word *beau* makes it possible to operate important dissociations. These will prove decisive for the sense and evolution of the idea of literature. The estheticizing of literature progresses and gains importance.

We repeat that the term is a direct heritage from the Renaissance and Humanism. Hence, there is the tendency of seeing a similitude (of identifying them, even) between *belles lettres* and *bonnes lettres, lettres humaines, humanités* (1685),[231] which it tends to absorb and eventually replace. In the long run, these *belles lettres* become the synonym for any kind of *lettres*: "grammar, languages, profane authors, orators, historians and poets."[232] *Polite letters, polite learning, amene lettere* have an identical meaning. Again, the stress is on the idea of "knowledge" ("of the orators, poets, historians"), as the dictionaries of the time point out.[233] The basic meaning remains the traditional, cultural one: "study," "learning."[234] At this stage, letters cannot go beyond *savoir*. *Belles lettres* continue to be considered, primarily, a specific teaching object, a means of methodically acquiring culture.[235]

At the same time, one notices a meaningful semantic evolution. Upon reaching this stage, *belles lettres* waver between two poles. On the one hand, to know them means to be cultivated, well-read, while not to know them means to be "ignorant."[236] On the other, *belles lettres* take on the meaning "erudition,"[237] great culture (= *grande, immense littérature*). Thus, *homme des belles lettres* (1680) = *savant* ("a great savant, both in law and in *belles lettres*").[238] Step by step, the erudite meaning tends to take over, which definitively pulls the sciences into the semantic and lexical field of "beautiful letters." Hence, a new combination: *belles lettres et les sciences*,[239] even *belles sciences*.[240] Simultaneously, as the adjective *beau* seems to be increasingly suitable for what we call *belles-lettres* today—especially under the influence of the idea of *beautiful literature* and *poetry* in full ascent (see subsequently)—*belles lettres* tends to become a term that is more appropriate for sciences: "*Belles lettres,* consisting of the sciences of history, mathematics, cartography, chronology, languages, heraldry, genealogy and of the nice qualities of poets."[241] The dictionaries (Richelet, Furetière) maintain the ambiguity by consecrating the formula *la science des belles lettres*. The fact that exact sciences encroach upon the idea of literature further consolidates its cultural content, which becomes more technical, more specialized.

The science of philology seems to be ideally suited to the concept *belles lettres* in this acceptation. A natural semantic selection seems to preside over the entire operation. In the final analysis, it is not a question of just any "knowledge," but first of all a knowledge of "old manuscripts," "ancient languages," "hieroglyphs," etc. These disciplines are indispensable to an "understanding of Antiquity."[242]

The specific range of *belles lettres,* in their erudite hypostasis, is thus clearly delineated: the study of Antiquity in all its forms (archeology, epigraphy, philology, history). Hence the decidedly classical penchant of such research, precisely formulated as early as the *Querelle*.[243] Becoming increasingly more learned and academic, this tendency has continued to this day. It is one of the most stable classical meanings of *literature*.

Beautiful Literature

The parallel, synonymous term, *beautiful literature*, which gradually replaces *beautiful letters*, is destined to an even greater career. Eventually, its significations will be purely esthetic. For the time being, however, the original, strong, cultural sense of the idea of literature predominates, hence, the continuity in the old terminology, inherited from the Renaissance and Humanism.

There is no innovation, then, in this respect, on the plane of lexicography. Literature is now *politioris literatura*, now *elegantioris literatura*. The terms are often met in didactic, philological and academic circles.[244] Its "modern" correspondent, richly attested throughout the seventeenth century,[245] *la belle littérature*, is in the same situation. The learned, erudite meaning remains essential. But an extremely important semantic shift has occurred. The graphical, Latin etymology of literature (*litterae*) vanishes completely from the epoch's philological-grammatical treatises (G. J. Vossius, for instance). It is a sign that the idea of literature, in its "modern" acceptations, has broken completely free of its old etymon. The new values that define it confer upon it a new content and new significations, in a more and more active way.

Clearly, the first to reappear is the idea of the beautiful. On one level, its forms are still modest, current, marginal. The concern for calligraphy continues: among Colbert's projects there is one of an *Académie des belles mains*. The epoch's calligraphy textbooks (Italian, French, German) propagate the familiar notion of "beautiful writings" and "beautiful books." *Belle lettere* also has the meaning of handsomely written graphic signs.[246] The esthetic revaluation of literature is even more important. Encyclopedic culture ("this universality") is "the most beautiful" (Pascal).[247] For La Bruyère, too, "beautiful things" are creations of the spirit.[248] The direct relationship between "beautiful letters," the "works of the spirit," and the "beauty of the works of the spirit" seems to be ever more obvious.[249] It is still more usual to include literary works, *letters* in general (in the present-day sense of *belles-lettres*) in this category. Sometimes it is a truism (for example, *beau roman*).[250]

The progress of "the beautiful spirit" is also verified by the fact that a new sort of intelligentsia asserts itself. *Docte* is replaced by *le bel esprit* in every domain linked to letters and arts.[251] Some literary works are defined as being *toute(s) de littérature et de bel esprit*.[252] Treatises are published that define this spirit (for example, F. de Callières, *Du bel Esprit*, 1695). It is a combination of *honnêteté*, *Gelehrsamkeit*, *beauté de l'esprit*, *bon goût* and *galanterie*.[253] A creator and consumer of literature, cultivated and fashionable—a cultural and social phenomenon quite typical of the age. The French Academy, of course, is also an *Académie des beaux esprits*.[254]

Literature or Poetry?

The divorce between *poetry* and *literature*—a process that is characteristic of the entire biography of the idea of literature—becomes more radical during this period. This crucial situation results in fact in two parallel biographies that are already identifiable. The history of the idea of *poetry* will prove to be much more important and meaningful than the history of the idea of *literature*. The essence of the phenomenon is to be searched for in the switch from the purely cultural to the esthetic criterion in the field of *letters*.

At the same time, however, one cannot ignore the fact that the "grammatical," cultural tradition of poetry—predominant from Antiquity to the Renaissance—continues to be strong. "Poetry is a part of learning."[255] Poets and philosophers are part of "one and the same learning,"[256] two worlds that *fraternisent ensemble*: "poetry and grammar."[257] The view that poetry is "beautiful letters" written in verse also remains current; moreover, it is viewed as an "ornament of beautiful letters."[258] But more and more often poetry is singled out, considered separate from the rest of the writings. The official Jesuit doctrine, *ratio studiorum*, continues to speak of *humanitas sive poesis*.[259] Within this sphere, the domains continue to overlap. To M. Costin also, who had a strong feeling for poetry ("*care eleneşte ritmos se cheamă, iară slavoneşte stihoslovi*" [called *ritmos* in Greek and *stihoslovie* in Slavonic], Ovid continues to be a "teacher."[260]

The dissociations now being made—at the beginning, very timidly, as we have seen for the previous century—are therefore all the more relevant. During the Renaissance, it is divine inspiration that provides the master solution of poetic creation *sans art, sans savoir*.[261] The battle is fought especially around this increasingly devalued notion. A contemporary poet is described in the following terms: "He knew nothing but he was a poet."[262] Two distinct planes, perceived as such, the same judgment is passed on another poet: "It is the poetry of a learned man, but not of a poet."[263] "Learned" poetry (= literature) is no longer considered poetry proper. It is the origin of a precise dissociation between "ignorance" and "erudition."[264] The former is characteristic of "barbaric" nations, preeminently poetical. The idea will be amplified in the following century and then by Romanticism.

The consequences of this neat delineation of poetry from culture-literature will be far-reaching. As our demonstration advances, they will be seen more and more clearly. Let us note, for the moment, that the distinction between "knowledge" (culture, erudition) and poetic vocation paves the way for what will be called the "autonomy" of literature. The rejection of Aristotelian rules and of the Aristotelian tradition, frequent especially with Baroque poets,[265] anticipates the question of "antiliterature," resumed with new and ever more powerful arguments. Finally, the rise, success, and general use of the notion *poet*, applied, at the beginning, to any author that "writes well,"[266] but then as distinct from *gens de belles lettres*, consecrates an activity whose specific character is now acknowledged. Its evolution can also be traced in the terminology of the texts.[267]

In spite of all this, poetry cannot break from the "wholeness" of literature. It goes on being a part of literature, and its ever more marked specificity continues to be taken in stock, so to say, within the inevitable category of the totality of written works. Quantitatively and literarily, poetry is more and more aware of itself. This status has been preserved to this day.

Poetic Literature

In the Renaissance, poetry is completely identified with "literary art." That age has no room for the intermediate category of "poetic literature." This can only be the product of a transitional period, in which the idea of poetry, more and more sharply defined, is on the rise, while literature cannot hold its traditional domineering position. Thus, the conditions of the implicit acceptation of "poetic literature" are met. An increasingly insistent transfer of poetry upon literature begins now. The awareness of the fact that literature becomes poetic makes real progress. Poetry, which both overshadows and substitutes for literature, incorporates, and adopts it, tending to assimilate it completely. Thus, in the pair *literature/poetry* the balance is tipped, decisively, in favor of the latter. This situation is clearly mirrored by the terminology of the age.

A first indication is the coupling of the idea of *lettres* and *poésie* (in dictionaries)[268] with that of writing (*scrittura*) and poetic text (*testura poetica*),[269] by the fact that poetry takes over almost all of the attributes of writing and literature. The phenomenon is discernible especially with critics, for instance Dryden.[270] In the guise of versification (*escrivir versos*), poetry constitutes the most delectable activity in "all the field of letters."[271] Thus, *letters = poetry*. Poetry of any genre (dramatic, tragic, etc.), in the well-known spirit of totalizing letters, is the sum-total of all literary genres, of the "genres of writing" (R. Rapin).[272] The statement has indeed been made that in the seventeenth century the term *poetry* defines everything we call *literature* today, with the exception of the novel.[273]

The period witnesses, of course, a great interfusion of concepts. The notion *bien écrire* (typical of the literary theory and practice of Jesuit colleges) is applicable, in modern terms, to both poetry and literature, to verse and prose. But it already becomes closely associated with the idea of *écrivain*; similarly, the idea of *style* and its qualities (Abbé de Bellegarde,

Réflexions sur l'élégance et la politesse du style, 1695). The theory of an ornate, figurative style, held in high esteem by Baroque artists, also has a twofold use: in literature and poetry, domains with a totalizing character which, nevertheless, continue to be well apart. They all fall under the category *science galante*.[274] A proof is one of the epoch's definitions of poetry as an "agreeable science that combines gravity of precepts and sweetness of language."[275] The basic dissociation, then, is again operated: "science" = literature/"agreeable," "sweetness of language" = poetry.

Literary Art

In this chapter, too, there is a notable terminological tradition and redundancy. From Antiquity to the Renaissance, art has a predominantly technical sense: execution according to plan. It is, first and foremost, a craft, ideally one that implies highly skilled labor. The classics will hold the same opinion: "Making a book is a craft, like making a clock" (La Bruyère).[276] The second, better known acceptation is that of *liberal arts*, among which "poetics," that is, poetry,[277] is included alongside grammar and rhetoric. The traditional, purely technical nature is overshadowed by the new signification, more capacious and much more open to esthetic treatment.

This concept makes it possible to pass from scholastic letters to "artistic,"[278] ones and then on to the "art of writing well,"[279] etc. Hence to *art poétique* (Boileau), *Künstliche Tichterey* (David Czepko)[280] and other such formulae, all rapidly classicized.

The significations gather, overlap, and eventually become synonymous, tautological, redundant even, a phenomenon that is, after all, typical of the idea of literature. So, *literary art* = any *"well-written discourse."* This formula dominates the century (*bien écrire*,[281] good writing, elaborate writing, etc.)[282] We also witness the resurrection of the traditional notion *of writing* (*écriture*), still inseparable from literature, but having resurfaced with an esthetic hue.[283] Finally, other variants of the same idea can be encountered: *The fairy way of writing* (Dryden's title), *charmante manière d'écrire* (Scarron), and so on.

What does this manner consist of? To begin with, one must be endowed with "style," "an agreeable manner," "wit."[284] The concept of style, in particular, is on the rise. "To write well" and to have a "good style," a "beautiful style" become the synonymous[285] expressions of a lofty literary ideal. A "treatise" by Ben Jonson is entitled *De stilo et optimo scribendi genere*.[286] The artistic style is "embellished," "ornate," rich in imagery. They are the "ornaments of beautiful letters," or (which is the same thing) "ornate beautiful letters."[287] The learned content is eclipsed, and soon will be eliminated completely.

Although this question only casts an indirect light upon the explicit idea of literature, we shall remember that in this period the concept of literary art and that of verbal art tend to overlap completely, the latter indistinguishable from the virtuosity of literary imagery. Needless to say, the fundamental pattern remains unchanged: a poetic language radically dissociated from the vulgar, ordinary one; a refined, artificial, "erudite" language, as we find it defined in a classical text of the time, signed by Luis Carrillo y Sotomayor: *Libro de erudición poética* (1611).[288] Its characteristics are preciosity, artificiality, constant invention—the very opposite of classical style, which is simple and laconic, unaffected. What it aims at is to create the emotion of surprise, an *enchanting language*.[289] This effect can be achieved through what poeticians call *concetti, acutezza, agudeza*, figures and devices treated theoretically in famous treatises by Matteo Pellegrini, Baltasar Gracián, et al.[290] The main feature of what would be called *concettismo* or *concettosità* is the ingenuity of antithetical associations, generating perpetual novelty. The Spanish variant *culteranismo* says even more about its essentially literary origin, one of high refinement. The concept is typically Baroque.[291]

Literary Versus Poetic Specificity

During Classicism and the Baroque, what is understood today by "literariness"—defined and dissociated in the previous periods by terms that were far from precise—displays ever more radical tendencies. The final outcome is the gradual fusion and, ultimately, identification with its opposite, "poetic specificity." What we see, in fact, is the completion on every plane of a process that is characteristic of the idea of *literature*: Its being challenged and eventually absorbed, that is, annihilated, by the idea of *poetry*. Clearly, a "literary," that is, "cultural specificity," continues to exist. It is more and more ignored and marginalized in favor of the "poetic" one.

   Defining literature and literary activity in noncultural or general poetic terms is the most obvious sign of this orientation. An ironical piece of advice ("let us all write, men of learning or not")[292] demonstrates, first of all, that being "learned" (well-read, educated, with "great literature") no longer is an essential prerequisite for writing. This quality no longer enjoys prestige as such. *Literature* is not a "cultural work" any more, but a "work of the spirit," that is, a creative, imaginative work (Bouhours, La Bruyère: *ouvrage de l'esprit*, Dryden, to write with "spirit" *with writing*,[293] which is something else entirely. On the other hand, the "poet" is the "creator," the author of any kind of literature.[294] Poetry, in its turn—in a reiteration of the Renaissance point of view—must not "only teach and instruct, like the other liberal arts, but also recreate through the same means.[295] This way, literature is converted to a new regimen, one that is esthetic, subjective, emotional, delectable. "The pleasure of literature" is rediscovered; even more, its rights are vouchsafed again.

   The concept of "literature for its own sake" is also "specific" (*la vérita-*

ble . . . littérature, litteratura stessa).[296] Its being extended to cover poetry as well (*les belles Lettres et la Poésie même*)[297] shows how tightly the two ideas are intertwined. No doubt, the concept of an intrinsic quality (*an ihr selbst, per se stessa*), which becomes fully structured only now, is applicable to literature in its totality, seen as synthesis: letters + poetry. For this reason, all of the definitions of poetry are, retroactively, applicable to "literature." But the problem is not that simple.

Without going into details that would exceed the scope of this study, let us specify that this necessity of defining poetry, the poetical, poetic emotion, etc., is the cause of the first really severe terminological crisis of the idea of literature. The facts are known: poetry is defined, by Baroque writers especially, as *je ne sais quoi, non so che, no se qué, choses ineffables*, etc., in other words, as an undefinable, unspeakable, unutterable emotion. In fact, the crisis has continued to this day and we enter it as soon as we leave the restricted, but firmly and clearly defined area of the hermeneutics of *letters*. No progress can be made in this direction; one can only obtain variation on the same theme. The problem is still topical. The sacred versus profane dissociation, in fact, introduces the first specific criteria.

Literature—poetry reveals its identity even more precisely when we appeal to another genre of concepts, controlling both "literature" and "poetry." That it was a question of an art of speech was quite clearly understood as early as the Renaissance and Humanism. The same idea is now expressed—reinforcing the epoch's conception of "literary art"—as *l'art des paroles*,[298] *belles lettres . . . arts of eloquence, arte de imitar con palabras*,[299] etc. The idea of "genius," of a creator in the "field of *belles lettres*,"[300] is also notable. *Belles lettres* no longer are, no longer can be, learned and erudite par excellence.

Other qualities of poetry, identified in or transferred to general literature, expand ideas known to us since the Renaissance. Poetry is creation, it is a "natural" (spontaneous, intimate, instinctual) work of "fiction."[301] This last attribute is particularly important, as it is an etymon of the future concept of "literature of the imagination." It ensures, of course, a specific place for literature in the system of the arts, as has been pointed out.[302] Its terminology, however, derives from its quality as a "work of witt" (*witt-written, . . . product of imagination*).[303]

When he condemned "*Alexandria . . . plină de basne şi scornituri*"[304] (*Alexandria* full of tall tales and fabrication), Miron Costin had the same idea in mind (it can be found in other sources as well). The notion of a literary style with certain esthetic qualities was not unknown in these lands either; see Varlaam, "*scrie cu meşteşug*" (he writes skillfully).[305] Also in *Viaţa Sfîntului Nifon* (*iscusit la scris*-deft with the plume), in which we also come across—assuming the translation is correct—the distinction (or synonymy) "*cele-poetice şi literare*" (things poetical and literary).[306]

The Autonomy of Literature

As in the previous periods, the incipient awareness of literary specificity determines more and more precise dissociations from concurrent values. The classicizing spirit, however, cannot encourage, let alone carry out, such an operation, the sense of which only becomes clear from the perspective of the entire biography. The integrating spirit of autonomy is, after all, a discovery of the Baroque. The Baroque alone is predisposed to radical dissociations (B. Guarini: "Not instruction, but delight"),[307] to formal accents and exercises (surprise, novelty, esthetic treatment; G. Marino, "To tickle the readers' ears with the oddity of novelty"),[308] which is not to say that certain tendencies of autonomy had not appeared, as we have seen, before that.

The separation of the sacred from the profane will once again prove to be quite instrumental, with far-reaching consequences upon the spirit. The idea appears under various guises: the Sorbonne has no sway over the Parnassus (Pascal); there are "witty books that can be read with great pleasure, though without faith" (Mme de Sévigné), "it is impossible to put together the profane laurels of the Parnassus and the sacred palm leaves of Lebanon."[309] In this instance, rejecting profane poetry means an explicit acknowledgment of the existence of an autonomous realm of its own.

Some terminological indications in the field of *letters* are even more specific. To begin with, we frequently come across the dissociation *les lettres et les sciences* or, put differently, *sciences et belles lettres*.[310] This wavering is not without cause, but rooted in a twofold process, followed by an increasingly precise polarization:

a) In a first acceptation, what prevails is the gradual estheticizing of the idea of *belles lettres*, which are less and less often defined and cultivated as *belles connaissances*.[311] The latter are reserved for the sphere of sciences. The former take on all of the traditional attributes, known since Antiquity: *piacevoli, dilettevoli, litterarum otio*,[312] *le loisir*, etc. The purpose, once again, is not acquiring knowledge, not cultural accumulation, but gratuitous, intrinsic, autotelic satisfaction. As a matter of fact, the entire idea of literature will advance in this direction from now on.

b) In the second acceptation, the cultural and scientific tradition of the idea of *lettres*—which is still strong and will not yield without a fight—predominates. Hence the protest of the so-called "old-fashioned" lexicographers: the equation *belles lettres* = *lettres humaines* is an "abuse;" "the true belles lettres are physics, geometry and solid (exact) sciences."[313] Only this, and nothing more.

All these keep us well within the tradition. *Literature*'s true autonomy is achieved through the radical dissociation *art/non-art*. This is a component of the Baroque esthetic mentality and is plainly expressed by one of its exponents, B. Fioretti: "I repudiate and condemn tragicomedy, not because it is outside Aristotle's *Poetics*, but because it is outside Art" (*fuori dell' Arte*).[314] Tragedy is a non-artistic literary genre, the very existence and essence of which are denied. Artistic literature claims to have a specific area that is asserted with increasing intransigence. All "literary" writings devoid of this quality are excluded.

As the idea of poetry absorbs and replaces *literature*, the autonomy process will be taken over, reformulated and given ampler scope by the theory of poetry. At this stage, the idea of *literature* is only implied, and the struggle for autonomy will take the form of asserting and praising "poetical literature." The road is paved with all the arguments, which, though quite numerous and intense, do not concern us here, on prose versus poetry, natural poetry versus artificial poetry, poetry versus versification, etc. All these dissociations are effectuated within the sphere of poetry, which has become a key concept. *Letters* remain associated forever with prose, with the rules[315] of classicized, academic culture.

THE HETERONOMY OF LITERATURE

By contrast, literature is ever more currently conceived of in "heteronomic" terms. This can be explained by the social hierarchy, stratification, discipline, and standardization, typical of the seventeenth century, especially in France. At this level especially, it is paradigmatic for all Western culture.

"The Republic of Letters"

The communitarian, social dimension of *letters* is defined, first, by a successful, prestigious syntagm, inherited from the Renaissance and Humanism: *república literaria*. Its frequency is again high, and it has numerous equivalents in the European languages of wide circulation: *république des lettres, Gelehrten Republik, repubblica letteraria, commonwealth of learning*. Some new, related combinations belong, nevertheless, to this age: *pays des lettres*,[316] *empire des lettres, lettered world*. An even more modern syntagm, entirely adapted to the new formula of letters on the rise, is *la république des belles lettres*[317] and its doublet, *l'empire des belles lettres*.[318] Its specific notes have been known to us since the previous period.

The prestige of the scientific, intellectual, and literary community becomes greater and greater. The *republic of letters* is at the same time academic, learned, erudite (*republica eruditorum, Literati orbis Academiam*)[319] and cultural-literary, in the sense that it comprises the "entire body of men of letters" ("all the men who study"),[320] *la république des beaux esprits*.[321] Its members have a strong *esprit de corps*. They have great moral solidarity and countless professional ties. Just as before, there is a constant exchange of news, information, ideas, opinions, and verdicts. Successes, achievements, losses, and deaths are recorded. Scientific and literary publicity becomes ever more intense, and an idyllic concept prevails. "All learned men must consider themselves brothers and be on excellent terms with one another."[322] Learned journals justify their existence by the necessity to inform "about what is new in the republic of letters" (*Journal des Savants*, 1665), about what happens of note in these "boroughs of literature."[323] Other publications keep readers informed about what is "strange" in the "republic of letters." Literature turns partly into attractive journalism, sometimes into sensational journalism. Thus, a new, incipient form of popular literature appears, the vulgarization of science.

The spatial and temporal dimensions of the "republic of letters" are also characteristic. The republic includes all the writers "of all ages"[324] and of all countries. The old idea of the totality and universality of letters resurfaces in institutional, categorizable forms (dictionaries, repertoires, catalogues, "universal introductions"). Mankind's whole culture becomes contemporary, and a dialogue with the geniuses of Antiquity becomes possible (M. Pellegrini).[325]

For this reason, the "republic of letters" can only be "cosmopolitan." The reader in the ideal library is "cosmopolitan—"[326] a concept summed up and reformulated in accordance with the well-known ancient acceptation ("universal fatherland," "citizens of the world," "the whole world is the fatherland," *literatura patria*).[327] The universal character of literature emerges much stronger from such a concept. It also projects dreams of social organization, of "liberty"[328] and "equality."[329] The "republic of letters"—a revealing detail—consists of "free" and "equal" citizens. *Letters* overtly begin to show their militant ideological propensity.

The first accurate, acute, critical observations concerning what is to be called "literary life" (specific interests, manners, shortcomings, tendencies, etc.) refer to the selfsame "republic." It is troublesome, chockfull of "disorder," "wars," "battles,"[330] agitated by "parties," torn asunder by "criticism," often oppressed by a "permanent dictatorship," "usurped by the undeserving, without the consent of the people."[331] To speak of letters in such terms is also something new. In the forthcoming century, this language will become even more widespread.

The first projects of socioliterary organization are also inspired by this mentality of activism. Some are of esoteric-religious inspiration (*Fama Fraternitatis*, 1614; J. V. Andreae: *Christianopolis*, 1619). The "republic of letters" needs "parliamentary representation" (*dieta generale di letterati*, as the organ of a *generale congregazione di letterati*),[332] it needs a constitution, reforms, new institutions. There is no dearth of projects. Leibniz' are the best known (*Semestria literaria, Societas eruditorum Germaniae*).[333] The idea of royal patronage also appears. Finally, the "republic" also accommodates satirical utopia (Diego de Saavedra Fajardo, *La república literaria*, 1617, 1655).

Society

Another kind of considerations is made, closely related to the study of the relationships between letters and society, later what will be called the "sociology of literature." It is a sociable century par excellence. To write a brilliant book is not enough; one must also know how to "make conversation and live." In other words, one must master the art of living in society (Boileau),[334] hence an entire theory of the "gentleman of the world."[335] All representative texts (Nicolas Faret, *L'honeste homme ou l'art de plaire à la court*, 1630) debate the part played by letters in the education of the perfect gentleman. For the first time, literature is invested with a well-defined, specialized social function: molding the ideal social type. The old dichotomy, *arms* versus *letters* is left behind: one cannot be an *honnête, galant homme* "with no knowledge of good letters."[336] What is more, a "man of the world must be universal."[337] The culture of letters renders life civilized, human, urban. It conveys *la galanterie*[338] and *la politesse des lettres*. *Le commerce du monde* is improved. Socioliterary relations are defined in the same way: *un commerce étroit de littérature*.[339] The social dimension of literature is more and more widely acknowledged.

The thinking of the age goes one step further: from the educational norms of one social class to the pedagogy of the whole society. The great subject of the usefulness of "beautiful letters" for the "republic" begins to be debated,[340] "whether letters or doctrines are necessary to states."[341] The answer can only be in the affirmative. The skepticism of Molière (*Les femmes savantes*, IV, 3) or Malherbe, according to which the poet (a mere *arrangeur de syllabes*!) is not more useful to the states than a . . . ninepins player, has become obsolete. Richelieu's political testament is the best proof.[342] The idea gains clarity: heads of state must encourage letters. Moralists rediscover the figure of Mecena, of the "enlightened prince," lover of letters.[343] The idea of an illustrious patron, of royal protection is re-launched in force, backed by notorious ancient examples. The moment is of crucial importance: political power begins to enslave literature, to handle it, to transmit to it, in an authoritative manner, its "social command." The phenomenon can be seen with the naked eyes, especially in France, where the ruling absolute monarchy creates its corresponding institutions, beginning with the French Academy (1636). Official literary policy is constituted now. It aims to shape public taste, to influence literary opinion, to decree a literary hierarchy from the top. That literature is subservient to social prestige, whether major or minor, has become an important reality.

The profession of "literature,"[344] the "profession of letters,[345] is also clearly formulated. The term defines the social status of all professional handlers of "letters," from copyists and secretaries to writers. A distinctive note is contributed by organized, specialized, professional studies and activities. The notion of a "public," closely related to the "profession of letters," also reappears in force now. The French classics, in particular, are well aware of it.[346] The idea of reception (favorable or not) asserts itself as well. Also highlighted are the social organizations of this public, the "court," the "town." Libraries also assume such a function (G. Naudé, C. Clément, *Musei, sive bibliotheca tam privatae quam publicae*, 1635). The encyclopedia must also become a "public thesaurus of erudition."[347] The social circulation of letters is observed, described, praised.

Commentaries on "success" increase in number, with a marked switch from traditional (classical) "glory" to (modern) literary "reputation." The latter implies reaching a wide audience, a strategy of success, professionalism, the idea of a literary career. The conviction (and preconception) that a literary work that the public does not like is "a very bad work"[348] also comes into being now. In fact, this principle anticipates the "industrial literature" of the nineteenth century. "Written for many, read by many,"[349] it is a brutal, but realistic statement of fact. The more immediate the response of the public, as in the theater, the greater and more immediate the "reputation" of the author.[350] Elizabethan playwrights have a very clear notion of success, as do the French poets, who know that the "plume" is more enduring than the "voice."[351] The picture of the "implicit" or "explicit" reader, directly invoked by authors,[352] also takes on specific contours now. The idea of the writer who creates opinion, anticipated in the Renaissance by P. Aretino, can also be perceived, for instance in the work of B. Gracián.[353] The social life of literature becomes generally recognized.

Instant success depends on satisfying public taste. This social coordinate of literature is discussed theoretically and appropriated for the first time. The "taste at court" comes to be the supreme authority. Success is the outcome of synchronization: "If the subject does not cater to the spectators' feelings and expectations, it can never be successful" (D'Aubignac, *La Pratique du théâtre*, 1657). The *Querelle des Anciens et des Modernes* is but an effort to make modern public taste legitimate. Baroque writers in particular stake a lot on the idea of fashion (*alla moda*, of "new models." G. Marino declares that he will only write the kind of poetry that is "liked today by his century," *al secol vivente*. Modern language causes controversy and apology (François de Callières, *Des mots à la mode*, 1692).

Success is just one facet of the social status of literature. The other one is much more somber: many of the previous considerations of the writer's "drama" are expatiated upon. The plight of the man of letters is evoked in all its complexity: his isolation, persecution, suffering, alienation, his great "unhappiness" (I. P. Valeriano, *De literarum infelicitate*, 1620; Theophilus Spizelius, *Infelix literatus*, 1680). The subject is treated at length during Romanticism. But the cornerstones are set in place now: an acute analysis of wicked ways, macabre statistics (murders, suicides, and other vices), the classical description of poverty, the ephemeral character of success, the "obstacles of erudition," etc.[354] One can sense a pre-romantic attitude: "Misery induces melancholy."[355] It goes without saying that the writer becomes the object of satire (Boileau, etc.). Such opinions appear in the Romanian cultural life of the age as well. But here social and historical circumstances are rough, not very favorable to the advancement of letters: "*Ce sosiră asupra noastră cumplite aceste vremi de acmu, de nu stăm de scrisori, ce de griji și suspinuri*" (But these hardest of times have come upon us, so that we have no time for writing, but only to worry and sigh [Miron Costin]).[356] Such laments—almost always justified—will inevitably continue to be heard.

Economy

Literature's professional self-awareness also evolves during the seventeenth century. To "work for a reward," or to "write for bread"[357] become very current notions. The writer turns, in effect, into a professional and, beginning with calligraphers and such artisans, is aware of it. Hence his increasing concern with the money due him, with "royalties," with the "merchandise to be sold,"[358] with profit-making and advertising.

There are two diverging attitudes about this problem. Some believe the market can absorb any printed text (G. Pelletier: "Let us just write . . . paper will sell anyway").[359] According to others, sales are proportional to the "beauty" of the written text (Juan de Robles: A beautifully written book has "greater value and sells better than a badly written one").[360] Such considerations, even though not frequent, confer on literature a new dimension: it changes, slowly but steadily, into a lucrative activity, one which is economically interesting. The writer knows that he will be paid by the "bookseller," according to empirical market laws (Furètiere and Sorel have, in France, a clear view of this problem, which is also well-known in Elizabethan England).[361] A book has a "price tag" (A. Baillet).[362] Hence, the necessity of publicity, of "advertising." Book fair catalogues, especially the one of the Frankfort book fair, fulfill this task as well.

The old, constant tension between "liberal" and "servile" professions reappears. Even "booksellers" will part from the representatives of "mechanical arts,"[363] "men of letters," even more so. Even translation is considered "a very slavish thing" (Ch. Sorel).[364] Not even Shakespeare looks at himself as a professional writer (*never writer*). At any rate, the opposition to, disdain for, and indictment of the "mercenary profession"[365] are still great. The expression is quite currently used.[366] The preconception that it is "shameful to make verse for money" (D. Huet)[367] is still strong and widespread.

Ideology

The literary heteronomy of the age clearly presupposes the existence of a set of active social and political ideas, deeply involved with the conjuncture. The process will gain momentum during the following century, with the development of the idea of literature. It is already a well-established fact, however, that literature is assimilated by ideology. The difference is that ideas are no longer launched and discussed exclusively by a humanist elite, but are often taken over by the "professional" writer.

The idea of the progress of "letters," and of general progress, influenced by "letters"—formulated in the previous periods, too—becomes systematic and takes the form of a real "pre-philosophy of history." One of the basic texts in this respect is F. Bacon's *The Advancement of Learning*, (1605). It seems that a vague Hegelianism is in the air: the history of "letters," that is, of the spirit, anticipates the history of social-political communities. This conception is an intrinsic part of the idea of "Republic," which "we call the furthering of letters."[368] "Good letters" pull nations out of barbarity and restore them to "humanity."[369] The thesis of the "translation of studies" also reappears. Renaissance means installing the "civility of letters" in Rome.[370]

When the "Republic of letters" is described or commented upon, additional political and social ideas are formulated. It experiences "tyranny" and "troubles," equivalents of the idea of "revolution" (protests, opposition movements, etc.) and especially—an interesting phenomenon that will take on future importance—manifestations of an aspiration to "freedom." Baroque and mannerist artists champion the right of creators (B. Varchi: the "liberty of [painters] to do what they please")[371] to achieve creative freedom. But more is at stake now: the free conscience of "authors," much more important than that of "preachers," as with Pierre Bayle[372] and others. Miron Costin also knew that for such writing concerns *"gîndu slobod şi fără strînsoare trebuieşte"* (one's thoughts must be free of coercion.[373] This seems to be the first time that freedom of conscience and free literary expression are both claimed by Romanian culture.

Needless to say, the opposite ideology is, predominant: that of a controlled literary education, of the theater and of literature as a "school" of good manners (providing examples of virtues, in the spirit of the old adage, *utile dulci*).[374] Due to the counter-Reformation, this ideology can even become one of repression. It is now that the conception of bowdlerizing texts (*Ad usum Delphini*), of ideological and pedagogical censorship is organized on solid foundations. Official and academic dogma is flourishing, such as the reference book by A. Possevino, *Bibliotheca selecta* (1593), especially book one, *De cultura ingegnorum*, directly related to *lectio librorum* (§46), *Censura librorum* (§51), *Disseminatio librorum bonorum* (§52), etc. At the same time, the age produces "pedagogical" novels and "exemplary" novellas (Cervantes, etc.).

HIERARCHY IN LITERATURE

In a strictly stratified society and in a despotic political regime, the criteria for establishing a literary hierarchy will be equally rigid. First, the old dichotomy of the idea of literature is again underlined: *culture/non-culture*. Culture is "up," lack of culture is "down." Once again, this principle is the backbone of all the "literary" descriptions and judgments of the age.

In the chapter "styles, genres," the classical schema resurfaces quite naturally as *genus humile, medium, grave*; sublime, medium and humble poetry; lofty and average poetry; the philosopher would be "humble" (?), the historian "medium," the poet "great." Such classifications circulate throughout Western culture, from Portugal to Germany. The "low" style is that of satire; the "Pont-Neuf style," also inferior, belongs to *colportage*, etc. The hierarchy is established according to an axiological paradigm. At the opposite end is *le haut savoir, la haute éloquence, la haute poésie, die hohere Rede,*[375] *Teutschen Hauptsprache,*[376] etc. The equivalent schema, *superior/inferior*, rigorously symmetrical, is based on the same criteria. The "moderns"—again we refer to the famous *Querelle*—deem themselves superior to the "ancients," the French are better than the Greeks, and so on. A hierarchy, applied to the idea of literature, presupposes an identical value scale. The absolute superiority of literary creation (Shakespeare can hardly be surpassed *in literature*)[377] is defined as: "What is most beautiful and profound in beautiful literature" (*la belle littérature*).[378] Medium quality is labeled *mediane letteratura,*[379] etc. *Les belles lettres* are classified accordingly, while poetry becomes the "foremost art." The criterion of superiority implies one of "size," that is, its contrary (G. F. Cresci, *L'Idea per voler legittimamente possedere l'arte maggiore e minore dello scrivere*, 1622). But it is not simply a question of calligraphy. It is especially that there is a "great literature" (*grande littérature*)[380] and a "lesser literature" (*petites lettres*): romances and comedies, according to the classical, restrictive taste of Mme de Sévigné,[381] which establishes representative hierarchies.

The literary hierarchy derives from the prevailing social realities and social criteria. The interferences are obvious. Once more, the idea of literature is conferred a social dimension. Literary fame (*le prix*) is preeminently social, and moralists begin to notice the phenomenon.[382] The settings are well-known: *la cour* and *la ville*. The "court" forces its criteria, taste and judgment on the "town." Every pressure comes from the top.[383] This is an elitist view, of course. Royalty is at the top of the hierarchy (the "king's language," the king "re-establishes letters," etc.), followed by the intellectual elite: "The men of learning and of taste, forming the smallest, but the most valuable part of the Republic of Letters."[384] This is what the "nobleness of letters"[385] consists of. For that reason, the "noble" should not leave the "letters, particularly the sciences" "in the hands of the plebeian."[386] Everything that is superior (genres, themes, styles, imagery) becomes, by implication, noble, *opus nobile*. Poetry is the "noble" art[387] by definition, an *Edlen Dicht-Kunst*.[388]

Needless to say, this is all based on the fundamental dissociation, contradiction, and typology encountered over and over again in the course of the biography of the idea of literature: *cultivated/uncultivated* (= popular), that is, *refined culture/popular culture*, or *dominant/dominated culture*. In the seventeenth century this is still a historical reality,[389] an invariant in its essence of the pair of opposites *los cultos/el volgo*, in French *le vulgaire*, particularly typical of the Spanish Baroque writers (Góngora, Carrillo y Sotomayor,[390] B. Fioretti: "Poetry is not an entertainment for the uncouth,"[391] etc.

Viewed from this perspective, popular poetry, popular literature in general, can only continue to be deprecated, minimized, banished from the *Politia literaria*. Perrault hardly dares defend his "tales," *ces bagatelles*. Classical taste excludes Rabelais; because of this, he is temporarily forgotten.

THE SCHOOL OF LITERATURE

Literature with Literature

In such a century as the seventeenth, fully cultivated and academic, saturated with classical models, the idea of literature can only be "literary." In this respect, therefore, we shall encounter no new ideas, but only ideas that are definitively classified, assimilated and integrated. Literature becomes explicitly and predominantly cultivated. The idea of literature is identified with literature as a cultural—literary product. This conviction, clearly expressed and insistently disseminated, is one of the most important contributions made by the seventeenth century to the idea of literature. The poets writing in a classical manner, especially Baroque and mannerist poets, are *"litterati"* rather than "poets." The dissociation *poetry/literature* is never more obvious than at this moment in history.

The basic ideas are the well-known, classical ones, fully integrated into the idea of literature: "Things that fraternize: poetry and grammar;"[392] there cannot be a "great poet who is not a great humanist as well."[393] A poet = a humanist, a learned man, a *scholar*. School = "the seedbed of literature."[394] Literature can be learned. Poetry is a "noble study."[395] To write well, one must first "read the best authors."[396] No other idea is more widely attested in the period, or in greater agreement with the system of the idea of literature.

What, through the process of estheticizing literature, has been dubbed *culteranism, cultamente, escritura in culto,* etc., reappears now with utmost vigor. Spanish Baroque literature provides the best examples of cultivated style (*hablar culto*), of cultivated poets (*los poetas cultistas*), of eulogizing cultivated expression (*exprimir cultamente sus conceptos*). Baltasar Gracián is the great theoretician of poetic culture (*Agudeza y arte de ingenio,* 1642,[397] but in other works as well see *Oráculo Manual, El discreto,* etc.). Identical ideas can be found with Lope de Vega, Carrillo y Sotomayor, Juan de Jáuregui, etc.

The synonym *erudición, el arte de erudición, docta erudición* is also in current use: a literary notion that evidently encompasses the creative capacity as well, that of cultivating "discourse," "conversation," "books,"[398] and making them increasingly subtle. The most systematic treatment of the problem is provided by Luis Carrillo y Sotomayor, in the work mentioned above, *Libro de erudición poética* (1611). The notion circulates in France as well, with some precious and mannerist writers.[399] Its equivalent is *poeta doctus, les plus doctes poètes,* "cultivated," "learned poets," *die gelehrten Poeten,*[400] another pan-European idea. It is closely associated with encyclopedic literature, a general source of knowledge and inspiration. As a matter of fact, the idea of encyclopedia is often referred to in a creative sense[401] and cultivated by Baroque poets in such works as *Adone* by G. Marino (considered to be "a kind of encyclopedia of the new times").[402] It is also discussed theoretically by the poeticians of the age.[402] Poetry means—and comprises, in effect—all arts and all sciences. Homer, of course, continues to be the archetype of a unique master of wisdom, the sum of all sciences, the "ultimate scholar," etc.[403] He is the founder of all arts and sciences, the absolute literary prototype.

One more time, literature is born out of and through literature. Natural talent is not excluded, but it means nothing without "art." Hence the widespread principle of *naturaleza y arte,*[404] *arte, naturaleza y doctrina.*[405] Doctrine = the art of studying "good letters"[406] without surcease. Knowing the "rules," the "science," is a universal article of poetic doctrine. We find it in France,[407] Germany,[408] and England.[409] At this stage in its history, it can be reduced to two essential trends:

1. The old principle of imitation is reaffirmed and redefined. A marked shift from imitating nature to imitating literature can be noticed. Literature imitates literature as a matter of necessity, in a spontaneous, organic manner. It follows the "lesson of books" and is invention only inasmuch as it confers "new shape to old things and old shapes to new things" (G. Marino).[410] This preeminently Baroque thesis assimilates the lesson of classicism (imitating Greek and Latin poets) in the sense of emulation and dissimulation. For the rest, "any writing is imitation" (John Florio).[411] Everything has been said. In its essence, literature is a series of

"typical commonplaces" (G. Marino). Modern topic, then, has its forerunners. The usefulness, superiority even, of the "commonplaces textbooks," including the ones for oratory, letter writing, etc., is reaffirmed on the basis of this principle.

2. Literary texts resume and incorporate, in various manners, preexistent literary texts. What has been called, in the last decades, "intertextuality" already exists, in both theory and empirical practice. The procedure is well-known and likened to the chemist's *mixture*.[412] All the classics start from ancient texts. The tragedy of the age has acknowledged Greek and Latin sources. The Baroque and precious authors make poetry out of poetry, programmatic variations on given subjects[413] Góngora writes an *Oda Centón*. Literature perpetrates, reiterates or processes the literature of the previous age, and this meets with general approval. A great "number of books" originate "from other books."[414] Montaigne is praised for the same technique.[415]

Reflection on the proceedings that make the writing of literature possible becomes more intense and widespread in this period. They have almost all been known since the Renaissance, so we shall just enumerate them. There are precise references, some of them quite lengthy, for each of the following procedures: translation, copying, quotation, compilation, "selection," the *centon*, macaronic language and poetry, summary, epigram, parody, pastiche, paraphrase, *travestie*, and plagiarism. There is a special mention for the "method" of using "commonplaces" in oratory.[416]

The Romanian chroniclers, those who only continue the work of their predecessors or interpolate passages in it work in the same spirit. To give just one example, Mihail Moxa has a very keen sense of compilation, summary, "sources," and translation.[417] Such techniques are also used in cultural and poetic compilations (*Mărgăritărele* [Pearls] and anthologies (*Antologhion*). The "encyclopedia" also gains ground, in the form of miscellanies. Similarly, paraphrase, as a didactic versification drill (*stihuri de dragoste Aretusăi* [love-lines to Aretusa]).[418] The Romanian refraction of these European literary procedures and their specific terminology have not yet been studied thoroughly.

Literature on Literature

Due to the tradition of the preceding period and to the book-oriented cultural and historical context of the seventeenth century, not to mention the inner dynamics of the idea of literature, the perennial subject of "literature" as the object of literature becomes topical again. Though the results are modest, this fact is extremely relevant. In one way or another, *literature* continues to be the focal point of the theoretical and creative concerns of the age.

It all "begins," one more time, by praising "letters" and study, a subject cultivated not only by Marinian Baroque lyrical poetry (Giuseppe Battista, *Lo Studio delle Lettere*),[419] but also by a long series of "libraries," "eulogies," "theaters," "portraits," and "galleries." Grammar is also set to verse (for example, *Le Jardin des Racines grecques mises en vers français*, 1657). Printing is eulogized in both prose (Christian Gueintz, *Lob der Drukerey-Kunst*, 1640) and Latin verse (Du Fresnoy, *De arte graphica*, 1668). At the core of these concerns we find, as always, the book, a theme that is very popular not just with Marinian poets (Giuseppe Battista, *Ai libri*),[420] and the library (Fulvio Frugoni).[421] It is also now that the concept *Bibliofilia* (C.L.A. Saldenus, 1681) is more thoroughly defined. The same theme can be identified in numerous (and savory) formulas referring to literary and editorial property.[422] In manuscript form, they can be found in Romania, too, beginning with this century. The eulogy of Romanian printing made in various *predoslovii* (forewords) is also worth mentioning.

Poetry written on poetry makes this trend seem even more spectacular. This kind of poetry is typical of the Baroque, of precious, mannerist authors. A widespread conviction holds that one must "Speak poetically of poetry" (Mlle de Gournay).[423] Impressionism is thus anticipated. It is what poets like G. Marino often do, sometimes in a serial manner. In *La Galeria*, one comes across the "portraits" of Anacreon, Dante, Ariosto, T. Tasso, etc. Poetic composition, the way in which poetry is made (as we shall see, the demonstration can also be negative), is the subject of one of Lope de Vega's celebrated sonnets, *Un Soneto me manda hacer Violante*, imitated in a famous *Rondeau* by Voiture. The image of the ephemeral writing on sand is also cultivated.[424] The *legend* (as "caption") is attested in French in 1611.[425]

The theory and practice of the didactic literature of the age is profoundly "literary," in the basic, cultural meaning of the word. There is a direct connection between the "didactic work" or the "book of learning" and the "curious book lovers."[426] Boileau establishes the same relationship between literature and "savant lessons."[427] Philosophical-didactical-scientific poetry—in the old spirit of the Renaissance and of Humanism—continues to be cultivated in France, England, etc.[428] The term *Lehrgedicht* appears in Germany in 1646 (G. Th. Harsdörffer).[429] It is applied to a large poetic-didactic output that enjoys tremendous success, especially in the forthcoming age, the Enlightenment.

Critical Literature

The great humanistic and philological tradition of the Renaissance is carried on in the seventeenth century in a more organized manner. Now there is an intense preoccupation with "learning" literature, which provides criticism, "critical literature," with a predominantly didactic function and motivation. It is called upon, first of all, to provide lessons and methods for the reading of books, for interpreting literature. The basic patterns are disseminated, particularly by the *Ratio studiorum* (1599) of the Jesuits.

Grammar, with its traditional chapters, *lectione, enarratione, emendatione,* and *judicio,*[430] continues to be, in the truest cultural European spirit, at the heart of literary study. As we know, such chapters originate in Antiquity and define the essence of traditional critical activities. In fact, the two domains, grammar and criticism, are plainly seen as one: *grammatica literaria* (Bacon)[431] and *critica addit grammatica* (Vossius).[432] The same explicit homogeneity is encountered in the *critic*'s case, associated or identified with the *grammarian (grammaticis . . . criticisque)*. Malherbe passes for "France's foremost grammarian" (Guez de Balzac); the "critics of grammar"[433] are great experts in "letters," in "beautiful letters." The critic-grammarian deals with *De librorum lectione in genere,*[434] that is, with "lessons" and "readings." In mid-century (after 1654) the concept of "reading" is used in this predominantly didactic sense: to teach, to explain an author in the classroom.[435] Dictionaries, however, retain the classical acceptation: *reading = erudition.*[436]

The closely related idea of *philology,* which Humanism gave to European culture, preserves the same traditional basic meanings.

The first is preeminently cultural and didactic—liberal studies, the science of "beautiful letters," especially the ancient ones. In the encyclopedic spirit, the concept is identified with *polymatheia* (the universal science "of all liberal arts")[437] (see also J. Johnston, *Polymatheia Philologica,* 1667). This is a current acceptation found in all the great philologists of the age, from Casaubon to Scaliger and Vossius. Obviously, its equivalent in modern languages will be a "mixture of various knowledge," a "world literature." At this stage, philology cannot be told apart from the study of all the manifestations of the spirit in time and space, from the general field of *belles lettres.* A philologist is "he who has written on beautiful letters."[438] The homogeneity of the definitions is obvious: in French, *belles lettres,* in Greek and Latin, *philologia;* philology is the "love of beautiful letters."[439] The great prestige of "beautiful letters" remains dominant and determinative.

The second meaning is no less prestigious and traditional: text criticism, the emendation of "corrupted letters" (C. Scioppius, *Suspectarum lectionum,* 1664), correcting texts, in the best Alexandrian tradition. Again, the philologist and critic becomes the traditional editor, annotator and commentator of classical texts.[440] *Literature = textual criticism.* The school produced famous works, among them Jean Mabillon's *De re diplomatica* (1671). When applied to literature in general, philology tends to be seen as "varied erudition," as in *Cartas filológicas* by Francisco Cascales, and in other works (1634).[441]

The interpretative operation, also characteristic of philological criticism has, in turn, a double origin and significance. First, sacred hermeneutics is consolidated and made systematic, *tum stylys et literatura*, as in Salomon Glasius' *Philologia Sacra* (1683). Some texts, like *Tractatus Theologico-Politicus* by Spinoza (1670), are quite famous. This operation marks the beginnings of the autonomy of criticism, through its separation from grammar. Biblical exegesis becomes explicitly "critical" (J. Clericus, *Ars Critica*, 1697). "Methods of studying and learning, in a methodical, Christian way, human letters in their relationship with sacred letters and with the Bible" are also being published (P. Thomassin, 1681).

At the same time, the evolution of literature and development of Baroque poetry set criticism new and difficult tasks of decoding and interpretation. In this period, expression becomes increasingly obscure and symbolic; polyvalent language is in its heyday, as are "mottoes" and "enigmas" or "new and mysterious significations." There is even a budding theory of a *poétique de l'énigme* (1694).[442] Enigmatic, obscure, ambiguous imagery calls for a "key," so that Cesare Ripa's preoccupations in the *Iconology* (1593) are carried on. In his *Agudeza y arte de ingenio* (1642), Baltasar Gracián responds to this tendency.

The decoding operation, *exegetica*, belongs in equal measure to sacred and profane classical philology (Vossius, *De exegetica*). Translated, it turns into paraphrase—a "text explanation."[443] As we have seen, the term comes from the lexis, of "literature with literature." Literary "fables," Góngora's "obscurity," etc., also require an explanation. The most concentrated text-explanation theory is probably that of La Bruyère.[444] "Paraphrase" equals "interpretation."[445] Critics become "interpreters and commentators,"[446] "decipherers of letters.[447] A hermeneut is a *Descifrador* (Baltasar Gracián).[448] Some authors, such as Scarron,[449] provide the "key" for the "understanding" of the text themselves. Generally speaking, however, the hermeneutical method of the day is systematized, so that it may be applied universally. We shall not go into details now.

The term *criticism* itself purports to be of similar cultural-literary descent. Conceived and practiced under the form of philology, criticism is seen, first of all, as a "literary" genre or species.[450] Books of criticism (of erudition, commentaries) are, at the same time, books of literature, the evidence of "Vast and profound literature."[451] The general conception of the age, also mirrored in dictionaries,[452] sees in criticism a "science" of letters and of handling the text, from editing to explaining it. In his turn, the *critic*—a character who has been on the stage for a century—is a savant, a *litterator* with a well-defined role in the organization of literary studies.[453] Grammarians, philologists, and "men of letters"[454] are—according to one widespread definition—his counterparts and colleagues. "Good criticism" backs "good literature." It presupposes a thorough reading, universal knowledge,[455] "many letters" and—a novel exigency in the history of critical literature—an entire deontology: impartiality (John Dennis, *The Impartial Critick*, 1693), assuming the reader's and the writer's frame of mind. Such novel demands will then be resumed and given ampler scope. Eventually, they will constitute a set of well-defined "rules,[456] in the codified spirit of Classicism.

Circulation of these ideas is ensured by a complex network of publications, book reviews—it is the dawn of European literary journalism[457]—collections of abstracts, critical journals (*Journal des Savants, Acta Eruditorum*, etc.). Titles such as *Mélanges de littérature* or P. Bayle's celebrated publication *Nouvelles de la République des Lettres* (first series: 1684–1689) proves that everything continues to remain within the sphere of (critical) "literature." In fact, all titles have erudite, learned denotations (Ch. Sorel, *Bibliothèque française*, 1664; Adrien Baillet, *Jugements des Savants sur les principaux ouvrages des auteurs*, 1685, etc.).

A fact that passes, as a rule, unnoticed[458] is that *almost* all the ends, methods, and basic functions of "modern" literary criticism, so aptly formulated in the nineteenth century, are prefigured now. Concepts like "selection" (*choix*) and "value judgment" (*jugement*) are more and more current (Ch. Sorel, A. Baillet, P. D. Huet, G. Naudé, etc.). Criticism exerts "censorship."[459] It operates through analysis ("decomposition," "dismantling,"[460] it singles out the "particular features of every author" by "penetrating" or "entering the spirit" of the writer, that is, by becoming identified with it (B. Lamy).[461] One could say that *Einfühlung* esthetics already has forerunners, as does modern esthetic irrationalism.[462]

A crucial event, heralded by many previous empirical reactions, is the explicit separation of criticism from culture (that is, science, philology, hermeneutics). It is a symmetrical and synchronized operation with the split between *literature* and *poetry*; criticism claims to be mere "reading," a term heavily attested in this period. More than that, it can provide pure satisfaction by catering to "taste," it can titilate one's sensitivity and create emotion which, along with intellectual pleasure, constitutes *Les Plaisirs de la lecture* . . . (Paris, 1681). Thus, the subjectivity of criticism begins to take shape. Even the term "impression" (R. Rapin) belongs to this age. It is one more occasion for us to see that "impressionism"—*verbi gratia*—is not an entirely "modern" invention.

One must insist, however, that the predominant and general trend continues to be cultural and dogmatic. The classicizing of criticism and of theoretical literary reflection—begun during the Renaissance—is now fully consolidated. Aristotelian tradition provides "norms" of creation and "rules for judging well.[463] All Classicism is mastered by the idea of prototype, of model. "Letters," "good letters," literature must be learned, while rhetoric is the "science" that teaches us how to "speak and write correctly."[464] All the (very numerous) rhetorics of the epoch have an overt pedagogical and normative character. The Jesuit textbooks of the Counter-Reformation play an important part. So does poetics, the "art that teaches us how to make poems,"[465] a *Libro de la erudición poética*, a "body of doctrines" (Le Bossu), a "grammar" even (F. Cascales). All of German poetics of the seventeenth century is, in essence, *Lehrbücher*.

At the same time, the idea of poetry becomes "national," a phenomenon that runs parallel with the emergence of *national literature*. There is a universal poetics, certainly, but it is also applicable to German poetry (M. Opitz).[466] In the case of oratory, the same national delineation becomes effective (La Mothe Le Vayer, *De l'éloquence française*, 1684). Even more remarkable, of great consequence to "modern times," is the tendency of doing away with the tyranny of "rules." *La Querelle du Cid* is the symbolic climax of this tension. G. Marino expressed it in these memorable words: "The true rule . . . is to know how to break the rules, function of time and place; adapting to general custom and to the taste of the century."[467] Baroque writers ignore norm in a consistent manner.

During the seventeenth century, a small part of these literary critical notions enters Romanian culture. To expect more would be to lack a sense of history and proportion. The idea of reading, "*cetania cărților*," "*cetitul cărților*," especially as "*zăbavă*" (pastime), has an enthusiastic champion in Miron Costin.[468] The fundamental motivation, of course, is cultural in nature, but traces of "entertaining" reading also appear (Theodora, the Empress of Byzantium, "liked to read the Scriptures").[469] Rhetoric is an object of Greek education.[470] Poetics becomes known as "*poesis*," the "art of putting together verses."[471] The "writer"[472] and—*verbi gratia* again—the critic and hermeneut also appear now. There are even preoccupations for "understanding poetry," "parables,"[473] understanding what this or that text "means," the "deep meaning of the Scriptures,"[474] even for criticizing those who "*tîlcuiesc rău*" (teach badly), for having a "canon,"[475] etc. For the time being, everything is embryonic and occasional.

DENYING LITERATURE

Literature inevitably produces negative reactions, every time a level of saturation or an excessive amount is reached; this phenomenon is recurrent in every age, though its intensity and frequency may be variable. This is even more true in an extremely cultural period, such as Classicism and the Baroque. We shall overlook the well-known antiliterary arguments of a religious, moral or social nature, reiterated to one's distraction, to dwell only upon those of a literary nature, which are very numerous. As before, we shall only deal, synthetically, with some typical reactions.

The anticulture theme is intensely exploited. An excess of "science" and "letters" makes of France, in particular, an irritating *nation grammair-*

ienne. Malherbe has only sired "poets-grammarians."[476] There is an identical reaction in Germany.[477] In the meantime, *encyclopedia* has become an "old-fashioned word."[478] The "scourge of universal people,"[479] who exaggerate their competence, is deplored. On the other hand, the devaluation of erudition—which has the power to single out and isolate people, serious defects in a supersocial age—is the direct outcome of the fashionable *moeurs* of the century, which propagate the "shame of being erudite."[480] Erudition becomes a "boring," "vain" occupation,[481] often an act of deception (Peter Poiret, *De eruditione solida et falsa*, 1692). For many, "savant and pedant are synonyms."[482] Pedanticism is "our common enemy."[483] Disgust at erudition acquires dangerous proportions and becomes equally excessive, when exclusively stylistic and fashionable concerns become predominant. Another "taste" takes the place of "the reign of critics and of philology" (P. Bayle).[484]

The book loses a great deal of its traditional prestige in such circles (fashionable, *bel esprit,* "esthetic," "modern"). Like Descartes in his famous *Discours. . . ,* philosophers declare that they learn only from the "great book of the world," an old, illustrious *topos,* while the *honnête homme* is ostentatiously content with the "book" of society. Fashionable civility and an abuse of books have become incompatible. The most erudite books are not necessarily the most *senses.* In their turn, the skeptics cast their "methodological doubt on whether the idea of beautiful letters is preferable to any other concern" (La Mothe Le Vayer).[485] The conclusion they reach is, needless to say, negative. *Bibliomania* (Fr., 1654; *bibliomane,* Fr., 1660), is indicted by moralists;[486] the burning of Don Quixote's books is a famous scene. *Misobiblia* becomes an object of study.[487] An obvious saturation by the printed word is promptly denounced.[488] Editorial production reaches alarming proportions.[489] Callimachus' ancient malicious remark is revived: "Great book, great sin."

It is altogether natural, then, that bookish literary devices should be questioned. Literature out of literature is condemned in its essence. The old controversy, *spirit/letter,* becomes topical again (Pascal, Spinoza, etc.). Compilation, plagiarism, the abuse of quotations,[490] the excess of references, excerpts, collections of texts, borrowed ideas, *les larcins,*[491] are especially irritating. On a higher plane, rules, norms,[492] restrictive literary pedagogy[493] are rejected. As a direct consequence of the polemics between the Ancients and the Moderns, the idea of a classical model—sterile, inhibiting—seems to be definitely compromised: "The moderns are not blinded by paganism."[494] Rhetoric passes for an unbearable artifice. On the other hand, the "Moderns" are saturated with Jesuit Baroque as well. As a conclusion, the "man of taste" and the "pedant" are irreconcilable. Erudition is considered *farouche, fort ennuyeuse, fastidiosa,*[495] etc. It is the other pole of the idea of literature; we have come full circle, to the negative pole.

The conflict and dissociation, *poetry* versus *literature* (V), are pushed to their final stage. All the possible conclusions are drawn regarding the incompatibility of culture, science, reflection, reason, spirit, and taste,[496] lyricism, and poetry in general. The clear awareness of "philosophy" ("R. Descartes' method"), "science" and "erudition" as declared antipoetry appears now. "False erudition" and an excess of grammar are to blame for the "decadence"[497] and sterility of letters. The most radical conclusion, formulated for the first time in the history of the idea of literature, is that one can write poetry "without letters." More than that: some Baroque writers (Scudéry, Théophile)[498] openly, ostentatiously praise uneducated poetry ("without letters," "without art"). Critical eulogies of the type, "He knew nothing, but was a poet" are encountered.[499] Pascal himself was persuaded that "real eloquence mocks at eloquence" (that is, rhetoric). The remark is made, in insidious, polemical tones, that the epoch of "great, deep literature" (= culture) is gone. A "more refined spirit"[500] has appeared instead.

Contesting "letters" has other portentous consequences. "Natural" qualities are brought to the fore. Shakespeare was "naturally learned."[501] The poet reads "inwards," not from books. The theory of "the true nature poetry" raises its head.[502] The idea of "genius" is evoked, that of a subjective creation, of poetry of the "heart," an outright, unsophisticated expression. The "pompous and sublime" style, *le faux brillant*,[503] is repulsed. Even the notion "antistyle" appears. The denial of the Gongoric, cultivated, neologistic, affected, obscure style can perhaps be seen most clearly in Baroque Spain (see Juan de Jáuregui's, *Discurso poético*, 1623). The accusations against literature in general are reiterated: sterility, platitudes (of a neoclassical nature), flatness, scholasticism, loss of esthetic pleasure. Denouncing the lack of creativity also becomes commonplace.[504] Many writers (Ben Jonson, Lope de Vega, etc.) are annoyed by chicanery and pedantry, and declare criticism incompetent and useless. Anti-critical reactions, some of them quite violent, appear from other quarters, too. The pleasure of criticizing is denounced: it keeps us from experiencing literary emotions, from "being moved by very beautiful things."[505] The critic's ways (corrupt, mercenary) are also condemned,[506] tunes that will be played again.

Finally, subtle forms of antiliterature, destined to a great "modern" career, also appear: saturation[507] and the excess of writing,[508] irony and mistrust in literature, revealing the devices (for example, Scarron, *Francion*, I, XVI). A new literary term, *l'anti-roman* (Ch. Sorel) is, for the moment, used only with satirical intent, similarly, *Adieu to poetry*.[509] The poetry that denies itself in the making—a Baroque irony (Lope de Vega, *Un Soneto me manda hacer Violante*, imitated by Voiture)—rediscovers and relaunches, even if only accidentally, marginally, the idea "literature on nothing." In the same spirit, the Earl of Rochester writes his poem *Nothing*, giving negation a positive sense. The French poet Jean Passerat also composes Latin verses about *Nihil*. The theme will become very fashionable much later, in the twentieth century, which abounds in Alexandrine, Baroque, and mannerist features. Radical repudiations of letters also appear,[510] as well as displays of total indifference to the origin, prestige, and traditional functions of poetry. The dilettantish, blasé literary spirit, that ruins poetry from the inside, takes a firm stand.[511] Here, Miron Costin is, for the time being, the only one to "question" the *Alexandria* as being "full of lies."[512] Epic fabulation is not yet appreciated for what it is.

CONCLUSIONS

Our conclusion is easily reached: the Classical and Baroque period in the biography of the idea of literature is neither fertile, nor creative. There are no new, bold, revolutionary interpretations. Moreover, in the area of literary ideas, *literature* becomes a marginal term. However, *literature* is much more stable and increasingly institutional; it is made "banal" through dogma and an excess of academic spirit. The great dictionaries of the age accurately define the term and give it official sanction. Definitions are clear and explicit. The hierarchy of significations is modified: the group of "humanist" meanings tends to grow weak, atrophied, to stop circulating altogether. The idea of literature is classicized throughout. It becomes increasingly normative and paradigmatic,[513] which is to say that its social character is amplified.

The only vivid, creative, original moment, *La Querelle des Anciens et des Modernes*, makes *literature* even more marginal and valueless as compared to *poetry*. The "literary" consequences, though indirect, are nonetheless important: the idea of literature becomes more liberal and relative, as a function of time, space and milieu. Literature expands and becomes universal, which paves the way for the idea—and so for the theory—of a world literature. The Baroque makes the dissociation *poetry/literature* more energetically emphasized. Poetry and literature split definitively, with two other important consequences. On the one hand, denying literature acquires unexpected proportions. On the other, *literature*'s autonomy and its specificity make great progress. The process will gain unforeseen complexity, as a result of the more and more intense, progressively esthetic and poetic, character of *literature*. But this will be the work of centuries to come.

Notes

PREFACE

1. Only some indications: "No treatment of the history of the concept of literature is known," René Wellek justly remarks, "Literature and
cognates," in Philip P. Wiener, ed., *Dictionary of the History of Ideas. Studies
of Selected Pivotal Ideas* (New York: Scribner's, 1973), III, p. 88. The idea
is resumed by Tzvetan Todorov in *Les genres du discours* (Paris: Seuil,
1978), p. 13: "*On n'a pas encore fait l'histoire complète de ce mot et de ses
équivalents dans toutes les langues.*" The history of the word "literature" has
not been written yet, also says Klaus Weimar, *Enzyklopädie der Literaturwissenschaft* (München: Franke Verlag, 1980), p. 42, etc.

2. The best known: Robert Escarpit: *La définition du terme Littérature.
Le Littéraire et le Social* (Paris: Flammarion, 1970), pp. 259–272; reprinted
in *Dictionnaire international des termes littéraires* (The Hague/Paris: Mouton,
1973), L 47–L 53.

3. For example, Gerhard Goebel, *Literaturgeschichte als Geschichte des
Literaturbegriffs an französischen Beispielen des 20. Jahrhunderts.* Rolf Kloeper,
hrsg. *Bildung und Ausbildung in der Romania* (München: Wilhelm Fink,
1979), I, pp. 211–233.

4. Helmut Arntzen, *Der Literaturbegriff. Geschichte. Komplementärbe-
griffe. Intention. Eine Einführung* (Münster: Aschendorff, 1984).

5. Arthur O. Lovejoy, *Essays in the History of Ideas* (1948. New York:
G. P. Putnam, 1960), p. 9.

6. Adrian Marino, *Hermeneutica ideii de literatură* ('the Hermeneutics
of the Ideas of Literature') (Cluj-Napoca: Dacia, 1987. Italian translation
by Marco Cugno, *Teoria della letteratura*, Bologna: Il Mulino, 1994).

7. T. S. Eliot, *Tradition and the Individual Talent. Selected Essays* (1932.
London: Faber and Faber, 1966), p. 14.

8. For instance, René Wellek, *A History of Modern Criticism* (New
Haven and London: Yale University Press, 1986), 5, pp. 85, 184, etc.

9. J. G. Herder, *Sämmtliche Werke*, hrsg. Bernard Suphan, completed by C. Redlich *et al.*, vol., 1877–1913 (Berlin 1880), 12, pp. 8, 10.

ANTIQUITY

1. Sextus Empiricus, *Adversus mathematicos*, I, 99. Plato, *Cratylos*, 424 d.

2. E. G. Turner, *Athenian Books in the Fifth and Fourth Century B.C.* (1952; London: 1954), pp. 8, 11. David Diringer, *The Alphabet, A Key to the History of Mankind*. 3rd ed., completely revised with the collaboration of Reinhold Regensburger (London: Hutchinson, 1968), I, p. 164. The basic dictionaries are, of course: E. Ernout and G. W. H. Lampe, *s.v.* A convenient recent interpretation: Jean Jrigoin, "Les Grecs et l'écriture", *Corps écrit*, I, 1982, p. 32.

3. St. Augustine, *Princip. dial.*; *P.L.*, 32, c.1410. *De Trinitate*, X; *P.L.*, 42, c. 972–973.

4. In a similar manner, G. Kaibel, *Sententiarum liber Quintus, Hermes*, XXV (1890), 102–103.

5. St. Augustine, *De Doctrina Christiana*, III, 29; *P.L.*, 34, c. 80.

6. On their use in Roman Dacia: G. Popa-Lisseanu, *Tablete cerate descoperite în Transilvania* (Bucureşti, 1926).

7. Cicero, *Partitiones Oratoriae*, VII, 26; *Philipp.*, II, 116.

8. Friedrich Nietzsche, *Werke*, hrsg. von Hans Joachim Mette und Karl Schechta (München: C. H. Beck'sche Verlagbuch, 1937), 4, p. 617.

9. Tacitus, *Annales*, XI, 13, 14. *The Annals and the Histories*. Translated by A. J. Curch and W. J. Brodribb. Edited and abridged with an introduction by Hugh Lloyd-Jones (New York: Twayne Publishers, 1964), p. 151.

10. Cf. Ludwig Jeep, *Zur Geschichte der Lehre von den Redeltheilen bei dem Lateinischen Grammatikern* (Leipzig: 1893), p. 107.

11. Details in Adrian Marino, *Hermeneutica ideii de literatură* (Cluj-Napoca: Dacia, 1987), pp. 44–45. Italian translation by Marco Cugno, *Teoria della letteratura* (Bologna: Il Mulino, 1994), pp. 44–45.

12. Cicero, *Ad Familiares*, V, 12. *The Letters to His Friends*. Tr. W. Glynn Williams (Cambridge, Mass.: Harvard University Press, 1927), pp. 364–365.

13. Livy (Titus Livius), *Ab urbe condita*, VI, 1. *Livy in Fourteen Vol-*

umes. Tr. B. O. Foster (Cambridge, Mass.: Harvard University Press, 1924), III, pp. 194–195.

14. Theodor Birt, *Das antike Buchwesen in seinem Verhältniss zum Literatur* (Berlin: 1882), p. 170. G. W. H. Lampe, *A Patristic Greek Lexicon* (Oxford: 1972), pp. 322–323. Andrei Cornea, *Scriere şi oralitate în cultura antică* (Bucureşti: Cartea românească, 1988), pp. 97–98.

15. Cicero, *Brutus*, III, VII. St. Augustine, *litteris meis*. *De Trinitate*, III, 2; *P.L.*, 42, c. 869.

16. Cicero, *Pro Archia*, 15.

17. St. Augustine, *De vera religione*, III, 4; *P.L.*, 34, c. 124.

18. Tertullian, *De Testimonio animae*, 5; *P.L.*, I, c. 615.

19. Martianus Capella, *De nuptiis Mercurii et Philologiae*, III, 229. *Martianus Capella and the Seven Liberal Arts*. Tr. William Harris Stahl and Richard Johnson, with E. L. Burge (New York: Columbia University Press, 1977), II, p. 67.

20. R. Reitzgenstein, *Epigramm und Skolien. Ein Beitrag zur Geschichte der Alexandrinischen Dichtung* (Giessen: 1893), pp. 87, 88, 104. Paul Friedländer, with the collaboration of Herbert B. Hoffeit, *Epigrammata—Greek Inscriptions in Verse. From the Beginnings to the Persian Wars* (Berkeley and Los Angeles: 1988), pp. 1, 3, 16. Adrian Marino, *Hermeneutica. . .* , p. 369. *Teoria della Letteratura*, pp. 406–407.

21. Cicero, *Ad Familiares*, V, 8, 5.

22. Pliny the Elder, *Naturalis historia*, XXX, 2; Seneca, *Ad Polybum*, XVIII, 2.

23. Terence, *Adelphi*, 1.

24. H. Baron, *"La notion d'intellectuel à Rome."* *Studii clasice*, XIII (1971), 99. E. G. Sihler, "The *Collegium Poetarum* at Rome." *American Journal of Philology*, XXVI (1905), 4–5.

25. Cicero, *De Oratore*, II, 15. Quintilian, *Institutio oratoria*, V, 10, 120.

26. Cicero, *De Oratore*, I, 20.

27. My translations. See also: Gorgias, *Encomium of Helen*, 8–10, 14. Tr. D. M. MacDonnel (Bristol: Bristol Classical Press, 1932), pp. 23, 25.

28. Quintilian, X, 1, 3: I, 4, 2.

29. Gorgias, *Encomium of Helen*, 9.

30. Aristotle, *Rhetoric*, III, 12, 1413.

31. Cicero, *De Oratore*, I, XVI. Tr. E. W. Sutton. Introd.: H. Rackham (Cambridge, Mass.: Harvard University Press/London: William Heinemann, 1988), p. 51.

32. Diodorus Siculus, *Bibliotheca*, I, II, 6. *Diodorus of Sicily in Twelve Volumes*. Tr. C. H. Oldfather, *et al.* (Cambridge, Mass.: Harvard University Press/London: William Heinemann, 1968), I, pp. 11, 13. Plato, *Gorgias*, 501 a. Plato's *Gorgias*. Tr. W. C. Helmbold (New York: Liberal Arts Press, 1952), p. 75.

33. George A. Kennedy, *Classical Rhetoric and Its Christian and Secular Tradition from Ancient to Modern Times* (Chapel Hill: University of North Carolina Press, 1980), pp. 109–110, Vasile Florescu, *La Rhétorique et la Néorhétorique. Genèse-Evolution-Perspectives*. Traduit du roumain par Melania Munteanu (Bucureşti: Editura Academiei/Paris: "Les Belles Lettres," 1982), p. 53.

34. Cicero, *De Oratore*, III, 27.

35. Tacitus, *Dialogus de oratoribus*, X, 4.

36. Cf. Gaston Boissier, *La fin du paganisme* (Paris: Hachette, 1891), I, p. 224, n. 1.

37. Cf. Eduard Norden, *Die Antike Kunstprosa* (Leipzig: 1893), I, p. 330.

38. Quintilian, XII, 10, 55; X, 1, 2.

39. Cf. Karl Vossler, *Poetische Theorien in der italienische Frührenaissance* (Berlin: 1900), p. 42, n. 2.

40. Euripides, *Hippolytus*, v. 874–875. Euripides *Hippolytus*. Tr. Gilbert and Sarah Lawall (Bristol: Bristol Classical Press, 1986), p. 59.

41. Quintilian, XII, 10, 55; X, 1, 2.

42. Plato, *Laws*, 810 b.

43. Cicero, *De Orat.*, I, 33.

44. Cf. Marvin T. Herrick, *The Fusion of Horatian and Aristotelian Literary Criticism* (Urbana: 1946), p. 64.

45. Plato, *Phaedrus*, 258 d.

46. Quintilian, IX, 4, 17–18.

47. Quintilian, XII, 10, 55.

48. Aristotle, *Rhetoric*, III, XII, 2.

49. Pliny the Younger, *Epistulae*, I, 20.

50. A. Ernout, *"Dictare, "dicter", allem. Dichten,"* *Revue des études latines*, XXIX (1954), 155–156. Claude Calame, *Le récit en Grèce ancienne, Énonciations et représentations de poètes* (Paris: 1986), pp. 31–32, 35–37.

51. *Genesis*, 1, 5; 2, 19–20.

52. *John*, I, 1, 14.

53. Walter J. Ong, *The Presence of the Word. Some Prolegomena for Cultural and Religious History* (1967. Minneapolis: University of Minnesota Press, 1981), pp. 182–183, *passim*.

54. Homer, *Odyssey*, XXII, 347–348.

55. Plato, *Phaedrus*, 245 a. *Ion*, 533 a.

56. Ovid, *Fasti*, VI, 5.

57. Franz Dornseiff, *Der Alphabet in Mystik und Magie* (Leipzig-Berlin: 1925), p. 9.

58. *Exodus*, XXIV, 12; XXXII, 16; XXXIV, 1. *Deuteronomy*, IV, 13; X, 2.

59. *Jeremiah*, XXXII, 40. *Proverbs*, III, 3.

60. II. *Corinth.*, III, 2–3. *Hebrews*, X, 16.

61. *Odyssey*, VIII, 43, 47. Ovid, *Amores*, III, 3.

62. Tacitus, *Annales*, IV, 43.

63. Democritus, 21.

64. Hesiod, *Theogony*, 31.

65. Seneca, *De tranquilitate animi*, IX, 7.

66. Liselotte Dieckmann, *Hieroglyphics. The History of a Literary Symbol* (St. Louis: Washington University Press, 1970).

67. Herodotus, *Historiae*, V, 59.

68. St. Jerome, *Epistulae*, 70; *P.L.*, 22, c. 666.

69. For example, Diogenes Laertius, *The Lives and Opinions of the Eminent Philosophers*, III, 63; VIII, 15; IX, 6, etc.

70. Cicero, *De orat.*, II, 12.

71. Servius, *Aeneid*, IV, 577.

72. St. Augustine, *De doctrina Christiana. Prol.*, 1; *P.L.*, 34. c. 15.

73. Lactantius, *De origine erroris*, liber II; *P.L.*, 6, c. 313.

74. St. Augustine, *Confessiones*, III, 5. *De Trinitate. Proem.*, 12; *P.L.*, 42, c. 869.

75. Vincenzo Loi, "*Oralità e tradizione letteraria nelle latinità di età patristica. Oralità e scrittura nel sistema letterario.*" *Atti del Convegno Cagliari 14–16 aprile 1980.* A cura di Giovanna Cerina, Cristina Lavinio, Luisa Mulas (Roma: Bulzoni, 1982), pp. 186–195.

76. Tertullian, *Adversus Haeret.*, XXXIX; *P.L.*, 34, 2, c. 52.

77. Tertullian, *De idolatria*, X; *P.L.*, 1, c. 675.

78. St. Augustine, *De doctrina Christiana*, IV, 3; *P.L.*, 34, c. 90. *De civitate Dei*, 20, 4; *P.L.*, 34, c. 93.

79. Prudentius, *Apotheosis*, 436; *P.L.*, 59, c. 954.

80. Prudentius, *Peristephanon*, XIV, v. 54; *P.L.*, 60, c. 585.

81. Isidore of Seville, *Etymologiae*, 7, 12, 15; *P.L.*, 82, c. 291.

82. Tacitus, *Dialogus de oratoribus*, X, 4.

83. Emile Benveniste, "*Profanus et profanare.*" *Hommage à G. Dumézil. Latomus* (Coll. *Latomus*, XLV) (Bruxelles: 1960), pp. 46–53. *Le vocabulaire des institutions indo-européennes* (Paris: Editions de Minuit, 1969), II, pp. 197–198. Mircea Eliade, *Le Sacré et le Profane* (1957. Paris: Gallimard, 1965).

84. Plato, *Phaedrus*, 245 a.

85. Martial, X, 4.

86. Tertullian, *De idolatria*, IX; *P.L.*, 26, c. 399.

87. Cassiodorus, *Institutiones Divinarum et Humanarum Lectionum. Praef.*; *P.L.*, 70, c. 1241.

88. Tertullian, *De testimonio animae*, 5; *P.L.*, 1, c. 616.

89. Tertullian, *De praescriptionibus haereticorum*, XXXIX; *P.L.*, 2, c. 52.

90. Tertullian, *De corona*, 7; *P.L.*, 1, c. 84. *De testimonio animae*, 5; *P.L.*, 1, c. 617.

91. St. Jerome, *Liber de viris illustribus*, CXIX; *P.L.*, 23, c. 709.

92. Cassiodorus, *Institutiones*. . . , *P.L.*; 70, c. 1204.

93. Minucius Felix, *Octavius*, 5, 4.

94. Tertullian, *De spectaculis*, XVIII; *P.L.*, 1, c. 650.

95. Cassian, *De coenob. institut.*, V. XXXIII; *P.L.*, 49, c. 250.

96. St. Jerome, *Adv. Iov.*, I, 4; *P.L.*, 23, c. 215.

97. For details: Eduard Wölfflin, *"Litteratura,"* *Archiv für lateinische Lexikographie und Grammatik*, V (1888), 53–55. Adrian Marino, *"Hermeneutica ideii de literatură,"* I, "Sacrul;" II, *"Profanul,"* *Revista de istorie si teorie literară*, XXXII (1984), 4, 23–29; XXXIII (1985), 1, 73–79. Adrian Marino, *"Mircea Eliade et la sécularisation de la littérature,"* *Dialogue* (1982), 8, 81–92; *Cahiers roumains d'études littéraires* 1985, 3, 92–104; a summary, *Hermeneutica ideii de literatură*, 61–72; *Teoria della letteratura*, pp. 59–68.

98. Livy (Titus Livius), *Praefatio*.

99. Quintilian, *Institutio oratoria*, II, 1, 4, 14, 3.

100. Varro, *De Lingua latina*, I, 107, 91. My translation. Seneca, *Ad Lucilius*, 88.

101. St. Augustine, *De Ordine*, II, 12, 37; *P.L.*, 32, c. 1012.

102. Martianus Capella, *De nuptiis Mercurii et Philologiae*, III, 229.

103. H. Keil, *Grammatici Latini* (Lipsiae: 1864), I, p. 42; III, p. 522; IV, pp. 486–487. *Corpus grammaticarum Latinorum veterum*. Adiecit Fridericus Lindemannus (Lipsiae: 1831), I, pp. 41, 309.

104. Seneca, *Ad Lucilius*, 88.

105. Pliny the Elder, *Naturalis historia*, XIV, 1.

106. St. Augustine, *Confessiones*, I, XIII. *The Confessions of Augustine*. Ed. by John Gibb and William Montgomery (Cambridge: University Press, 1908).

107. E. W. Bower, "Some technical terms in Roman education." *Hermes*, 89 (1961), p. 475.

108. Plato, *Philebus*, 18 d.

109. Cassiodorus, *Variorum libri XII*, IX, Ep. 21; *P.L.*, 69, c. 788. My translation.

110. Diomedes, *Ars grammatica*, II. H. Keil, *Grammatici Latini*, I, p. 421.

111. Cicero, *De oratore*, I, 3.

112. Suetonius, *De grammaticis et rhetoribus*, XIII. *The Lives of Illustrious Men. On Grammarians*. Tr. T. C. Rolfe (London: William Heinemann/New York: Macmillan, 1914), p. 417.

113. Tertullian, *Adversus Nationes*, II, 7; *P.L.*, I. c. 595.

114. Cassian, *P.L.*, 70, c. 1107.

115. Alain Hus, *Docere et les mots de la famille docere* (Paris: Presses Universitaires de France, 1965), pp. 304, 320, 322.

116. Cf. Erich Bethe, *Buch und Bild in Altertum*. Aus dem Nachlass herausgegeben von Ernst Kirsten (Amsterdam: 1964), p. 33.

117. Vitruvius Pollio, *De architectura*, VI, 1.

118. Aulus Gellius, *Noctes Atticae*, XIV, VI, 1.

119. Cicero, 2, *Phil.*, 45.

120. Cassiodorus, *Variorum libri* XII, IX, c. 21. My translation.

121. Aulus Gellius, *Noctes Atticae*, III, III, 1. *The Attic Nights of Aulus Gellius*. Tr. John C. Rolfe (London: William Heinemann/New York: G. P. Putnam, 1925), I, p. 245.

122. Seneca, *Ad Lucilius*, XV.

123. Cicero, *Ad Herennius*, IV, 4.

124. Henri-Irénée Marrou, *Saint-Augustin et la fin de la culture antique* (Paris: De Boccard, 1938), p. 4; for details, *L'idée de culture antique*, pp. 549–560. "*Culture, civilisation, décadence.*" *Revue de synthèse*, X, 3 (1938), pp. 133–160.

125. Cicero, *Tusculanum Disputationis*, I, 13.

126. Henri-Irénée Marrou, *Histoire de l'éducation dans l'antiquité* (Paris: Seuil, 1948; 1981, I–II).

127. Aristotle, *Poetics*, 1447 b. *The Poetics of Aristotle*. Edited with critical notes and a translation by S. H. Butcher (4th ed., London: Macmillan, 1917), p. 9.

128. Plato, *Theaetetus*, 152 e.

129. Cf. Ernst Zellner, *Die Wörter auf -ura* (Gotha: 1930), p. 44. Eduard Wölfflin, *ibid.*, p. 53. A. Ernout-A. Meillet, *Dictionnaire étymologique de la langue latine* (Paris: 1967), p. 363.

130. Cf. Gabriel R. F. Nuchelmans, *Studien über φιλόλογοδ, φιλολογία und φιλολογείη* (Zwolle: 1950), p. 35.

131. Cicero, *Acad. prim.*, II, 2.

132. Pindar, *Isthmians*, IX, 26.

133. Plato, *Republic*, X, 598. Plato, *The Republic*. Tr. Paul Shorey (Cambridge, Mass.: Harvard University Press, 1935), II, p. 431.

134. Tertullian, *Ad. Nat.*, II, 12; *P.L.*, 1, c. 603; see also: *P.L.*, 1, c. 588.

135. Cf. Eduard Wölfflin, *ibid.*, p. 52.

136. Theodor Birt, *Das antike Buchwesen in seinem Verhältniss zur Literatur* (Berlin: 1882), p. 22.

137. Cassiodorus, *Institutiones* . . . II, *Praef.*, 2; *P.L.*, 70, c. 1151.

138. Plato, *Phaedrus*, 275 c. Tr. C. I. Rowe (Warminster: Aris and Philipps, 1986), p. 125.

139. Minucius Felix, *Octavius*, 7, 2.

140. St. Jerome, *Liber de vir. ill.*, CXVI; *P.L.*, 23, c. 707.

141. St. Jerome, *Ep.*, XXII, 30; *P.L.*, XXII, c. 417.

142. Cf. Theodor Birt, *ibid.*, p. 115.

143. Aulus Gellius, XIV, II, 1. *The Attic Nights of Aulus Gellius*, III, p. 21.

144. *Inscripţiile Daciei romane* (Bucureşti: Ed. Academiei române, 1977), II, p. 390.

145. Ernst Robert Curtius, *Europäische Literatur und Lateinisches Mittelalter* (1948. Bern und München: Franke Verlag, 1984), pp. 308–315.

146. Wilhelm Schubart, *Das Buch bei den Griechen und Römern* (1921. Heidelberg: 1968), p. 33.

147. Aristophanes, *Frogs*, v. 1114.

148. Cf. Leonid Arbuzov, *Colores Rhetorici* (1948. Göttingen: Vandenhoek-Rupecht, 1963), p. 17.

149. Pliny the Younger, *Letters*, I, 2, 6. Martial, II, 8.

150. Isidore of Seville, *Etymologiae*, VI, 1, 3; *De bibliotecis*; *P.L.*, 82, c. 135.

151. Martial, II, 8.

152. Edward Alexander Parsons, *The Alexandrian Library. Glory of the*

Hellenic World (London: 1952), pp. 6, 8ff., 18. Mustafa El-Abbadi, *"La Bibliothèque et le musée d'Alexandrie à l'époque des Ptolémées".* Diogène, (1988), 141, 24–40.

153. Tertullian, *Apologeticus*, 18; *P.L.*, 1, c. 379.

154. Aulus Gellius, *Noctes Atticae*, VII, XVII, 1.

155. Pliny the Elder, *Naturalis Historia*, VII, 30, 115. Tr. H. Rackham (Cambridge, Mass.: Harvard University Press/London: William Heinemann, 1942), pp. 580–581.

156. St. Jerome, *Prob. in Divin. S. Hier. Bibl.*; *P.L.*, 28, c. 31; *Ep.*, V; *P.L.*, 22, c. 337.

157. Cf. Anscari Mundó, "Biblioteca, Bible et lecture du Carême d'après Saint Benoît." *Revue Bénédictine*, LX (1950), p. 78.

158. Tacitus, *Dialogus de oratoribus*, 2.

159. Cf. *Monumenta Germaniae Historica*, 53, III, p. 638.

160. Cf. M. Bonamy, *Dissertation historique sur la bibliothèque d'Alexandrie. Mémoire de l'Académie Royale des Inscriptions et Belles Lettres* (Paris: 1736), IX, p. 400.

161. Quintilian, X, 1, 104. *The Institutio Oratoria of Quintilian.* Tr. H. E. Butler (London: William Heinemann/New York: G. P. Putnam, 1922), IV, pp. 60–61.

162. Ernst Robert Curtius, *ibid.*, pp. 253–265.

163. Edward Alexander Parsons, *ibid.*, p. 206.

164. Eusebius, *Ecclesiastical History*, V, VIII, 11. *The Ecclesiastical History.* Tr. Kirsopp Lane (Cambridge, Mass.: Harvard University Press, 1926), I, p. 459.

165. Quintilian, X, 1, 57.

166. St. Jerome, *Liber de viris ill.*; *P.L.*, 23, c. 631–730.

167. Rudolf Pfeiffer, *History of Classical Scholarship. From the Beginnings to the End of the Hellenistic Age* (1968. Oxford: Clarendon, 1976), p. 123.

168. Cassiodorus, *De Orth. Praef.*, *P.L.*, 7, c. 1239.

169. Henri-Irenée Marrou, *Histoire de l'éducation dans l'antiquité,* pp. 244–245.

170. Vitruvius Pollio, *De architectura*, VI, *Praefatio*.

171. Quintilian, I, 10, 1; cf. also Cicero, *De orat.*, 15.

172. Eric A. Havelock, *Preface to Plato* (Cambridge, Mass.: Belknap Press, 1963), pp. 61–86. *The Literate Revolution in Greece and its Cultural Consequences* (Princeton: Princeton University Press, 1982), p. 125.

173. Pliny the Elder, *Hist. Nat. Praef.*, 11.

174. Francesco della Corte, *Enciclopedisti latini* (Genova: 1946), pp. 13–14, 16.

175. Pierre Courcelle, *Les lettres grecques en Occident de Macrobe à Cassiodore* (Paris: 1948), pp. 326, 340.

176. Isidore of Seville, *Etymologiae*, I, II, 1; *P.L.*, 82, c. 70–71.

177. St. Augustine, *De doctrina christiana*, 29; *P.L.*, 34, c. 807.

178. St. Augustine, *Confessiones*, IV, 16.

179. Cassiodorus, *Institutiones . . .* , II, *Praef.*, 11.

180. Isidore of Seville, *Etymologiae*, I, 4, 2; *P.L.*, 82, c. 77–78.

181. Seneca, *Naturales quaestiones*, I, 12.

182. Seneca, *Ad Luc.*, XI, 88.

183. Cf. A. H. L. Haeren, *Geschichte des Studium der griechischen und romanischen Literatur* (Göttingen: 1797), I, p. 24. *Thesaurus Linguae Latinae* (Lipsiae: 1929), VI, IX, c. 2170.

184. Seneca, *Ad Polybum*, XXI, 5. St. Augustine, *De ord.*, II, 16, 44; *P.L.*, 32, c. 1015.

185. Cf. James Westfall Thompson, *The Literacy of the Laity in the Middle Ages* (New York: 1960), p. 102.

186. Cassiodorus, *De Artibus et Disciplinis liberalium Artium*; *P.L.*, 32, c. 1015. Isidore of Seville, *Etymologiae*, I, 5; *P.L.*, 88, c. 81.

187. Seneca, *Ad Luc.*, 88, 23.

188. Virgilius Maro Grammaticus, *Epitomae*, III, 6.

189. *Inter alia*: Gregory I, The Great, *In prim. Reg. Exp.*, V, III § 30; *P.L.*, 79, c. 355.

190. Cicero, *De officiis*, I, 42; Seneca, *Ad Luc.*, 88, 12.

191. Seneca, *Ad Luc.*, 88, 2.

192. Aulus Gellius, *Noctes Atticae, Praef.*, 13. *The Attic Nights of Aulus Gellius*, pp. XXXI, XXXIII.

193. St. Augustine, *De ordine*, II, 16, 44; *P.L.*, 32, c. 1015.

194. Seneca, *Ad Luc.*, 88, 1.

195. Aulus Gellius, *Praef.*, 13; XVII, 5, 10.

196. A general introduction: N. I. Herescu, *"Homo-Humus-Humanitatis. Préface à un humanisme contemporain."* Bulletin de l'Assoc. G. Budé (1948), 5, 64–76.

197. Cicero, *Pro Archia*, 2, 3, 9. *Tusculanae Disputationes*, V, 66.

198. Cassiodorus, *De orth.*, *Praef.*; *P.L.*, 70, c. 1241.

199. Cassiodorus, *De orth.*, III; *P.L.*, 79, c. 1167.

200. Cicero, *Pro Archia*, 2, 3, 4; *De Legibus*, 3, 1.

201. Cf. St. Augustine, *De ord.*, II; *P.L.*, 32, c. 1016.

202. Aulus Gellius, *Noctes Atticae*, XIII, XVII, 1. *The Attic Nights of Aulus Gellius*, II, p. 457.

203. Cicero, *De finibus bonorum et malorum*, V, 54.

204. Cicero, *Pro Archia*, 7.

205. Cicero, *ibid.*, 16. Cicero, *The Speeches*. Tr. N. H. Watts (Cambridge, Mass.: Harvard University Press, 1923), p. 24.

206. Cicero, *De Re Publica*, I, XVII, 28. *Cicero in Twenty-Eight Volumes*. Tr. Clinton Walker Keyes (Cambridge, Mass.: Harvard University Press, 1928), XVI, p. 51.

207. Aulus Gellius, *Noctes Atticae*, XIII, 17, 1.

208. Cicero, *De Officiis*, I, 8, 33. Caesar, *De bello gallico*, I, 4.

209. St. Augustine, *Disciplinae*, X, 12, cf. *Thesaurus Linguae Latinae*, VII, 2, c. 1529.

210. Apuleius, *Metamorphoses*, X, 2; Symmachus, *Ep.*, I, 79.

211. Aulus Gellius, XIII, 17, 1.

212. Tertullian, *De idolatria*, X; *P.L.*, 1, c. 675.

213. *Codex Theodosianus*, XIV, 1, 1; cf. Gaston Boissier, *La fin du paganisme* (Paris: Hachette, 1891), I, p. 230. My translation.

214. Tertullian, *De idolatria*, V; *P.L.*, 1, c. 667.

215. Plutarch, *De Pythiae oraculis*, 23.

216. Tacitus, *Dialogus de oratoribus*, 12.

217. Varro, *De Lingua Latina*, V, 143; VI, 33.

218. Plato, *Republic*, X, 595 c.

219. Horace, *Epistolae*, II, 1, v. 157.

220. Ernst Robert Curtius, *ibid.*, pp. 254–256.

221. Juvenal, *Saturae*, III, 76.

222. Wladyslaw Tatarkiewicz, *Istoria celor şase noţiuni*. Rom. transl. (Bucureşti: Meridiane, 1981), p. 160.

223. Anonymous fragment, *On comedy*, 11. *Comicorum Graecorum Fragmenta*. Ed. G. Kaibel (Berolini: 1899), I, fasc. 1. cf. Aristotle, *Poetica*. Studiu introductiv, traducere şi comentarii de D. M. Pippidi (Bucureşti: Editura Academiei, 1965), p. 193.

224. Horace, *Epistles*, II, 1, v. 36–45.

225. Horace, *ibid.*, II, 1, v. 35–36; Tacitus, *Dialogus de oratoribus*, XV.

226. For details: Adrian Marino, *"Aux sources de la dialectique sémantique ancien/nouveau."* *Cahiers roumains d'études littéraires* (1975), 1, 50–51, 53, *passim*. Albert Maréchal, *"Vetus, Novus, dans la Querelle des Anciens et des Modernes à Rome."* *Mélanges Vianey* (Paris: 1934), pp. 230–231. Ernst Robert Curtius, *ibid.*, pp. 256–261.

227. Quintilian, XII, 10, 16–17.

228. Horace, *Saturae*, I, 4, v. 63–65.

229. Aulus Gellius, *Noctes Atticae*, IV, 11, 3; XII, II, 1, etc.

230. Aulus Gellius, *ibid.*, XIX, IX, 7.

231. Virgilius Maro Grammaticus, *Epitomae*, I, 1, 1–2.

232. Macrobius, *Saturnalia*, I, 2.

233. Cicero, *Brutus*, I, 33.

234. Tacitus, *Annales*, XI, 13. *The Annals and the Histories*, p. 151. Fronto, *Epistulae*, II, 6, 2. Recensuit Samuel Adrianus Naber (Lipsiae: Teubner, 1867), p. 30.

235. Cicero, *De oratore*, I, 18.

236. St. Augustine, *En. Psalm.*, LXX; *P.L.*, 36, c. 888.

237. G. M. A. Grube, *The Greek and the Roman Critics* (London: Methuen, 1965), p. 41.

238. Tertullian, *De cultu Feminarum*, I, III; *P.L.*, I, c. 1358.

239. Cf. Brian Stock, *The Implications of Literacy. Written Language and Models of Interpretation in the Eleventh and Twelfth Centuries* (Princeton: Princeton University Press, 1983), p. 21.

240. Cicero, *Brutus*, LVI.

241. M. Ruch, *"Nationalisme culturel et culture internationale dans la pensée de Cicéron." Revue des Études Latines*, XXXVI (1958), 187–204.

242. Diodorus Siculus, I, I, 3.

243. Moses Hadas, "From Nationalism to Cosmopolitanism in the Greco-Roman World." *Journal of the History of Ideas* (1943), 4, 105–111. *Hellenistic Culture: Fusion and Diffusion* (New York: 1959), pp. 16–17.

244. Diogenes Laertius, II, 9.

245. Cicero, *De orat.*, II, 38, 159. *Cicero in Twenty-Eight Volumes, De oratore in Two Volumes*, I, Books I, II. Tr. E. W. Sutton (Cambridge, Mass.: Harvard University Press/London: William Heinemann, 1942), III, p. 313.

246. Quintilian, X, 1, 65. *The Institutio Oratoria of Quintilian*, IV, p. 37.

247. St. Augustine, *De ord.*, II, 13, 78; *P.L.*, 32, c. 1013.

248. Dionysius of Halicarnassus, *On Litrary Composition*, 11, 14–16. *Classical and Medieval Literary Criticism. Translations and Interpretations.* Ed. by Alex Preminger, O. B. Hardison Jr., Kevin Kerrane (New York: Frederik Ungar, 1974), pp. 172–175.

249. Hesiod, *Theogony*, v. 22–33.

250. Aristotle, *Rhetoric*, III, 1, IX.

251. Cicero, *De Officiis*, 1, 133.

252. Minucius Felix, *Octavius*, XIV, 3–4.

253. Plato, *Laws*, VII, 810 b.

254. Among the latest studies: Henryk Markiewicz, "Ut pictura Poesis. A History of the Topos and the Problem." *New Literary History*, (1987), 3, 525–538.

255. Plutarch, *Glory of Athens*, 3.

256. Aristotle, *Rhetoric*, III, I, VII.

257. Cicero, *Tusculanae disputationes*, V, XIII, 40. My translation.

258. Plato, *Laws*, II, 658 e. *Plato in Twelve Volumes*. Tr. R. G. Bury (Cambridge, Mass.: Harvard University Press/London: William Heinemann, 1976), X, p. 108.

259. Democritus, *Philologische Schriften*, 18. *Die Fragmente der Vorsokratiker*. Griechisch und Deutsch von Hermann Diels (1903. Berlin: Weidmansche Buchhandlung, 1912), II, p. 66.

260. Plutarch, *De Pythiae oraculis*, 5.

261. Cf. Frederick A. Norwood, "Attitude of the Ante-Nicene Fathers toward Greek Artistic Achievement." *Journal of the History of Ideas*, III (1947), 446–447.

262. V. V. Bîcikov, *Estetica antichităţii tîrzii*. Rom. transl. (Bucureşti: Meridiane, 1984), p. 274.

263. Silvio Accame, *"L'ispirazione della musa e gli albori della critica storica nell'età archaica."* *Rivista de filologia e d'istruzione classica*, CXII (1964), 131–132.

264. Plutarch, *De Pythiae oraculis*, 6.

265. Wolfgang Schadenwaldt, *Der Umfang des Begriffs der Literatur in der Antike. Literatur und Dichtung*. Hrsg. von Horst Rüdiger (Stuttgart-Berlin-Köln-Mainz: W. Kohlhammer, 1973), p. 15. In the same sense, briefly, Roland Barthes, *"L'Ancienne Rhétorique. Aide-Mémoire."* *Communications*, 1976 (16): 176.

266. Cicero, *In Pison*, 70.

267. Petronius, *Satyricon*, CXVIII, CXVI.

268. René Marache, *La critique littéraire de la langue latine et le développement du goût archaïsant au II-e siècle de notre ère* (Rennes: 1952), p. 263.

269. Cassiodorus, *Variarum libri XII*, IX, 21; *P.L.*, 69, c. 787.

270. *Inter alia*: Pliny the Elder, *Naturalis historia*, XXX, 2.

271. Léonid N. Stolovitch, *"L'étymologie du mot 'Beauté' et la nature de la catégorie du Beau."* Traduit du russe. *Revue d'Esthétique* 19 (1966), 243–257, particularly, 256. Pierre Monteil, *Beau et Laid en latin. Étude de vocabulaire* (Paris: 1964), p. 236, *passim*.

272. Quintilian, XI, 1, 11.

273. Plato, *Apology*, 22 c. *Plato in Twelve Volumes*. Tr. R. G. Bury (Cambridge, Mass.: Harvard University Press/London: William Heinemann, 1926), X, p. 85.

274. Horace, *Ars poetica*, v. 99; *Epistulae*, II, 1, 72.

275. Ladislas Tatarkiewicz, *"Deux mille ans de poétique."* *Diogène*, 38 (1962), 9.

276. Hesiod, *Theogony*, 27–28. *Hesiod's Theogony*. Tr. Richard S. Caldwell (Newburyport, Mass.: Focus Classical Library, 1987), p. 27. About imitation and fictionality: Aristotle, *Poetics*, XXIV, XXV. Subsequently: St. Augustine, *Confessiones*, I, 14: *fabelas, "omnes suavitate graecas fabularum narrationum"*.

277. Lucian, *Portraits*, 16 (*Essays in Portraiture*). *Lucian in Eight Volumes*. Tr. A. M. Harmon (Cambridge, Mass.: Harvard University Press, 1975), IV, p. 285.

278. D. A. Russell, *Theories of Literature and Taste*. *The Classical World*. (eds.) David Daiches, Anthony Thorlby (London: 1972), p. 426.

279. Plato, *Phaedrus*, 267 c. Tr. C. I. Rowe (Warminster-Great Britain: Aris and Phillips, 1986), p. 107.

280. Longinus, *On the Sublime*, 5, 30, 32. *Longinus on the Sublime*. Tr. Benedict Einarson (Chicago: Paccard and Co., 1945), pp. 11–12, 53, 58.

281. Cf. D. M. Pippidi, *Formarea ideilor în antichitate* (Bucureşti: Editura enciclopedică română, 1972), p. 151.

282. Quintilian, VIII, 3, 1. Diodorus Siculus, XII, 53.

283. Demetrius, *On Style*, 193. Aristotle, *The Poetics*. *"Longinus" On the Sublime*. Demetrius *On Style*. Tr. Rhys Roberts (Cambridge, Mass.: Harvard University Press/London: William Heinemann, 1927), p. 421.

284. Plato, *Gorgias*, 502 b.

285. Cf. Eduard Wölfflin, *"Litteratura."* *Archiv für Lateinische Lexikographie und Grammatik*, V (1888), 52.

286. Symmachus, *Epistulae*, 1, 8. Cf. Eduard Wölfflin, *ibid.*, p. 52.

287. Diogenes Laertius, *The Lives and Opinions of the Eminent Philosophers*, VII, 4, 167. *Lives of Eminent Philosophers*. Tr. R. D. Hicks (Cambridge, Mass.: Harvard University Press, 1975), II, p. 271.

288. Aristotle, *Poetics*, IX, 1451 b. *The Poetics of Aristotle*, pp. 35, 37.

289. Ovid, *Tristia*, IV, X, v. 25.

290. Henri Weil, *"De l'origine du mot 'poète'."* *Études sur L'Antiquité grecque* (Paris: 1900), pp. 236–245, particularly, p. 244.

291. Cf. D. M. Pippidi, *ibid.*, p. 148.

292. Plato, *Phaedrus*, 258 d. Tr. C. I. Rowe (Warminster-Great Britain: Aris and Phillips, 1986), p. 87.

293. Pliny the Younger, *Epistulae*, I, 10.

294. Silvio Accame, *ibid.*, pp. 147–148. Claude Calame, *ibid.*, pp. 25, 186.

295. St. Augustine, *Soliloquia*, I, 1; *P.L.*, 32 c. 869.

296. Aristotle, *Poetics*, IV, 1448 b. *The Poetics of Aristotle*, p. 21.

297. Lucretius Carus, *De rerum natura*, V, v. 1041–1090.

298. Plato, *Republic*, X, 601 d. *Sophist*, 219 a. *Aristotle, Poetics*, IV, 1448 b. *The Poetics of Aristotle*, p. 15.

299. Phaedrus, *Fabulae*, 1. *Prologus.*

300. H. Keil, *Grammatici Latini* (Lipsiae: Teubner, 1853), I, p. 475. Ernst Robert Curtius, *ibid.*, p. 440.

301. Isidore of Seville, *Etymologiae*, VIII, 7, 10.

302. St. Augustine, *De ordine*, II, 14, 40, 41; *P.L.*, 32, c. 1014.

303. Seneca, *De Tranquilitate Animi*, V, 5.

304. Cicero, *Tusculanae disputationes*, V, 30, 105.

305. Plato, *Phaedrus*, 277 e.

306. Aristotle, *Poetics*, I, 1447 a. *The Poetics of Aristotle*, p. 9.

307. Aristotle, *Poetics*, VI, 1449 b. *The Poetics of Aristotle*, p. 23.

308. Jacqueline Duchemin, *"La joie de la création poétique chez les poètes grecs." Revue d'esthétique*, 105(3), 236–268, particularly 246.

309. John Forskyde, *Greece before Homer. Ancient Chronology and Mythology* (London: 1956), pp. 140–141.

310. Plutarch, *De Pythiae oraculis*, 23.

311. Quintilian, VII, 3, 56.

312. Quintilian, , II, 12. *Quintilian as Educator*. Tr. H. E. Butler. Ed. with Introduction and Notes by Frederick M. Wheelock (New York: Twayne Publishers, 1974), p. 110.

313. Cicero, *Pro Archia*, 8, 18.

314. Pindar, *Olympians*, VI, 86–90.

315. Diogenes Laertius, *ibid.*, IV, 14; *On Sublime*, VIII.

316. Quintilian, X, 1, 35. Cicero, *De orat.*, III, 16.

317. Aristotle, *Poetics*, I, 1447 a. *The Poetics of Aristotle*, p. 9.

318. Sidonius Apollinaris, LIII. Tr. Eugène Barat (Paris: 1887), p. 106.

319. Plato, *Apology*, 22. Cf. *Plato in Twelve Volumes*. Tr. R. G. Bury, X, p. 85.

320. Plato, *Phaedrus*, 277 e. Tr. C. I. Rowe, p. 129.

321. Aristotle, *Metaphysics*, 893–910.

322. Ovid, *Tristia*, 2, 1, v. 276ff.

323. Pliny the Younger, VI, IX. St. Augustine, *Confessiones*, IV, 15.

324. Clement of Alexandria, *Stromates*, VI, 150, 5. Cf. V. V. Bîcikov, *Estetica antichităţii tîrzii*, p. 264.

325. Tertullian, *De Test. Anim.*, 57; *P.L.*, 1, c. 747.

326. Xenophon, *Memorabilia*, I, 2, 33.

327. Roger Druet-Herman Grégoire, *La civilisation de l'écriture* (Paris: Fayard, 1976), p. 64.

328. For instance: Eva Mathews Sanford, "Propaganda and Censorship in the Transmission of Josephus." *T.P.L.A.*, LXVI (1935), 127–145.

329. Jean Collart, "A propos du mot 'Auctoritas'." *Helikon*, I (1961), 214.

330. Diogenes Laertius, IX, 45, 61.

331. Aristotle, *De interpretatione*, 2, 16 a.

332. A. M. Guillemin, *Le Public et la vie littéraire à Rome* (Paris: 1937), pp. 98–99.

333. Cicero, *De Oficiis*, I, 41; *Tusculanae disputationes*, I, 3.

334. Vitruvius Pollio, *De architectura*, VII, IX. *Praefatio*.

335. Seneca, *De Tranquillitate animi*, I, IX, 5, 7.

336. Strabo, *Geography*, XIII, 609.

337. Diogenes Laertius, VI, 21.

338. St. Jerome, *Ep.*, XLIX; *P.L.*, 22, c. 511–513.

339. Pliny the Younger, VII, XXI.

340. Cf. D. M. Pippidi, *ibid.*, p. 148.

341. C. Velleius Paterculus, *Historia Romana*, II, XXXVI. *Compendium of Roman History*. Tr. Frederick Shipley (London: William Heinemann/ New York: G. P. Putnam, 1924), pp. 128–129.

342. Cicero, *De orat.*, X, 4.

343. Plato, *Phaedrus*, 275 a–b.

344. Wladyslaw Tatarkiewicz, *Istoria celor şase noţiuni*, pp. 96–103.

345. Cicero, *De Oficiis*, I, 42.

346. Pliny the Younger, I, XX, 4.

347. *On the Sublime*, I, VIII. *Classical and Medieval Literary Criticism*, pp. 192, 196–197.

348. Cicero, *Ad Herennius*, IV, 8–10.

349. Cicero, *De oratore*, II, 128.

350. St. Augustine, *De doctrina Christiana*, IV, XX; *P.L.*, 34, c. 107.

351. St. Jerome, *Ep.*, LVII; *P.L.*, 22, c. 579.

352. Erich Auerbach, *Sermo humilis, Literatursprache und Publikum in der lateinischen Spätantik und im Mittelalter* (Bern: Franke, 1958), pp. 25–53.

353. Prudentius, *Peristephanon*, II, 574; *P.L.*, 60, c. 339.

354. Tacitus, *Dialogus de oratoribus*, 10.

355. Aristotle, *Poetics*, IX, 1451 b.

356. Valerius Maximus, *Factorum et dictorum memorabilium libri IX*, III, VII, in *Rom*. 11. Cf. Claude-Odon Reure, *Les gens de lettres et leurs protecteurs à Rome* (Paris: 1891), p. 9.

357. Sidonius Apollinaris, *Ep.*, VIII, 2; *P.L.*, 58, c. 590.

358. Cicero, *Pro Archia*, 6, 13; a central idea with Quintilian, 8, *Proem.*, 6, 20.

359. Cassiodorus, *Institutiones* . . . , II, 1; *P.L.*, 70, c. 1152.

360. Plutarch, *De Pythiae oraculis*, 22.

361. Cicero, *Ad Heren.*, III, 22.

362. Vitruvius Pollio, *De architectura*, I, 2, 7ff.

363. N. I. Herescu, "Poetae docti." *Revista clasică*, VI (T. II), 1930, 13–24.

364. Terence, *Andria*, *Prol.*, 18.

365. Macrobius, *Saturnalia*, I, 1, 6.

366. For details, Adrian Marino, *"Literatura cu literatură"*. *Hermeneutica ideii de literatură* (Cluj-Napoca: Dacia, 1987), pp. 368–386. *Teoria della letteratura*, pp. 406–421.

367. One point of view: Ferdinand Lot, *La fin du monde antique et le début du moyen âge* (1927; Paris: 1968), pp. 165–166, 169, 171, 175; see also: Henri-Irénée Marrou, *Décadence romane ou antiquité tardive? IIIᵉ–IVᵉ siècles* (Paris: Seuil, 1977).

368. Details in: Adrian Marino, *"Literatura despre literatură,"* *Hermeneutica ideii de literatură*, pp. 386–394. *Teoria della letteratura*, pp. 422–428.

369. Martianus Capella, *De nuptiis Mercurii et Philologiae*, III, 230–231.

370. Horace, *Odes*, XXX, 1, 6.

371. Quintilian, I, 4, 2.

372. Cf. Karl Barwick, *Remmius Palaemon und die römische Ars Grammatica* (Leipzig: 1922), pp. 220, 223. H. Keil, *Grammatici latini*, VII, p. 321.

373. Suetonius, *De grammaticis et rhetoribus*, 24.

374. *Grammaticae Romanae Fragmenta*. Collegit recensuit Hyginus Funaioli (Lipsiae: Teubner, 1907), I, p. 236 (fr. 236).

375. Cicero, *De orat.*, I, 42, 187.

376. Quintilian, I, 4, 2.

377. *Grammaticae Romanae Fragmenta*, I, p. 205. H. Keil, *ibid.*, I, p. 426; IV, pp. 486–487: (Sergii) *Explanationum in Artem Donati*.

378. H. Keil, *ibid.*, IV, pp. 446–447; IV, p. 4.

379. H. Keil, *ibid.*, V, p. 547; VII, 321. Karl Barwick, *ibid.*, p. 223. *Historicorum Romanorum Reliquiae*. Collegit . . . Hermannus Peter (Stuttgart: 1967), p. 40. K. Lehrs, *De vocabulis "filologos, grammatikós, criticós."* *Program des königlichen Friedrichkollegiums zu Königsberg in Ost Preussens* (Königsberg: 1838), pp. 5–6.

380. Pindar, *Olympians*, II, 93.

381. Plato, *Ion*, 554 e. *The Dialogues of Plato*. Translated into English with Analyses and Introduction by B. Jowett, M.A. (Oxford: Clarendon Press, 1892), I, pp. 502–503.

382. Diogenes Laertius, IX, 13: *Heraclitus*. Tr. R. D. Hicks, II, p. 421.

383. Demetrius, *On Style*, 76. *Classical and Medieval Literary Criticism*, p. 147.

384. Augusto Rostagni, *Classicità e spirito moderno* (Torino: Einaudi, 1939), p. 40.

385. Herodotus, *Historiae*, II, 53.

386. *Grammaticae Romanae Fragmenta*, I, p. 205.

387. Jean Pépin, *"L'Herméneutique antique." Poétique* (1975), 23, 291–300.

388. Vitruvius Pollio, *De architectura*, 8, 3, 25. Petronius, *Satyricon*, XXIX.

389. *Grammaticae Romanae Fragmenta*, I, pp. 185–186, 197. Gabriel R. F. Nuchelmans, *Studien über* φιλόλογοδ, φιλολογία *und* φιλολογείη (Zwolle: 1950). Heinrich Kuch, *Filologos* (Berlin: Akademie-Verlag, 1965), pp. 25, 37, 55, 62, 68.

390. Varro, *De Lingua Latina*, V, 7.

391. *Grammaticae Romanae Fragmenta*, I, p. 205.

392. Edward Alexander Parsons, *The Alexandrian Library. Glory of the Hellenic World* (London: 1952), p. 141.

393. G. M. A. Grube, *The Greek and Roman Critics* (London: Methuen, 1965), p. 132.

394. Edward Alexander Parsons, *ibid.*, pp. 220, 225.

395. Rudolf Pfeiffer, *History of Classical Scholarship. From the Beginnings to the Era of the Hellenistic Age* (Oxford: Clarendon, 1968), pp. 213, 219–220, 225–227. Mustafa El-Abbadi, *"La Bibliothèque et le Musée d'Alexandrie à l'époque des Ptolémées." Diogène*, 141 (1988), 32.

396. *Grammaticae Romanae Fragmenta*, I, p. 205.

397. Cicero, *De orat.*, I, 33, 177.

398. G. M. A. Grube, *ibid.*, p. 164.

399. Aristotle, *Poetics*, 1447 c.

400. Plato, *Phaedrus*, 275 c–d.

401. Plato, *ibid.*, 275–a–c.

402. II *Corinth*, III, 6.

403. St. Augustine, *De spiritu et littera*, XXI; *P.L.*, 44, c. 222.

404. St. Augustine, *En Psal.*, LXX; *P.L.*, 36, c. 890.

405. Plato, *Republic*, II, 264 b–d, 280 c; III, 292 a–b; X, 607.

406. Plutarch, *Lycurg.*, 13. Isocrates, *Areopagita*, 16.

407. Ezio Bolaffi, *La critica filosofica e letteraria in Quintiliano* (Bruxelles: 1958), p. 7. A general view: Tudor Vianu, *"Manierism și asianism."* *Studii de literatură universală și comparată* (1960. București: Editura Academiei R. S. România, 1963), pp. 611–620.

408. Tertullian, *De praescriptionibus haereticorum*, VII; *P.L.*, II, c. 20. For St. Augustine (*De Civitate Dei*, IV, 32) the "poet's religion" is superfluous, futile, harmful: "vain inventions under the name of religion" (*The City of God*, John Healey's translation . . . , (London: Dent, 1945), I, p. 141.

409. Cf. A. M. Guillemin, *"Les Querelles littéraires dans l'antiquité."* *Humanités*, IX (1932), 86.

410. Cf. Athenaeus, *Deipnosophistai* (*"Banquet of Sophists"*), III, 72. *The Deipnosophistas*. Tr. Charles Burton-Julick (London: William Heinemann/New York: G. P. Putnam, 1927), I, p. 315.

411. Martial, 5, 50. Aulus Gellius, XIII, XXI.

412. Seneca, *Ad Luc.*, XXXIII.

413. *On the Sublime*, II. *Classical and Medieval Literary Criticism*, p. 192.

414. Horace, *Epistulae*, I, 19 v. 19.

415. Tacitus, *Dialogus de oratoribus*, 20. Aulus Gellius, VI, XIV, 11.

416. Plato, *Republic*, II, 378 a.

417. Plato, *ibid.*, x, 607 c–d.

418. Seneca, *De brevitate vitae*, 13, 7.

419. *II Corint.* XII, 1–4. *Romans*, VI, 24–26.

420. For details, *"Antiliteratura."* Adrian Marino, *Hermeneutica ideii de literatură*, pp. 418–458. *Teoria della Letteratura*, pp. 449–482.

THE MIDDLE AGES

1. Prudentius, *Apotheosis*, 436; *P.L.*, 59, c. 954. Prudentius, *Peristephanon*, V, 186–187; *P.L.*, 60, c. 389; XIV; *P.L.*, 60, c. 585.

2. Isidore of Seville, *Etymologiae*, V, III; *P.L.*, 82, c. 236; *Libri carolini*, II, 30; *P.L.*, 98, c. 1105.

3. Eduard Wölfflin, *"Litteratura."* *Archiv für lateinische Lexicographie und Grammatik*, V (1888), 54. cf. also Ernst von Dobschütz, *De Decretum Gelasianum. De libris recipiendis et non recipiendis*. In kritischen Text. Hrsg. und untersucht (Leipzig: 1912), p. 225.

4. J. de Ghellinck, " *'Pagina' et 'Sacra Pagina'* " *Mélanges Auguste Pelzer* (Louvain, 1947), pp. 23–59.

5. *Monum. Germ. Historica Scriptores*, XXXIII (1905), cf. Etienne Gilson, *Les idées et les lettres* (Paris: Vrin, 1932), p. 222.

6. St. Augustine, *Quest. in Hept*; *P.L.*, 34, c. 547. St. Jerome, *Liber de viris illustribus*; *P.L.*, 23, c. 619.

7. Ernst Robert Curtius, *Europäische Literatur und lateinisches Mittelalter* (1948. Bern: Francke, 1984), p. 458.

8. J. de Ghellinck, " *'Originale' et 'Originalia'.* " *Archivum Latinitatis Medii Aevi*, XIV (1939), 101.

9. Ernst von Döbschutz, *Das Decretum Gelasianum . . .* , p. 225.

10. St. Augustine, *De Scriptura sacra Speculum*; *P.L.*, 34, c. 889.

11. Ernst Robert Curtius, *Europäische Literatur und lateinisches Mittelalter*, p. 458. Ernst von Döbschutz, *Das Decretum Gelasianum*, p. 325.

12. Gregory I, The Great, *Ep.*, XXII; *P.L.*, 20, c. 416.

13. Cf. Dom Jean Leclercq, *L'Amour des lettres et le Désir de Dieu* (Paris: 1957), p. 57.

14. Cf. Charles Thurot, *Notices et extraits de divers manuscrits latins pour servir à l'histoire des doctrines grammaticales au Moyen Âge* (Paris: 1868), XXII, p. 69.

15. Bede, *Historia ecclesiastica gentis Anglorum*, IV, 1; *P.L.*, 95, c. 172.

16. Hugo de St. Victor, *Excerptionum Allegoricarum*; *P.L.*, 177, c. 203.

17. *Inter alia*: Rabanus Maurus, *De cler. instit.*, III, 19; *P.L.*, 107, c. 396.

18. Cf. Pierre Riché, *Éducation et culture dans l'occident barbare*, VI–XIII siècles. (Paris: Seuil, 1962), p. 34.

19. Cf. James Westfall Thompson, *The Literacy of the Laity in the Middle Ages* (New York: Burt Franklin, 1960), pp. 103–104.

20. Alcuin, *Ep.*, 162; *P.L.*, 100, c. 441.

21. Conrad de Hirschau, *Dialogus super Auctores*. Ed. critique par R. B. C. Huygens (Bruxelles: Latomus, 1955), pp. 15, 29, 63, 65.

22. Ives Congar, *"Clercs et laïcs au point de vue de la culture au Moyen Âge: 'laicus' = sans lettres."* *Studia medievalia et mariologica P. Carolo Bolic O.E.M.* (Roma: 1971), pp. 326–327. A general synthesis: Georges de Lagarde, *La naissance de l'esprit laïque au déclin du Moyen Âge* (Louvain-Paris, 1956–1958), I–II.

23. F. J. E. Raby, *A History of Christian-Latin Poetry from the Beginnings to the Close of the Middle Ages* (Oxford: 1927), p. 193.

24. Daniel Poiron, *Le poète et le prince. L'évolution du lyrisme courtois de Guillaume de Machaut à Charles d'Orléans* (Paris: P.U.F., 1965), p. 117.

25. Sigismund Jakó şi Radu Manolescu, *Scrierea latină în evul mediu* (Bucureşti: Editura ştiinţifică, 1971). This work is quoted as it provides data on the spread of the Latin alphabet in the Romanian principalities also.

26. Paul Zumthor, *La lettre et la voix. De la "littérature" médiévale* (Paris: Seuil, 1987), p. 110.

27. *Inter alia:* G. Goetz, *Corpus Glossariorum Latinorum* (Lipsiae: 1882), III, 38. *Thesaurus Linguae Latinae* (Lipsiae: 1929), VI, Fasc. IX, c. 2169–2170, etc.

28. Isidore of Seville, *Etymologiae*, I, III, 9; *P.L.*, 82, c. 74–75. Alcuin, *De gramm.*; *P.L.*, 101, c. 855.

29. Cf. Harry F. Reijnders, *Aimericus, Ars lectoria. Vivarius*, 10 (1972), p. 86. *Novum Glossarium Mediae Latinitatis*. Ed. Franz Blatt (Hafniae: 1957): L. *Literatura*, c. 166–167.

30. Gregory I, the Great, *Moral.*, XV; *P.L.*, 75, c. 1105.

31. Philipp de Harveng, *Ep.*, XVIII; *P.L.*, 203, c. 159.

32. J. F. Niermeyer, *Mediae Latinitatis Lexicon Minus* (Leiden: 1976), p. 616.

33. *Nomenclature des écritures livresques du IXe au XVIe siècle*. B. Bischoff, G. I. Lieftinck, G. Battelli (Paris: C.N.R.S., 1954), pp. 17–18.

34. Walter von Wartburg, *Französisches Etymologisches Wörterbuch* (Basel: 1950), 5, p. 378.

35. Alcuin, *Disput.*; *P.L.*, 101, c. 975. John of Salisbury, *Polycr.*, I, *Prol.*; *P.L.*, 199, c. 385.

36. *Libri e lettori nel medioevo.* Guida, storia e critica a cura di Guglielmo Cavallo (Bari: Laterza, 1977), p. 135.

37. M. T. Clancy, *From Memory to Written Record: England 1066–1307* (Cambridge, Mass.: Harvard University Press, 1979), pp. 288ff.

38. F. Vigouroux, *Écriture, Écriture Sainte. Dictionnaire de la Bible* (Paris, 1926), II, c. 1572–1573. J. de Ghellinck, *Ibid.*, p. 34.

39. Marie-Madeleine Gauthier, *"Pulcher"* et *"Formosus,"* l'appréciation du beau en latin médiéval. *La Lexicographie du latin médiéval et ses rapports avec les recherches actuelles sur la civilisation du Moyen Âge* (Paris: 1981), p. 416.

40. St. Cassian, *De cenob. institut.*, V, XXXIV; *P.L.*, 49, c. 363.

41. St. Ferreol, *Regula Ad Monach.*, XXVIII; *P.L.*, 66, c. 969.

42. W. Wattenbach, *Das Schriftwesen von Mittelalter* (Leipzig: 1896), pp. 441–443, 495. Emile Lesne, *Les livres, "scriptoria" et bibliothèques du commencement du VIIIᵉ à la fin du XIᵉ siècle* (Lille: 1938). (= *Histoire de la propriété écclésiastique en France*, T. IV). Heinrich Fichtenau, *Mensch und Schrift im Mittelalter* (Wien: 1944), pp. 154, 156, 164. Ernst Robert Curtius, *Europäische Literatur. . . ,* pp. 319–323ff.

43. P. Hippolyte Delehaye, *"Note sur la légende de la lettre du Christ tombée du ciel."* Académie royale. *Bulletins de la Classe des lettres et de la Classe des Beaux-Arts*, 3ᵉ série, XXXIII, 2ᵉ partie (Bruxelles: 1899), 171–213. R. Stübe, *Der Himmelbrief* (Tübingen: 1918).

44. For example, Eugen de Toledo, *De inventoribus litterarum*, XXI; *P.L.*, 87, c. 568.

45. An immense bibliography. Some bearings: Hermann Güntert, *Von der Sprache der Götter und Geister* (Halle: 1921), pp. 46–49. R. A. Stewart Macalister, *The Secret Languages of Ireland* (Cambridge: 1937), pp. 15–19, 29. A short synthesis: David Diringer, *The Alphabet. A Key to the History of Mankind.* Third edition, completely revised, with the collaboration of Reinhold Regensburger (London: Hutchinson, 1968), I–II.

46. J. Loth, *"Le sort et l'écriture chez les anciens Celtes."* *Journal des Savants*, 9 (1911), 403–414, particularly 408.

47. Wilhelm Grimm, *Bericht über eine Inschrift auf einem in der Wallachei ausgegrabenen, golden Ring. Kleinere Schriften.* Hrsg. von Gustav Hinrichs (Berlin: 1883), III, pp. 132–134. David Diringer, *Ibid.*, I, p. 401. Ovidiu Drimba, *Istoria culturii și civilizației* (București: Editura enciclopedică, 1987), II, p. 128 (recent bibliography).

48. Rudolf Limmer, *Bildungszustände und Bildungsideen des 13. Jahrhunderts* (Berlin: 1928), p. 142.

49. Cf. Giuseppe Toffanin, *Storia dell 'Umanesimo* (Bologna: Zanichelli, 1964), I, p. 52.

50. Hugo de St. Victor, *Excerpt. Alleg.*, I, II, IV; *P.L.*, 177, c. 205.

51. J. H. Baxter-Charles Johnson, *Medieval Latin Word-List. From British and Irish Sources* (Oxford: 1934), p. 250. J. F. Niermeyer, *Ibid.*, p. 616. Ewald Flügel, "Bacon's Historia literaria." *Anglia*, XXI, B. IX (1899), 282. James Westfall Thompson, *ibid.*, p. 47.

52. Antonio da Tempo, *Delle Rime volgari . . .* Tratto per cura di Giusto Grion (Bologna: 1869), p. 174. Carl Sutter, *Aus Leben und Schriften des Magister Boncampagno* (Freiburg-Leipzig: 1894), p. 39.

53. Du Cange, Walter von Wartburg, Albert Dauzat, A.-J. Greimas, A. Walde, Tobler-Lommatzsch, *s.v.*

54. Charles Thurot, *"Documents relatifs à l'histoire de la grammaire au Moyen-Âge."* Académie des Inscriptions et Belles-Lettres, Comptes rendus. Nouv. série (Paris: 1870), VI, p. 250.

55. Petrus Blesensis (Pierre de Blois), *Epistolae*, LXVI; *P.L.*, 207, c. 198.

56. *Französische Literarästhetik des 12. und 13. Jahrhunderts. Prologe-Exkurse-Epiloge.* Ausgewählt von Ulrich Mölk (Tübingen: Max Niemeyer Verlag, 1969), pp. 59, 98.

57. Dante Alighieri, *Convivio*, II, 1, 2. *Tutte le opere.* A cura di Fredi Chiapelli. Edizione del Centenario, (Milano: U. Mursia, 1965), pp. 512–514.

58. Cf. Orazio Bacci, *La critica letteraria. Dell'Antichità classica al Rinascimento* (Milano: Vallardi, 1910), p. 158.

59. Walter von Wartburg, *Ibid.*, 5, p. 378. J. F. Niermeyer, *Ibid.*, p. 616. *Novum Glossarium Mediae Latinitatis*, L., c. 166–167.

60. Cassiodorus, *De Institutione Divinarum litterarum*, I, XXX; *P.L.*, 70, c. 1144.

61. J. M. Baxter-Charles Johnson, *Medieval Latin Word-List . . .* pp. 249–250. *Französissche Literarästhetik . . .* pp. 21, 41, 53, 87, 97, 103, etc.

62. Echart Conrad Lutz, *Rhetorica Divina. Mittelhochdeutsche Prolog-*

gebete und die rhetorische Kultur des Mittelalters (Berlin-New York: Walter de Gruyter, 1984), p. 49.

63. Dante Alighieri, *Convivio*, II, XII, (XIII), *Tutte le opere*, p. 532.

64. J. de Ghellinck, " '*Pagina*' *et* '*Sacra Pagina*'," pp. 28–29. *Französische Literarästhetik* . . . , p. 71.

65. Cassiodorus, *De Institit. Div. Litt.*, XV; *P.L.*, 70; c. 1126–1151.

66. W. Wattenbach, *Das Schriftwesen von Mittelalter*, pp. 317–323. Emile Lesne, *Les livres*, "*scriptoria*" *et bibliothèques du commencement du VIII*e à la fin du XIe siècle, pp. 405, 407–408.

67. Lucien Musset, *Introduction à la runologie* (Paris: 1965), pp. 369, 377, 378, 381, 406–407. M. T. Clancy, *From Memory to the Written Record*, p. 243.

68. Ernst Robert Curtius, *"Nennung des Autornamens in Mittelalter." Europäische Literatur*. . . ., pp. 503–505.

69. Bernard Cerquilini, *Éloge de la variante. Histoire critique de la philologie* (Paris: Seuil, 1989), pp. 57–69.

70. For example, Paul Zumthor, *"Y a-t-il une 'littérature' médiévale?" Poétique*, 66 (1986), 131–133. *ibid.*, *La lettre et la voix*, pp. 299–322.

71. John of Salisbury, *Metalogicus*, I, XIII; *P.L.*, 199, c. 880.

72. Hugo de St. Victor, *Erud. Didasc.*, I, 12; *P.L.*, 176, c. 750.

73. Th. M. Charland, *Artes Praedicandi. Contribution à l'histoire de la rhétorique au Moyen Âge* (Paris-Ottawa: 1936), p. 24.

74. David F. Hult, *"Vers la société de l'écriture. Le Roman de la Rose." Poétique*, 50 (1982), 170.

75. Brian Stock, *The Implications of Literacy. Written Language and Models of Interpretation in the Eleventh and Twelfth Centuries* (Princeton: Princeton University Press, 1983), pp. 3, 10–11.

76. Emile Lesne, *ibid.*, 337.

77. Dante Alighieri, *De vulgari eloquentia*, II, VI. *Tutte le opere*, p. 680.

78. Manfred Günther Scholz, *Hören und Lesen. Studien zur primären Rezeption der Literatur im 12. und 13. Jahrhundert* (Wiesbaden: Franz Steiner Verlag, 1980), pp. 25, 124–125.

79. *Französische Literarästhetik* . . . , p. 72. Some other examples: M. T. Clancy, *From Memory to Written Record*, p. 164. H. J. Claytor, *From Script to*

Print: An Introduction to Medieval Vernacular Literature (Cambridge: 1945), pp. 5–21, 115.

80. Edgar de Bruyne, *Études d'esthétique médiévale* (1946. Genève: Slatkine Reprints, 1975), II, p. 117.

81. Maurice Delbouille, *Les chansons de geste et le livre. La Technique littéraire des chansons de geste* (Paris: 1959), pp. 297, 299, 307, 334, 337, 339. W. Wattenbach, *Das Schriftwesen von Mittelalter*, p. 575. Paolo Merci, *Circolazione orale e tradizione scritta delle "Chansons de Geste." Oralità e scrittura*, pp. 197–204.

82. Geoffrey de Vinsauf, *Poetria nova*, I, VI. *Classical and Medieval Literary Criticism. Translations and Interpretations.* Ed. by Alex Preminger, O. B. Hardison Jr., Kevin Kerrane (New York: Frederick Ungar, 1974), pp. 389, 403.

83. John Lough, *Writer and Public in France from the Middle Ages to the Present Day* (Oxford: Clarendon Press, 1978), pp. 26–27. Michèle Perret, *"De l'espace romanesque à la matérialité du livre." Poétique*, 50 (1982), 175, 176, 179.

84. Miko Kos, "Carte sine litteris." *Mitteilungen des Instituts für österreichische Geschichtsforschung*, 62 (1954), 97, 99.

85. *Novum Glossarium Mediae Latinitatis*, L., c. 167.

86. *Französische Literarästhetik* . . . , pp. 15, 65, etc.

87. H. J. Claytor, *ibid.*, pp. 144–145.

88. Marbode, *Decem capitulorum*, I; *P.L.*, 171, c. 1693.

89. Edgar de Bruyne, *ibid.*, pp. 46, 93–95.

90. Ernest Langlois, éd. *Recueil d'arts de seconde rhétorique* (1902. Genève, Slatkine Reprints, 1974): Paul Zumthor, *Le masque et le visage. La poétique des grands rhétoriqueurs* (Paris: Seuil, 1978).

91. For example, Hugo de St. Victor, *Eruditionis Didascaliae*, V, VII; *P.L.*, 176, c. 795.

92. St. Augustine, *En Psal.*, LXX, 19; *P.L.*, 36, c. 888.

93. Abelard, *Introductio ad Theologiam*; *P.L.*, 178, c. 1043, who quotes Isidore of Seville, *Sent.*, 3, 13, 11.

94. *Visio Godeschalci.* cf. Aaron I. Gurevich, "Oral and Written Literature of the Middle Ages: Two 'Peasant Visions' of the Late Twelfth–Early Thirteenth Century." *New Literary History*, XVI (1) 1984, 61.

95. Henri-Irénée Marrou, *Décadence romaine ou antiquité tardive? III–VIᵉ siècle* (Paris: Seuil, 1977), p. 154.

96. Isidore of Seville, *Etymologiae*, I, 4, 1; *P.L.*, 83, c. 688.

97. St. Pierre Damien, *Ep.*, 22; *P.L.*, 189, c. 235.

98. *P.L.*, 106, c. 121–278.

99. Saint Basile, *Aux jeunes gens sur la manière de tirer profit des lettres helléniques.* Texte établi et traduit par l'abbé Fernand Boulanger (Paris: Les Belles Lettres, 1935).

100. Honorius d'Autun, *Spec. eccl.*, XI; *P.L.*, 172. c. 1056.

101. St. Jerome, *Ep.*, LXX; *P.L.*, 22, pp. 665–666.

102. Pierre Riché, *Education et culture dans l'occident barbare*, pp. 343, 442. André Cantin, *Les Sciences séculières et la foi. Les deux voies de la science au jugement de S. Pierre Damien (1007–1072)*. (Spoleto: 1975), pp. 299–374.

103. Cf. Antonio Garzya, "*Ideali e conflitti di cultura alla fine del mondo antico.*" *Maia*, XX (1968), 314.

104. Walter von Wartburg, *Französisches Etymologisches Wörterbuch* . . . , 5, p. 377.

105. David Kuhn, *La poétique de François Villon* (Paris, 1969), p. 257.

106. *Oxford English Dictionary* (Oxford: 1933), VI, p. 372. Frédéric Godefroy, *Dictionnaire de l'ancienne langue française* (Paris: 1888), IV, p. 764.

107. Alcuin, *Grammatica*; *P.L.*, 101, c. 854.

108. Philipp de Harveng, *De Dignitate Clericorum*; *P.L.*, 203, c. 693: II, *De scientia clericorum*.

109. cf. Hans Robert Jauss, *Alterität und Modernität der mittelalterlichen Literatur* (München: Wilhelm Fink Verlag, 1977), p. 127.

110. Dante Alighieri, *De Monarchia*, II, 4. *Tutte le opere*, p. 807.

111. Rabanus Maurus, *Carmina XXIX, Ad Bonosum, Carmina XXX*; *P.L.*, 112, c. 1606–1609.

112. Alcuin, *Capitulare de Imaginibus*; *P.L.*, 98, c. 1104, 1099–1109, 1164.

113. Gregory I, the Great, *Ep.*, LIII; *P.L.*, 77, c. 991. Isidore of Seville, *Etymologiae*, XIX, XLI; *P.L.*, 82, c. 676.

114. Cf. Edgar de Bruyne, *Études d'esthétique médiévale*, I, p. 290–291.

115. Gregory I, the Great, *Ep.*, IX; *P.L.*, 77, c. 1027–1028, 1128.

116. Rosario Assunto, *La critica d'arte nel pensiero medievale* (Milano: Il Saggiatore, 1961), p. 266.

117. Yves Congar, *Clercs et laïcs au point de vue de la culture au Moyen Âge*, p. 317. L. Gougauld, *"Muta praedicatio."* *Revue bénédictine*, XLII (1930), 168–169.

118. David Diringer, *The Hand-Produced Book* (London-New York: 1967). *Ibid.*, *The Illuminated Book*. New ed . . . , with the assistance of Dr. Reinhold Regensburger (London: 1967), pp. 21–22. Kurt Weitzmann, *Ancient Book Illumination* (Cambridge, Mass.: Harvard University Press, 1959), pp. 12, 81–101, 130ff.

119. Dante Alighieri, *Purgatorio*, XXXIII, v. 76. *Tutte le opere*, p. 240.

120. Walter Ong, "Orality, Literacy and Medieval Textualisation." *New Literary History*, XVI (1984), 1, 3.

121. John William Adamson, *The Illiterate Anglo-Saxon* (Cambridge: 1946), p. 85.

122. Manfred Günther Scholz, *Hören und Lesen*, pp. 36–52.

123. Jacques Le Goff, *Les Intellectuels au Moyen Âge* (Paris: 1957), pp. 69, 95. L. Gougauld, *ibid.*, pp. 170–171.

124. Isidore of Seville, *Etymologiae*, I, 3; *P.L.*, 82, c. 74.

125. *Glossaria latina* (Paris: 1931), V, p. 67; H. Grundmann, *"Litteratus-Illiteratus."* *Archiv für Kulturgeschichte*, 40 (1958), 48. J. H. Baxter-Charles Johnson, *Medieval Latin Word-List*, p. 249.

126. R. W. Hunt, *The History of Grammar in the Middle Ages*. Ed. by G. L. Bursill-Hall (Amsterdam: 1980), p. 89.

127. Cassiodorus, *Variarum libri*, III, *Ep.* XXXII; *P.L.*, 69, c. 595.

128. Alcuin, *Grammatica; De Syll.*; *P.L.*, 101 c. 857.

129. Hugo de St. Victor, *De sacramentis*, III, VII; *De Lectoribus*, *P.L.*, 176, c. 424.

130. Philipp de Harveng, *Ep.*, XVI; *P.L.*, 203, c. 149.

131. Petrus Venerabilis, *Ep.*, XXI; *P.L.*, 189, c. 347.

132. Ulrich Ricken, *"Gelehrten" und "Wissenschaft" im Französischen.*

Beiträge zu ihrer Bezeichnungsgeschichte von 12–17. Jahrhundert (Berlin: 1961), pp. 184–195. *Novum Glossarium* . . . , L.; c. 167.

133. Cf. Henri de Lubac, *Exégèse médiévale* (Paris: 1961), II, 1, p. 294.

134. H. Keil, *Grammatici Latini* (Lipsiae: Teubner, 1864), VIII, p. 91.

135. St. Augustine, *De ordine*, II, 37, c. 1012.

136. István Hajnal, *L'Enseignement de l'écriture aux Universités Médiévales* (Budapest: Academia Scientiarum Hungarica, 1954), p. 109. J. F. Niermeyer, *Mediae Latinitatis Lexicon Minus*, p. 616.

137. Isidore of Seville, *Etymologiae*, I, 2; *P.L.*, 82, c. 74.

138. *Ibid.*, III, 13, 6, 9; *P.L.*, 88, c. 688.

139. *Monumenta Germaniae Historica. Poetae* . . . , IV, 1, p. 77. Abelard, *Hist. calam.*; *P.L.*, 178, c. 1459.

140. Paul Lehmann, "Fuldaer Studien. Neue Folge, I, Karolus Magnus, De litteris colendis." *Sitzungsberichte der Bayerischen Akademie der Wissenschaften*, Phil.-Philologische und Historische Klasse (München: 1927), 9.

141. Wilhelm von Malmesbury, *De gestis pontificarum Anglorum*, I; *P.L.*, 179, c. 1459.

142. J. H. Baxter-Charles Johnson, *ibid.*, p. 250.

143. Cf. John William Adamson, *ibid.*, p. 59.

144. Alcuin, *Grammatica*; *P.L.*, 101, c. 857.

145. Among others: John of Salisbury, *Metalogicon*, I, 18; *P.L.*, 199, c. 847.

146. *Regula S. Benedicti*, LVIII; *P.L.*, 66, c. 807.

147. Giraldus Cambrensis, *Gemma eccl.*, XXXVII. Ed. J. S. Brewer (London: 1862), II, pp. 341, 348.

148. Camille Tihon, "Les expectatives 'in forma pauperum' particulièrement au XVᵉ siècle." *Bulletin de l'Institut historique belge de Rome*, 1925, 5ᵉ fascicule, 76. Frédéric Godefroy, *ibid.*, V, 3.

149. *Dicţionar al ştiinţelor speciale ale istoriei* (Bucureşti: Editura ştiinţifică şi enciclopedică, 1982), pp. 157–158.

150. Walter von Wartburg, *ibid.*, 5. pp. 377–379. M. T. Clancy, *ibid.*, pp. 15–16, 65–69.

151. Ludwig Schütz, *Thomas-Lexicon* (1895. Reprint, Stuttgart: 1958), pp. 448–449.

152. W. Wattenbach, *Das Schriftwesen im Mittelalter*, p. 148. Ernst von Dobschütz, *Das Decretum Gelasianum*, p. 57.

153. René Wellek, "Literature and Its Cognates." *Dictionary of the History of Ideas. Studies of Selected Pivotal Ideas.* Philip P. Wiener, ed. (New York: Charles Scribner's, 1973), III, p. 81.

154. John of Salisbury, *Polycraticus*, VII, 9; *P.L.*, 199, c. 655.

155. Heinrich Bechtold, *"Der französische Wortschatz im Sinnbezirk des Verstandes."* *Romanische Forschungen*, XLIX (1935), 33–35, 37, 47, 57, 69, 79.

156. Gregory of Tours, *Historia Francorum, Praefatio. Monumenta Germaniae Historica. Scriptores rerum Merovingiarum* (Hannoverae, 1885), I.

157. *Monumenta Germaniae Historica, S.S.*, VI, p. 474.

158. *Ibid.*, *Epistolae Saeculi*, XIII (Berlin: 1880), II, p. 500.

159. Isidore of Seville, *Etymologiae*, VI, c. 3; *P.L.*, 82, c. 236.

160. Beryl Smalley, *The Study of the Bible in the Middle Ages* (Oxford: 1952), p. 22.

161. Tobler-Lommatzsch, *Altfranzösisches Wörterbuch* (Wiesbaden; 1963), V, p. 525.

162. Petrus Cellensus (Pierre de Celle), *Ep.*, I, *Ll*; *P.L.*, 202, c. 476.

163. F. J. E. Raby, *A History of Latin Poetry in the Middle Ages* (1927. Oxford: 1953), II, p. 159.

164. Beryl Smalley, *ibid.*, p. 41.

165. J. de Ghellinck, *L'Essor de la littérature latine au XII*ᵉ *siècle* (Bruxelles: 1953, 2ᵉ éd.), p. 139.

166. H. Grundmann, *"Litteratus-Illiteratus,"* 8–9; Yves Congar, *Clercs et laïcs* . . . , p. 313.

167. Henri de Lubac, *Exégèse médiévale*, II, 1, pp. 68–69.

168. *Französische Literaturästhetik* . . . , p. 101. Pierre-Yves Badel, *"Rhétorique et polémique dans les prologues de romans au Moyen Âge." Littérature*, (1975), 20, 93.

169. Dante Alighieri, *Convivio*, I, IX. *Tutte le opere*, p. 502.

170. Cassiodorus, *Variarum* . . . , IX, 21; *P.L.*, 69, c. 787.

171. Isidore of Seville, *Etymologiae*, I, V, 1; *P.L.*, 82, c. 81.

172. John of Salisbury, *Metalogicus*, I, 13; *P.L.*, 199, c. 840.

173. *Ibid.*, I, 21; *P.L.*, 199, c. 199: "*Clavis est omnium scripturarum et totius sermonis mater et arbitra.*"

174. *Ibid.*, I, 24; *P.L.*, 199, c. 856.

175. Hans Blumenberg, *Die Lesbarkeit der Welt*, (1981. Frankfurt a. Main: Suhrkamp, 1983), p. 55.

176. Petrus Blesensis (Pierre de Blois), *Ep.*, I; *P.L.*, 207, c. 312.

177. Harry Thurston Peck, *A History of Classical Philology* (New York: 1911), p. 229.

178. Jacques Fontaine, *Isidore de Seville et la culture classique dans l'Espagne visigothique* (Paris: 1959), II, pp. 869–870.

179. Hugo de St. Victor, *Eruditionis Didascalorum*, III, 4; *P.L.*, 176, c. 768–769: "*De duobus generibus scripturam.*"

180. E. P. Goldsmith, *Medieval Texts and Their First Appearance in Print* (1943. New York: 1969), p. 98.

181. Ludwig Rockinger, "*Briefsteller und Formelbücher des elften bis vierzehnten Jahrhunderts.*" *Quellen zur Bayerischen und Deutschen Geschichte* (München: 1863), I, p. 9.

182. Hugo de St. Victor, *Erud. Didasc.*, VII, 30; *P.L.*, 176, c. 814.

183. Gregory I, the Great, *Homil.*, IX; *P.L.*, 76, c. 882.

184. Hugo de S. Victor, *De scriptibus*, VII; *P.L.*, 175, c. 16–17.

185. Dante Alighieri, *Monarchia*, III, IV, 11: "*dictator est Deus*"; *Paradiso*, XXIX, 41: "*scrittor de lo Spirito Santo.*" *Tutte le opere*, pp. 345, 770.

186. John of Salisbury, *Polycr.*, VII; *P.L.*, 199, c. 659.

187. St. Jerome, *Ep.*, *XXII*; *P.L.*, 22, c. 416.

188. cf. L. Gougauld, "*Muta praedicatio*," p. 169.

189. Manfred Günther Scholz, *Hören und Lesen*, pp. 130–132.

190. Yves Congar, *Clercs et laïcs* . . . , p. 322.

191. Petrus Lombardus, *Liber Sententiarum. Prologus*; *P.L.*, 192, c. 522.

192. Serge Lusignan, *Préface au "Speculum Maius" de Vincent de Beauvais: réfraction et diffraction* (Montréal-Paris: 1979), p. 33.

193. Dante Alighieri, *Paradiso*, XXXIII v. 85–87. *Tutte le opere*, p. 361.

194. The fundamental study continues to be: *Das Buch als Symbol.* Ernst Robert Curtius, *Europäische Literatur*, pp. 300–352.

195. Jean Leclercq, *"Aspects spirituels de la symbolique du livre au XVIe siècle." L'Homme devant Dieu. Mélanges . . . Henri de Lubac* (Paris: Aubier, 1964), II, p. 70.

196. St. Bonaventura, *Collatio in Hexameron*, 12, 17. *Opera Omnia,* Ed. Quaracchi, (1891) V, p. 387.

197. Erich Rothacker, *Das "Buch der Natur," Materialien und Grundsätzliches zur Metaphernageschichte* (Bonn: Bouvier, 1979).

198. Johannes Trithemius, *In Praise of Scribes. De laude scripturorum.* Ed. with Introduction by Klaus Arnold. Tr. by Roland Behrendt (Lawrence, Kans.: Coronado Press, 1974), ch. III–V.

199. *Französische Literarästhetik . . . ,* p. 40.

200. Serge Lusignan, *ibid., P.L.,* 58.

201. Anscari Mundó, *"Bibliotheca, Bible et lecture du Carême d'après Saint Benoît." Revue bénédictine,* LX (1950), 74–77.

202. St. Jerome, *Prolegomenon,* I; *P.L.,* 28, c. 31; *Ep.,* 5, 2; *P.L.,* 82, c. 235.

203. J. de Ghellinck, *"Un évêque bibliophile au XIVe siècle: Richard Aungerville de Bury"* (1345). *Revue d'histoire ecclésiastique,* 18 (1922), 501.

204. Isidore of Seville, *Etymologiae,* VI, I, 31: *De bibliothecis; P.L.,* 82, c. 235.

205. W. Wattenbach, *Das Schriftwesen im Mittelalter*, pp. 154–157.

205b. Charles Merritt Carlton, *Studies in Romance Lexicology, based on a Collection of Late Latin Documents from Ravenna* (A.D. 445–700). Chapel Hill: The University of North Carolina Press, 1965, pp. 17–19.

206. Helen Waddell, *The Wandering Scholars* (London: 1932, 6th ed.), pp. 242–243.

207. Photius, *Bibliotheca,* I, 1–22. *Bibliothèque.* Texte établi et traduit par René Henry. Paris: Les Belles Lettres, 1959, I.

208. Cassiodorus, *Institutiones divinarum et humanarum lectionum,* 5; *P.L.,* 70, c. 1116.

209. J. Destrez, *La Pecia dans les manuscrits universitaires du XIIIe et du XIVe siècles* (Paris: 1935), p. 48, Paul Lehmann, "Literaturgeschichte im Mittelalter, I," *Germanisch-Romanische Monatsschrift,* IV (1912), 618.

210. St. Bonaventura, *Collatio in Hexameron*, 6. *Opera Omnia*. Ed. Quaracchi (1891), V, p. 421.

211. Hugo de St. Victor, *De Scripturis* . . . , *XII, De bibliothecae interpretatione et variis librorum nominibus*; *P.L.*, 175, c. 18–19z.

212. Theodor Gottlieb, *Über mittelalterliche Bibliotheken* (Leipzig, 1890. Abdruck, Graz: 1955), p. 209.

213. Hugo de St. Victor, *De Scripturis* . . . , *P.L.*, 175, c. 20.

214. Theodore Besterman, *The Beginnings of Systematic Bibliography* (London: Oxford University Press, 2nd ed. revised, 1936), p. 214.

215. Isidore of Seville, *Etymologiae*, I, 5; *P.L.*, 82, c. 81–82.

216. Albert Appuhn, *Das Trivium und Quadrivium in Theorie und Praxis*, I, Theil: *Das Trivium* (Erlangen: 1900), p. 24.

217. Brunetto Latini, *Li livres dou tresor*. Ed. Chabaille (Paris: 1863), pp. 727–728.

218. Michel de Boüard, *"Encyclopédies Médiévales. Sur la 'connaissance de la nature et du monde' au moyen âge." Revue des questions historiques*, 58 (1930), 283. Serge Lusignan, *Préface au "Speculum Maius,"* p. 94.

219. cf. Ciro Trabalza, *Storia della grammatica italiana* (Bologna: Arnaldo Forni, 1963), p. 199.

220. Heinrich Bechtold, *Das französische Wortschatz*, p. 107. *Novum Glossarium* . . . , *L*, c. 167. Paul Renucci, *L'Aventure de l'humanisme européen au Moyen Âge* (Paris: Les Belles Lettres, 1953), I, p. 175.

221. Cassiodorus, *Institutiones* . . . , XXXIII; *P.L.*, 70, c. 1149.

222. John of Salisbury, *Metalogicus*, I, 12; *P.L.*, 199, c. 859.

223. Bede, *Historia ecclesiastica* . . . , V, 18; *P.L.*, 95, c. 261.

224. Johannes Scotus Erigena, *Super Ierarhia Caelestem S. Dionysii*; *P.L.*, 122, c. 139.

225. Clement of Alexandria, *Stromates*, I, 30, 1ff. cf. Antonio Garzya, "Ideali e confliti . . . ," p. 314.

226. E. Gilson, *La servante de la théologie. Etudes de philosophie médiévale* (Strasbourg: 1921), pp. 30–35. Henri de Lubac, *Exégèse médiévale*, I, 1, p. 175. Franco Simone, *"La 'Reductio Artium ad Sacram Scripturam' quale espressione dell'umanesimo medievale fine al secolo XII." Convivium* (1949), 887, 927.

227. Cassiodorus, *De artibus ac disciplinis liberalium artium. Praef.*; *P.L.*, 70, c. 1151.

228. Rabanus Maurus, *De cler. instit.*, III, 18; *P.L.*, 107, c. 295.

229. John of Salisbury, *Metalogicus*, I, 13; *P.L.*, 199, c. 840.

230. Hugo de St. Victor, *Eruditionis Didascalicae*, III, 5; *P.L.*, 176, c. 709: in artibus cohaerentia.

231. Gregory of Tours, *Historia Francorum, Praefatio Monumenta Germaniae historiae. Scriptores rerum Merovingiarum* (1885), I, p. 31.

232. Cassiodorus, *Variarum, Ep.*, XXI; *P.L.*, 69, c. 788.

233. Isidore of Seville, *Etymologiae*, I, IV, 2; *P.L.*, 82, c. 777–778.

234. Alcuin, *Ep.*, 185; *P.L.*, 82, c. 73.

235. Isidore of Seville, *Etym.*, I, II, 2; *P.L.*, 82, c. 73.

236. Alcuin, *Grammatica*; *P.L.*, 101, c. 853.

237. Scotus Erigena, *Sup. ier. cael . . .* , *P.L.*, 122, c. 139.

238. Cassiodorus, *De artibus . . .* , III; *P.L.*, 70, c. 1167.

239. St. Augustine, *De ord.*, II, 16, 44; *P.L.*, 32, c. 1015. Tertullian, *De idolatria*, 10; *P.L.*, 1, c. 851.

240. Anselm of Canterbury, *De grammaticis*, VIII; *P.L.*, 158, c. 560.

241. Cf. A. Clerval, *Les écoles de Chartres au moyen âge, du Ve au XVIe siècle* (Chartres: 1895), p. 12.

242. Jacques Le Goff, *Les Intellectuels au Moyen Âge*, p. 181.

243. Dante Alighieri, *Monarchia*, I, III. *Tutte le opere*, p. 730.

244. Cassiodorus, *Var.*, IX, *Ep.*, XXI; *P.L.*, 69, c. 789.

245. Carl Appel, *Provenzalische Chrestomatie* (Leipzig: 1895), p. 191.

246. Walter Freund, *Modernus und andere Zeitbegriffe des Mittelalters* (Köln-Graz: Böhlau Verlag, 1957). Wilfrid Hartmann, *"Modernus" und "Antiquus:" Zur Verbreitung und Bedeutung dieser Bezeichnungen in der wissenschaftlichen Literatur von 9, bis zum 12. Jahrhundert. Antiqui und Moderni* (= *Miscellanea Medievalia*). Hrsg. von Albert Zimmermann . . . (Berlin-New York: Walter de Gruyter, 1974), pp. 21–39.

247. F. N. Cornford, *Principium Sapientiae. The Origins of Greek Philosophical Thought* (London: 1952), pp. 199, 201.

248. John of Salisbury, *Metalogicus*, I, 3; *P.L.*, 199, c. 829.

249. Priscian, *Instit.*, H. Keil, *Grammatici latini*, II, 1.

250. Heinrich Fichtenau, *Mensch und Schrift im Mittelalter* (Wien: 1944), p. 212. Adrian Marino, *"Aux sources de la dialectique sémantique ancien/nouveau."* Cahiers roumains d'études littéraires, 1, 1975, 53–55.

251. Francesco Sabatini, *"Dalla 'scripta romana rustica' alle 'scriptae' romanze."* Studi medievali, IX (1968), 334.

252. Theodor Gottlieb, *Über mittelalterliche Bibliotheken*, pp. 162–163.

253. Cf. M. S. Batts, "The 'Emergence' of Medieval German Literature." *Mosaic*, VIII (1975), 4, 139.

254. Paul Lemerle, *Élèves et professeurs à Constantinople au Xe siècle* (Paris: 1969), p. 282.

255. Hans Rheinfelder, *"Nationalismus und Kosmopolitismus im Werk Dantes."* Actes . . . du IVe Congrès de L'A.L.L.C. (Paris-La Haye: 1966), I, pp. 474–480.

256. Gregory I, the Great, *Moral.*, XV, 41; *P.L.*, 75, c. 1105.

257. Ernst Robert Curtius, *ibid.*, pp. 387–391. Yves Congar, *ibid.*, pp. 311, 314–315; Jacques Le Goff, *ibid.*, p. 306.

258. Guillaume de Lorris, *Le roman de la rose*, v. 1599; cf. Nancy Freeman Regalado, " 'Des contraires choses' . . ." *Littérature*, 41 (1981), 62.

259. Gregory of Tours, *Historia Francorum. Praefatio.*

260. Dante Alighieri, *Vita Nuova*, XXV, 4. *Convivio*, I, VII, 5. *Tutte le opere*, pp. 397, 499.

261. Einhard, *Vita Caroli Magni*, 29. *Monumenta Germaniae Historica*, S.S., II, p. 458.

262. Cf. Paul Zumthor, *La poésie et la voix dans la civilisation médiévale* (Paris: Presses Universitaires de France, 1984), p. 95.

263. Carl Sutter, *Aus Leben und Schriften des Magisters Boncompagno* (Freiburg-Leipzig: 1894), p. 39.

264. Douglas Kelly, *Obscurity and Memory: Sources for Invention in Medieval French Literature. Vernacular Poetics in the Middle Ages*, Ed. Lois Ebin = "Studies in Medieval Culture," No. 16 . . . (Western Michigan University: 1984), pp. 37, 47.

265. Joan M. Ferrante, "Was Vernacular Poetic Practice a Response to Latin Language Theory?" *Romance Philology*, 35 (1982), 587, 593, 595.

266. Cassiodorus, *Variarum*, IX, 21; *P.L.*, 69, c. 787.

267. A recent synthesis: Marie-Madeleine Gauthier, *Pulcher et Formosus* . . . , pp. 410–418.

268. Edgar de Bruyne, *ibid.*, I, pp. 358–364. St. Augustine, *De Pulchro*, cf. Ananda K. Coomarswamy, *Christian and Oriental Philosophy of Art* (New York: Dover Publications, 1956), p. 102.

269. Among others: Theodulf, *Carmina*; *P.L.*, 105, c. 513.

270. Rosario Assunto, *La critica d'arte nel pensiero medievale* (Milano: Il Saggiatore, 1961), p. 167. Edgar de Bruyne, *ibid.*, I, pp. 264, 265, 280.

271. Cassiodorus, *De Artibus ac Disciplinis Liberalium Literarum*, I; *P.L.*, 70, c. 1152.

272. A. Clerval, *Les écoles de Chartres* . . . , p. 11.

273. St. Augustine, *De ordine*, II, 4, 13; *P.L.*, 32, c. 1000.

274. L. J. Paetow, *Morale Scholarium of John of Garland* (Berkeley: 1927), p. 23.

275. Chrétien de Troyes, *Erec et Enide*, v. 13–14. Ed. Mario Roques (Paris: Champion, 1966).

276. For the last quotation: *Vita Johannis Gorziensis*. *Monumenta Germaniae Historica*, IV, p. 339.

277. Edmond Faral, *Les arts poétiques du XIIe et du XIIIe siècles* (Paris: Champion, 1924), pp. 153, 158–159.

278. Marbode, *De apto genere scribendi*; *P.L.*, 171, c. 1687–1692.

279. Dante Alighieri, *Inferno*, I, 87. *Convivio*, II, XI, 9; II, XI, 4. *Tutte le opere*, pp. 7, 531, 532.

280. John of Salisbury, *Metalogicus*, I, 34; *P.L.*, 199, c. 816.

281. Dante Alighieri, *Convivio*, II, XI, 9; *Tutte le opere*, 532.

282. *Ibid.*, *De vulgari eloquentia*, I, I; I, II. *Vita nuova*, XV. *Tutte le opere*, 397, 655, 656.

283. *Glossaria latina* (Paris: 1926), II, p. 98. *Recueil général de lexiques français du Moyen Âge* (XIIe–XVe siècles) publié par Mario Roques I, *Lexiques Alphabétiques* (Paris, 1938), II, p. 319.

284. Giraldus Cambrensis, *Gemma ecclesiastica*, XXXVII, cf. *Les Oeuvres de Siger de Courtrai*. Ed. critique et textes inédits par G. Wallerand (Louvain, 1913), p. 41.

285. Edgar de Bruyne, *ibid.*, II, p. 11. Giovanni Mari, *I Trattati medievali di ritmica latina* (Milano: 1899), p. 883. Hans H. Glunz, *Die Literarästhetik des europäischen Mittelalters* (Frankfurt/M: V. Klostermann, 1963), p. 239.

286. Edgar de Bruyne, *ibid.*, I, p. 207.

287. Dante Alighieri, *De vulgari eloquentia*, II, VIII, 6. *Tutte le opere*, p. 682.

288. *Purchardi Gesta Witigowis. Monumenta Germaniae Historica*, IV, p. 622.

289. *Glossaria latina*, I; *Glossarium Ansilenbi* (Paris: 1926), p. 449.

290. Mathieu de Vendôme, *Ars versificatoria*, III, 1–2. Ed. E. Faral, *Les arts poétiques du XIIe et du XIIIe siècles*, pp. 167–168.

291. Dante Alighieri, *Convivio*, II, XIII. *Tutte le opere*, p. 535.

292. Donald Lemen Clark, *Rhetorik and Poetry in the Renaissance. A Study of Rhetorical Terms in English Renaissance Literary Criticism* (New York: 1922), pp. 48–50.

293. St. Augustine, *De civitate Dei*, XI, 18; *P.L.*, 41, c. 333.

294. Cassiodorus, *De artibus* . . . , II, 1; *P.L.*, 70, c. 1152.

295. Alcuin, *Ep.*, CLXIV; *P.L.*, 100, c. 430.

296. John of Salisbury, *Metalogicus*, II, IX; *P.L.*, 199, c. 867.

297. John of Garland, *The "Parisina Poetria."* Ed. with Introduction, Translation and Notes by Traugott Lawler (New Haven and London: 1974), p. 89.

298. Paulin de Nola *(Poema X)*; *P.L.*, 61, c. 453.

299. *Poetae latini aevi Carolini*, M.G.H., I. Recursuit Ernest Duemmerer (Berlin: 1881), I, pp. 543–544.

300. Dante Alighieri, *De vulgari eloquentia*, II, IV, 2. *Tutte le opere*. p. 677.

301. *Ibid.*, *Convivio*, II, 1, 3. *Tutte le opere*, p. 513.

302. Cf. Umberto Eco, *Il problema estetica in San Tommaso* (Torino: 1956), p. 194.

303. Cf. Paul Zumthor, *Essai de poétique médiévale* (Paris: Seuil, 1972), p. 101.

304. John of Garland, *ibid.*, pp. 62–63.

305. Prudentius, *Apotheosis*, 396, 407, 409; *P.L.*, 59, c. 916, 925, 927.

306. S. Thomae Aquinatis, *Questiones quodlibetales* (Paris: 1926), p. 280.

307. Edgar de Bruyne, *ibid.*, II, p. 206.

308. *Decretum Gratiani*; *P.L.*, 187, c. 204.

309. Ulrich Mölk, *Trobar clus trobar leu. Studien zur Dichtungstheorie des Trobadors* (München: 1968), pp. 46, 53. See also: Mircea Eliade, *"Limbajele Secrete."* *Revista Fundațiilor Regale*, 1 (1938), 124–141. *"Alegorie sau 'limbaj secret'."* ibid., 3 (1938), 616–632.

310. Dante Alighieri, *Inferno*, IX, 61–63. *Tutte le opere*, p. 33.

311. Mircea Eliade, *"Le 'Dieu Lieur' et le symbolisme des noeuds."* *Images et symboles* (Paris: Gallimard, 1952), pp. 120–122. Roger Dragonetti, *Aux frontières du langage poétique* (Gand: 1961), pp. 54–55, 80–81.

312. Paul Zumthor, *"Note sur les champs sémantiques dans le vocabulaire des idées."* *Neophilologus*, 39 (1955), 181.

313. John of Salisbury, *Entheticus, De dogmata philosophorum*; *P.L.*, 199, c. 966.

314. Paul Lemerle, *"L'Encyclopédie à Byzance à l'apogée de l'Empire et particulièrement sous Constantin VII Porphyrogénète."* *Cahiers d'histoire médiévale*, IX (1966), 615.

315. Paulin de Nola, *Poema*, XVI, v. 121; *P.L.*, 67, c. 479.

316. Prudentius, *Apotheosis*, 415; *P.L.*, 59, c. 933.

317. Isidore of Seville, *Etymologiae*, VIII, VII, 9; *P.L.*, 82, c. 309.

318. Hans H. Glunz, *Die Literarästhetik des europäischen Mittelalters*, pp. 175ff.

319. Edgar de Bruyne, *ibid.*, III, p. 344.

320. Peter Dronke, *Fabula. Explorations into the Uses of Myth in Medieval Platonism.* (Leiden und Köln: E. J. Brill, 1974), pp. 13–78.

321. Dante Alighieri, *Purgatorio*, IX, 112–122. *Tutte le opere*, p. 155.

322. *Ibid.*, *De vulgari eloquentia*, I, VI, 5 *Tutte le opere*, p. 659.

323. Klaus von See, *"Skop und Skald. Zur Auffassung des Dichters bei den Germanen."* *Germanisch-Romanische Monatschrift*, XIV (1964), 8, 14.

324. *Vita Maiorli*; *P.L.*, 137, c. 755.

325. Dante Alighieri, *Convivio*, II, 1, 4. *Tutte le opere*, p. 513.

326. Cf. Karl Vossler, *Poetische Theorien in der italienischen Frührenaissance* (Berlin: 1900), p. 5.

327. Richard de Bury, *Philobiblion, sive de Amore librorum*, 1473. *Philobiblion excellent traité sur l'amour des livres*. Tr. fr. par Hippolyte Cocheris (Paris: Aubry, 1857), ch. XIII.

328. Richard McKeon, "Poetry and Philosophy in the Twelfth Century. The Renaissance of the Rhetoric." *Critics and Criticism. Ancient and Modern*. Ed. with Introduction by R. S. Crane (1952. Chicago and London: University of Chicago Press, 1965), pp. 305, 309.

329. John of Salisbury, *Metalogicus*, I, 17; *P.L.*, 199, c. 847.

330. Cf. Edgar de Bruyne, *ibid.*, III, p. 87; II, 146, 152.

331. J. de Ghellinck, *"Neotericus, Neoteric."* *Archivum Latinitatis Medii Aevi*, XV (1940), 120.

332. John of Salisbury, *Metalogicus*, I, 3; *P.L.*, 199, c. 829.

333. Dante Alighieri, *Ep.*, XIII, 16. *Tutte le opere*, p. 864.

334. F. J. E. Raby, *A History of Secular Latin Poetry in the Middle Ages* (1934. Oxford: 1957), II, p. 30.

335. Petrus Blesensis (Pierre de Blois), *Epistolae*, LXVI; *P.L.*, 207, c. 198.

336. Bede, *Historia ecclesiastica gentis Anglorum*, V, 18; *P.L.*, 95, c. 261; Dante Alighieri, *De vulgari eloquentia*, I, X, 2. *Tutte le opere*, p. 664.

337. L. J. Paetow, *The Battle of the Seven Arts* (Berkeley: 1914).

338. Alcuin, *Ep.*, 28; *P.L.*, 100, c. 184.

339. Loup de Ferriere, *Epistula ad Eginhardum*; *P.L.*, 119, c. 433.

340. Cf. Pierre Riché, *Education et culture dans l'occident barbare*, pp. 272–273.

341. Paulinus de Nola, *Ep.*, 16; *P.L.*, 61, c. 232.

342. John of Salisbury, *Polycr.*, I, *Prol.*; *P.L.*, 199, c. 388.

343. Hugo de St. Victor, *Erud. Didasc.*, III, 4; *P.L.*, 176, c. 768–769.

344. Edgar de Bruyne, *ibid.*, I, pp. 226–227.

345. Roger Dragonetti, *La vie de la lettre au Moyen Âge* (Paris: 1985), p. 112.

346. Cf. Guglielmo Cavallo, *"Il libro come oggetto d'uso nel mondo bizantino." Jahrbuch der öster. Byzantinistik*, 31 (1982), 2, 410 (= XVI, *Internationaler Byzantinisten Kongress*).

347. Riccardus de S. Victor, *Benj. Min.*, II, 5, *P.L.*, 196, c. 83.

348. Ulrich Mölk, *Trobar clus trobar leu*, pp. 99–101, 105, 177–195.

349. Jean Frappier, *"Aspects de l'herméneutique dans la poésie médiévale." Cahiers de l'Association internationale des études françaises*, 15 (1963), 13.

350. Dante Alighieri, *De vulgari eloquentia*, II, IV. *Tutte le opere*, pp. 677–678.

351. Edgar de Bruyne, *ibid.*, I, p. 193.

352. Dante Alighieri, *Convivio*, I, IX, 3. *Tutte le opere*, p. 503.

353. Cf. Giuseppe Valli, *"Cultura e 'imitatio' nel primo Boccaccio." Annali della scuola normale superiore di Pisa*, serie II, XXXVII, (1968), 78.

354. Isidore of Seville, *Etymologiae*, 42; *P.L.*, 82, c. 762.

355. Hugo de S. Victor, *Erud. Didasc.*, II, XXVIII, *P.L.*, 176, c. 762.

356. Philipp de Harveng, *Ep. ad Heroaldum; P.L.*, 203, c. 31.

357. Cf. Jacques Le Goff, *Les Intellectuels au Moyen Âge* (Paris: 1957), p. 53.

358. Dante Alighieri, *Monarchia*, I, III. *Tutte le opere*, p. 730.

359. Honorius d'Autun, *De animae . . .* , *P.L.*, 172, c. 1243.

360. Hans Theinfelder, *Kultsprache und Profansprache in der romanischen Ländern* (Genève-Firenze: 1933), p. 152. Yves Congar, *ibid.*, pp. 326–327.

361. J.-B. La Curne de Sainte-Pelaye, *Dictionnaire historique de l'Ancien Langage Français* (Niort-Paris: 1880), VII, p. 184.

362. James Westfall Thompson, *The Literacy of the Laity in the Middle Ages* (New York: Burt Franklin, 1960), p. 193.

363. Abundant references and a good synthesis in Raymond Williams, *Culture and Society* (London: 1958), pp. 93, 100, 105, 125–127, etc.

364. John Lough, *Writer and Public in France. From the Middle Ages to the Present Day*, pp. 16–18, 27–28.

365. Isidore of Seville, *Diff. libri*, I, 3, 8; *P.L.*, 83, c. 11.

366. H. Pirenne, *"L'Instruction des marchands au moyen âge."* Annales d'histoire économique et sociale, I (1929), 13–28. ibid., *"De l'état de l'instruction des laïques à l'époque mérovingienne."* Revue Bénédictine, 46 (1934), 164–177.

367. Jacques Le Goff, *ibid.*, p. 68.

368. Dante Alighieri, Convivio, I, IX, 5. Tutte le opere, p. 503.

369. Carla Bozzolo et E. Ornato, Pour une histoire du livre manuscrit au Moyen Âge (Paris: C.N.R.S., 1980), p. 24. ibid., Supplément (Paris: C.N.R.S., 1983), p. 364.

370. Glossaria latina (Paris: 1926), II, p. 84; G. Goetz, Corpus glossariorum latinorum (Lipsiae: 1889), IV, p. 361.

371. Conrad von Hirschau, Dialogus super Auctores. Ed. critique par R. B. C. Huygens (Bruxelles: 1953), p. 58 (= Latomus).

372. Rabanus Maurus, De instit. cler., III, 1; P.L., 107, c. 377.

373. Philipp de Harveng, Ep., XVIII; P.L., 203, c. 159.

374. Dante Alighieri, De vulgari eloquentia, I, 1, 4. Tutte le opere, p. 655.

375. Yves Congar, Clercs et laïcs . . . , pp. 320, 324.

376. St. Pietro Damiani, De vera felic., III; P.L., 145, c. 833.

377. William de Conches, De phil. mundi, IV, 4, I; P.L., 172, c. 100.

378. Charles Thurot, Notices et extraits de divers manuscrits latins . . . , p. 45.

379. Recueil général des lexiques français du Moyen Âge . . . , II, p. 172.

380. Dante Alighieri, Paradiso, XII, 138. Tutte le opere, p. 287.

381. Charles Thurot, *ibid.*, p. 249. Ernst Robert Curtius, Europäische Literatur und Lateinisches Mittelalter, pp. 439–460.

382. Yves Congar, *ibid.*, pp. 314, 331.

383. Robert Browning, *"L'Alfabetizazione nel mondo byzantino."* Libri e lettori nel medioevo. Guida storica e critica. A cura di Guglielmo Cavallo (Bari: Laterza, 1977), p. 14.

384. Gregory of Tours, Historia Francorum, Praefatio.

385. Othloh, De adm. cleric. et laic.; P.L., 146, c. 246.

386. Alcuin, Ep., I; P.L., 100, c. 141.

387. *Poetria magistri Johannis Anglici de arte prosayca metrica et rithmica.* Ed. by Giovanni Mari. *Romanische Forschungen,* XIII (1902), 888, 900, 920. For the problem as a whole see Erich Auerbach, *Sermo humilis. Literatursprache und Publikum in der lateinischen Spätantike und im Mittelalter* (Bern: 1958), pp. 25–52. Franz Quadlbauer, "Die antike Theorie der genera dicendi im lateinischen Mittelalter." *Österreichische Akademie der Wissenschaften. Phil.-hist. Kl. Sitzungsberichte,* 24, Bd. 2 (Wien: 1962), pp. 114, 127, 272, 278. Leonid Arbuzov, *Colores Rhetorici* . . . (1948. Göttingen: Vandenbeck-Ruprecht, 1963), pp. 15–17.

388. Ernst Robert Curtius, *ibid.,* pp. 477–478.

389. Dante Alighieri, *De vulgari eloquentia,* I, 1. *Tutte le opere* p. 655.

390. Isidore of Seville, *Etymologiae,* II, III, 2; *P.L.,* 82, c. 125.

391. Hugo de St. Victor, *Erud. Didasc.,* III, 7; *P.L.,* 176, c. 777.

392. Edgar de Bruyne, *ibid.,* I, p. 226.

393. James S. Aldermann, "*Ars sine scientia nihil est*—Gothic Theory of Architecture of the Cathedral of Milan." *The Art Bulletin,* XXXI (1949), 100–101.

394. Guilbert de Nogent, *De vita sua,* XVII; *P.L.,* 156, c. 872.

395. Dante Alighieri, *Inferno,* I, 83; see also: *De vulgari eloquentia,* II, IV, 9–10. *Tutte le opere,* pp. 7, 678.

396. Henri-Irénée Marrou, *Décadence romaine ou antiquité tardive?* p. 134.

397. Domenico Comparetti, *Virgilio nel Medio Evo* (Firenze: 1896, 2nd ed.), II, pp. 13–14.

398. Paul Salmon, "*Über den Beitrag des grammatischen Unterrichts zur Poetik des Mittelalters.*" *Archiv für das Studium der neueren Sprachen und Literaturen,* 119 (1962–1963), 75.

399. Chrétien de Troyes, *Erec et Enide,* II, v. 6736–6743.

400. Cf. Ernst Robert Curtius, *ibid.,* p. 390.

401. Cf. Eugène Vinaver, "From Epic to Romance." *Bulletin of the John Rylands Library,* 46 (1963–1964), 491.

402. John of Salisbury, *Metalogicus,* I, 17; *P.L.,* 199, c. 847.

403. Cassiodorus, *De art.; P.L.,* 70, c. 1152.

404. Albon de Saint-Germain, *Impeditur* . . . , *P.L.,* 132, c. 754.

405. Cf. Paul Salmon, *ibid.*, p. 71.

406. Rich bibliography. Among others: Larry D. Benson, "The Literary Character of Anglo-Saxon Formulaic Poetry." *P.M.L.A.*, LXXXI (1966), 334–341. A recent synthesis: Franz H. Bäuml, "Medieval Texts and Two Theories of Oral-Formulaic Composition: A Proposal for a Third Theory." *New Literary History*, XVI (1984), 1, 91–94.

407. Cassiodorus, *Instit.*, XXX; *P.L.*, 70, c. 1144–1146.

408. Marie de France, *Lais. Prologue*, V, 15. Ed. A. Ewert (Oxford: Blackwells, 1963).

409. Bernard Cerquiglini, *Éloge de la variante*, pp. 36, 41–42, 58–59, 60.

410. Friedrich Panzer, *"Vom mittelalterlichen Zitieren." Sitzungsberichte der Heidelberger Akademie der Wissenschaften. Phil. Hist. Klasse* (XXXV), 1950 (Heidelberg: 1950), pp. 14, 26, 28, 36.

411. Isidore of Seville, *Etymologiae*, I, 39, 25; *P.L.*, 82, c. 121.

412. Cf. Alfredo Schiaffini. *" 'Poesis' e 'Poeta' in Dante." Studia filologica in honorem L. Spitzer.* Editerunt A. G. Hatcher et K. L. Selig (Bern: Francke Verlag, 1958), p. 384.

413. Marie de France, *Lais*, verses 9–16. St. Bonaventura, *Opera Omnia*, ed. Quaracchi (1888), I, pp. 14–15.

414. M. B. Parkes, "The Influence of the Concepts of 'Ordinatio' and 'Compilatio' in the Development of the Books." *Medieval Learning and Literature. Essays Presented to Richard William Hunt.* Ed. by J. J. Alexander and M. T. Gilson (Oxford: 1976) pp. 128, 130, 132.

415. St. Bonaventura, *Comment. in I. Liber Sent.*, Ed. Quaracchi (1882), I, pp. 14–15.

416. Brunetto Latini, *Li livres dou Tresor*, I, I, 1. ed. P. Chabaille (Paris: 1863).

417. Cf. Paul Lehmann, *Pseudo-Antike Literatur des Mittelalters* (1927. Darmstadt: 1964), p. 36. Douglas Kelly, *"Les inventions ovidiennes de Froissart: réflexions intertextuelles comme imagination." Littérature* (1981), 41, 84.

418. Léon Gautier, *Histoire de la poésie liturgique au moyen âge*, I, *Les Tropes* (Paris: 1886), pp. 1–2.

419. E. P. Goldsmith, *Medieval Texts and Their First Appearance in Print* (Oxford: 1943), p. 115.

420. Paul Lehmann, *ibid.*, particularly pp. 96–97.

421. Salvatore Battaglia, "Dall 'esempio alla novella. L'Esempio medievale." *La Coscienza letteraria del Medioevo.* (Napoli: Liguori, 1965), pp. 447–485, 487–547. *Rhétorique et histoire. L'"Exemplum" et le modèle de comportement dans le discours antique et médiéval. Mélanges de l'École Française de Rome. Moyen Âge et Temps Modernes*, T. 92 (1980), 1.

422. A synthesis: Paul Lehmann, *Die Parodie im Mittelalter* (1923. Stuttgart: 1963).

423. Hubert Silvestre, *"Le problème des faux au Moyen Âge." Le Moyen Âge*, 66 (1960), 351–370.

424. Peter Wunderli, *"Die ältesten romanischen Texte unter dem Gesichtswinkel von Protokoll und Vorlesen." Vox romanica*, 24 (1965), 46–47.

425. W. Wattenbach, *Das Schriftwesen im Mittelalter*, pp. 70–78, 124, 128–129. Ernst Robert Curtius, *ibid.*, pp. 316–319 (but references are far more numerous).

426. *Poetae latini aevi Carolini*, I, p. 294.

427. Theodulf, *Carmina*, II, 1; VII, 27; *P.L.*, 105, c. 299–305, 376.

428. *Ibid.*, *Carmina*, IV, II; *P.L.*, 105 c. 333–335.

429. Bernhard Sowinski, *Lehrhafte Dichtung des Mittelalters* (Stuttgart: 1971).

430. John of Salisbury, *Metalogicus*, I, 24; *P.L.*, 199, c. 853. Hugo de St. Victor, *Didasc.*, III, 3, *P.L.*, 176, c. 768.

431. Helmut Rosenfeld, *Legende*. 3 verbesserte und vermehrte Auflage (Stuttgart: Metzler, 1972). Walter von Wartburg, *Ibid.*, 5, p. 244.

432. Diodorus Siculus, *Bibliotheca*, IV, V, 4; IV, VII, 1. *Diodorus of Sicily in Twelve Volumes.* Tr. C. H. Oldfather *et al.* (Cambridge, Mass.: Harvard University Press/London: William Heinemann, 1968), IV.

433. *Monumenta Germaniae Historica. Auctores Antiquissimi*, VII, pp. 238–239.

434. Rabanus Maurus, *Ad Bonn.*, 30; *P.L.*, 112, c. 1608.

435. Theodulf, *Carmina*, II, 13; *P.L.*, 105, c. 314–315.

436. *Poetae Latini aevi Carolini*, I, pp. 224, 288–293; II, p. 691.

437. Rabanus Maurus, *De cler. instit.*, III, 18; *P.L.*, 107, c. 314–315.

438. Louis John Paetow, *The Art Course at Medieval Universities with Special Reference to Grammar and Rhetoric* (Urbana-Champaign: 1910).

439. John of Salisbury, *Metalogicus*, I, 23; *P.L.*, 199, c. 853; I, 24; *P.L.*, 199, c. 854.

440. Dante Alighieri, *De Vulgari Eloquentia*, I, IX, 11. *Tutte le opere*, p. 663.

441. *Poetria magistri Johannis Anglici* . . . , p. 899.

442. Hennig Brinkmann, *Mittelalterliches Hermeneutik* (Tübingen: Max Niemeyer Verlag, 1980), pp. 3–4. Conrad de Hirschau, *Dialogus super auctores*, pp. 16, 104–105.

443. Conrad de Hirschau, *ibid.*, p. 27.

444. Thomas d'Aquino, *Quodlib.*, VII, *Questio*. VI, Art. XIV. *Summa Theologiae*, I, q. 1, art. lo, ad 3 m.

445. Talbot Donaldson, *Patristic Exegesis in the Criticism of Medieval Literature: The Oppositions. Literary Criticism, Idea and Art*. Edited with Introduction by W. K. Wimsatt (Berkeley-Los Angeles-London: University of California Press, 1974), pp. 170–188.

446. Mircea Eliade, *"Alegorie sau 'limbaj secret'?" Revista Fundaţiilor Regale*, 1938, 3, 618. Hans Merker, *Schriftauslegung als Weltauslegung. Untersuchungen zur Stellung der Schrift in der Theologie Bonaventuras* (München-Padeborn-Wien: 1971), pp. 16–20.

447. Some references in Ferdinand Lot, *La fin du monde antique et le debut du moyen âge* (Paris: 1968), p. 398.

448. B. Lanfrancus, *Comment. Epist. II ad Cor.*, III; *P.L.*, 150 c. 223–224.

449. *Regula Sancti Benedicti*. Regula 8; *P.L.*, 82, c. 867.

450. St. Bernard, *Sermo*, XXXVI; *P.L.*, 183, c. 967.

451. Etienne Langdon, *Sermo*, 18; *P.L.*, 212, c. 633.

452. Honorius d'Autun, *Spec. Eccl.*, XI; *P.L.*, 172, c. 1056.

453. Paulus Allarus, *Ep.*, 5, 4; *P.L.*, 121, c. 451.

454. John of Salisbury, *Polycr.*, VII, XII; *P.L.*, 199, c. 662.

455. Isidore of Seville, *Sent. libri*, III, 13; *P.L.*, 83, c. 688.

456. Cf. Girolamo Tiraboschi, *Storia della letteratura italiana* (Firenze: 1779), IV, p. 364.

457. Mitropolit Nicolae Corneanu, *"Critica literară în epoca patristică." Patristica Mirabilia. Pagini din literatura primelor veacuri creştine* (Timi-

şoara: Editura Mitropoliei Banatului, 1987), pp. 16–26. Nicolae V. Dură, *Mitropolia Banatului*, iulie–august 1988, 140.

458. Cf. F. J. Raby, A *History of Secular Latin Poetry in the Middle Ages* (1934. Oxford: 1957), I, p. 371.

459. Gregory I, the Great, *Epist. ad Leander.* cf. A. F. Ozanam, *Des écoles et de l'instruction publique en Italie aux temps barbares* (Paris: 1850), p. 7.

460. St. Pietro Damiani, *Ep.*, 8; *P.L.*, 144, c. 476. *De perf. Monach.*, XI; *P.L.*, 145, c. 306.

461. Guilbert de Nogent, *De Pignarum Sanctorum*; I, 4, 2; *P.L.*, 156, c. 630.

462. M.-D. Chenu, *"Grammaire et théologie au XII*e *et XIII*e *siècles."* *Archives d'histoire doctr. et litt. du Moyen Âge*, 10–11 (1935–1936), 5–28.

463. Umberto Eco, *Il problema estetico in San Tommaso*, pp. 202, 203.

464. Friedrich Ohly, *"Vom geistigen Sinn des Wortes im Mittelalter."* *Zeitschrift für deutsches Altertum und deutsche Literatur*, 89 (1958–1959), 20.

465. Helen Waddell, *The Wandering Scholars* (London: 1932, 6th ed.).

466. *Carmina Burana*. Hrsg. Otto Schumann (Heidelberg: 1930), I, 1–2, II, 1–2; (1970), I, 3.

467. (Charles) Thurot, *"Documents relatifs à l'histoire de la grammaire au moyen âge."* *Académie des Inscriptions et Belles Lettres. Comptes rendus.* Nouv. série, T. VI (Paris: 1870), p. 248 (Aimericus, *De arte lectoria*).

468. Alfred Jeanroy, *Les origines de la poésie lyrique en France au Moyen Âge* (Paris: H. Champion, 1904), II, p. 37.

469. Geoffrey Chaucer, *The Franklin's Prologue. The Complete Works* (1894. Oxford: 1972), IV, pp. 482–483.

470. Cassian, *Coll.*, IX, *De Oratione*, XXXVI; *P.L.*, 49, c. 817–818.

471. Dom Jean Leclercq, *L'Amour des Lettres et le Désir de Dieu* (Paris: 1957), pp. 146–147.

472. André Pézard, *"Le dit du muet (Purgatoire, XIII, 76)."* *Letteratura e critica*, I, 306.

473. Cf. Marian Papahagi, *Intelectualitate şi poezie. Studii despre lirica lui Ducento* (Bucureşti: Cartea Românească, 1985), p. 358.

The Renaissance and Humanism

1. Lorenzo Valla, *Opera Omnia*. Con una premessa di Eugenio Garin (Torino: Bottege d'Erasmo, 1962), II, p. 473.

2. cf. Eugenio Garin, *Geschichte und Dokumente der abendländischer Pädagogie*, II, *Humanismus* (Reinbeck bei Hamburg: Rowohlt, 1966), p. 207.

3. Muret, Marc-Antoine (M. Antonii Mureti), *Orationes* (Venetiis: 1576), p. 18.

4. Cf. Jean Plattard, " 'Restitution des Bonnes Lettres' et 'Renaissance.'" *Mélanges . . . Gustave Lanson* (Paris: 1922), p. 129.

5. Erasmus, Desiderius (Desiderii Erasmi Roterodami), *Opera omnia ex recensione Joannis Clerici* (Lugduni Batavorum: 1701–1706), VII, p. 15. *Opus epistolarum Des. Erasmi Roterodami*, ed. P. S. Allen (Oxford: 1928), IV, p. 11.

6. *Ibid.*, VI, p. 133 (letter dated 1591).

7. Joseph Niedermann, *Kultur: Werden und Wandlungen des Begriffs und seiner Ersatzbegriffe von Cicero bis Herder* (Firenze: Bibliopolis, 1941), p. 77.

8. Edmond Hugnet, *Dictionnaire de la langue française du seizième siècle* (Paris: 1946), IX, p. 540.

9. Ulrich von Hutten, *Epistolae obscurorum virorum. Operum Supplementum 1515–1516*. Ed. Böcking (Lipsiae: 1864), I, p. 259.

10. For example, Hans Baron, *The Crisis of the Early Italian Renaissance* (Princeton: 1965), II, pp. 212, 224. August Buck, "Die 'studia humanitatis' und ihre Methode." *Die humanistische Tradition in der Romania* (Bad Homburg-Berlin-Zürich: 1968), pp. 133–150.

11. Mihai Berza, "Autour d'un 'humanisme' sud-est européen." *Pentru o istorie a vechii culturi românești*. Culegere de studii editată, cu o introducere și note de Andrei Pippidi (București: Eminescu, 1985), pp. 104–111.

12. Erich König, " 'Studia humanitatis' und verwandte Ausdrucke bei den deutschen Frühhumanisten. Beiträge zur Geschichte der Renaissance und Reformation." *Joseph Schlecht. Am 16 Januar 1917 als Festgabe zum 60. Geburtstag* (München und Freising: 1917), p. 253. Giuseppe Toffanin, *Storia dell 'Umanesimo (dal XIII al XVI Secolo)* (Napoli: 1933), p. 142.

13. Paul Oskar Kristeller, *Renaissance Thought* (New York: Harper Torchbook, 1961), I, pp. 110, 159.

14. Francisco Martinez, *Grammaticae artis integris institutio. Ejusdem de grammatica professione declamatio* (Salamanca: 1575). *Prologus.*

15. Cf. Fritz Schalk, *Exempla romanischen Wortgeschichte. Humanitas in Romanischen* (Frankfurt am Main: 1966), p. 269.

16. *Journal d'un bourgeois de Paris sous François Ier.* Texte choisi, établi et présenté par Philippe Joutard (Paris: Union génerale d'Éditions, 1963), p. 126.

17. Baldassare Castiglione, *Il libro del Cortegiano.* A cura de Ettore Bonora. Commento di Paolo Zoccola (Milano: Mursia, 1972), I, 44, p. 87.

18. Giuseppe Toffanin, *Storia dell'Umanesimo* (Bologna: Zanichelli, 1964), II, pp. 151–152.

19. Cf. Karl-Heinz Gerschmann, "*Antiqui-novi-moderni in den 'Epistolae obscurorum virorum'.*" *Archiv für Begriffsgeschichte*, XI (1967), 25.

20. Augusto Campana, "The Origin of the Word 'Humanist'." *Journal of the Warburg and Courtauld Institutes*, IX, (1946), 60–73. Peter M. Brown, "A significant sixteenth-century use of the word 'Umanista'." *The Modern Language Review*, 64 (1969), 565–575.

21. *Trattatisti del Cinquecento.* A cura di Mario Pozzi (Milano-Napoli: 1978), I, pp. 770–771.

22. Tomasso Garzoni, *Piazza universale di tutte le professioni del mondo* (Venetia: 1587), pp. 956–958.

23. Eckhard Kessler, *Das Problem des frühen Humanismus. Seine philosophische Bedeutung bei Coluccio Salutati* (München: 1968), p. 121, *passim.*

24. L. Bruni Aretino, *Humanistisch-philosophische Schriften.* Hrsg. von H. Baron (Leipzig-Berlin: 1928), p. 19, etc.

25. *Dulce bellum inexpertis. Dissertatio Des. Erasmi Rotterdami* (Brunsvigae: 1672), pp. 24, 25, 58.

26. Guillaume, Budé (Gulielmus Budaeus), *De Philologia. De Studio Litterarum (recte et comoda instituendo).* Faksimile-Neudruck der Ausgabe von Paris 1532, mit einer Einleitung von August Buck (Stuttgart-Bad Cannstatt: 1964), p. XVI v.

27. Aulus Gellius, *Noctes Atticae*, XIII, 17, 1–2.

28. Giuseppe Toffanin, *ibid.*, II, pp. 151–152.

29. *Vocabulario degli Accademici della Crusca* (Firenze: 1900. Quinta Impressione), IX, Fasc. I: *Litteratura*, pp. 261–262.

30. Berthold L. Ullman, *The Humanism of Coluccio Salutati* (Padova: 1963), pp. 58, 74. Simon Roths, *Fremdwörterbuch*. Herausgegeben von Emil Öhmann (Helsinki: 1936, p. 316), (= Mémoires de la Société néophilologique de Helsingfors").

31. Erich König, *ibid.*, p. 205.

32. August Buck, *ibid.*, p. 135.

33. Rudolf Pfeiffer, *Humanitas Erasmiana* (Leipzig-Berlin: 1931), pp. 6, 8.

34. Cf. Mircea Frînculescu, *"Primele noţiuni de artă oratorică în cultura românească."* Revista de istorie şi teorie literară, XXXV (1987), 1–2, 287.

35. *Vocabulario* . . . , IX, Fasc. L, p. 261.

36. Erasmus, *Opus epistolarum*, II, p. 368.

37. Guillaume Budé, *Le livre de l'instruction du prince* (Paris: 1547), p. 68 r.

38. Fritz Schalk, *ibid.*, pp. 257–258.

39. Cf. Eckhard Kessler, *ibid.*, p. 202.

40. Erasmus, *Opera Omnia*, X, c. 1704.

41. G. Budaeo, *De studio litterarum de commode instituendo* (Parisii: 1532), p. XXXVII v.

42. Eugenio Garin, *Geschichte und Dokumente* . . . , II, p. 207.

43. Erasmus, *Opera Omnia*, X, c. 1744.

44. L. Valla, *Opera Omnia*, II, p. 9.

45. G. Budaeo, *De philologia*, p. LXV.

46. *Ibid.*, *De studio litterarum*, p. XII v.

47. Plutarque, *Les oeuvres morales et meslées*, translatées . . . , par Jacques Amyot (Paris: 1582), II, p. 4 v.

48. Ferdinand Brunot, *Histoire de la langue française* (Paris: 1966), VI, 1, fasc. 1, p. 680.

49. Plutarque, *ibid.*, II, p. 668 r.

50. Plutarque, *ibid.*, II, p. 655 r. *Oeuvres* (Paris: 1784), VIII, p. XI.

51. P. P. Vergerio, *L'Umanesimo.* A cura di E. Garin (Firenze: 1958), p. 30.

52. *Elisabethan Critical Essays.* Edited with an introduction by G. Gregory Smith (Oxford: 1904), I, p. 67.

53. Eugenio Garin, "Gli *'Studia Humanitatis'* e la pedogogia italiana del *Rinascimento."* *Saggi di filologia e filosofia.* Raccolti e pubblicati a cura di un comitato editoriale (Bucureşti: Bucovina, 1946), pp. 89, 92.

54. Cf. Ernesto Grassi, *Verteidigung des individuellen Lebens. Studia humanitatis als philosophische Überlieferung* (Bern: 1947), p. 138.

55. John William Aldridge, *The Hermeneutics of Erasmus* (Winterthur: 1966), pp. 17, 20.

56. Erasmus, *Opus Epistolarum,* II, p. 325; III, pp. 548, 927; VI, p. 379.

57. G. Budaeo, *De studio litterarum . . .* , p. XXXIII v.

58. Gulielmi Budaei, *Opera Omnia* (Basileae: 1557), I, pp. 155, 239, 294.

59. Leon Battista Alberti, *De Commodis literarum atque Incommodis. Defunctus.* Testo latino, traduzione italiana. Introduzione e note a cura di Giovanni Farris (Milano: Marzorati, 1971), p. 255.

60. Among many: Cr. Mylaeus, *De scribenda universitatis rerum* (Basileae: 1551), p. 4.

61. Erasmus, *Opera Omnia,* IV, c. 628.

62. Erasmus, *Opus Epistolarum,* II, p. 214; IX, p. 225.

63. Erasmus, *ibid.,* VII, pp. 16, 495.

64. Erasmus, *ibid.,* IV, pp. 346, 347; V, p. 451; VI, p. 328; VII, p. 360.

65. Erasmus, *ibid.,* VI, p. 202.

66. Larry D. Benson, "The Literary Character of Anglo-Saxon Formulaic Poetry." *P.M.L.A.,* 81 (1950), V, 378.

67. Jacques Amyot, *Aux Lecteurs.* Plutarque, *Les oeuvres morales et méslées . . .* , I.

68. Erasmus, *Opera Omnia,* II, c. 1052.

69. Walter von Wartburg, *Französisches Etymologisches Wörterbuch* (Basel: 1950), V, p. 378.

70. Jehan de Nostre Dame, *Les Vies les plus célèbres et anciens poètes provenceaux . . .* (Lyon: 1575), pp. 145, 177.

71. *Trattatisti del Cinquecento.* A cura di Mario Pozzi (Milano-Napoli: 1978), I, pp. 107, 586.

72. Cf. Ulrich Ricken, *"Gelehrter" und "Wissenschaft". Beiträge zu ihrer Bezeichnungsgeschichte von 12–17. Jahrhundert* (Berlin: 1961), p. 147.

73. Jacques Chomarat, *Grammaire et Rhétorique chez Erasme* (Paris: Les Belles Lettres, 1981), I–II. Robert J. Clements, *Picta Poesis. Literary and Humanistic Theory in Renaissance Emblem Books* (Roma: 1960), p. 160.

74. Edmond Hugnet, *Dictionnaire de la langue française du seizième siècle* (Paris: 1946), IV, p. 33.

75. Cf. Ewald Flügel, "Bacon's *Historia Literaria*." *Anglia*, XXI, B. IX (1899), 283.

76. Pico della Mirandola, *Opera quae extant omnia* (Basileae: 1601), III, p. 1ff.

77. J. Bale, *Illustrium maioris Britannie scriptorum* (1547), f. 73 r.

78. L. Valla, *Opera Omnia*, II, p. 285 r.

79. J. Bale, *ibid.*, f. 73.

80. Edmond Hugnet, *Dictionnaire de la langue française* . . . , IV, p. 520.

81. Francis Bacon, *The Advancement of Learning and New Atlantis* I, *To the King.* With a preface by Thomas Case (1906. London: Oxford University Press, 1960), p. 5.

82. Erasmus, *Opus Epistolarum*, V, p. 520.

83. G. Budé, *De Asse* (1514. Paris: 1541), p. 202.

84. Lorenzo Valla, *Elegantiarum Linguae Latinae* (1471. Cantabrigiae: 1688), 1, IV. *Praefatio*, p. 276.

85. Erasmus, *Opera Omnia*, X, c. 1713.

86. J. Bale, *ibid.*, f. 39.

87. Cf. Ewald Flügel, *ibid.*, p. 284.

88. Louis Le Roy, *De la vicissitude ou variété des choses de l'univers* . . . (A Paris: 1584), p. 69 r.

89. Cf. J. Lough, *Writers and Public in France. From the Middle Ages to the Present Day* (Oxford: Clarendon Press, 1978), p. 42.

90. *Thesaurus Linguae Latinae* (Lipsiae: 1929), VII, 2, c. 1539. Albert Dauzat, Jean Dubois, Henri Mitterand, *Nouveau Dictionnaire Etymologique et Historique* (Paris: Larousse, 1964), p. 420.

91. Robert Estienne, *Thesaurus Linguae Latinae* (1532. Editio Nova; Londini: 1872), III, *s.v.*, p. 521. Charles Estienne, *Dictionnaire latino-graecum* (Lutetiae: 1554), p. 521.

92. L. Valla, *Elegantiarum Linguae Latinae*, 1, III, V, p. 199, etc.

93. Robert Estienne, *Thesaurus . . .* , III, *s.v.*; A. Calepinus, *Dictionarum undecim linguarum* (1514. Basileae, 1605), II, p. 828.

94. Oscar Bloch-Walter von Wartburg, *Dictionnaire étymologique de la langue française* (Paris: Presses Universitaires de France, 1975), p. 372.

95. Erasmus, *Opus Epistolarum*, I, pp. 321, 375; II, pp. 78, 218; III, p. 505, etc.

96. Liselotte Dieckmann, *Hieroglyphics. The History of a Literary Symbol* (St. Louis: Washington University Press, 1970), pp. 38–39, 86–89, 94. Rudolf Wittkower, *Hieroglyphics in the Early Renaissance. Developments in the Early Renaissance.* Ed. by Bernard S. Levy (Albany: 1972), pp. 65–66, 70. François Rigolot, *"La figure de la lettre: graphisme et paradigmatisme à l'aube de la Renaissance."* *Revue des sciences humaines*, LI (1980), 47.

97. Alison Saunders, *"Picta Poesis.* The Relationship Between Figure and Text in the Sixteenth-Century French Emblem Book." *Bibliothèque d'Humanisme et Renaissance*, XLVIII (1986), 3, 651.

98. Erik Iversen, *The Myth of Egypt and Its Hieroglyphs in European Tradition* (Copenhagen: 1961), p. 74. Robert Klein, *"La Théorie de l'expression figurée dans les traités italiens sur les 'Imprese,'* 1555–1612." *Bibliothèque d'Humanisme et Renaissance*, XIX (1957), 320–341.

99. Fernand Halleyn, *"Les Emblèmes de Délie."* *Revue des Sciences Humaines* (1980), 179, 61–75.

100. Ludwig Volkmann, *Bilderschriften der Renaissance. Hieroglyphik und Emblematik in ihren Beziehungen und Fortwirkungen* (Leipzig: 1923), pp. 35, 41.

101. Robert Estienne, *Les mots français selon l'ordre des lettres* (Paris: 1544. Slatkine Reprints: 1972), *s.v.*

102. Terence Cave, *The Cornucopian Text. Problems of Writing in the French Renaissance* (Oxford: Clarendon Press, 1979), p. XI.

103. Lynn Thorndike, *Science and Thought in the Fifteenth Century* (New York-London: 1963), p. 237.

104. The problem of the beginnings of writing in Romanian is controversial. At any rate, it began before the sixteenth century. For the last

stage of the problem (with bibliography) see: I. C. Chiţimia, "Inceputurile scrisului în limba română," *Noi Tracii* (1989), 174, 1–11; (1989), 175, 14–19.

105. *Crestomaţie de literatură română veche.* Coordonatori I. C. Chiţimia şi Stela Toma (Cluj-Napoca: Dacia, 1984), I, pp. 32–33, 35.

106. Silvia Rizzo, *Il Lessico filologico degli umanisti* (Roma: 1973), pp. 101–104, 321–322.

107. Simon Roths *Fremdwörterbuch*, p. 325.

108. J. C. Scaliger, *Poetices libri septem* (1561. Editio secunda: 1581), III, 25, p. 113.

109. Silvia Rizzo, *ibid.*, pp. 9–10; François Rigolot, *"La Renaissance du Texte."* *Poétique* (1982), 50, 182–193.

110. *Dichtungslehren der Romania aus der Zeit der Renaissance und des Barock.* Hrsg. und eingeleitet von August Buck, Klaus Heitmann, Walter Mettmann (Frankfurt/M: 1972 = Dokumente zu Europäischen Poetik, B. 3), p. 352.

111. Adam Bohorizh, *Arcticae horulae succisivae. De latino carniolana literatura . . .* (Wittenbergae: 1584), *Praefatiuncula*, p. 2.

112. W. Wattenbach, *Das Schriftwesen im Mittelalter* (Leipzig: 1896), p. 298.

113. J. C. Scaliger, *Poetices . . .* , I, 4, 3, pp. 3, 6. G. Budé, *Lexicon graecolatinum seu Thesaurus Linguae Graecae* (Genevae: 1534), *s.v.*

114. (Etienne Dolet) Stephani Doleti, *Commentariorum linguae latinae . . .* (Lugduni: 1536), I, c. 1160: *Literatura.*

115. August Buck, *Italienische Dichtungslehren vom Mittelalter bis zum Ausgang der Renaissance* (Tübingen: 1952), p. 99. *Thesaurus linguae latinae,* VII, 2, c. 1531.

116. Dante Alighieri, *Convivio,* I, 9. *Tutte le opere.* A cura di Fredi Chiapelli (Milano: Mursia, 1965), p. 503.

117. Lorenzo Valla, *Opera Omnia.* Con una premessa d'Eugenio Garin (Torino: Bottega d'Erasmo, 1962), II, pp. 441–442.

118. Walter J. Ong, *Orality and Literacy. The Technologizing of the World* (London and New York: Methuen, 1982), pp. 26, 120.

119. *Oral Literature. Seven Essays.* Edited by Joseph J. Duggan (Edinburgh and London: Scottish Academic Press, 1975), pp. 92–93.

120. Francesco Tronci, *"Aspetti della simulazione dell'oralità nel Decameron." Oralità e scrittura nel sistema letterario. Atti del Convegno Cagliari, 14–16 aprile 1980.* A cura di Giovanna Cerina, Cristina Lavinio, Luisa Mulas (Roma: Bulzoni, 1982), pp. 283–303. Giulio Herczeg, *"Sintassi e stile dei Dialoghi nelle Novelle di Matteo Bandello," ibid.,* pp. 265–281. Luisa Mulas, *"La Scrittura del Dialogo. Teorie del Dialogo tra Cinque e Seicento," ibid.,* pp. 245–263.

121. Cf. Christian Bec, *Les marchands écrivains. Affaires et Humanisme à Florence, 1375–1434* (Paris-La Haye: Mouton, 1967), p. 390.

122. Pedro de Navarra, *Diálogos de la differencia del Hablar al Escrivir* (Tolosa: 1560? D. O. Chambers, Ed.: 1968), p. 11.

123. Juan de Valdés, *Diálogo de la lengua.* Edición, introducción y notas de José F. Montesinos (1535–1536. Madrid: 1969), pp. 154–155.

124. O. B. Hardison, Jr., "The Orator and the Poet: The Dilemma of Humanist Literature." *The Journal of Medieval and Renaissance Studies,* I (1971), 1, 35. J. A. Burrow "Bards, Minstrels and Men of Letters." *The Medieval World.* Ed. David Daiches, Anthony Thorlby (London: 1973), p. 361.

125. Jean Lemaire de Belges, *Oeuvres* publiées par J. Stecher (Louvain: 1885), II, p. 468.

126. Jehan de Nostre Dame, *Les vies des plus célèbres et anciens poètes provenceaux . . . ,* p. 65.

127. Cf. Nathalie Zonn Davis, *Society and Culture in Early Modern France* (London: 1965), p. 347.

128. Johannes Trithemius, *In Praise of Scribes. De laude scripturorum.* Ed. with Introduction by Klaus Arnold. Translation by Roland Behrendt (Lawrence, Kans.: Coronado Press, 1974), ch. VI, p. 59.

129. Cf. Ernst Mehl, *"Deutsche Bibliotheksgeschichte." Deutsche Philologie im Aufriss.* Hrsg. von Wolfgang Stammler (Berlin-Bielefeld: 1952), c. 323.

130. Speroni Sperone, *Dialoghi . . .* (In Venetia: 1596), pp. 546, 555.

131. R. Glynn Faithfull, "The Concept of 'Living Language' in *Cinquecento* Vernacular Philology." *Modern Language Review,* XLVII (1953), 289.

132. Juan de Valdés, *ibid.,* p. 8.

133. Pedro de Navarra, *ibid.,* pp. 13, 14.

134. Giuseppe Toffanin, *Storia dell'umanesimo*, II, pp. 116–124, 262–272. Eugenio Garin, *"Umanesimo e rinascimento."* *Questioni e correnti di storia letteraria* (Milano: Marzorati, 1949), III, p. 13.

135. Erasmus, *Opera Omnia*, V, c. 383. *Opus Epistolarum*, II, p. 378; IV, p. 372.

136. Giovanni Boccaccio, *Genealogie deorum gentilium*, XII. *Prose latine.* A cura di Pier Giorgio Ricci (Milano-Napoli: 1965), p. 982.

137. *Crestomaţie de literatură română veche*, I, pp. 63, 67, 102, 106, 211.

138. August Buck, *Die humanistische Tradition in der Romania* (Homburg, D.H.-Berlin-Zürich: 1968), p. 159.

139. Leon Battista Alberti, *De commodis litterarum atque incommodis*, p. 136.

140. D. Murăraşu, *La poésie néolatine et la renaissance des lettres antiques en France (1500–1539).* *Mélanges de l'école roumaine en France* (Paris, 1926), I, pp. 291, 316. Dario Cecchetti, "L'elogio delle arti liberali nel primo Umanesimo francese." *Studi francesi*, X (1966), 5.

141. Guillaume Budé, *Le livre de l'institution du prince* . . . (Paris, 1547), p. 8 r.

142. Augustin Renaudet, *Humanisme et Renaissance* (Genève: 1958), p. 47. Fritz Caspari, "Erasmus on the social functions of Christian Humanism." *Journal of the History of Ideas*, VIII (1947), 78–106.

143. Erasmus, *Opera Omnia*, I, c. 683. *ibid.*, I, c. 1017.

144. Heinrich Fichtenau, *Mensch und Schrift im Mittelalter* (Wien: 1944), p. 208.

145. Erasmus, *Ciceronianus*, *Opera Omnia*, I, c. 1017.

146. G. Budé, *De transitu Hellenismi ad Christianismum* (Paris: 1535), L.3, fol. 132 r.

147. Giraldi, Lelio Gregorio (Lilii Gregorii Gyraldi), *Progymnasma adversus literas et literatos* (Florentiae: 1551), p. 183.

148. Ulrich von Hutten, *Epistolae obscurorum virorum*, I, p. 289.

149. Lorenzo Valla, *Opera Omnia*, II, p. 285.

150. Ambrosius Calepinus, *Dictionarium undecim linguarum*, I, p. 624.

151. *Ibid.*, I, p. 624.

152. Etienne Dolet, *Comentariorum linguae latinae*, I, *Literae*, c. 1156.

153. Erasmus, *Opus Epistolarum*, I, p. 345.

154. Dan-Horia Mazilu, *Proza oratorică în literatura română veche* (Bucureşti: Minerva, 1986), I, p. 143.

155. Among others: Tomasso Garzoni, *Piazza universale di tutte le professioni del mondo*, p. 87.

156. G. Balbus, *Catholicon* (Mainz: 1460), *s.v.*

157. G. A. Padley, *Grammatical Theory in Western Europe, 1500–1700* (Cambridge: 1976), pp. 30–31.

158. M.-A. Muret, *Oratio de laude litterarum* (1554. *De studiis literarum*, Venetiis: 1555).

159. Robert Estienne, *Thesaurus Linguae Latinae*, II, *s.v.*

160. A. Rey, *Littérature. Dictionnaire des littératures de langue française* (Paris: Bordas, 1984), II, p. 1309. Walter von Wartburg, *ibid.*, V, p. 376.

161. G. Budé, *Le livre de l'instruction du prince*, pp. 10, 67.

162. Plutarque, *Les oeuvres morales et meslées . . .* II, p. 666 v.

163. Edmond Hugnet, *Dictionnaire de la langu?ge française du seizième siècle*, V, p. 329. Walter von Wartburg, *ibid.*, V, pp. 378–379. U. Ricken, "Remarques sur l'évolution du vocabulaire français des idées." *Revue de linguistique*, 8 (1963), 28–29, 33.

164. Albert Dauzat, etc., *ibid.*, p. 420.

165. Josef Niedermann, *Kultur . . .* , p. 64.

166. Tomasso Garzoni, *ibid.*, p. 130.

167. Josef Niedermann, *ibid.*, pp. 135, 138.

168. Ewald Flügel, "Bacon's *Historia literaria*," 270–271.

169. Richard Newald, *Humanitas, Humanismus, Humanität* (Essen: 1947), p. 33.

170. Erasmus, *Opus Epistolarum*, I, p. 121.

171. G. Budé, *De Philologia*, I, p. XXII r.

172. Balbus, *Catholicon*, *s.v.*

173. Cf. Andrei Pippidi, "Early Modern Libraries and Readers in South-Eastern Europe." *Revue des études sud-est européennes*, XIX (1981), 716.

174. *Pravila Ritorului Lucaci.* Text stabilit, studiu introductiv şi indice de I. Rizescu (Bucureşti: Editura Academiei R.S.R., 1971), p. 174.

175. Mircea Frînculescu, *"Primele noţiuni de artă oratorică în cultura românească."* 282, 288.

176. Edmond Hugnet, *ibid.*, V, p. 799.

177. Giuseppe Toffanin, *Storia dell'umanesimo*, II, p. 190.

178. *Carta de Juan de Lucerna, exhortatoria à las lettras. Opúsculos literarios de los siglos XIV à XVI.* Ed. A. Paz y Mélia (Madrid: 1892), p. 212.

179. Cf. Ewald Flügel, *ibid.*, 253.

180. Cf. Dan Simonescu, *"Puncte de vedere."* Glasul Bisericii (1958), 4, 348.

181. Erasmus, *Opus Epistolarum*, I, p. 121. E. Dolet, *Commentariorum . . .* , I, c. 1161–1162.

182. Lorenzo Valla, *Opera Omnia*, II, p. 284.

183. Curio Lancillotto Pasio, *De litteratura non volgari* (1518. Augusto Taurinorum: 1528), fol. I, v; V r. Juan Luis Vives, *Opera Omnia* (Valentiae Edeltanorum: 1785), VI, p. 70 (reprint London: The Gregg Press, 1964).

184. Pietro Crinito, *De honesta disciplina*, XVI, 8. A cura di Carlo Angeleri (1504. Roma: 1955), p. 332.

185. Curio Lancillotto Pasio, *ibid.*, fol. XXVIII v, XXXII r.

186. Erasmus, *Opera Omnia*, III, c. 937. *Opus Epistolarum*, IV, p. 594, IX, p. 117.

187. Cf. A. H. L. Heeren, *Geschichte des Studiums der griechischen und römischen Litteratur* (Göttingen: 1797), I, p. 307.

188. Lilio Gregorio Gyraldus Ferrariensis, *Dialogi duo de Poetis nostrorum temporum* (1551. *Operum quae extant omnium* (Basileae: 1580), II, p. 427.

189. L. Valla, *De linguae latinae elegantia*, 2, XIX (1471). Cantabrigiae: 1688), p. 52.

190. Erasmus, *Opus Epistolarum*, II, p. 491.

191. Cf. Eugenio Garin, *ibid.*, II, p. 170.

192. Cf. Albert Hyma, *The Christian Renaissance. A History of the "Devotio Moderna"* (Hamden: 1965), p. 394.

193. J. Bale, *Illustrium maioris Britanniae* (1548), f. 90 r.

194. *Vocabulario degli Accademici della Crusca*, IX, I, pp. 261–262.

195. Guillaume Budé, *Lexicon graeco-latinum seu Thesaurus linguae graecae* (Genevae: 1534), *s.v.* Etienne Dolet, *Commentariorum linguae latinae*, I, c. 1160.

196. Robert Estienne, *Dictionariolum puerorum tribus linguis latina, anglica et gallica* (Londini: 1552), *s.v.*

197. Robert Estienne, *Thesaurus linguae latinae*, III, *s.v.*

198. Barnabae Brissonii, *De verborum . . . significatione* (1559. Halae Magdeburgicae: 1743), p. 744.

199. L. Valla, *Opera Omnia*, I, XVIII; *Praefatio*, III.

200. René Wellek, "Literature and Its Cognates." *Dictionary of the History of Ideas. Studies in Selected Pivotal Ideas*. Philip P. Wiener, ed. (New York: Charles Scribner, 1973), III, p. 81.

201. Albert Dauzat, *ibid.*, p. 420, etc. Oscar Bloch-Walter von Wartburg, *ibid.*, p. 372. Walter von Wartburg, *ibid.*, V, p. 379.

202. Walter von Wartburg, *ibid.*, V, pp. 378–379. Edmond Hugnet, *ibid.*, IV, pp. 32–33.

203. Xenophon, *L'Histoire du voyage que fit Cyrus à l'encontre du Roi de Perses Artaxerxe*, tr. Claude de Seyssel, 1529; Ms. fr. B. N. 702 (p. 16).

204. G. Budé, *Le livre de l'instruction du Prince*, p. 30 v.

205. Plutarque, *Les vies des hommes illustres*. tr. Jacques Amyot (1559. Paris: 1575) (dedication: *Au très puissant et très Chrestien Roy de France . . .*)

206. Louis Le Roy, *De la vicissitude . . .* , pp. 84–85 r.

207. Jean Lemaire de Belges, *Oeuvres*, II, pp. 268, 409.

208. Antoine Du Verdier, *La Bibliothèque avec un discours sur les bonnes lettres servant de préface* (Lyon: 1585), p. XV.

209. Cf. Raymond Williams, *Keywords. A Vocabulary of Culture and Society* (New York: Oxford University Press: 1976), p. 151.

210. Cf. Hanna-Barbara Gerl, *Rhetorik als Philosophie, Lorenzo Valla* (München: 1974), p. 242.

211. Victor Manuel de Aguiar e Silva, *Teoria da literatura* (4ª Edição. Coimbra: Livreria Almedina, 1982), pp. 1–2.

212. *Deutsches Fremdwörterbuch*. Begonnen von Hans Schulz, fortgeführt von Otto Basler (Berlin: Walter de Gruyter, 1942), II, p. 34.

213. *Oxford English Dictionary* (Oxford: University Press, 1933), VI, p. 342.

214. Cf. Ewald Flügel, *ibid.*, 283.

215. Aldo Scaglione, *Comparative Literature as Cultural History: The Educational and Social Background of Renaissance Literature. The Comparative Perspective on Literature*. . . . Edited with an introduction by Clayton Koelb and Susan Noakes (Ithaca and London: Cornell University Press, 1988), pp. 147–161.

216. Aldo D. Scaglione, *Ars Grammatica* (The Hague-Paris: Mouton, 1970), p. 92.

217. Antonio Galateo, *De educatione (1504–1505). Scritti inediti e rari di diversi autori*. Ed. Francesco Casotti (Napoli: 1865), p. 17.

218. Among others: Christofle de Savigny, *Tableaux accomplis de tous les arts libéraux* (Paris: 1587).

219. Leonardo Bruni Aretino. *De studiis et litteris*. Hans Baron: *Leonardo Bruni Aretini humanistische-philosophische Schriften* (Leipzig-Berlin: 1928), p. 19.

220. Louis Le Roy, *ibid.*, p. 84 v.

221. Pontus de Tyard, *Oeuvres*, II, *Solitaire premier*. Ed. critique Silvio F. Baridon (Genève-Lille: 1950), p. XXIX.

222. Francis Bacon, *The Advancement of Learning. To the King.* p. 5.

223. Cf. Ewald Flügel, *ibid.*, 284. In German: *Deutsches Fremdwörterbuch*, II, p. 34.

224. Johannes Trithemius, *In Praise of Scribes. De laude scripturorum*. Ed. with Introduction by Klaus Arnold. Translation by Roland Behrendt (Lawrence, Kans.: Coronado Press, 1979), ch. XIV, p. 9.

225. Jürgen Henningsen, " 'Enzyclopädie'. Zur Sprach- und Bedeutungsgeschichte eines pädagogisches Begriffs." *Archiv für Begriffsgeschichte*, B. 10 (1966), 243.

226. Etienne Dolet, *ibid.*, I, c. 1156.

227. cf. J. G. Schelhorn, *Amoenitates literariae* . . . (Francofurti et Lipsiae: 1725), II, p. 338.

228. Cf. Ulrich Dierse, *Enzyklopädie. Zur Geschichte eines philosophischen und wissenschaftstheoretischen Begriffs.* (Bonn: 1977), p. 14.

229. Pietro Crinito, *ibid.*, III, p. 112.

230. J. Bale, *ibid.*, p. 10.

231. Among others: Jean Bodin, *Methodus ad Facilem Historiarum Cognitionem, Oeuvres philosophiques.* Texte établi, traduit et publié par Pierre Mesnard (Paris: Presses Universitaires de France, 1951), I, pp. 122, 290.

232. Bernhardt Wendt, *Idee und Entwicklungsgeschichte der enzyklopädischen Literatur. Eine literarisch-bibliographische Studie* (Würzburg: 1941), p. 2.

233. Alain Rey, *Encyclopédies et dictionnaires* (Paris: Presses Universitaires de France, Que sais-je, 1982), p. 12.

234. August Buck, *Studia humanitatis* (Wiesbaden: 1981), p. 133.

235. G. Budé, *De Studio litterarum*, p. XX v.

236. *Panepistemon* Angeli Poliziani, *hoc est omnium scientiarum* (1532).

237. Robert Collison, *Encyclopaedias: Their History Throughout the Ages* (New York-London: 1966), p. 79.

238. Cf. Jean Jehasse, *La Renaissance de la critique. L'essor de l'Humanisme érudit de 1560 à 1614.* (Saint-Etienne: 1976), p. 233.

239. G. Budé, *De philologia*, I, p. XXI v.

240. Jürgen Henningsen, *ibid.*, pp. 281, 284.

241. Jean Jehasse, *ibid.*, p. 18. Franco Simone, *"La notion d'Encyclopédie, élément caractéristique de la Renaissance française."* French Renaissance Studies. Ed. by Peter Sharratt (Edinburgh: 1976), pp. 234–262.

242. Guillaume Budé, *Le livre de l'instruction du prince*, p. 67 v.

243. Pontus de Tyard, *ibid.*, p. 4.

244. Joachim du Bellay, *La Deffence et Illustration de la Langue Française* (1549), ch. X. (Paris: 1904), p. 124.

245. Jean Edouard Du Monin, *"Discours philosophique et historial de la Poésie philosophique." Nouvelles Oeuvres* (Paris: 1582), p. 50.

246. Louis Le Roy, *ibid.*, p. 19 v.

247. Cf. Silvia Rizzo, *Il Lessico filologico degli umanisti*, p. 69. Curt F.

Bühler, *The Fifteenth Century Book. The Scribes, The Printers, The Decorators* (1966. Philadelphia: University of Pennsylvania Press, 1961), p. 41.

248. Elisabeth L. Eisenstein, *The Printing Press as an Aspect of Change, Communications and Cultural Transformations in Early Modern Europe* (Cambridge: Cambridge University Press, 1979), I, p. 168. Curt F. Bühler, *ibid.*, pp. 16, 96 (numerous other references).

249. *Crestomație de literatură română veche*, I, pp. 67, 102.

250. Ulrich von Hutten, *Epistolae obscurorum virorum. Operum Supplementum*, I, p. 245.

251. Leo S. Olschki, *"Incunables illustrés imitant les manuscrits. Le passage du manuscrit au livre imprimé."* *Bibliophilia*, 15 (1913–1914), 245–246. Curt F. Bühler, *ibid.*, pp. 580–583.

252. Johannes Trithemius, *ibid.*, pp. 34–37, 62–65.

253. Dolf Sternberger, *Über die Verbindlichkeit des Schrifttums* (Frankfurt am Main: 1954), pp. 38–39.

254. Jean Bodin, *ibid.*, p. 430.

255. Nathalie Zonn Davis, *Society and Culture in Early Modern France*, p. 308.

256. Jean de La Caille, *Histoire de l'imprimerie et de la librairie où l'on voit son origine et son progrès jusqu'en 1689* (Paris: 1689), pp. 10–16.

257. Henri Estienne, *Artis Typographicae Querimonia* (Paris: 1569), *Plainte de la Typographie contre certains imprimeurs ignorants qui lui ont attiré le mépris où elle est tombée, poème latin . . . par . . .* (Paris: 1785), p. IX.

258. Cf. Curt F. Bühler, *ibid.*, p. 49; other references in Elisabeth L. Eisenstein, *ibid.*, I, pp. 304, 311, 326, 340, etc. Lucien Febvre et Henri-Jean Martin, *L'apparition du livre* (Paris: 1971), pp. 248–259.

259. Lucien Febvre et Henri-Jean Martin, *ibid.*, p. 378.

260. A. F. Doni, *Ragionamento della stampa. I Marmi* (Venezia: 1552), pp. 5–23.

261. Rudolf Hirsch, *Printing, Selling and Reading, 1450–1530* (Wiesbaden: Otto Harrassowitz, 1967), pp. 179, 181.

262. Erasmus, *Opus Epistolarum*, I, p. 448.

263. Rudolf Hirsch, *ibid.*, p. 19.

264. Elisabeth L. Eisenstein, *ibid.*, I, pp. 89, 217. James B. Wadsworth,

Lyons 1473–1503. The Beginnings of Cosmopolitanism (Cambridge, Mass., 1962), p. 21. A correction of this widespread idea in Etiemble, *"Le chef-d'oeuvre de l'imposture européocentriste: Gutenberg serait l'inventeur de l'imprimerie." L'Europe chinoise* (Paris: Gallimard, 1988), I, pp. 27–41.

265. Silvia Rizzo, *ibid.*, pp. 3–9.

266. Cf. Fr. Heinrich Reusch, *Die "Indices librorum prohibitorum"* des *sechzenten Jahrhunderts*. Gesammelt und herausgegeben . . . (Tübingen: 1886), I, pp. 260, 495.

267. Giovanni Boccaccio, *La Teseide*. Tratta dal Manoscritto del Conte Guglielmo Camposempiero (Milano: 1819), p. 432.

268. Johannes Trithemius, *ibid.*, III, pp. 44, 46; IV, p. 88.

269. Cf. Werner Krauss, *Gesammelte Aufsätze zur Literatur und Sprachwissenschaft* (Frankfurt am Main: 1949), p. 153.

270. Francis Bacon, *Essays, L, On Studies*. With an Introduction by Oliphant Smeaton (London: J. M. Dent, 1914), p. 150.

271. Cf. Rudolf Hirsch, *ibid.*, p. 152.

272. *Emblemata. Handbuch zur Sinnbildkunst des XVI. und XVII. Jahrhunderts*. Herausgegeben von Arthur Henkel und Albrecht Schöne (Stuttgart: 1978), c. 1287–1290.

273. Cf. *Storia d'Italia. Annali 4. Intelletuali e potere*. A cura di Corrado Vivanti (Torino: 1981), pp. 198, 331, 335.

274. *Oxford English Dictionary*. Suppl. I, p. 299.

275. Alexio Vanegas, *Primera parte de las differencias de libros que ay en el universo* (1545. Madrid: 1569), p. 5.

276. Cf. Fritz Schalk, *Exempla romanischer Wortgeschichte* (Frankfurt am Main: 1966), pp. 138–139, 141. Hans Blumenberg, *Die Lesbarkeit der Welt* (Frankfurt am Main: Suhrkamp, 1981), pp. 58–59.

277. Alexio Vanegas, *ibid.*, pp. 5–6.

278. Eugenio Garin, *"Le livre comme symbole à la Renaissance." Le Débat* (1982), 12, 111.

279. Hugo von Trimberg, *Das "Registrum Multorum Auctorum." Untersuchungen und Komentierte Textausgabe von Karl Langosch* (Berlin: 1942), p. 195.

280. Basic references: Ernst Robert Curtius, *"Das Buch der Natur." Europäische Literatur und Lateinisches Mittelalter* (1948. Bern und München:

1984), pp. 323–329. Erich Rothacker, *"Das Buch der Natur."* *Materialien und Grundsätzliches zur Metapherngeschichte* (Bonn: Bouvier, 1979), pp. 90–99, 109–120. Fritz Schalk, *ibid.*, pp. 137–140.

281. Cf. M. T. Jones-Davies, *Victimes et rebelles: l'écrivain dans la société élisabéthaine* (Paris: 1986), p. 117. *Deutsche Wortgeschichte.* Hrsg. von Friedrich Maurer u. Friedrich Stroh. 2. neu bearbeitete Auflage (Berlin: Walter de Gruyter, 1959), I, p. 379.

282. Lorenzo Valla, *Opera Omnia*, II, p. 291.

283. Robert Estienne, *Dictionariolum* . . . , *s.v.*

284. Angelo Decembrio, *De politia literaria* (1462. Basileae: 1562), pp. 9, 103.

285. Beriah Botfield, *Prefaces to the First Editions of the Greek and Roman Classics and of the Sacred Scriptures.* Collected and edited by . . . (London: 1861), p. 529.

286. Antoine Du Verdier, *La Bibliothèque* . . . , p. XXX.

287. Pietro Crinito, *ibid.*, II, 2, p. 485.

288. A. Francesco Doni, *La libraria . . . nella quale sono scritti tutti gl'autori vulgari* . . . (Vinegia: 1550).

289. Henri-Jean Martin, *Classement et conjectures. Histoire de l'édition française* (Paris: 1982), I, p. 435.

290. Rudolf Blum, *"Vor-und Frühgeschichte der nationalen Allgemeinbibliographie." Archiv für Geschichte des Buchwesens*, II (1958), 234–235. Louise-Noëlle Malclès, *La Bibliographie* (1956. Paris: Presses Universitaires de France, Que sais-je, 1977), pp. 26–27, 32.

291. Luigi Balsamo, *Introduzione alla bibliografia* (Modena: 1978), p. 11. Rudolf Blum, *ibid.*, p. 238. *"Bibliographia. Ein Wort- und Begriffsgeschichtliche Untersuchung. Archiv für Geschichte des Buchwesens*, X (1970), c. 1009–1246.

292. Theodore Bestermann, *The Beginnings of Systematic Bibliography* (London: Oxford University Press, 1936. 2nd ed. revised).

293. Lloyd W. Daly, *Contributions to a History of Alphabetisation in Antiquity and the Middle Ages* (Bruxelles = Latomus, 1971), pp. 77, 79.

294. Giovanni Getto, *Storia delle storie letterarie* (1942. Milano: Sansoni, 1969), pp. 10, 11, 13. Peter Brockmeier, *Darstellungen der französischen Literaturgeschichte von Claude Fauchet bis Laharpe* (Berlin: Akademie Verlag, 1963), pp. 15–23.

295. Cf. Hans Robert Jauss, "Aesthetische Normen und geschichtliche Reflexion in der 'Querelle des Anciens et des Modernes.' " Parallèle des Anciens et des Modernes en ce qui regarde les arts et les sciences par M. Perrault de l'Académie Française (1688. München: Eidos Verlag, 1974), p. 60.

296. Richard de Bury, Philobiblion, sive de Amore librorum (1473. Philobiblion . . . , Paris: 1856), ch. XVI.

297. Joannis Pici Mirandulae, Epist, I. Opera Omnia (Basileae, 1601), II, p. 85.

298. José Antonio Maravall, Antiguos y Modernos. La idea de progreso en el desarrollo inicial de una sociedad (Madrid: Sociedad de estudios y publicaciones, 1966), p. 215.

299. Rachel Giese, "Erasmus on Tradition and Imitation." Actes du IVᵉ Congrès de l'A.I.L.C. (The Hague-Paris: 1966), II, pp. 747–750.

300. Rabelais, Pantagruel, 1. II, ch. 8. Oeuvres (Paris, Didot, 1857), I, p. 268.

301. Cf. J. J. Baebler, Beiträge zu einer Geschichte des lateinischen Grammatik in Mittelalter (Halle: 1885), p. 148.

302. Erasmus, Opus Epistolarum, II, p. 49.

303. Erasmus, cf. J. Huizinga, Parerga (Basel: 1945), p. 81.

304. Rabelais, ibid., 1, II, ch. 8. Oeuvres, pp. 268–269.

305. Louis Le Roy, ibid., p. 96 v.

306. Erasmus, Opus Epistolarum, II, pp. 539, 541.

307. B. L. Ullman, The Origin and the Development of the Humanistic Script (Roma: 1960), p. 23. Silvia Rizzo, ibid., p. 141.

308. Henri Cornelius Agrippa, De Incertitudine et Vanitate Scientiarum et Artium (1530. Tr. en françois du latin, Paris: 1582), ch. II, pp. 13–17.

309. Louis Le Roy, ibid., ch. II, pp. 17 v–24 v.

310. Nathalie Zonn Davis, ibid., p. 326.

311. Francesco Patrizio, Della poetica. La Deca disputata. (Ferrara: 1586), c. I, p. 2ff.

312. Louis Le Roy, ibid., pp. 113 v–115 r.

313. A general introduction: Giacinto Margiotta, Le origini italiane de la Querelle des Anciens et des Modernes (Roma: Editrice Studium, 1953).

Adrian Marino, *"Aux sources de la dialectique sémantique ancien/nouveau."* *Cahiers roumains d'études littéraires*, 1975, 1, 50–59.

314. Erasmus, *Opus Epistolarum*, II, p. 223.

315. Lorenzo Valla, *De linguae latinae elegantia*, III. *Praefatio* (1440, 1471); 59 editions to 1536 (Cantabrigiae: 1688), p. 184.

316. G. Budé, *De Philologia*. (Another edition, Bâle: 1533, p. 155.)

317. Cf. Beriah Botfield, *ibid.*, p. 381.

318. Cf. Giuseppe Toffanin, *ibid.*, II, p. 177.

319. Speroni Sperone, *Dialogo delle Lingue. Dialoghi . . .* , p. 105.

320. R. Glynn Faithfull, "The Concept of 'Living Language' in *Cinquecento* Vernacular Philology." *Modern Language Review*, XLVIII (1953), 249. Henri Chamard, *Les origines de la poésie française de la Renaissance* (Paris: 1920), pp. 288–289.

321. Leon Battista Alberti, *La prima grammatica della lingua volgare*. A cura di Cecil Grayson (Bologna: 1964).

322. Etienne Dolet, *Préfaces françaises*. Textes établis, introduits et commentés par Claude Longeon (Genève: 1979), p. 183.

323. Ferdinand Brunot, *"Un projet d''enrichir, magnifier et publier' la langue française en 1509."* *Revue d'Histoire littéraire de la France*, I (1894), 31.

324. Clément Marot, *Oeuvres complètes*. Avec préface, notes et glossaires par Pierre Janet (Paris: Flammarion, 1900), IV, p. 192.

325. Pierre Villey, *Les sources italiennes de la "Défense et illustration de la langue française" de Joachim du Bellay* (Paris: Bibliothèque de la Renaissance, No. 386, 1908).

326. Cf. John William Adamson, *The Illiterate Anglo-Saxon* (Cambridge: 1946), p. 451.

327. Cf. Ciro Trabalza, *ibid.*, p. 68.

328. Cf. Hans Baron, *The Crisis of the Early Italian Renaissance* (Princeton: 1955), I, p. 362.

329. Philippus Villanus, *Liber de civitatis Florentiae famosis civibus . . . et de Florentinorum litteratura principes fere synchroni scriptores*. Ed. G. C. Galletti (Firenze: 1847).

330. Franco Simone, *"Une entreprise oubliée des humanistes français de*

la prise de conscience historique du renouveau culturel à la naissance de la pre-mière histoire littéraire." Humanism in France, at the End of the Middle Ages and in the Early Renaissance. Ed. by A. H. T. Levi (New York: Manchester University Press, 1970), pp. 118, 121.

331. Vernon Hall, Jr., *Renaissance Literary Criticism. A Study of its So-cial Content* (New York: Columbia University Press, 1945), pp. 36, 158.

331 b. Max Wehrli, *"Der Nationaldgedanke im deutschen und schweizer-ischen Humanismus,"* Nationalismus in Germanistik und Dichtung (Berlin, 1971), 126.

332. Bartolomeo Ricci, *De Imitazione* (Venetiis: 1525), p. 32 r.

333. Cf. Eugenio Garin, *Umanesimo e Rinascimento. Questioni e corre-nti di storia letteraria.* (Milano: Marzorati, 1949), III, pp. 385–386.

334. *Ibid., "Gli 'Studia Humanitatis' e la pedagogia italiana del Rinasci-mento."* Saggi di filologia e filosofia, pp. 95, 98.

335. Terence Cave, *The Cornucopian Text. Problems of Writing in the French Renaissance* (Oxford: Clarendon Press, 1979), p. 175.

336. Cf. Robert Ranc, *"La Foire de Francfort telle que la vit Henri Estienne."* Gutenberg-Jahrbuch, 53 (1958), 177.

337. Jehan de Nostre Dame, *ibid.*, p. 205.

338. *Crestomaţie . . .* , I, pp. 60, 70, 103, 107.

339. Sir Philip Sidney, *An Apologie for Poetrie.* Ed. by Evelyn S. Shuckburgh (Cambridge: University Press, 1938), p. 60.

340. R. Glynn Faithfull, *ibid.*, pp. 208, 212–213.

341. Pietro Bembo, *Prose della volgar lingua. I classici italiani nella storia della critica.* Opera diretta da Walter Bini, I, *Da Dante a Tasso* (Firenze: 1971), pp. 180, 181.

342. Etienne Dolet, *Préfaces françaises . . .* , p. 14.

343. R. Glynn Faithfull, *ibid.*, pp. 281, 283.

344. Cf. Eugenio Garin, *Il Rinascimento italiano* (Milano: 1941), p. 85.

345. Peter Burke, *Popular Culture in Early Modern Europe, 1500–1800* (London: 1978), pp. 3–22, 287–288.

346. François Furet-Jacques Ozouf, *Lire et écrire. L'alphabétisation des Français de Calvin à Jules Féry* (Paris: Editions de Minuit, 1977), I, pp. 50, 70ff, 176ff.

347. Erasmus, *Opus Epistolarum*, III, p. 488.

348. Grigorie Reis, *Margarita philosophica* (Basileae: 1535), p. 1137.

349. Erasmus, *Opus Epistolarum*, IV, 593; VII, p. 14.

350. Cf. Erich König, " '*Studia humanitatis*' *und verwandte Ausdrucke bei den deutschen Frühhumanisten.*" *Beiträge zur Geschichte der Renaissance und Reformation* . . . (München und Freising: 1917), p. 257.

351. J. Bale, *Illustrium maioris Britannie scriptorum*, f. 98 v.

352. Edmund Hugnet, *ibid.*, IV, p. 520.

353. Antoine Du Verdier, *La Bibliothèque*, . . . p. VI, XIII.

354. Torquato Tasso, *Discorsi dell'arte poetica*, I, *Prose*, a cura di Ettore Mazzoli (Milano-Napoli: 1959), p. 309.

355. Pico della Mirandola (Joannis Pici Mirandulae), *Epistolarum Liber. Ep. IV* (Cizae: 1652), p. 36.

356. Erasmus, *Opus Epistolarum*, I, p. 375; IV, pp. 181, 391, 394; VI, pp. 90, 132, etc.

357. Beriah Botfield, *ibid.*, pp. 171, 417, 652.

358. J. C. Scaliger, *De causis linguae* (Lugduni: 1540), *Praefatio*.

359. Joannes Murmelius, *Scoparius* . . . *ad juvanda politioris literaturae studia* . . . (Coloniae: 1518).

360. Paul Zumthor, *Le masque et la lumière. La Poétique des grands rhétoriqueurs* (Paris: Seuil, 1978). *Ibid.*, *Anthologie des grands rhétoriqueurs* (Paris: Union générale d'éditions, 1978).

361. Plentiful references and bibliography: *Scribes and Sources. Handbook of the Chancery Hand in the Sixteenth Century. Texts from Writing-Masters*, selected, introduced and translated by A. S. Osley (London-Boston: 1980).

362. Cf. Emanuela Cassamassima, *Trattati di scrittura del cinquecento italiano* (Milano: 1966), p. 450.

363. G. Budé, *Opera Omnia* (Basileae, 1557), I, p. VII r.

364. Erasmus, *Opus Epistolarum*, VI, p. 133.

365. G. Budé, *ibid.*, I, p. 238.

366. Erasmus, *ibid.*, II, pp. 223, 489; III, p. 529; VI, p. 249.

367. G. Budé, *ibid.*, I, p. XXXII r.

368. Louis Le Roy, *ibid.*, p. 118 r.

369. Pietro Bembo, *Prose della volgar lingua*, III, 1. Cf. *Dichtungslehre der Romania aus der Zeit der Renaissance und des Barock*, p. 98.

370. Antoine Du Verdier, *La Bibliothèque* . . . , p. XVI.

371. Pietro Bembo, *ibid.*, *I Classici italiani nella storia della critica* . . . , p. 38.

372. Edmund Hugnet, *ibid.*, IV, p. 520.

373. Cf. Orazio Bacci, *La critica letteraria* (Milano: 1910), pp. 175, 191.

374. G. Budé, *De Asse* (Parisiis: 1541), p. CCVII.

375. Plutarch, *Les Vies des Hommes illustres* . . . (Paris: 1575), *Aux lecteurs*.

376. Clément Marot, *ibid.*, I, p. 217.

377. *Dichtungslehren der Romania* . . . , p. 381.

378. Cf. Ewald Flügel, *ibid.*, 284–286.

379. Ciro Trabalza, *La critica letteraria* (Milano: Valardi, 1915), p. 266. G. Toffanin, *Storia dell'umanesimo* (Bologna, Zanichelli, 1964), II, p. 153.

380. Christophoris Mylaeus, *De Scribendo Universitatis rerum* (Basileae: 1551), p. 245.

381. Plutarque, *Les oeuvres morales et meslées*, translatées du Grec en Français par Messire Jacques Amyot (Paris: 1572), p. 95.

382. Cf. Karl Vossler, *Poetische Theorien in der italienischen Frührenaissance* (Berlin: 1900), pp. 65–66. Hans Baron, *The Crisis of the Early Italian Renaissance*, II, pp. 541–542 (abundant references and bibliography), etc.

383. Dante Alighieri, *Vita nuova*, XXV, 3. *Tutte le opere*, p. 397.

384. *Elisabethan Critical Essays*. Ed. with an introduction by G. Gregory Smith (Oxford: 1904), I, p. 277.

385. Ulrich von Hutten, *Epistolae obscurorum virorum*, I, p. 10.

386. Speroni Sperone, *Dialoghi* . . . , p. 266.

387. Pietro Bembo, *ibid.*, p. 29.

388. Francesco Petrarca, *Le Familiari*. Traduzione, note e saggio introduttivo di Ugo Dotti (Urbino: Argalia editore, 1970), p. 583.

389. B. Daniello, *Della Poetica. Trattati di poetica e retorica del Cinquecento.* A cura di Bernard Weinberg (Bari: Laterza, 1970), I, p. 272.

390. B. Castiglione, *ibid.*, I, 46.

391. Ulrich von Hutten, *ibid.*, I, p. 277.

392. Augusto Campana, "The Origin of the Word 'Humanist'," 62, 64.

393. Cf. L. J. Paetow, *Morale Scolarium of John of Garland* (Berkeley: 1927), p. 94.

394. Pietro Bembo, *ibid.*, p. 31.

395. Bernard Weinberg, *A History of Literary Criticism in the Italian Renaissance* (Chicago: 1961), II, p. 730.

396. Cf. Adriana Mauriella, *"Cultura e società nella Siena del Cinquecento."* Filologia e letteratura, XVII (1971), 29.

397. Bernardo Tasso, *Delle lettere* (Vinegia: 1569), p. 80.

398. B. Castiglione, *ibid.*, I, 36.

399. Peter M. Brown, "A Significant Sixteenth-Century Use of the Word 'Umanista'," 566.

400. Antonio Possevino, *Coltura degli ingegni*, c. II (Vicenza: 1598), p. 101.

401. Tomasso Garzoni, *La Piazza Universale* . . . , p. 284.

402. Pietro Bembo, *ibid.*, p. 38. B. Castiglione, *ibid.*, I, 32. Claudio Tolomei, *Delle Lettere* (Vinegia: 1548), p. 9.

403. Jehan de Nostre Dame, *Les vies des plus célèbres* . . . , p. 222.

404. G. B. Giraldi Cinzio, *Lettere a Bernardo Tasso sulle poesia epica* (1557). *Trattati* . . . , II, p. 463.

405. Ulrich von Hutten, *ibid.*, I, pp. 32–33.

406. Hugo von Trimberg, *Das "Registrum Multorum Auctorum"* . . . , pp. 185, 817.

407. Cf. Käte Hamburger, *"Das Wort 'Dichtung'."* Literatur und Dichtung. Hrsg. von Horst Rüdiger (Stuttgart-Berlin-Köln-Mainz: Kohlhammer, 1973), p. 35.

408. Orazio Toscanella, *Precetti della poetica* (1562). *Trattati* . . . , II, p. 571.

409. Jehan de Nostre Dame, *ibid.*, p. 169.

410. Cf. Ewald Flügel, *ibid.*, 285. Annie Parent, *Les Métiers du livre à Paris au XVIe siècle (1535–1560)*. (Genève-Paris: 1974), p. 173.

411. Jehan de Nostre Dame, *ibid.*, p. 180.

412. Erasmus, *Opera Omnia*, 1, c. 709.

413. Just one example of ten possible ones: B. Tasso, *ibid.*, p. 81.

414. Bernard Weinberg, *ibid.*, I, p. 142.

415. Cf. John Lough, *Writer and Public in France from the Middle Ages to the Present Day* (Oxford: Clarendon Press, 1978), p. 33.

416. A. L. Pinciano, *Filosofía Antigua Poética* (Madrid: 1596), cf. *Historia general de las literaturas hispánicas* (Barcelona: 1953), III, p. 605.

417. Dante Alighieri, *Convivio*, I, IX. *Tutte le opere*, p. 503.

418. Pietro Aretino, *Tutte le opere. Lettere. Il primo e il secondo libro.* A cure di Francesco Flora (Milano: Mondadori, 1960), p. 193.

419. *Dichtungslehren der Romania . . .* , pp. 203, 204, 271.

420. Ulrich von Hutten, *ibid.*, I, p. 51.

421. Francesco Berni, *Poesie e prose*. Criticamente curate de E. Chiorboli (Genève-Firenze: 1934), p. 261.

422. *Dichtungslehren der Romania*, p. 146.

423. Plutarque, *Oeuvres. . . .* (Paris: 1784), VIII, pp. 85–86.

424. William Webbe, *A Discourse of Englishe Poetrie* (1586). *Elisabethan Critical Essays*, I, p. 226.

425. *Ibid.*, I, p. 230. Jochen Linck, *Die Theorie des dichterischen Renaissance* (München: 1971), p. 154.

426. Torquato Tasso, *Discorsi dell'arte poetica e in particolare sopra il poema eroico. Prose.* A cure di Ettore Mazzoli (Milano-Napoli: 1959), p. 354.

427. Cf. Karl Borinski, *Die Poetik der Renaissance und die Anfänge der literarischenkritik in Deutschland* (Berlin: 1886), p. 18.

428. Cf. Sigismund von Lempicki, *Geschichte der deutschen Literaturwissenschaft bis zum Ende des 18. Jahrhunderts* (Göttingen: 1920), pp. 102–103.

429. B. Castiglione, *ibid.*, I, 29.

430. Cf. August Buck, *Humanistische Lebensformen. Die Rolle der italienischen Humanisten in der Zeitgenössischen Gesellschaft* (Basel-Frankfurt/M.: 1981), p. 131.

431. Francesco Patrizio, *Della poetica. La Deca disputata.* (Ferrara: 1586), p. 4.

432. Lodovico Castelvetro, *Poetica d'Aristotele volgarizzata et sposta* (Basel: 1576), p. 13.

433. A. L. Pinciano, *ibid.*, p. 606.

434. Bernard Weinberg, A *History of Literary Criticism in the Italian Renaissance*, I, p. 37.

435. *De Dignitate disciplinarum ad Pancratium. La disputa delle arte nel Quattrocento.* A cura di Eugenio Garin (Torino: 1947), pp. 134–135.

436. W. S. Howell, "Poetics, Rhetoric and Logic in Renaissance Criticism." *Classical Influences on European Culture. A.D. 1500–1700.* Ed. by R. R. Bolgar (Cambridge: 1976), pp. 157–159.

437. Francesco Berni, *ibid.*, p. 268.

438. Tomasso Garzoni, *ibid.*, p. 921.

439. François Rigolot, *"La Figure de la lettre. Graphisme et paradigmatisme à l'aube de la Renaissance."* *Revue des sciences humaines*, LI (1980), 47–59.

440. Cf. *Dichtungslehren der Romania . . .* , p. 111.

441. Cf. Eugenio Garin, *Il Rinascimento italiano* (Milano: 1941), p. 175. Michael B. Kline, *Rabelais and the Age of Printing* (Genève: Droz, 1963), p. 20.

442. Giordano Bruno, *Opere* (Milano-Napoli: 1956), pp. 572–573.

443. Pontus de Tyard, *Oeuvres*, II, p. 27.

444. Cesare Segre, *"Edonismo linguistico nel Cinquecento."* *Giornale storico della letteratura italiana*, 130 (1953), 157. Baxter Hathaway, *The Age of Criticism. The Late Renaissance in Italy.* (Ithaca: Cornell University Press, 1962), p. 454.

445. Richard (George?) Puttenham, *The Arte of English Poesie (1589).* *Ancient Critical Essays upon Poets and Poësy.* Ed. by Joseph Haslewood (London: 1811), I, p. 7.

446. Francesco Patrizio, *Della poetica*, 1.V: *De poesia si possa fare in prosa*, pp. 93ff.

447. Sir Philip Sidney, *ibid.*, p. 36.

448. Lorenzo Valla, *Opera Omnia*, II, p. 421.

449. Bernard Weinberg, *ibid.*, I, p. 389; II, p. 729, etc.

450. Torquato Tasso, *Prose*, pp. 498, 587.

451. Erich Köhler, " '*Je ne sais quoi*'. Ein Kapitel aus der Begriffsgeschichte des Unbegreiflichen." *Romanisches Jahrbuch*, VI (1953–1954), 22, 25, 32.

452. Cf. Beriah Botfield, *ibid.*, p. 309.

453. Cf. Gino Funaioli, *Studi di letteratura antica* (Bologna: 1951), I, p. 282.

454. *De Dignitate disciplinarum ad Pancratium*, p. 126.

455. Guarino Veronese, cf. Mircea Eliade, *Contribuţii la filosofia Renaşterii* (Bucureşti: Colecţia "Capricorn," 1984), p. 152.

456. L. G. Gyraldi, *Progymnasma adversus literas et literatos* (Florentiae: 1551), p. 159.

457. Ernst Robert Curtius, *Europäische Literatur* . . . , p. 532. *Dichtungslehren der Romania* . . . , pp. 59ff.

458. Elisabeth L. Eisenstein, *The Printing Press* . . . , I, p. 137.

459. Angelo Decembrio, *De Politia literaria libri septem* (1462. Basileae: 1562), 1, II.

460. Erasmus, *Opera Omnia*, X, c. 1704.

461. G. Toffanin, *Storia dell'Umanesimo (Dal XIII al XVI Secolo)*. (Napoli: 1933), p. 72.

462. Erasmus, *Opus Epistolarum*, I, p. 332.

463. The basic orientation in Fritz Schalk, "*Von Erasmus Res Publica Literaria zur Gelehrtenrepublik der Aufklärung.*" *Studien zur französischen Aufklärung.* (Frankfurt/M.: Vittorio Klosterman, 1977), pp. 145, 147–148, 155. Jean Jehasse, *La Renaissance de la critique*, p. 61.

464. Angelo Decembrio, *ibid.*, p. 6.

465. L. G. Gyraldi, *ibid.*, p. 172.

466. Philippe Monnier, *Le Quattrocento* (Paris: Perrin, 1912), I, pp. 49, 247.

467. Speroni Sperone, *Trattatisti del Cinquecento*, I, p. 728.

468. Cf. A. Renaudet, *Études érasmiennes*, 1521–1529 (Paris: Droz, 1939), p. 4. Frances A. Yates, *The Art of Memory* (London and Henley: 1966), p. 318.

469. *Trésor de la langue française* (Paris: 1978), VI, p. 259 A.

470. Paul Hazard, "'Cosmopolite'." *Mélanges* . . . *F. Baldensperger* (Paris: 1930), I, pp. 354–364.

471. Leon Battista Alberti, *De commodis litterarum atque incommodis. Defunctus*. Testo latino. Traduzione italiana. Introduzione e note a cura di Giovanni Farris (Milano: Marzorati, 1971), pp. 138–139.

472. Dario Cecchetti, "L'elogio delle arti liberali nel primo Umanesimo francese." *Studi francesi*, X (1966), 6.

473. Charles Trinkans, "A Humanist's Image of Humanism: The Inaugural Orations of Bartolommeo della Fonte." *Studies in the Renaissance*, VII (1960), 119.

474. Erasmus, *Opus Epistolarum*, V, p. 562.

475. Samuel Daniel's *Musophilus: Containing a General Defense of All Learning*. Ed. by Raymond Himelinck (West Lafayette: 1965), pp. 68, 207.

476. Giovanni Vidari, *Il Pensiero pedagogico italiano nel suo sviluppo storico* (Paravia: 1924, 2nd ed.). August Buck, *"Die 'studia humanitatis' und ihre Methode." Die humanistische Tradition in der Romania*. (Bad Homburg: 1968), pp. 133–150.

477. Hans Baron, *The Crisis of the Early Italian Renaissance*, II, p. 435.

478. Anibale Romei, *Della precedenza dell'Arme o delle Lettere. Discorsi* . . . (Ferrara: 1586), pp. 196–215.

479. R. J. Clements, "Pen and Sword in Renaissance Emblem Literature." *Modern Language Quarterly*, V (1944), 131–141.

480. Erasmus, *Opus Epistolarum*, VIII, p. 24.

481. Walter Rüegg, I, *Die vergnügliche Familie der Bücher*, II, *Die gespenstliche Welt der Väter. Geistige Väter des Abendlandes*. Hrsg. von G. Finsteren Stüber (Stuttgart: 1960), p. XVI. Berthold L. Ullman and Philip A. Stadter, *The Public Library of Renaissance. Florence* . . . (Padova: 1972).

482. Frances Yates, *The French Academies of the Sixteenth Century* (London: 1947).

483. Etienne Dolet, *Préfaces françaises* . . . , pp. 54, 57.

484. Henri Estienne, *Apologie pour Herodote*. Ed. P. Ristelhuber (1566. Paris: 1879), I, p. 35.

485. *Ibid.*, *L'Art de faire les Devises* (Paris: 1645), p. 14.

486. Cf. Albert Flocon, *L'Univers des livres* (Paris: 1961), p. 288. Sebastian Brandt, *Das Narrenschiff*. Hrsg. von Friedrich Zarncke (1497. Leipzig: 1854), pp. 8–10.

487. Bernard Weinberg, *ibid.*, II, p. 859.

488. Leon Battista Alberti, *Opere volgari*, II, *Rime e trattati morali*. A cura di Cecil Grayson (Bari: 1966), p. 55.

489. Cf. Jean Jehasse, *ibid.*, p. 322.

490. *Ibid.*, p. 42.

491. Giovanni Boccaccio, *Genealogia deorum gentilium. Opere in versi. . . . Prose latine . . .* A cura di Pier Giorgio Ricci (Milano-Napoli: 1966), p. 895.

492. Leon Battista Alberti, *ibid.*, pp. 32–36, 140–142.

493. Cf. Joël Lefebvre, "*Le poète, la poésie et la poétique. Éléments pour une définition et une datation de l'humanisme allemand.*" *L'Humanisme allemand 1450–1540. Actes du XVIIIe Colloque International de Tours* (München und Paris: 1979), p. 288.

494. Robert J. Clements, "Condemnation of the Poetic Profession in Renaissance Emblem Literature." *Studies in Philology*, 43 (1946), 213–232. M. T. Jones-Davies, *Victimes et rebelles: L'écrivain dans la société élisabéthaine* (Paris: 1980), pp. 36, 54, 57, 106.

495. Henri Estienne, *Artis Typographicae Querimonia* (1560. Fr. translation: *Plainte de la typographie . . .* , pp. 6–7.

496. Dolf Sternberger, *Über die Verbindlichkeit des Schrifttums* (Frankfurt/M: 1954), p. 97.

497. Rudolf Hirsch, *ibid.*, pp. 46, 48. cf. Jean Jehasse, *ibid.*, p. 268.

498. Pietro Aretino, *Tutte le opere. Lettere*, p. 306.

499. Christian Bec, *Les marchands écrivains . . .* , p. 387.

500. Cf. Albert Cim, *Le Livre* (Paris: 1905), I, p. 111.

501. A. F. Doni, *I Marmi* (Vinegia: 1552), p. 150.

502. Rudolf Blum, *Vor und Frühgeschichte . . .* , II, pp. 237, 239. Jean

Vial, "Formules publicitaires dans les premiers livres français." *Gutenberg-Jahrbuch*, 33 (1958), 149–154.

503. Rudolf Hirsch, *Printing, Selling and Reading*, p. 83.

504. Elisabeth L. Eisenstein, *The Printing Press* . . . , I, p. 121. Annie Parent, *Les métiers du livre à Paris, 1435–1560* (Genève-Paris: 1974), pp. 103, 116. Glauco Sanga, *"Modi di produzione e forme di tradizione: dall' oralità feudale alla scrittura capitalistica." Oralità e scrittura nel sistema letterario*, pp. 31–48.

505. Al. Piru, *Istoria literaturii române de la origini pînă la 1830* (Bucureşti: Editura ştiinţifică şi enciclopedică, 1977), p. 70.

506. Pico della Mirandola, *De dignitate hominis. L'Humanesimo.* A cura di E. Garin (Firenze: 1958), pp. 141, 151.

507. Erasmus, *Opus Epistolarum*, II, pp. 492–493; VI, p. 51; IX, p. 233.

508. Jacob Burckhardt, *Kultur und Kunst der Renaissance in Italien*. Ungekürzte Textausgaben (1860. Berlin: Deutsche Buch-Gemeinschaft G.M.b., 1936), p. 140.

509. N. Herman-Mascard, *La censure des livres à Paris à la fin de l'Ancien Régime* (Paris: 1968), p. 5.

510. Adrian Marino, *"Erasmus, critic al 'armelor'." Secolul 20*, (1966), 11, 155–162.

511. A text very seldom quoted: Guy de Brues, *Les Dialogues contre les nouveaux académiciens* (Paris: 1557). Ed. P. P. Mophos (Baltimore: 1953), p. III.

512. Henri Estienne, *ibid.*, p. 177.

513. Cf. Joël Saugnieux, *Cultures populaires et cultures savantes en Espagne du Moyen âge aux Lumières*, (Paris: C.N.R.S., 1982), pp. 59ff.

514. For example, John Colet, *Opera*. With a translation, introduction, and notes by J. H. Lupton (London: 1873), I, p. 32.

515. Fr. Heinrich Reusch, *Die "Indices librorum Prohibitorum" des sechzehnten Jahrhunderts*. Gesammelt und herausgegeben . . . (Tübingen: 1886), I, pp. 123, 260, 495. John Lough, *ibid.*, p. 40.

516. Leon Battista Alberti, *Opere volgari. Rime e trattati morali*, I, p. CXXV.

517. Curt F. Bühler, *The Fifteenth Century Book. The Scribes, The Printers, The Decorators* (1960. Philadelphia: University of Pennsylvania

Press, 1961), p. 17. S. F. Steinberg, *Five Hundred Years of Printing* (London: A Pelican Book, 1955), p. 54.

518. Alfred Gudeman, *Grundriss der Geschichte der klassischen Philologie* (Leipzig und Berlin: 1909), pp. 188, 189.

519. Clément Marot, *Oeuvres complètes*, IV, p. 190.

520. Erasmus, *Opus Epistolarum*, II, p. 489. *Opera Omnia*, IX, c. 1699.

521. Claudio Tolomei, *Delle lettere* (Vinegia: 1547), p. 35.

522. Joannis Sturmi (Sturmius), *Nobilitas Literata liber Unus* (1547). *Institutionis literae* (Toruni Bonussorum: 1586), I, pp. 301–354.

523. Francesco Tateo, *"Sulla formazione del canone degli scrittori nella scuola umanistica," Il "Minore" nella storiografia letteraria.* Convegno internazionale Roma, 10–12 marzo 1983, a cura di Enzo Esposito (Ravenna, 1984), pp. 203–217. Fritz Nies, *Genres mineurs. Texte zur Theorie und Geschichte nicht-kanonischen Literatur (von 16. Jahrhundert bis zum Gegenwart)*, (München: 1978), p. 20.

524. Ruggiero Romano et Alberto Tenenti, *"L'Intellectuel dans la société italienne des XVe et XVIe siècles." Niveaux de culture et groupes sociaux* (Paris-La Haye: 1967), p. 61.

525. Leon Battista Alberti, *ibid.*, II, p. 56.

526. John William Adamson, *The Illiterate Anglo-Saxon* (Cambridge: 1946), p. 41.

527. Plutarque, *Les oeuvres morales et meslées* . . . , p. 666 v.

528. Dante Alighieri, *Paradiso*, XII, *Tutte le opere*, p. 287.

529. Peter Burke, *Popular Culture* . . . , pp. 24–29, 58, 270. William Beik, "Popular Culture and Elite Repression in Early Modern Europe." *Journal of Interdisciplinary History*, XI (1980), 98–99; Joël Saugnieux, *Cultures populaires* . . . , *passim*.

530. Giorgio Voigt, *Il risorgimento dell'antichità classica*. Tr. italiana D. Valbuso (Firenze: Sansoni, 1888), II, pp. 400–404.

531. Cf. Marjorie Donker and George M. Muldrow, *Dictionary of Literary-Rhetorical Conventions of the English Renaissance* (Westport-London: 1982), p. 248.

532. Benedetto Croce, *La poesia popolare e la poesia d'arte* (Bari: Laterza, 1933, p. 25.

533. Among others: Marques de Santillana, *Proemio al Condestable de Portugal* (Madrid: B.A.E., 1870), 62, p. 12.

534. Cf. John Link, *ibid.*, p. 70.

535. D. Murăraşu, *La poésie néolatine* . . . , passim. Günter E. Grimm, *Literatur und Gelehrtum in Deutschland* . . . (Tübingen: Max Niemeyer Verlag, 1983), pp. 80, 99ff.

536. August Buck, *"Der Begriff der 'poeta eruditus' in der Dichtungstheorie der italienischen Renaissance." Die humanistische Tradition in der Romania* (Homburg v.d. H.-Berlin-Zürich, 1968), pp. 227–243.

537. Ulrich von Hutten, *Epistolae obscurorum virorum*, I, 5, 3.

538. Joachim du Bellay, *La Défense et Illustration de la langue française.* Nouvelle édition revue et annotée par Louis Humbert (1549. Paris: Garnier, 1948), p. 8.

539. Etienne Dolet, *Préfaces françaises*, p. 68.

540. Frances D. Yates, *The Art of Memory* (London and Henley: 1966).

541. Ulrich von Hutten, *Epistolae obscurorum virorum*, I, 7, 28.

542. Cf. Gyula Alpár, *Streit der Alten und Modernen in der Deutschen Literatur bis um 1750* (Pécs: 1939), p. 18.

543. Albert-Marie Schmidt, *La poésie scientifique en France au XVIᵉ siècle* (Lausanne: Editions Rencontre, 1970), pp. 15, 28, 93, 103, 189.

544. Gabriele Zinano, *Il sogno, overo della poesia* (1590). *Tratatti* . . . , II, p. 672.

545. Terence Cave, *The Cornucopian Text*, p. 181. Raoul Morçay, *La Renaissance* (Paris: 1934), II, p. 59. Peter W. Hurst, "The Encyclopaedic Tradition. The cosmological epic and the validation of the medieval romance." *Comparative criticism* (1979), I, 55–71.

546. Terence Cave, *ibid.*, pp. 10–14, 70–71. Marjorie Donker and George M. Muldrow, *ibid.*, pp. 58–60.

547. Dan-Horia Mazilu, *Proza oratorică în literatura română veche* . . . , I, pp. 106, 109.

548. The term is expressly used by Boccaccio, *La Teseide*, XII, 86.

549. Joël Blanchard, *"Compilation et légitimation au XVᵉ siècle." Poétique* (1988), 74, 139–158.

550. *Crestomaţie* . . . , I, p. 111. Ion-Radu Mircea, *"Florilegii din gînd-*

irea antică în manuscrise slavo-române." *Revista de istorie şi teorie literară* (1982), 2, 164–170.

551. Lee A. Sonnino, *A Handbook to the Sixteenth Century Rhetoric* (London: 1968), pp. 2–3.

552. Michael Metschies, *Zitat und Ziterkunst in Montaignes "Essais"* (Genève-Paris: 1966). Bernard Beugnot, *"Un aspect textuel de la réception critique: la citation"* Oeuvres et critiques (1976), I, 2, 8.

553. (Henri Estienne), *Centonum et Parodiarum exempla ab . . . selecta et illustrata* (Genevae: 1575), pp. 3–4.

554. Cf. Al. Piru, *Istoria literaturii române*, p. 30.

555. Pierre Galand, *"Ange Politien et l'équivoque intertextuelle, Nutricia, v. 34–138."* Poétique (1989), 77, 35–51.

556. Jean Bodin, *Oeuvres philosophiques*, I, pp. 207, 273.

557. F. Robortello, *Explicationes de satyra, de epigrammata, de comedia, de elegia.* Trattati . . . , I, p. 509. J. C. Scaliger, *Poetices libri septem* (1561), I, 56.

558. Richard (George?) Puttenham, *The Art of English Poesie* (1589), I, ch. 30. *Ancient Critical Essays* . . . , II, pp. 60–61.

559. Ronsard, *Abrégé de l'art poétique français* (1565). *Oeuvres complètes*, XIV, p. 6.

560. Harold Ogden White, *Plagiarism and Imitation During the English Renaissance. A Study in Critical Distinctions* (Cambridge: Harvard University Press, 1935). Ferruccio Ulivi, *L'Imitazione nella poetica del Rinascimento* (Milano: Marzorati, 1959). Erich Welslau, *Imitation und Plagiat in der französischen Literatur von der Renaissance bis zur Revolution* (Schäuble Verlag: 1976).

561. Cf. Fritz Nies, *Genres mineurs*, p. 109.

562. Cf. M. T. Jones-Davies, *Victimes et rebelles*, p. 69. Erich Welslau, *ibid.*, p. 99.

563. F. W. Genthe, *Geschichte der macaronischen Poesie und Sammlung ihrer vorzüglichsten Denkmäle* (Halle und Leipzig: 1829).

564. (Henri Estienne), *ibid.*, pp. 132, 133.

565. J. C. Scaliger, *ibid.*, I, 42, p. 114.

566. Raymond Lebègue, *"Rabelais et la parodie."* Mélanges Augustin Renaudet (Genève: Droz, 1952), pp. 193–204.

567. Walter L. Bullock, "The Precept of Plagiarism in the Cinquecento." *Modern Philology*, XXV (1927–1928), 301, 310, 312. Harold Ogden White, *ibid.*

568. Joachim du Bellay, *Défense et Illustration* . . . , I, 8; cf. also Fr. Duarenus, *De Plagiariis et Scriptorum Compilationibus* (Francofortis: 1592).

569. George Haven Putnam, A. M., *Books and Their Makers During the Middle Ages* (New York-London: 1897), II, pp. 343–416. Erich Welslau, *ibid.*, pp. 135, 137–139, 173.

570. Augustin-Charles Renouard, *Traité des droits d'auteurs dans la littérature, la science et les beaux-arts* (Paris: 1838), I, p. 42.

571. Geoffroy Tory, *Champs Fleury ou l'Art et Science de la Proportion des Lettres* (1592. Ed. Gustave Cohen, Paris: 1931).

572. Gilles Corozet, *Les Blasons domestiques* (1539. Nouvelle édition, Paulin Paris: 1865), pp. 33–35.

573. Samuel Daniel's *Musophilus: Containing a General Defense of All Learning* (1599. Ed. by Raymond Himelinck (West Lafayette, Indiana, 1965), pp. 67–68.

574. A. S. Osley, *Scribes and Sources. Handbook of the Chancery Hand in the Sixteenth Century* (London-Boston: Faber and Faber, 1980), pp. 233–237.

575. Robert J. Clements, *Picta Poesis*, pp. 33, 36, 47, 61ff., 85.

576. Walter von Wartburg, *ibid.*, V, p. 244. Edmond Hugnet, *ibid.*, 4, p. 790.

577. *Deutsches Fremdwörterbuch* (Berlin: 1942), II, p. 18.

578. G. Budaeo, *De Studio litterarum recte de commode instituendo* (Parisii: 1532), p. XIX v.

579. *Ibid.*, *De Philologia. Libri II* (Parisii: 1532), p. XXXV v.

580. Gulielmus Budaeus, *De Philologia. De Studio litterarum (recte et commode instituendo)*. Faksimile Neudruck der Ausgabe von Paris 1532, mit einer Einleitung von August Buck (Stuttgart-Bad Cannstatt: 1964), I, p. XXV v.

581. *Deutsche Wortgeschichte*, I, p. 408.

582. A. Delboulle, *"Historique de trois mots: Pindariser, Philologia et Sycophante."* *Revue d'Histoire littéraire de la France*, IV (1895), 285–286.

583. L. Valla, *Elegantiarum Linguae Latinae*, p. 184.

584. Raymond Williams, *Keywords. A Vocabulary of Culture and Society* (New York: Oxford University Press, 1976), p. 151.

585. Cristóbal de Villalón, *Ingeniosa comparación entre lo antiguo y lo presente* (1539. Madrid: La Sociedad de bibliófilos españoles, 1898), p. 164.

586. Cf. Pierre Villey, *Les sources italiennes de la "Défense et illustration de la langue française" de Joachim du Bellay* (Paris: 1908), pp. 92–93.

587. Remigio Sabbadini, *Storia e critica di testi latini* (Catania: 1914), pp. 35, 41–42, 47, 56. E. J. Kenney, "The Character of Humanist Philology." *Classical Influence on European Culture. A.D. 500–1500.* Ed. by R. R. Bolgar (Cambridge: 1971), pp. 123–125.

588. J. C. Scaliger, *Poetices libri septem* (Genevra: 1561), 1. V.

589. J. L. Vives, *De Disciplinis* (1531), 1, II, c. VI. *Opera Omnia* (Valentiae Edentanorum: 1755), II, pp. 373ff.

590. Silvia Rizzo, *Il lessico filologico degli umanisti,* pp. 209–213, 246, 249, 255. Antonio Bernardini e Gaetano Righi, *Il Concetto di filologia e di cultura classica nel moderno pensiero europeo* (Bari: 1953, 2nd ed.), pp. 46–47.

591. Jean Jehasse, *ibid.,* p. 309; for the entire problem, also see René Wellek, "Term and Concept of Literary Criticism." *Concepts of Criticism.* Ed. and with an introduction by Stephen P. Nichols, Jr. (1963. New Haven and London: Yale University Press, 1965), pp. 23–24, 26.

592. (Francisco Martinez), *Grammaticae artis integra institutio. Ejusdem de grammatica professione declamatio.* (Salamanca: 1575): "*Grammatica finis emendatio oratio*" (p. 1).

593. Aldo Scaglione, "The Humanist as Scholar and Politian's Conception of 'Grammaticus'." *Studies in the Renaissance,* VIII (1961), 49–70.

594. J. L. Vives, *ibid.,* 1. II, c. 1.I, p. 400.

595. Tomasso Garzoni, *La Piazza universale . . . ,* pp. 92, 467–474.

596. J. L. Vives, *De causis corruptarum artium,* 1. II, c. IV. *Opera Omnia,* VI, p. 93.

597. *Ibid.,* VI, p. 78. Curio Lancillotto Pasio, *De litteratura non vulgari,* f. V r.

598. Silvia Rizzo, *ibid.,* pp. 96–98.

599. L. Valla, *ibid.,* IV, CXX, pp. 305–306.

600. *Der Kommentar in der Renaissance.* Herausgegeben von August Buck und Otto Herding (Bonn-Bad Godesberg: 1973), pp. 7–19.

601. Peter M. Schon, *Vorformen des Essays in Antike und Humanismus. Ein Beitrag zur Entstehungsgeschichte des Essais von Montaigne* (Wiesbaden: 1954).

602. Cf. Eugenio Garin, *Geschichte und Dokumente der abendländische Pädagogik* (Reinbeck bei Hamburg: Rowohlt, 1967), III, p. 85.

603. Mathias Flacius Illyricus, *Clavis Scripturae S. seu de Sermone Sacrarum literarum* (Basileae: 1567), pp. 1–6.

604. Clément Marot, *Oeuvres complètes,* IV, p. 184. Boccaccio, *De genealogia deorum gentilium,* I, 3.

605. B. Weinberg, *A History of the Literary Criticism in the Italian Renaissance,* II, p. 854.

606. François Cornillat, *"Le commentaire a-t-il horreur du vide? L'attribution du sens chez Barthélemy Aneau." Poétique* (1989), 77, 17–34.

607. Robert Klein, "La Théorie de l'expression figurée dans les traités italiens sur les 'Imprese', 1555–1562." *Bibliothèque d'Humanisme et Renaissance,* XIX (1957), pp. 320–341.

608. Richard de Bury, *Philobiblion,* ch. XII.

609. L. G. Gyraldi, *Progimnasmo* . . . , p. 155.

610. J. C. Scaliger, *ibid.,* I, 1, p. 3.

611. Cf. August Buck, *Die humanistische Tradition in der Romania,* pp. 131–137.

612. B. Hauréau, *Notices et extraits de quelques manuscrits latins de la Bibliothèque Nationale* (Paris: 1890), I, p. 300.

613. Antonio Bernardini e Gaetano Righi, *ibid.,* pp. 40, 42. Jean Jehasse, *ibid.,* p. 140.

614. Pedro de Navarra, *Diálogo de la differencia del Hablar al Escrivir* (1560. Ed. D. O. Chambers: 1968), p. 14.

615. Peter Ramus, *Scholae in liberales artes* (Basileae: 1569), c. 238, 255. Petrarca, *De studi eloquentiae, Fam.,* I, 9.

616. Aurelio Brandolino Agostiano, *De ratione scribendi* (Basileae: 1549), p. 15.

617. Erasmus, *Opus Epistolarum,* III, p. 384. J. L. Vives, *ibid.,* II, p. 388.

618. Jehan Molinetti, Ernest Langlois, *De artibus Rhetoricae Rhythmicae* (Paris: 1890), pp. 55, 56.

619. Aldo Scaglione, *The Classical Theory of Composition. From Its Origins to the Present. A Historical Survey* (Chapel Hill: 1972), p. 2. William J. Kennedy, *Rhetorical Norms in Renaissance Literature* (New Haven and London: 1978).

620. Mircea Frînculescu, *"Primele noțiuni de artă retorică în cultura română,"* 282–289.

621. Francesco Patrizio, *Della Poetica. La Deca disputata* (Ferrara: 1586), p. 213.

622. Enrique de Villena. Marcelino Menendez Pelayo, *Historia de las ideas estéticas en España* (1940. Tercera Edición. Madrid: Consejo superior de investigaciones científicas: 1962), I, Apendice I, pp. 482–487.

623. Bernard Weinberg, *ibid.*, I, pp. 1–37, 41.

624. J. C. Scaliger, *ibid.*, VII, 2, 1.

625. Francesco Robortello, *Paraphrasis in librum Horatii qui Vulgo de Arte Poetica ad Pisones inscribitur* (Florentiae: 1548).

626. Aurel Sasu, *Retorica literară românească* (București: Minerva, 1976), pp. 75, 82–83. Dan-Horia Mazilu, *Proza oratorică*, I, pp. 138, 141.

627. G. Trissino, *Trattati . . .* , I, p. 30.

628. Gilbert Ouy, *"Le thème du 'Taedium Scriptorum Gentilium' chez les humanistes, particulièrement en France au début du XVᵉ siècle."* *Cahiers de l'Association Internationale des études françaises* (1971), 23, 9–26.

629. J. L. Vives, *De tradendis disciplinis*, I, VI.

630. Erasmus, *Opus Epistolarum*, I, p. 375; IV, pp. 542, 594; VI, pp. 51, 163, 321, 323.

631. Robert J. Clements, *Picta Poesis*, p. 71.

632. Cf. Roger Caillois, *Au coeur du fantastique* (Paris: Gallimard, 1965), p. 70.

633. Nicolas de Cusa, *De Docta Ignorantia* (1440. Tr. fr. Paris: Alcan, 1930), I, § 1, pp. 36–38, 104.

634. Le *"De Ignota Litteratura"* de Jean Wenck de Harenberg. *Contre Nicolas de Cuse*. Texte inédit et étude par E. Vansteenberghe (München: 1910), p. 8.

635. Erasmus, *Opera Omnia*, IX, c. 1696.

636. Sander L. Gilman, *The Parodic Sermon in European Perspective. Aspects of Liturgical Parody from the Middle Ages to the Twentieth Century* (Wiesbaden: 1974), p. 47. E. Vaucheret, *"Références au sacré dans les farces des XVe et XVIe siècles."* Romania (1979), 100, 223–256.

637. Henri Cornelius Agrippa, *Déclamation sur l'incertitude, vanité et abus des sciences*, III (Tr. en français du latin, Paris: 1582), pp. 30, 35.

638. Pietro Aretino, *Tutte le opere. Lettere. Il primo e il secondo libro.* A cura di Francesco Flora (Milano: Mondadori, 1960), pp. 124, 224.

639. Joachim du Bellay, *Poésies françaises et latines.* Avec notice et notes par E. Courbet (Paris: Garnier, 1918), II, pp. 171–172.

640. Francesco Berni, *Poesie e prose*, criticamente curate da E. Chiorboli (Genève-Firenze: 1934), pp. 267–289.

641. Jean Bodin, *Oeuvres Philosophiques*, I, pp. 189, 270.

642. Rabelais, *De la volupté.* Ed. Jacques Saint Germain (Paris: 1949), p. LXV.

643. Robert Elbrodt, *L'Inspiration personnelle et l'esprit du temps chez les poètes métaphysiques anglais* (Paris: 1960), p. 96.

644. Robert J. Clements, *ibid.*, Studies in Philology (1946), 43, 213–232.

645. Adelio Noferi, *"Caos, simulazione e scrittura nella teoria bruniana dell'imaginazione."* Letteratura e critica, I, 378.

646. On the "vanities" and perils of study and learning: Francis Bacon, *The Advancement of Learning and New Atlantis.* With a preface by Thomas Case (London: Oxford University Press, 1960), I, IV, 2, p. 28.

647. Sebastian Brandt, *Das Narrenschiff*, pp. 4–5, 29–30, 76–77.

648. Cf. Walter J. Ong, *Orality and Literacy. The Technologizing of the World* (London and New York: Methuen, 1982), p. 81. Robert J. Clements, *Picta Poesis*, p. 223.

649. Hans Blumenberg, *Die Lesbarkeit der Welt*, pp. 59, 64, 72. André Lefevere, *Literacy Knowledge* (Assen-Amsterdam: 1977), p. 107.

650. Thomas Frognall Dibdin, *Bibliomania, or Book Madness. A Bibliographical Romance* (1809, London: 1842), p. 651.

651. Juan Luis Vives, *De disciplinis. Obras completas* (Madrid: 1948), I, 1.I, c. X, II, pp. 392–393.

652. Cf. Giuseppina Fumagalli, *Leonardo omo senza lettere* (Firenze: 1952), p. 38.

653. Cf. Giacinto Margiotta, *Le origini italiane de la Querelle des anciens et des modernes*, pp. 40–41.

654. Cf. Paul Zumthor, *Le Masque et la Lumière* (Paris: Seuil, 1978), p. 68. Lionello Sozzi, "Parole come cose: Sartre e l'autonomia delle scritture." *Sigma* (1985), 1, 56, 58.

655. Bernardo Tasso, *Delle Lettere* (Vinegia: 1569), *Al reverendiss. et illustriss. Monsignor d'Ares.*

656. Agrippa D'Aubigné, *Les Tragiques. Aux Lecteurs. Oeuvres.* Ed. H. Weber (Paris: 1969), p. 3.

657. Lodovico Castelvetro, *Poetica d'Aristotele volgarizzata et sposta* (1570. Basel: 1576), p. 29.

658. Ion Iliescu, *Geneza ideilor estetice în cultura românească* (Timişoara: Facla, 1972), p. 36.

659. Raoul Morçay, *ibid.*, I, p. 189.

660. Bernardo Tasso, *ibid.*, p. 38. Pietro Aretino, *ibid.*, p. 192.

661. cf. Giuseppina Fumagalli, *ibid.*, p. 38.

662. cf. Werner Forrest Patterson, *Three Centuries of French Poetic Theory. A Critical History of the Chief Arts of Poetry in France* (1328–1630). (Ann Arbor: University of Michigan Press, 1935), I, p. 822.

663. Giordano Bruno, *De gli eroici furori. Dialogo*, I, *Opere* (Milano-Napoli: 1956), p. 573.

664. Robert Elbrodt, *L'inspiration personnelle et l'esprit du temps chez les poètes métaphysiques anglais*, p. 368. Hanna H. Gray, "Renaissance Humanism: The Pursuit of Eloquence." *Journal of the History of Ideas*, XXIV (1963), 503.

665. Henri Estienne, *Projet du livre intitulé de la precellence du langage français* (1579, Ed. L. Humbert. Paris: Garnier), p. 139. Sir Philip Sidney, *ibid.*, pp. 57, 58.

666. Christian Bec, *ibid.*, pp. 16–18, 54–55, 175, 178.

667. Cf. Pierre Voltz, *La Comédie* (Paris: A. Colin, 1964), p. 198.

668. Cf. Hubert Gillot, *La Querelle des anciens et des modernes* (Paris: Champion, 1914), p. 352.

669. Louis Le Roy, *De la vicissitude ou vanité des choses de l'univers*
..., p. 250.

670. A. F. Doni, *I Marmi*, p. 162.

671. Pietro Aretino, *Tutte le opere. Le Lettere*, pp. 193, 207, 716.

672. V. L. Saulnier, *"Le silence de Rabelais et le mythe des paroles gelées.
François Rabelais"* (Genève-Lille: 1953), pp. 241–246. Jerrold E.
Seigel, *Rhetoric and Philosophy in Renaissance Humanism. The Union of Eloquence
and Wisdom* (Princeton: 1968), pp. 43, 45.

CLASSICISM AND THE BAROQUE

1. Francisco Cascales, *Cartas filológicas*, III, 3 (1634. Ed. Justo García
Soriano. Madrid: 1954–1969), III, p. 5.

2. Gerardus Joannis Vossius, *De Philologia liber* (Amstelodami: 1650),
p. 24. Johann Friedrich Alsted, *Encyclopaedia* . . . (Herborn: 1630), I,
p. 265.

3. G. J. Vossius, *De arte grammatica* (Amstelodami: 1635), p. 2. Gregorio de Andres, *El Maestro Baltasar de Céspedes* . . . *y su Discurso de las letras
humanas* . . . , *Estudio biográfico y edición crítica* (*El Escorial:* 1965), pp. 170,
211, etc.

4. One example: Gerardus Joannis Vossius, *Aristarchus sive De arte
Grammaticae*, I, 3, (Amstelodami: 1695), p. 4.

5. G. A. Padley, *Grammatical Theory in Western Europe. 1500–1700.*
(Cambridge: 1976), p. 155.

6. Du Cange, *Glossarium Mediae et Infimae Latinitas* (1678. Niort:
1885), V, p. 127. Antoine Furetière, *Dictionnaire universel* . . . (1691. La
Haye et Rotterdam: 1694), II, *s.v.*

7. Alessandro Tassoni, *Varietà di pensieri*, VII, 2 (Modena: 1612),
p. 321.

8. G. Naudé, *Advis pour dresser une bibliothèque* (Paris: 1627), p. 23.

9. Ulrich Ricken, *"Gelehrter" und "Wissenschaft" im Französischen.
Beiträge zu ihrer Bezeichnungsgeschichte von 12–17. Jahrhundert* (Berlin:
1961).

10. Walter von Wartburg, *Französisches Etymologisches Wörterbuch*
(Basel: 1920), V, pp. 379, 380. E. Littré, *Dictionnaire de la langue française*
(Paris: 1863), II, p. 283.

11. Antoine Furetière, *ibid.*, II, *s.v.*, p. 17. *Le dictionnaire de l'Académie Française* (Paris: 1694), I, p. 640. Du Cange, *ibid.*, IV, p. 127.

12. Gerardus Joannis Vossius, *De Philologia*, p. 24.

13. Gui Patin, *Lettres*. Ed. J.-H. Réveillé-Parise (Paris: 1846), III, p. 178.

14. D. G. Morhof (Danielis Georgii Morhofii), *Polyhistor, sive de Notitia auctorum et rerum commentarii* (Lubecae: 1688), II, p. 219.

15. Cf. Josef Niedermann, *Kultur: Werden und Wandlungen des Begriffs und seiner Ersatzbegriffe von Cicero bis Herder* (Firenze: Bibliopolis, 1941), pp. 107, 111, 118, 124.

16. I. Pierio Valeriano (I. P. Valeriani Bellunensis), *De litteratorum infelicitate* (Venetia: 1620), p. 82.

17. Philippe Beneton, *Histoire de mots. Culture et civilisation* (Paris: 1975), pp. 24–25.

18. An accurate gloss: cf. Ewald Flügel, "Bacon's Historia Literaria." *Anglia*, XXI, B. IX (1899), 288.

19. A little-known example: Juan de Robles, *Primera parte del culto sevillano* (1631. Sevilla: Sociedad de bibliófilos andaluces, XIV, 1883), pp. 10, 34.

20. Cf. Joseph Niedermann, *ibid.*, p. 178. Franz Rauhut, "Die Herkunft der Worte und Begriffe 'Kultur', 'Civilisation' und 'Bildung'." *Germanisch-Romanische Monatschrift*, XXXIV (1953), 82–83.

21. Baltasar Gracián, *Oráculo Manual*, § 22. Edición, introducción y notas de E. Correa Calderón (1647. Madrid: Anaya, 1968), p. 62. *Agudeza y arte de ingenio*, IX. Edición, introducción y notas de Evaristo Correa Calderón (1642–1648. Madrid: Editorial Castalia, 1969), II, p. 221.

22. La Mothe Le Vayer, *Observations diverses sur la composition et sur la lecture des livres* (Paris: 1668), p. 152. Charles Sorel, *De la connaissance des bons livres ou examen de plusieurs auteurs* (Paris: 1671), p. 337.

23. Pierre Bayle, *Dictionnaire historique et critique* (1697. Amsterdam-Leiden-La Haye-Utrecht: 1740), I, p. 66.

24. Chapelain, *Mélanges de littérature, tirez des lettres manuscrits* (Paris: 1726), p. 216.

25. Saint-Évremont, *Oeuvres* (Amsterdam: 1739), VI, p. CXLIII.

26. English domain: *Oxford English Dictionary* (Oxford: 1933), VI, p. 342.

27. Du Cange, *ibid.*, V, p. 127.

28. Antoine Furetière, *ibid.*, II, *s.v.*

29. P. Philibert Monet, *Inventaire de deux langues, française et latine* . . . (Lyon: 1635), pp. 427, 504. Adam Littleton, *Linguae latinae liber dictionarius quadripartibus. A Latine Dictionary in Four Parts* (London: 1678), *s.v.*

30. Jean-Claude Chevalier, "La pédagogie des collèges jésuites." *Littérature* (1972), 71, 120–128.

31. A few indications in Dan Simonescu, "Idei despre educaţie în literatura română." *Contribuţii* (Bucureşti: Eminescu, 1984), pp. 5–20.

32. *Crestomaţie de literatură română veche.* Coordonatori: I. C. Chiţimia şi Stela Toma (Cluj-Napoca: Dacia, 1984), I, p. 165 (1989), II, pp. 34, 189.

33. Ole Worm (Olaus Wormius) ᚱᚤᛉᛣᛒ *seu Danica Literatura antiquissima vulgo gothica dicta* (Hafniae: 1636), pp. 1, 37, 55, 65, etc.

34. D. Ge. Schubart, *Litteraturae apud Germanos primordiis* . . . (23 apr. 1679). *Miscellanea Lipsiensia* (1717), V, p. 42.

35. Gerardus Joannis Vossius, *Etymologicon linguae latinae* (Lugduni: 1664), p. 292.

36. Louis Ferrand, *Réflexions sur la religion chrétienne* (Paris: 1679), II, p. 256.

37. Hermannus Hugo, *De prima scribendi origine et universa rei litterariae antiquitate*, c. XXXI (Antverpiae: 1697), pp. 185–199.

38. Giovanni Pozzi, *La parola dipinta* (Milano: 1981), p. 239.

39. Du Cange, *ibid.*, V, p. 127.

40. Pierre Borel, *Trésor de recherches et antiquitez gauloises et françaises* (Paris: 1655), p. 303.

41. Rudolf Blum, "*Vor-und Frühgeschichte der nationalen Allgemeinbibliographie.*" *Archiv für Geschichte des Buchwesens*, II (1958), 245.

42. Guillaume Colletet, *L'art poétique* . . . (Paris: 1658. Slatkine Reprints, 1970), p. 22.

43. Justus Lipsius (Justi Lipsii), *Opere Omnia* (Antverpiae: 1637), II, p. 533.

44. Antoine Furetière, *ibid.*, *s.v.* Du Cange, *ibid.*, V, p. 127. *Dictionnaire de l'Académie Française*, p. 639.

45. Hermannus Hugo, *ibid.*, p. 203. Alain Viala, *Naissance de l'écrivain: sociologie de la littérature à l'âge classique* (Paris: Les Editions de Minuit, 1985), pp. 276–277.

46. Madeleine V.-David, *Le débat sur les écritures et l'hiéroglyphe aux XVIIe et XVIIIe siècles* . . . (Paris: 1965), pp. 13, 65.

47. Elisabeth Cook, "Figured Poetry." *Journal of Warburg and Courtauld Institutes* 42 (1979), 1–15, especially p. 112. Peter Daly, *Literature in the Light of the Emblem. Structural Parallels Between the Emblem and Literature in the Sixteenth and Seventeenth Centuries* (Toronto, Buffalo, London: 1979), passim.

48. Rosemary Freeman, *English Emblem Books* (1948. London: 1967), pp. 14–18.

49. Cesare Ripa, *Introduction à l'Iconologie.* Traduction et présentation de H. Damisch. *Critique,* XXIX (1973), 801–819.

50. Henri Etienne, *L'Art de faire des devises* (Paris: 1645), pp. 30–31.

51. (P. Bouhours), *Les Entretiens d'Ariste et d'Eugène,* VI, *Des Devises* (Paris: 1661), pp. 258–445.

52. C. A. Du Fresnoy, *De arte graphica* . . . , II, 1–16 (Lutetiae Parisiorum: 1688).

53. Gerardus J. Vossius, *De Quatuor Artibus popularibus* . . . (Amstelaedam: 1650), pp. 62–94.

54. Peter M. Daly, *ibid.*, pp. 6–8.

55. Antoine Furetière, *ibid.*, art. *Auteur.* P. Richelet, *ibid.*, I, p. 266.

56. Varlaam, *Opere. Răspunsul împotriva catihismului calvinesc* Ed. critică, studiu filologic şi studiu lingvistic de Mirela Teodorescu (Bucureşti: Minerva, 1984), pp. 36, 145.

57. *Crestomaţie de literatură română veche,* I, p. 181, II, p. 182.

58. Miron Costin, *Opere.* Ed. P. P. Panaitescu (Bucureşti: Editura pentru literatură, 1966), II, pp. 10, 12.

59. *Ibid.,* I, p. 3.

60. L. Volovici, *Apariţia scriitorului în cultura românească* (Iaşi: Junimea, 1976), pp. 11–21.

61. Cf. Alexandru Duţu, *Coordonate ale culturii româneşti în secolul XVIII* (Bucureşti: Editura pentru literatură, 1968), p. 32.

62. Antoine Furetière, *ibid.*, art. *Orateur, s.v.*

63. Charles Sorel, *De la connaissance des bons livres ou examen de plusieurs auteurs* (Paris: 1671), p. 291.

64. Nicole Gueunier, *"Pour une définition du conte."* *Roman et lumières au 18ᵉ siècle*, (Paris: Editions Sociales, 1971), p. 424.

65. Blaise de Vigenere, *Traité des chiffres ou secrètes manières d'escrire* (Paris: 1587), p. 2.

66. Baltasar Gracián, *El oráculo manual*, § 148, p. 152.

67. William Wotton, *Reflections upon Ancient and Modern Learning* (London: 1694), p. 23.

68. Peter France, "The Writer as Performer." *Essays on the Age of Enlightenment in Honor of Ira O. Wade* (Genève: Droz, 1977), pp. 113–114.

69. Du Plaisir, *Sentiments sur les lettres et sur l'histoire avec des scrupules sur le style* (Paris: 1683), p. 5.

70. Juan de Jáuregui, *Discurso poético* (1623. Madrid: 1978), pp. 116–117, 122–123. Also: Juan de Valdés, Juan de la Cueva, etc.

71. Martin Opitz, *Buch von der deutschen Poeterei*. Abdruck der ersten Ausgabe (1624). (Halle: 1913), p. 19.

72. Ben Jonson, *Timber: or Discoveries* (1640). *The Works.* Ed. by C. H. Herford Perry and Evelyn Simpson (Oxford: 1970), VIII, p. 615.

73. Bruno Markwardt, *Geschichte der Deutschen Poetik* (Berlin-Leipzig: 1964), I, p. 249.

74. *Lettre de Monsieur Huet à Monsieur de De Segrais sur l'origine des romans* (1670. Paris: 1678), p. 129.

75. Baltasar Gracián, *Agudeza y arte de Ingenio*, Disc. LXII: *Ideas de hablar bien*, II, pp. 245–246.

76. Charles Sorel, *Histoire comique de Francion*, I. V. Ed. Emile Roy (Paris: 1926), II, p. 84.

77. R. Glynn Faithfull, "The Concept of 'Living Language' in Cinquecento Vernacular Philology." *Modern Language Review*, XLVIII (1952), 278–292.

78. Joachim Dyck, *"Philosoph, Historiker, Orator und Poet. Rhetorik als Verständnisshorizont der Literaturtheorie des XVII. Jahrhunderts."* *Arcadia* (1969), 4, 12.

79. Dan-Horia Mazilu, *Proza oratorică în literatura română veche* (Bucureşti: Minerva, 1986), I.

80. Mathias Flacius Illyricus, *Clavis Scripturae, seu de sermone sacrarum litterarum* (Bâle: 1618).

81. J. Cave (Guillielmi Cave), *Scriptorum Ecclesiasticorum Historia Literaria* (Londini: 1688), p. 2.

82. I. Bianu-N. Hodoş, *Bibliografia românească veche* (Bucureşti: Ediţiunea Academiei Române, 1903), I, p. 145.

83. Mihail Moxa, *Cronica Universală*. Ediţie critică, însoţită de izvoare, studiu introductiv, note şi indici de G. Mihailă. (Bucureşti: Minerva, 1989), pp. 112, 121, 176. *Crestomaţie* . . . , II, p. 189.

84. Lorenzo Crasso, *Elogii d'huomini letterati* (Venetia: 1666), II, p. 156.

85. T. Tasso, cf. August Buck, *Die humanistische Tradition der Romania* (Berlin-Zürich: 1968), p. 240.

86. Saint-Cyran, cf. Sainte-Beuve, *Port-Royal*. Texte présenté et annoté per Maxime Leroy (Paris: Gallimard, 1952), I, p. 527.

87. Antoine Godeau, *Discours de la poésie chrétienne. Oeuvres chrétiennes* (Paris: 1633), p. 26.

88. Helmut Hatzfeld, *Estudios sobre el barroco*. Versión española (Madrid: Editorial Gredos, 1973. Tercera edición aumentada), pp. 76–78. René Bray, *La formation de la doctrine classique en France* (Paris: Nizet, 1966), p. 300.

89. Boileau, *Art poétique*, III, v. 165–170. *Oeuvres poétiques*. Ed. E. Geruzez (Paris: Hachette, 1866), pp. 222–223. *Réflexions sur Longin*, (1694, 1713).

90. René Bray, *ibid.*, p. 130.

91. Cf. Raoul Morçay, *La Renaissance* (Paris: 1935), II, p. 125.

92. Antonius Possevinus, *Bibliotheca Selecta* . . . (1593. Venetiis: 1603), I, p. 533.

93. Salomon Glass (Glassius), *Philologia Sacra* . . . Tract. IV (Jena: 1623).

94. Cf. Giuseppe Zonta, *"Rinascimento, aristotelismo e barocco."* *Giornale storico della letteratura italiana*, LII (1934), 199–200.

95. Justus Lipsius, *Opera Omnia*, III, p. 637.

96. P. L. Thomassin, *La méthode d'étudier et d'enseigner chrétiennement*

et solidement les lettres humaines par rapport aux lettres divines et aux écritures (Paris: 1681), I, *Préface.*

97. Cf. Bruno Markwardt, *ibid.*, I, p. 153.

98. Nicolas Faret, *L'honeste homme ou l'art de plaire à la court* (Paris: 1630), pp. 64–65.

99. Boileau, *Art Poétique*, III, v. 195–204. *Oeuvres poétiques*, p. 224.

100. René Bray, *ibid.*, pp. 293, 294, 298.

101. Saint-Évremont, *Critique littéraire.* Introduction et notes de Maurice Wilmotte (Paris: 1921), pp. 65, 106–107, 111.

102. Henry Reynolds, *Mythomystes* (1632). *Critical Essays of the Seventeenth Century.* J. E. Spingarn, ed. (Oxford: 1957), I, pp. 144, 158–160.

103. A. Tassoni, *Pensieri diversi* (Venezia: 1646), p. 327.

104. E.g., Mircea Eliade, *Les Mythes et les contes de fées. Aspects du mythe* (Paris: Gallimard, 1963), pp. 233–244.

105. Madeleine V.-David, *ibid.*, pp. 23, 26–28. Gabriel Germain, "Du sacré au fantastique." *Bull. de l'Assoc. G. Budé*, 27 (1968), 4, 498.

106. Cf. Alexandru Duţu, *Coordonate ale culturii româneşti în secolul XVII*, p. 32.

107. *Crestomaţie* . . . , II, p. 66.

108. D. G. Morhof, *Polyhistor*, I, c. XIV, I, p. 150.

109. Gui Patin, *Lettres*, I, p. 72.

110. *Inter alia*: Thomas-Pope Blount, *Censura celebriorum authorum* (Londini: 1690), p. 700.

111. Francis Bacon, *The Advancement of Learning and New Atlantis. To the King*, I, 2. With a preface by Thomas Case (London: Oxford Press, 1960), p. 5.

112. Paul Colomiès, *Bibliothèque choisie* (La Rochelle: 1687), p. 159.

113. (O.) Patru, *Plaidoyers et oeuvres diverses* (Paris: 1681), pp. 50, 81, 178.

114. Girolamo Ghilini, *Teatro d'huomini letterati* (Venezia: 1647), *Lettori.*

115. Antoine Furetière, *ibid.*, *Auteur*, *s.v.* Pierre Richelet, *Dictionnaire français* (Genève: 1680), p. 151.

116. Cf. Heinz Ischreyt, *Welt der Literatur. Einführung in Gesetze und Formen der Dichtung* (Gütersloch: 1961), p. 26.

117. Adrianus Junius, *Nomenclator octolingvis omnium rerum propria nomina continens* (Genevae: 1602), p. 191. Hermannus Hugo, *ibid.*, p. XXXV.

118. Hans Blumenberg, *Die Lesbarkeit der Welt* (Frankfurt/M.: Suhrkamp, 1981), pp. 88–89. Giovanni Pozzi, *ibid.*, pp. 311, 313–314. Eugenio Garin, "Le livre comme symbole à la Renaissance," *Le Débat* (1982), 22, 106–107.

119. Sir Thomas Browne, *Religio Medici and Other Writings*. Ed. M. R. Ridey (1642. London-New York: 1969), pp. 17–18.

120. Saint-Évremont, *Oeuvres*, IV, pp. 131–135.

121. Waldemar Voiré, *"Le livre 'instrument primaire de l'éducation' aux yeux des adeptes de Comenius."* *Revue française d'histoire du livre*, V (1975), 221–227.

122. Geneviève Bollème, *Les Almanachs populaires aux XVIIᵉ et XVIIIᵉ siècles* (La Haye: Mouton, 1969), p. 63.

123. Cf. C. A. Sainte-Beuve, *Causeries du lundi* (Paris: Garnier), II, pp. 170–171.

124. Cf. Albert Cim, *Le Livre* (Paris: Flammarion, 1905), II, p. 7.

125. Antoine Furetière, *ibid.*, II, p. 36.

126. John Milton, *Of Education* (1650). *The Works* (New York: Columbia University Press, 1931), IV, p. 277–278.

127. Cf. Albert Cim, *ibid.*, I, pp. 149, 240.

128. Alexandru Duţu, *Cărţile de înţelepciune în cultura română* (Bucureşti: Editura Academiei R.S.R., 1972. Fr. transl. Bucarest: Association internationale d'Études du Sud-Est Européen, 1971).

129. *Crestomaţie . . .* , II, pp. 85, 190.

130. D. H. Morhof, *Polyhistor*, I, c. IIIff.

131. Justus Lipsius, *De bibliothecis syntagma* (Antverpiae: 1602).

132. André Masson, *"La Bibliothèque temple des muses au dix-septième siècle."* *Humanisme actif. Mélanges . . . Jules Cain* (Paris: 1968), II, pp. 135–139.

133. Leibniz, *Oeuvres*. Ed. A. Foucher de Careil (Paris: 1775), VII, p. 21.

134. G. Naudé, *Advis pour dresser une bibliothèque* (Paris: 1627), pp. 21, 31.

135. Etienne Pasquier, *Choix de lettres sur la littérature, la langue et la traduction.* Publié et annotées par D. Thickett (Genève: Droz, 1956), p. 25.

136. Jean de La Caille, *Histoire de l'Imprimerie et de la librairie où l'on voit son origine et son progrès jusqu'en 1689* (Paris: 1689), p. 303. Also, G. Naudé: "choix et triage," p. 68, Mabillon, *Projet de bibliothèque ecclésiastique* (Paris: 1691), pp. 425–476.

137. La Mothe Le Vayer, *Petits traitez en formes de lettres écrites à diverses personnes studieuses* (Paris: 1648), *Lettre XIII*, pp. 149–163.

138. La Mothe Le Vayer, *ibid.*, p. 160.

139. A general introduction: Theodore Bestermann, *The Beginnings of Systematic Bibliography* (London: Oxford University Press, 1936, 2nd ed., revised). Louise-Noëlle Malclès, *La Bibliographie* (1956. Paris: Presses Universitaires de France, 1977, 4ᵉ éd.). *Ibid., Manuel de bibliographie* (Paris: 1969, 2ᵉ éd.): "Définition du mot bibliographie," pp. 16–19. André Stegmann, "Bibliographie," *Dictionnaire International des Termes Littéraires* (Berne: Franke, 1970, 2, pp. 158–161. Rudolf Blum, "Bibliographia. Ein Wort-und Begriffgeschichteliche Untersuchung." *Archiv für Geschichte des Buchwesens*, X (1970), c. 1009–1246.

140. (Adrien Baillet), *Jugements des sçavans sur les principaux ouvrages des auteurs* (Paris: 1685), II, 1, p. 26.

141. Rudolf Blum, *"Vor- und Frühgeschichte der nationalen Algemeinbibliographie." Ibid.*, II, 1958), 274.

142. Thomas-Pope Blount, *Censura Celebriorum Authorum* (Londini: 1690), *Ad Lectori*.

143. Ewald Flügel, *ibid., Anglia*, XXI, B. IX (1899), 259–288. Peter Brockmeier, *Darstellungen der Französischen Literaturgeschichtsschreibung von Claude Fouchet bis Laharpe* (Berlin: Akademie Verlag, 1963).

144. Miron Costin, *Opere*, II, p. 12. *Crestomaţie . . .* , II, pp. 88–89.

145. Guillielmo Cave, *Scriptorum ecclesiasticorum Historia Literaria* (Londini: 1688), p. IX.

146. Benedetto Accolti, *Dialogo de praestantia virorum sui aevi* (Parma: 1689), p. 29.

147. Charles Sorel, *La Science Universelle* (Paris: 1668), I, p. 31.

148. Claude Cristin, *Aux origines de l'histoire littéraire* (Grenoble: 1973), p. 100.

149. C. Suárez de Figueroa, *Plaza universal de todas scientias y artes* (1615. Perpiñan: 1629), p. 371.

150. Jürgen Henningsen, " '*Enzyklopädie*'. *Zur Sprach- und Bedeutungsgeschichte eines pädagogischen Begriffs.*" *Archiv für Begriffgeschichte* B. 10 (1966), 295.

151. Cf. Ulrich Dierse, *Enzyklopädie. Zur Geschichte eines philosophischen und Wissenschaftlichen Begriffs* (Bonn: 1977), p. 25.

152. M. Magendie, *La Politesse mondaine et les théories de l'honnête homme, en France au XVIIe siècle, de 1600 à 1660* (Paris: Presses Universitaires de France, 1925).

153. Blaise Pascal, *Pensées*, I, 42. *L'Oeuvre*. . . . Texte établi et annoté par Jacques Chevalier (Paris: Gallimard, 1936), p. 833.

154. Nicolas Faret, *L'Honeste homme ou l'art de plaire à la court* (Paris: 1630). Thèse complémentaire pour le doctorat ès lettres par M. Magendie (Paris: Presses Universitaires de France, 1925), p. 361.

155. Leibniz, *Oeuvres*, VII, p. 160.

156. Henri Bremond, *Histoire littéraire du sentiment religieux en France* . . . , I, *L'Humanisme dévot* (Paris: Blond et Gay, 1929).

157. E.g., P. L. Thomassin, *La méthode d'étudier et d'enseigner chrétiennement et solidement les lettres humaines par rapport aux lettres divines et aux écritures* (Paris: 1681–1682), I–III.

158. Rudolf Blum, *ibid.*, *Archiv für Geschichte des Buchwesens* II (1958), 284.

159. P. Philibert Monet, *Inventaire de deux langues* . . . , p. 457. Cf. also Walter von Wartburg, *ibid.*, V, p. 378.

160. Pierre Bayle, *Nouvelles de la République des Lettres* (Amsterdam: 1684), I, p. 79. (Adrien Baillet), *Jugements des sçavans* . . . II, 2, pp. 259, 281.

161. Antoine Furetière, *ibid.*, I, p. 737.

162. Gregorio de Andres, *ibid.*, pp. 157, 204, 226.

163. Antonio Bernardini e Gaetano Righi, *Il concetto di filologia e di cultura classica nel moderno pensiero europeo* (Bari: 1953, 2nd ed.), p. 131. Robert J. Clements, "The Cult of the Poet in Renaissance Emblem Literature." *P.M.L.A.*, LIX (1944), 674.

164. Cf. Jean Jehasse, *La Renaissance de la critique* (Saint-Etienne: 1976), p. 157.

165. Cf. Jürgen Henningsen, *ibid.*, p. 289.

166. Justus Lipsius, *ibid.*, IV, p. 428.

167. Valentin Henri Vogler, *Introductio universalis in notitiam cujus-cumque generis bonorum scriptorum* (Helmstadii: 1691), p. 2.

168. (Guez) de Balzac, *Les lettres diverses* (Paris: 1663), II, p. 28.

169. Cf. Roger Charlier, Dominique Julie, Marie-Madeleine Compère, *L'Éducation en France du XVIᵉ au XVIIIᵉ siècle* (Paris: 1976), p. 171.

170. Alain Viala, *Naissance de l'écrivain* . . . , p. 288.

171. (Adrien Baillet), *ibid.*, II, 2, p. 108.

172. Gio. Pietro Belloni, *Vite dei Pittori, Scultori ed Architetti moderni* . . . (1672. Pisa: 1821), I, p. 255.

173. Gui Patin, *ibid.*, I, p. 595. Etienne Pasquier, *Recherches de la France*, 1. IX, ch. XVIII (Paris: 1621).

174. Lorenzo Crasso, *Elogii d'huomini letterati* . . . , I, pp. 8, 258; II, p. 151.

175. Cf. Albert Collignon, *La religion des lettres* (Paris: 1896), pp. 159, 162.

176. Du Cange, *Glossarium mediae et infimae latinitatis*, digessit G. A. Henschel (Paris: 1845), IV, pp. 129–132.

177. Madeleine V.-David, *Le débat sur les écritures et l'hiéroglyphe aux XVIIᵉ et XVIIIᵉ siècles* (Paris: 1965).

178. Hermannus Hugo, *De prima scribendi origine et universa rei litterariae antiquitate* (Antverpiae, 1617), p. 5. D. Ge. Schubart, *Literaturae apud Germanos* (1679). *Miscellanea Lipsiensia*, V (1717), 41–56.

179. (Adrien Baillet), *ibid.*, II, 1, p. 15.

180. M. Mich. Lilienthal, *De historia literaria certae cujusdam gentis scribende* (1690. Lipsiae et Roshchii: 1710).

181. Etienne Pasquier, *Recherches de la France*, 1. IX, ch. I., p. 725.

182. Giovanni Getto, *Storia delle storie letterarie* (1942. Firenze: Sansoni, 1969. Nuova edizione riveduta), pp. 23–30. Peter Brockmeier, *Literaturgesschichtsschreibung von Claude Fauchet bis Laharpe* (Berlin: Akademie Verlag, 1963), pp. 25–37.

183. Paul Pellisson et Abbé d'Olivet, *Histoire de l'Académie française* (Paris: 1743, troisième édition), II, p. 11.

184. M. Mich. Lilienthal, *ibid.*, p. 9.

185. Abbé d'Olivet, *Huetiana ou Pensées diverses de M. Huet* (Paris: 1722), pp. 1–3.

186. For example, Adrian Marino, "*Aux sources de la dialectique séman-tique ancien/nouveau,*" *Cahiers roumains d'études littéraires* (1975), 1, 50–59.

187. Bernard Lamy, *La Rhétorique ou l'art de penser* (Paris: 1675), pp. 312ff.

188. E.g., Abbé d'Olivet, *ibid. Défense des Anciens contre les Modernes*, p. 28.

189. Charles Perrault, *Parallèle des Anciens et des Modernes en ce qui regarde les arts et les sciences.* Ed. H. R. Jauss (1688: München: Eidos Verlag, 1964), p. 116.

190. Cf. René Wellek, *The Rise of English Literary History* (1941. New York-London-Sydney-Toronto: McGraw-Hill Book Company, 1966), p. 12.

191. Cf. Lucette Desvignes-Parent, *Marivaux en Angleterre* (Paris: 1970), p. 137.

192. B. Fioretti, *Proginnasmi poetici* (Firenze: 1620), I, pp. 59–63.

193. Mihail Moxa, *ibid.*, p. 40.

194. René Bray, *ibid.*, p. 30.

195. Desmarets de Saint-Sorlin, *La Comparaison de la poésie française avec la Grecque et la Latine* (Paris: 1676), p. 232.

196. Noémi Hepp, *Homère en France du XVIIIᵉ siècle* (Paris: 1969), pp. 300–302, 418, etc.

197. Desmarets de Saint-Sorlin, *ibid.*, p. 5, 22.

198. Cf. Hubert Gillot, *La Querelle des Anciens et des Modernes en France* (Paris: Champion, 1914), p. 107.

199. (Adrien Baillet), *ibid.*, I, pp. 230 ff.

200. Hans Kohn, "The Genesis and Character of English National-ism." *J.H.I.*, I (1940), 69–94.

201. William Wotton, *Reflexions Upon Ancient and Modern Learning* (London: 1694), p. 2.

202. José-Antonio Maravall, *Antiguos y Modernos*, *La idea de progreso en el desarrollo inicial de una sociedad* (Madrid: Sociedad de estudios y publicaciones, 1966), pp. 329–331, 340–341.

203. Gyula Alpár, *Streit der Alten und Modernen in der Deutschen Literatur bis um 1750* (Pécs: 1939), pp. 34–35.

204. Vauquelin de la Fresnaye, *L'Art poétique* (1605. Paris: 1862. Publié par Arch. Genty) 129. Alessandro Tassoni, *Varietà di Pensieri* (Modena: 1612), IX, 15.

205. Desmarets de Saint-Sorlin, *ibid.*, p. 11.

206. Charles Sorel, *Bibliothèque française* (Paris: 1664), p. 12.

207. Suzanne Trocmé Sweany, *Etienne Pasquier (1529–1615) et le nationalisme littéraire* (Genève-Paris: Droz, 1985).

208. Cf. Jean Rousset, *La littérature à l'âge baroque en France. Circé et le paon* (154. Paris: José Corti, 1965), p. 270.

209. Christian Thomasius, *Von Nachahmung der Franzosen* (1687, 1701. Hrsg. von August Sauer. Stuttgart: "Deutsche Lit. Denkmale des 18. und 19. Jahrhunderts," 1894), p. VI.

210. P. Bouhours, *Manière de bien penser dans les ouvrages de l'esprit* (Paris: 1687), p. 40.

211. Charles Sorel, *De la connaissance des bons livres . . .* (Paris: 1671), p. 325.

212. (Adrien Baillet), *Jugements des sçavans sur les principaux ouvrages des auteurs* (Paris: 1685), I, p. VI.

213. H. B. Requeline de Longepierre, *Discours sur les Anciens* (Paris: 1687), p. 94. cf. Arnaldo Pizzorusso, "L'idea di 'critica' nel seicento francese." *Intersezioni*, V (1985), 58.

214. Etiemble, *L'Europe chinoise*, I, *De l'empire romain à Leibniz* (Paris: Gallimard, 1988).

215. Bernard Lamy, *ibid.*, p. 19.

216. Nicolas Trigault, *Histoire de l'expédition chrétienne au royaume de Chine par les P. P. de la Compagnie de Jésus, 1616.* cf. Madeleine V.-David, *ibid.*, p. 32.

217. Leibniz, *Oeuvres*, VII, pp. 20–23, 157–165.

218. Miron Costin, *ibid.*, II, pp. 113–114.

219. Luis Carrillo y Sotomayor, *Libro de erudición poética* (1611, Edition de Manuel Cardenal Iracheta (Madrid: 1946), p. 38.

220. Baltasar Gracián, *Agudeza y arte de Ingenio*, II, p. 197.

221. *Crestomaţie* . . . , I, p. 92.

222. Valentin Henri Vogler, *Introductio universalis in notitiam cujuscumque generis bonorum scriptorum* (Helmstadii: 1691), c. XV, pp. 79–83.

223. Gerardus J. Vossius, *De Quator artibus popularibus* (Amstelodami: 1650), pp. 2–4, passim.

224. John Taylor. cf. Rayner Unwin, *The Rural Muse. Studies in the Peasant Poetry of England* (London: 1954), p. 21. Victor E. Neuburg, *Popular Literature. A History and Guide. From the Beginning of Printing to the Year 1897* (London: Penguin Books, 1977), pp. 61, 76.

225. Cf. Benedetto Croce, *Poesia popolare e poesia d'arte* (Bari: Laterza, 1933), p. 26.

226. Mary Elisabeth Storer, *La Mode des contes de fées* (1685–1700). (Paris: Champion, 1928), pp. 226–234. Marc Fumaroli, *"Les enchantements de l'éloquence: 'Les Fées' de Charles Perrault ou de la littérature." Le Statut de la littérature. Mélanges offerts à Paul Bénichou* (Genève: Droz, 1982), pp. 59, 185–186. Raymonde Robert, *Le conte des fées littéraire en France de la fin du XVIIᵉ à la fin du XVIIIᵉ siècles* (Nancy: 1988).

227. Miron Costin, *ibid.*, p. 254.

228. Cf. Louis P. Betz, *Pierre Bayle und die "Nouvelles de la République des Lettres"* (*Erste populärwissenschaftliche Zeitschrift, 1684–1687*) (Zürich: 1896), p. 12.

229. Alessandro Tassoni, *ibid.*, X, 5.

230. Walter von Wartburg, *ibid.*, V, p. 387. (The other proposed dates for the first attestation, 1666, 1691, etc., are erroneous.)

231. A very explicit identification in Adrien Baillet, *ibid.*, II, 2, p. 439, etc.

232. Jean Mabillon, *Traité des études monastiques*. P. II, ch. XI: *De la connaissance des belles lettres* (Paris: 1691), p. 268.

233. P. Richelet, *ibid.* (1680), *s.v.*, A. Furetière, *ibid.*, I (1694), *s.v.*

234. Pierre Bayle, *Dictionnaire historique et critique* (1690. Amsterdam . . . , 1740, 5ᵉ éd.), II, pp. 195, 952.

235. J. Carré, *Les Pédagogues de Port-Royal* (Paris: 1887), p. 90.

236. Cf. *ibid.*, p. 205. M. Magendie, *ibid.*, p. 854.

237. *Huetiana* . . . (Paris: 1722), pp. 8, 9.

238. Gui Patin, *Lettres*, I, p. 70. Adrien Baillet, *ibid.*, II, 2, p. 216 (plenty of references).

239. *Mercure Galant*, mars 1690, p. 7.

240. Sieur Saunier, *Encyclopédie des beaux esprits, contenant les moyens de parvenir à la connaissance des belles sciences* (Paris: 1657).

241. La Chétardie, *Instructions pour un jeune seigneur sur l'idée d'un galant homme* (1683. Paris: 1688), I, p. 28.

242. Jean Mabillon, *ibid.*, p. 279. Jean Le Clerc, *Parrhasiana* . . . (Amsterdam: 1699), p. 261.

243. R. Rapin, *La Comparaison des grands hommes de l'antiquité qui ont plus excellé dans les belles lettres* (Paris: 1684), I, p. III.

244. D. G. Morhof, *ibid.*, p. 293. *Elegantioris litteraturae collegium* . . . (Halle: 1697). Theophilus Spizelius, *Felix literatus* . . . (Augustae Vindelicorum: 1676), p. 25. I. P. Valerianus Bellunensis, *De litteratorum infelicitate* (Venetia: 1620), p. 25.

245. Pierre Bayle, *Dictionnaire* . . . (Roterdam: 1720), IV, p. 2688. *Huetiana* . . . , p. 92. *Discours sur la vie de feu monsieur Ancillon* (Basle: 1698), p. 8.

246. P. Philibert Monet, *Inventaire de deux langues* . . . , p. 504.

247. Pascal, *Pensées*, I, 42. *L'Oeuvre*, p. 833.

248. La Bruyère, *Les Caractères. Des ouvrages de l'esprit*, 57. *Oeuvres complètes.* Texte établi et annoté par Julien Benda (Paris: Gallimard, 1953), p. 86.

249. (Abbé) Bouhours, *La manière de bien penser dans les ouvrages de l'esprit* (Paris: 1687). (Pierre Nicole), *Traité de la beauté des ouvrages de l'esprit et particulièrement de l'épigramme* . . . (Paris: 1659).

250. P. Richelet, *ibid.*, I, p. 71.

251. Peter-Eckhard Knabe, "Bel Esprit." *Schlüsselbegriffe des Kunsttheoretischen Denkens in Frankreich von der Spätklassik bis zum Ende der Aufklärung* (Düsseldorf: Verlag L. Schwann, 1972), pp. 93–94.

252. Gabriel Guéret, *Le Parnasse réformé* (Paris: 1671), p. 3.

253. Christian Thomasius, *Von Nachahmung der Franzosen*, p. 33.

254. Gui Patin, *Lettres*, II, p. 382.

255. Francis Bacon, *The Advancement of Learning*, II, IV, 1. (London: Oxford University Press, 1966), p. 96.

256. Henry Reynolds, cf. *Critical Essays of the Seventeenth Century*, J. E. Spingarn, ed. (Oxford: 1957), I, p. 153.

257. Etienne Pasquier, *Recherches de la France*, VII, 6, p. 610.

258. Girolamo Ghilini, *Teatro d'huomini letterati*, I, p. 233.

259. cf. Eugenio Garin, *Geschichte und Dokumente der abendländische Pädagogie* (Reinbeck bei Hamburg: Rowohlt, 1967), III, p. 19.

260. Miron Costin, *Opere*, II, p. 41.

261. cf. J. E. Spingarn, *La critica letteraria nel Rinascimento*, It. transl. (Bari: Laterza, 1905), p. 193.

262. Père Rapin, *Réflexions sur la poétique d'Aristote. Oeuvres diverses concernant les belles-lettres* (Amsterdam: 1686), p. 121.

263. cf. J. E. Fidao-Justiniani, *Qu'est-ce qu'un poète classique?* (1929. Paris: Firmin Didot, 1930), p. 161.

264. M. Huet, *Traité de l'origine des romans* (Paris: 1670), pp. 156–157.

265. Benedetto Croce, *Storia della età barocca in Italia* (Bari: Laterza, 1929), p. 570.

266. Alain Viala, *ibid.*, p. 276.

267. For example, D. Diego de Saavedra Fajardo, *La república literaria* (1612, 1653. Palermo: 1700, p. 47: "Los Letrados y los Poëtes."

268. P. Richelet, *ibid.*, *s.v.*: Poëte, Poëme.

269. B. Fioretti, *Proginnasmi poetici*, III, p. 278.

270. John Dryden, *An Essay of Dramatic Poesy* (1668). *Of Dramatic Poesy and Other Critical Essays*. Ed. with and introduction by George Watson (London: 1962), I, pp. 23, 24, 41–42.

271. Antonio Lopez de Vega, *Heraclito: Democrito de nuestro siglo . . .* (Madrid: 1641): "De las letras," p. 150.

272. Cf. Noémi Hepp, *"Esquisse du vocabulaire de la critique littéraire du Cid à la Querelle d'Homère." Romanische Forschungen* 69 (1957), 336.

273. A. Kibédi-Varga, *Rhétorique et littérature. Études de structures classiques* (Paris-Bruxelles-Montréal: 1970), pp. 8–9.

274. Alain Viala, *ibid.*, pp. 276, 281.

275. Jules de la Mesnadière, *La poétique* (Paris: 1639), I, *Préface*.

276. La Bruyère, *Des ouvrages de l'esprit*, 3. *Oeuvres complètes*, p. 65.

277. Bossuet, *De la connaissance de Dieu et de soi-même*, I, 15. *Oeuvres complètes* (Bar-Le-Duc: 1862), IV, p. 16.

278. Boileau, *Art poétique*, IV, v. 31. *Oeuvres poétiques*, p. 238.

279. Pellisson et d'Olivet, *ibid.*, I, p. 324.

280. Bruno Markwardt, *ibid.*, I, pp. 64, 130.

281. La Bruyère, *Des ouvrages de l'esprit*, 59. Scarron, *Le Roman comique*, I, XX. Buffon, etc.

282. Ben Jonson. Cf. J. E. Spingarn ed., *ibid.*, I, p. 32. John Dryden, *ibid.*, I, p. 70.

283. Chapelain, *Lettres*. Ed. Tamizey de Larroque (Paris: 1880), I, p. 176.

284. La Bruyère, *Des ouvrages de l'esprit*, 37. *Oeuvres complètes*, p. 76.

285. Charles Sorel, *De la connaissance des bons livres* (Paris: 1671), pp. 290, 323. B. Lamy, *ibid.*, *Préface*.

286. Ben Jonson, *Timber, or Discoveries. Works*, VIII, pp. 615–625.

287. Girolamo Ghilini, *ibid.*, I, p. 31.

288. Edición de Manuel Cardenal Iracheta (Madrid: 1946).

289. Cf. Robert Elbrodt, *L'inspiration personnelle et l'esprit du temps chez les poètes métaphysiques anglais* (Paris: 1960), p. 120.

290. Matteo Pellegrini, *Delle Acutezze, che altrimente Spirite, Vivezze e concetti volgarmente si appellano* (Genova-Bologna: 1693). Baltasar Gracián, *Agudeza y arte de Ingenio* (Huesca: Juan Nogués, 1648).

291. Benedetto Croce, "I Trattatisti italiani del concettismo e Baltasar Gracián" (1899). *Problemi di estetica* (1910. Bari: Laterza, 1966), pp. 311–346. *Storia della età barocca in Italia*, p. 200. Giuseppe Zonta, "Rinascimento, aristotelismo e barocco." *Giornale storico della letteratura italiana*, LII (1934), 62–63, 189, 204, 208, 311.

292. J. Peletier du Mans, cf. Nathalie Zonn Davis, *Society and Culture in Early Modern France* (London: 1965), p. 220.

293. John Dryden, *Essays*. Ed. W. P. Ker (Oxford: 1926), I, p. 14.

294. Ibid., *Of Dramatic Poesy and Other Critical Essays*, II, p. 451.

295. Paolo Rossi, cf. *Cultura popolare e cultura dotta nel seicento.* Convegno di Studio di Genova (22–23 novembre 1982). (Milano: 1983), p. 40.

296. (Adrien Baillet), *ibid.*, II, 2, p. 108. Giovanni Ciampoli, *Delle lettere sacre e profane. Prose* (Roma: 1649), p. 116.

297. P. L. Thomassin, *La méthode d'étudier et d'enseigner chrétiennement et solidement les lettres humaines par rapport aux lettres divines et aux écritures* (Paris: 1691), *Préface.*

298. Cf. Zobeidah Ioussef, *Polémique et littérature chez Guez de Balzac* (Paris: 1972), p. 297.

299. William Wotton, *Reflections Upon Ancient and Modern Learning*, p. 5. Francisco Cascales, *Tablas poéticas* (1617. Ed. Benito Francoforte, Madrid: 1975), p. 27.

300. Guillaume Colletet, *L'Art poétique* . . . , *De l'Epigramme* (Paris: 1658), p. 27.

301. For example, (Adrien Baillet), *Plan de l'ouvrage qui a pour titre: Jugements des Sçavans* . . . (Paris: 1694), II, p. 7.

302. René Wellek, *"Was ist Literatur?"* LILI, 30/31 (1978), p. 17.

303. John Dryden, *ibid.*, I, p. 14.

304. Miron Costin, *Opere.* Ed. P. P. Panaitescu (Bucureşti: E.S.P.L.A., 1958), p. 254.

305. *Crestomaţie* . . . , I, p. 118.

306. *Viaţa Sfîntului Nifon. O redacţie grecească inedită.* Editată, tradusă şi însoţită cu o introducere de V. Grecu (Bucureşti: M. O. Imprimeria Naţională, 1944), p. 39.

307. Cf. Benedetto Croce, *Storia della età barocca in Italia*, p. 14.

308. Cf. *ibidem*, p. 174.

309. Antoine Godeau, *Oeuvres chrétiennes* (Paris: 1633), p. 9.

310. (Adrien Baillet), *ibid.*, I, p. 319. La Bruyère, *Des jugements*, 17. *Oeuvres complètes*, p. 347.

311. A. Furetière, *Nouvelle Allégorique* . . . (Paris: 1658), p. 68.

312. Girolamo Ghilini, *ibid.*, I, pp. 50, 134, 322. I. P. Valeriani Bellunensis, *De Literatorum infelicitate* (Venetia: 1620), p. 29.

313. A. Furetière, *ibid.*, *Lettres*, *s.v.*, II, p. 21.

314. Cf. Benedetto Croce, *ibid.*, p. 102.

315. *Huetiana* . . . (Paris: 1722), pp. 42–43.

316. *Ibid.*, p. 1.

317. Gabriel Guéret, *Le Parnasse réformé* (Paris: 1671), p. 5.

318. Guillaume Colletet, *ibid.*, p. 115.

319. *Acta eruditorum* (Lipsiae: 1682). (Dedication.)

320. Current acceptations in dictionaries: P. Richelet, II, pp. 304, 557. A. Furetière, III, *s.v.*

321. J. P. Camus, *Conférence académique* (Paris: 1636), p. 36.

322. (Pierre Bayle), *Nouvelles de la République des Lettres* (Amsterdam: 1684), I, *Préface*.

323. Paul Dibon, "*L'Université de Leyde et la République des Lettres au 17ᵉ siècle.*" *Querendo*, V (1975), 27, 28. Ibid., "*Les échanges épistolaires dans l'Europe savante au XVIIᵉ siècle.*" *Revue de Synthèse*, XCVII (1976), 37.

324. Edward Phillips, J. E. Spingarn, ed. *Ibid.*, II, p. 258.

325. Cf. B. Croce, *ibid.*, p. 67.

326. G. Naudé, *Advis pour dresser une bibliothèque* (Paris: 1627), pp. 4, 21.

327. Ole Worm, . . . *Danica literatura antiquissima* (Hafniae: 1636), p. 43.

328. (Pierre Bayle), *ibid.*, II, pp. 101–102.

329. Cf. Paul Dibon, "*L'Université de Leyde . . . ,*" p. 27.

330. Charles Perrault, *Parallèle des Anciens et des Modernes . . .* , pp. 254, 370.

331. J. L. Guez de Balzac, *Lettres* (Paris: 1659), p. 164.

332. Traiano Boccalini, *De ragguagli di Parnasso* (Venetia: 1629), pp. 33, 43.

333. Leibniz, *Oeuvres*, VII, pp. 13, 21, 155–156.

334. Boileau, *L'Art poétique*, IV, v. 123–124. *Oeuvres poétiques*, p. 243.

335. M. Magendie, *La politesse mondaine et les théories de l'honêteté en France, au XVIIᵉ siècle, de 1600–1660* (Paris: P.U.F., 1925).

336. F. de Callières, *Du bel esprit* (Paris: 1695).

337. La Chétardie, *Instructions pour un jeune seigneur ou l'idée d'un galant homme* (Paris: 1688), I, p. 29.

338. Gabriel Guéret, *ibid.*, p. 202.

339. *Huetiana* . . . , p. 300. Chapelain, *Mélanges de littérature* . . . , (Paris: 1726), p. V.

340. La Bruyère, *Des jugements*, 17. *Oeuvres complètes*, p. 347.

341. Alessandro Tassoni, *Dieci libri di pensieri diversi* (Milano: 1628), 1. VII.

342. John Lough, *Writer and Public in France* . . . (Oxford: 1978), p. 74.

343. For example, Fénelon, *Dialogues des morts*, IV: *Achille et Homère* (1700, 1712, 1718. Paris: 1861), pp. 103–106.

344. G. M. Crescimbeni, *La bellezza della volgar poesia* (Roma: 1700), p. 155.

345. G. Naudé, *ibid.*, pp. 18, 31, 114–115.

346. Erich Auerbach, *Das französische Publikum des 17. Jahrhunderts* (München: 1933).

347. Leibniz, *Oeuvres*, VII, p. 160.

348. Boileau, *Ceuvres poétiques. Préface* (1701). Ed. E. Geruzez, p. 3.

349. Luis Carrillo y Sotomayor, *ibid.*, p. 42.

350. Erich Auerbach, *La cour et la ville. Vier Untersuchungen zur Geschichte der Französische Bildung* (Bern: 1951), pp. 12–50.

351. Etienne Pasquier, *Choix de lettres sur la littérature, la langue et la traduction*, publiés et annotés par D. Thickett (Genève: Droz, 1956), p. 64.

352. Francisco de Quevedo, *Sueños y discursos*. Edición, prólogo y notas de Francisco Abad (Madrid: Espasa-Calpe, 1980), pp. 56, 127. Grimmelshausen, *Simplicissimus Teutsch* (1669. Hrsg. von J. H. Scholte. Tübingen: 1954), I, 10, pp. 30–31.

353. Baltasar Gracián, *Oráculo Manual y Arte de Prudencia*, § 281, pp. 242–243.

354. *Huetiana* . . . , pp. 5–8, 95–198, 210, 213.

355. Robert Burton, *The Anatomy of Melancholy* (1621). Ed. by Rev. A. R. Schillet (London: 1893), I, pp. 348–378.

356. Miron Costin, *Opere*, I, p. 4.

357. Richard Bentley, *A Dissertation Upon the Epistles of Phalaris* . . . (London: 1699), pp. 8, 9.

358. Alain Viala, *Naissance de l'écrivain: sociologie de la littérature à l'âge classique*, pp. 183, 217.

359. Cf. Nathalie Zonn Davis, *ibid.*, p. 220.

360. Juan de Robles, *Primera parte del culto sevillano* (1631. Sevilla, Sociedad de bibliófiles andaluces, XIV, 1883), p. 316.

361. A text from 1611, cf. Peter Burke, *Popular Culture in Early Modern Europe* (London: 1978), p. 253. M. Nicolet, *"La condition de l'homme de lettres au XVIIe siècle à travers l'oeuvre de deux contemporains: Ch. Sorel et A. Furetière."* *Revue d'Histoire Littéraire de la France*, 63 (1963), 369–393. Phoebe Sheavyn, *The Literary Profession in the Elisabethan Age.* (New York-Manchester: 2nd ed., revised throughout by J. W. Saunders, 1967).

362. (Adrien Baillet), *ibid.*, I, p. 544.

363. Cf. Paul Delolain, *Étude sur le libraire parisien du XIIIe au XVe siècle* (Paris: 1891), p. XLI.

364. Charles Sorel, *Histoire comique de Francion* (1623. Ed. Emile Roy. Paris: Hachette, 1926), II, p. 80.

365. Boileau, *Art poétique*, IV, v. 132. *Oeuvres poétiques*, p. 244.

366. For example, Robert Burton, *ibid.*, I, p. XIII.

367. Hans Kortum, *Charles Perrault und Nicolas Boileau* (Berlin: 1966), p. 81.

368. Ben Jonson. J. E. Spingarn, *Critical Essays of The Seventeenth Century*, I, p. 27.

369. Sieur de Tournay, *L'Alliance des Armes et des Lettres* (Paris: 1648), p. 40.

370. Père Rapin, *Réflexions sur la poétique* (Paris: 1675), p. 132.

371. *Trattati di arte del Cinquecento tra Manierismo e Contrariforma.* A cura di Paola Barocchi (Bari: Laterza, 1960), I, p. 15.

372. Pierre Bayle, *Dictionnaire historique et critique*, I, p. 857.

373. Miron Costin, *Opere*, I, p. 4.

374. René Bray, *La formation de la doctrine classique en France*, pp. 64, 66, 70, 73, etc.

375. Cf. Joachim Dyck, *"Philosoph, Historiker, Orator und Poet. Rhetorik als Verständnisshorizont der Literaturtheorie des XVII. Jahrhunderts."* Arcadia, 4 (1969), 7, 12, 15. René Bray, *ibid.*, p. 13.

376. J. G. Schottel (1645. cf. Bruno Markwardt, *Geschichte der deutschen Poetik*, Berlin-Leipzig: 1964), I, p. 68.

377. Edward Phillips. J. E. Spingarn, *ibid.*, II, p. 271.

378. (Adrien Baillet), *ibid.*, II, 2, p. 472.

379. Traiano Boccalini, *Ragguagli di Parnasso*, XIII. A cura di Giuseppe Rua (Bari: Laterza, 1910), I, p. 47.

380. René Rapin, *Les Réflexions sur la poétique de ce temps et sur les ouvrages des poètes anciens et modernes* (1674, 1675. Ed. critique par E. T. Dubos. Genève-Paris: Droz, 1970), pp. 95–96.

381. Mme de Sévigné, *Choix de lettres* (15 janvier 1690. Paris: 1933), p. 334.

382. La Bruyère, *Des jugements*, 17. *Oeuvres complètes*, p. 347.

383. Erich Auerbach, *La cour et la ville. Vier Untersuchungen . . .* , pp. 16, 23, 28, 31, 48.

384. (Adrien Baillet), *ibid.*, I, p. 551.

385. Cf. M. Magendie, *ibid.*, p. 341.

386. T. Tasso. Cf. Guido Morpurgo Tagliabue, *"Aristotelismo e barocco." Retorica e barocco. Atti del III Congresso Internazionale di studi umanistici* (Roma: 1955), pp. 142–143.

387. Bruno Markwardt, *ibid.*, I, p. 155.

388. Cf. *Das Zeitalter der Barock. Texte und Zeugnisse.* Hrsg. Albrecht Schöne (München: C. H. Beck. Zweite verbesserte und erweiterte Auflage, 1968), p. 43.

389. *Cultura popolare e cultura dotta nel seicento . . .* (Milano: 1983).

390. Luis Carrillo y Sotomayor, *ibid.*, pp. 57–58.

391. Cf. Giuseppe Zonta, *"Rinascimento, aristotelismo e barocco,"* Giornale storico della letteratura italiana, LII (1934), 190.

392. Etienne Pasquier, *Les Recherches de la France*, l. VI, ch. VII, p. 739.

393. Gregorio de Andres, *ibid.*, p. 243.

394. Pierre Bayle, *Dictionnaire . . .* , II, p. 1657.

395. B. Fioretti, *Proginnasmi poetici*, I, p. 15.

396. Ben Jonson, *The Works*, VIII, p. 615.

397. Baltasar Gracián, *Agudeza y arte de Ingenio*, I, pp. 22, 138, 174; II, pp. 242, 245.

398. *Ibid.*, *Discurso LVIII: De la docta erudición y de las fuentes de que se saca*, II, pp. 217–221.

399. Roger Lathuillère, *La Préciosité. Étude historique et linguistique* (Genève: Droz, 1966), I, p. 631. René Bray, *ibid.*, p. 97.

400. Günter E. Grimm, *Literatur und Gelehrtentum in Deutschland. Untersuchungen zum Wandel ihres Verhältnisses vom Humanismus bis zur Frühaufklärung* (Tübingen: Max Niemeyer Verlag, 1983), pp. 154–185.

401. Vitruve, *Les dix livres d'architecture*. Traduction intégrale de Claude Perrault, 1673, revue et corrigée par les textes latins et présentée par André Salmas (Paris: Balland, 1979), p. 186.

402. Martin Opitz, *Buch von der deutschen Poeterei*, III.

403. Noémi Hepp, *Homère en France au XVIIIe siècle* (Paris: Klincksieck, 1969), pp. 49–50, 52, 91, 105–113ff.

404. Baltasar Gracián, *Oráculo Manual*, § 12, 87, pp. 59, 111.

405. Francisco Cascales, *Cartas filológicas*, III, 3; III, p. 47.

406. Traiano Boccalini, *ibid.*, I, 83.

407. René Bray, *ibid.*, pp. 91, 93–96, 108, etc.

408. Cf. Bruno Markwardt, *ibid.*, I, p. 33.

409. John Dryden, *Of Dramatic Poesy*, II, p. 267.

410. Giambattista Marino, *Epistolario*. A cura di Angelo Borzelli e Fausto Nicolini (Bari: Laterza, 1911), I, pp. 256, 259.

411. Cf. Erich Welslau, *Imitation und Plagiat in der französischen Literatur von der Renaissance bis zum Revolution* (Schäuble Verlag: 1976), p. 168.

412. Robert Burton, *Democritus junior to the Reader. Ibid.*, I, p. 23.

413. Jean Rousset, *La littérature de l'âge baroque en France*, pp. 115, 242, 246.

414. Charles Sorel, *De la connaissance des bons livres* (Paris: 1671), p. 4.

415. Etienne Pasquier, *Choix de lettres . . .* , p. 47.

416. Richesource, *La méthode des orateurs ou l'art de lire les auteurs, de les examiner, de dresser le plan d'un Discours, et de faire des Remarques et des Collections qu'on appelle Lieux-communs* (Paris: 1688).

417. Mihail Moxa, *ibid.*, pp. 48, 102, 203, 414.

418. Dan Simonescu, *Contribuţii* (Bucureşti: Eminescu, 1984), p. 8.

419. *Lirici marinisti.* A cura di Benedetto Croce (Bari: Laterza, 1910), p. 431.

420. Ariosto, *Orlando furioso*, XII, 14–15. Cervantes, *Don Quijote*, I, 2; I, 3; I, 4.

421. Benedetto Croce, *Storia della età barocca in Italia*, pp. 432–433.

422. José Simón Díaz, *La Bibliografía: conceptos y aplicaciones* (Barcelona: Planeta, 1971).

423. Cf. Arnaldo Pizzorusso, *ibid.*, p. 60.

424. Alexandre Ciorănescu, *Le Masque et le Visage. Du baroque espagnol au classicisme français* (Genève: Droz, 1983), pp. 186, 193.

425. Walter von Wartburg, *ibid.*, V, p. 244.

426. Guillaume Colletet, *L'art poétique* . . . (Paris: 1658), p. 28.

427. Boileau, *Art poétique*, IV, v. 87. *Oeuvres poétiques*, p. 242.

428. René Bray, *ibid.*, pp. 65, 77. Robert Elbrodt, "Scientific Curiosity and Metaphysical Poetry in the Seventeenth Century." *Modern Philology*, LXI (1964), 185.

429. L. L. Albertsen, *Das Lehrgedicht. Eine Geschichte der antikisieren dem Sachepik in der neueren dt. Literatur* (Aarhus: 1967), pp. 10–29.

430. For example, Phil. Jacobus Maussalus, *Dissertatio critica*, Harpocrationis, *Dictionarium* . . . (Parisiis: 1614), pp. 303–399.

431. Cf. Ewald Flügel, *ibid.*, *Anglia*, XII, B. IX (1899), 276–278.

432. Gerardus Joannis Vossius, *Aristarchus sive De arte Grammatica* cap. VI (Amstelodami: 1695), p. 9.

433. (Adrien Baillet), *ibid.*, II, 2, p. 45.

434. C. L. A. Saldenus, *Bibliophilia, sive De scribendis, legendis et aestimandis libris exercitatio parenetica* (Ultrajecti: 1681), pp. 199–214.

435. Walter von Wartburg, *ibid.*, V, p. 242. (synthesis in René Wellek, *Concepts of Criticism* (1963. New Haven and London: Yale University Press, 19, 1965), pp. 25, 28).

436. Antoine Furetière, *ibid.*, II, p. 17.

437. G. I. Vossius, *De Philologia liber* (Amstelodami: 1650), p. 1.

438. (Adrien Baillet), *ibid.*, II, 2, pp. 3, 5–6, 302, 439.

439. B. Lamy, *ibid.*, *Preface*. Fabienne Gégou, *Lettre-traité de Pierre-Daniel Huet sur l'origine des romans* . . . Ed. critique (Paris: 1971), p. 110.

440. Jean Jehasse, *La Renaissance de la critique. L'essor de l'Humanisme érudit de 1560 à 1614* (Saint-Etienne: 1976), pp. 197–198, 268, 334–335, 345.

441. Francisco Cascales, *Cartas filológicas* (1634. Ed. Justo García Soriano (Madrid: 1954–1969), I–III.

442. Claude-François Ménestrier, *Poétique de l'énigme*. Présentation, notes et commentaire de Michel Charles, *Poétique*, 45 (1981), 28–52.

443. Antoine Furetière, *ibid.*, II, *s.v.*

444. La Bruyère, *De quelques usages*, 72. *Oeuvres complètes*, pp. 430–431.

445. (Adrien Baillet), *ibid.*, II, 2, p. 589.

446. G. Naudé, *ibid.*, p. 40.

447. Guez de Balzac, *ibid.*, I, p. 362.

448. Baltasar Gracián, *El criticón*, III, 4. (1651. Edición al cuidado del P. Ismael Quiles, S.J. Madrid: Espasa-Calpe, 1968), p. 298.

449. Scarron, *Le roman comique*, I, VIII. Ed. Emile Magne (Paris: 1967).

450. Adrien Baillet, *ibid.*, I, p. 17.

451. Pierre Bayle, *Dictionnaire* . . . , I, p. 66. III, p. 1949. *Huetiana* . . . , p. 182.

452. Antoine Furetière, *ibid.*, II, p. 370.

453. D. G. Morhof, *Polyhistor*, 1. V, *Criticus* (1688. Lübeck: 1708), II, pp. 218–226.

454. (Adrien Baillet), *ibid.*, I, p. X, 364; II, 1, p. 5.

455. Juan de Robles, *ibid.*, p. 22. Luis Carrillo y Sotomayor, *ibid.*, p. 56.

456. La Bruyère, *Des ouvrages de l'esprit*, 56. *Oeuvres complètes*, p. 86.

Jean Mabillon, *Traité des études monastiques*, II, ch. XIII (Paris: 1691), pp. 200–302.

457. Hans Mattausch, *Die literarische Kritik der frühen französischen Zeitschriften* (1665–1748) (München: 1968).

458. René Wellek, *Term and Concept of Literary Criticism. Concepts of Criticism*, pp. 25–26. Arnaldo Pizzorusso, *"L'idea di 'critica' nell seicento francese,"* Intersezioni, V (1985), 49–61.

459. Charles Sorel, *De la connaissance des bons livres* (Paris: 1671), p. 85.

460. *Les Plaisirs de la lecture aux vives lumières du camouflet ou Maximes de la critique rectifiante raisonnée* (Paris: 1681), I, p. 3. Carel de Saint-Garde, *Réflexions académiques sur les orateurs et les poètes* (Paris: 1676), pp. 31–32.

461. Cf. Noémi Hepp, "Esquisse du vocabulaire de la critique littéraire du Cid à la Querelle d'Homère." *Romanische Forschungen*, 69 (1957), 333–334, 336–337.

462. Tudor Vianu, *Inceputurile iraționalismului modern. Opere* (1934. București: Minerva, 1980), 9, pp. 131–145.

463. Père Rapin, *Réflexions sur la poétique de ce temps . . .* (Paris: 1675), p. 75.

464. Charles Sorel, *ibid.*, pp. 250–251.

465. For example, P. Richelet, *ibid.*, II, p. 18. Antoine Furetière, *Dictionnaire Universel . . .* (1708), III, p. 1708.

466. Martin Opitz, *Buch von der deutschen Poeterei*. Abdruck der ersten Ausgabe, 1624 (Halle: 1913), p. 8.

467. G. Marino, *Poesie e prose varie* (Milano: 1930), p. 93.

468. Miron Costin, *Opere*, II, pp. 114–115, 119–120.

469. Mihail Moxa, *ibid.*, p. 179.

470. Vasile Florescu, *La Rhétorique et la Néorhétorique. Genèse. Evolution. Perspectives* (Paris-București: Les Belles Lettres-Editura Academiei, 1982), pp. 120–122.

471. Aurel Sasu, *Retorica literară românească* (București: Minerva, 1976). Dan-Horia Mazilu, *Proza oratorică în literatura română veche* (București: Minerva, 1986), I, p. X, XII, 146 ff.

472. L. Volovici, *Apariția scriitorului în cultura românească* (Iași: Junimea, 1976), pp. 19–21.

473. Miron Costin, *Opere*, II, pp. 114–115, 119–120.

474. *Crestomaţie* . . . , II, p. 189. Mihail Moxa, *ibid.*, p. 202.

475. *Crestomaţie* . . . , I, pp. 118, 132, 164.

476. René Bray, *ibid.*, pp. 41, 97.

477. Günter E. Grimm, *ibid.*, p. 741.

478. P. Richelet, *ibid.*, *s.v.*

479. Baltasar Gracián, *Oráculo Manual*, § 27, p. 69.

480. La Bruyère, *Des jugements*, 18. *Oeuvres complètes*, pp. 347–348.

481. Antoine Furetière, *ibid.*, II, s.v. Hubert Gillot, *La Querelle des Anciens et des Modernes en France* (Paris: Champion, 1944), pp. 333, 404.

482. La Bruyère, *Des jugements*, 17, *Oeuvres complètes*, p. 347. See also: Malabranche, *La recherche de la vérité* (Paris: 1674–1675), I, 26.

483. Charles Perrault, 1697. Cf. Louis P. Betz, *ibid.*, pp. 47–48.

484. Pierre Bayle, *Dictionnaire historique et critique* (1690, Amsterdam-Leide-La Haye-Utrecht, 1740), I, p. 60, IV, p. 2786. Also: M. Huet, *Traité de l'origine des romans* (1670. Paris: 1711), pp. 177–178.

485. F. de La Mothe Le Vayer, *Doubte sceptique si l'estude des belles-lettres est préférable à toute autre occupation* (Paris: 1667).

486. La Bruyère, *De la mode*, 2. *Oeuvres complètes*, p. 386. Gui Patin, *Lettres*, II, p. 144; III, p. 30.

487. C. L. A. Saldenus, *ibid.*, p. 268.

488. For example, Charles Sorel, *Le berger extravagant* . . . (Paris: 1627). *Préface*.

489. F. de La Mothe Le Vayer, *Observations diverses sur la composition et sur la lecture des livres* (Paris: 1668), p. 79.

490. La Bruyère, *Des ouvrages de l'esprit*, 62. *Des jugements*, 64. *Oeuvres complètes*, pp. 88–89, 364–365. (Adrien Baillet), *ibid.*, I, p. 449, 469. La Chétardie, *Instructions pour un jeune seigneur ou l'idée d'un galant homme* (Paris: 1688), II, p. 31.

491. Bernard Beugnot, *"Dialogue, entretien et citation à l'époque classique." Canadian Review of Comparative Literature*, 1 (1976), 44. *Ibid.* "Florilèges et Polyantheae. Diffusion et statut du lieu commun à l'époque classique." *Études Françaises*, 13 (1977), 1–2, 135. Antoine Compagnon,

La seconde main ou le travail de la citation (Paris: Seuil, 1979), pp. 313, 318, 320–321.

492. La Bruyère, *Des ouvrages de l'esprit*, 31. *Oeuvres complètes*, p. 75. T. Boccalini, *ibid.*, I, 28, etc.

493. Francis Gallaway, *Reason, Rule and Revolt in English Classicism* (1940. New York: Charles Scribner's Sons, 1965).

494. Charles Sorel, *ibid.*, p. 472.

495. Antonio Lopez de Vega, *Heraclito: Democrito de nuestro siglo* (Madrid: 1641), p. 129.

496. Père Rapin, *ibid.*, I, p. III.

497. *Huetiana* . . . , pp. 171–173.

498. Théophile, *Oeuvres complètes*. Ed. Alleaume (Paris: P. Janet, 1853), II, p. 183.

499. Cf. Noémi Hepp, "Esquisse du vocabulaire de la critique littéraire du Cid à la Querelle d'Homère," 350.

500. Pierre Bayle, *Dictionnaire* . . . , I, p. 66.

501. John Dryden, *Essays*. Ed. W. P. Ker (Oxford: 1926), I, p. 67.

502. Edward Philipps, *Theatrum Poetarum*, 1675. Allan H. Gilbert, *Literary Criticism. Plato to Dryden.* (Detroit: Wayne State University Press, 1962), p. 677.

503. Christian Thomasius, *Von Nachahmung der Franzosen* (1687, 1701. Stuttgart, 1894), p. VII.

504. Charles Perrault, *Parallèle des Anciens et des Modernes*, III, Ed. H. R. Jauss, p. 284.

505. La Bruyère, *Des ouvrages de l'esprit*, 20. *Oeuvres complètes* p. 70.

506. *Le procès de la critique contre les auteurs ignorants et mercenaires* (Paris: 1681).

507. La Bruyère, *Des jugements*, 21. *Oeuvres complètes*, p. 350.

508. Pietro Bembo-Francesco Loredano, cf. Giovanni Getto, *Barocco in prosa e in poesia* (Milano: 1969), p. 289.

509. Charles Sorel, *Le Berger extravagant, où parmy des fantaisies amoureuses on voit les impertinences des romans et de la poésie* (Paris: 1627), pp. 491–492.

510. Francisco Cascales, *Cartas filológicas*, Ep. II, I, pp. 35–54. Tanneguy Le Fèvre, *De futilitate poetices* (Amsterdam: 1697).

511. Robert Elbrodt, *ibid.*, p. 112.

512. Miron Costin, *Opere*, I, p. 66.

513. Hans Robert Jauss, *"Paradigmwechsel in der Literaturwissenschaft."* *Methoden der deutschen Literaturwissenschaft.* Viktor Žmegač (Hrsg.) (1971. Frankfurt am Main: Athenäum Fischer Taschenbuch Verlag, 1972), pp. 276–277.

Name Index

Congar, Ives 224, 230, 232, 233, 237, 242, 243
Conrad de Hirschau 38, 72, 79, 224, 243, 247
Constantine VII Porphirogenitus 59, 240
Constantine the Great 33
Cook, Elisabeth 290
Coomarswamy, Ananda K. 237
Coresi, Deacon 97, 106, 117, 142, 170
Cornea, Andrei 203
Corneanu, Metropolitan Nicolae 247
Cornford, F. N. 236
Cornillat, François 283
Corozet, Gilles 281
Correa Calderón, E. 288
Corte, Francesco della 211
Cortesius, Paulus 97
Costin, Miron 154, 156, 173, 174, 177, 181, 187, 188, 197, 200, 290, 295, 299, 302, 304, 307, 312, 313, 315
Courbet, E. 285
Courcelle, Pierre 211
Crane, R. S. 241
Crasso, Lorenzo 169, 292, 297
Crates of Mallos 32, 33
Cresci, Giovan Francesco 119, 189
Crescimbeni, Giovan Maria 172, 306
Crinito, Pietro 259, 262, 265
Cristin, Claude 296
Critias 27
Croce, Benedetto 278, 300, 302, 303, 304, 305, 310
Cueva, Juan de la 291
Cugno, Marco 201, 202
Curch, A. J. 202
Curtius, Ernst Robert xiii, 73, 209, 210, 213, 217, 223, 225, 227, 234, 237, 243, 244, 246, 264, 274
Cusa, Nicolas de (Cusanus, Nicolaus) 106, 144, 284
Cyrus 260
Czepko, David 179

Daiches, David 216, 256
Daly, Lloyd W. 265

Daly, Peter M. 290
Damisch, H. 290
Daniel, Samuel, 127, 139, 275, 281
Daniello, B. 105, 271
Danielo, Arnaldo, 117
Dante, Alighieri 41, 44, 46, 52, 55, 59, 62, 63, 65, 66, 67, 70, 72, 114, 117, 124, 134, 147, 193, 226, 227, 229, 230, 232, 233, 234, 236, 237, 238, 239, 240, 241, 242, 243, 244, 245, 247, 255, 268, 270, 272, 278
D'Aubignac, Abbé François Hédelon 186
D'Aubigné, Agrippa 286
Dauzat, Albert 226, 253, 258, 260
David, Madeleine V.- 290, 293, 297, 299
Davis, Nathalie Zonn 256, 263, 266, 303, 307
Decembrio, Angelo 118, 130, 265, 274
Dekker, Eduard 109
Delbouille, Maurice 228
Delboulle, A. 281
Delehaye, P. Hippolyte 225
Delolain, Paul 307
Demetrios of Phalerum 32
Demetrius 216, 221
Democritus 205, 215
Dennis, John 196
Descartes, René 152, 161, 199
Deschamps, Eustace 43, 74, 143
Desmarets de Saint-Sorlin, Jean 299
Desportes, Philippe 142
Destrez, J. 234
Desvignes-Parent, Lucette 298
Díaz, José Simón 310
Dibdin, Thomas Frognall 285
Dibon, Paul 305
Dieckmann, Liselotte 205, 254
Diels, Hermann 215
Dierse, Ulrich 262, 295
Diodorus Siculus 3, 14, 110, 204, 214, 216, 246
Diogenes Laertius 27, 205, 214, 216, 218, 219, 221
Diomedes 9, 25, 31, 32, 56, 61, 207

Thematic Index